Allen C. Hughes

D0456367

SPEAKING THE CHRISTIAN GOD

WITHDRAWN

DATE DUE

12/13/04	
10/25/05	

DEMCO, INC. 38-2931

DATE DUE

Speaking the Christian God

*The Holy Trinity and the
Challenge of Feminism*

Edited by

Alvin F. Kimel, Jr.

WILLIAM B. EERDMANS PUBLISHING COMPANY
GRAND RAPIDS, MICHIGAN

Gracewing.

LEOMINSTER, ENGLAND

First published 1992 in the United States by
Wm. B. Eerdmans Publishing Co.,
255 Jefferson Ave. S.E., Grand Rapids, Michigan 49503
and in Europe by Gracewing,
2 Southern Avenue, Leominster, HR6 0QF, UK

Printed in the United States of America

Library of Congress Cataloging-in-Publication Data

Speaking the Christian God : the Holy Trinity and
the challenge of feminism / edited by Alvin F. Kimel.
p.   cm.
Includes bibliographical references.
ISBN 0-8028-0612-0 (pbk.)
1. Trinity. 2. Nonsexist language — Religious aspects — Christianity.
3. God — Knowableness. 4. Feminist theology. 5. Feminist theology —
Controversial literature.   I. Kimel, Alvin F.
BT111.2.S64   1992
231'.044 — dc20   92-17173
                                                        CIP

Gracewing ISBN 0 85244 213 0

Contents

Contents

Contributors

ELIZABETH ACHTEMEIER, Adjunct Professor of Bible and Homiletics, Union Theological Seminary in Richmond, Virginia

RAY S. ANDERSON, Professor of Theology and Ministry, Fuller Theological Seminary

J. A. DINOIA, O.P., Professor of Systematic Theology, Dominican House of Studies

GERHARD O. FORDE, Professor of Systematic Theology, Luther Northwestern Theological Seminary

ROLAND M. FRYE, Felix E. Schelling Professor of English Literature Emeritus, University of Pennsylvania

GARRETT GREEN, Professor of Religious Studies, Connecticut College

COLIN GUNTON, Professor of Christian Doctrine, King's College, University of London

THOMAS HOPKO, Professor of Dogmatic Theology, St. Vladimir's Orthodox Theological Seminary

BLANCHE JENSON, Private scholar and theologian

ROBERT W. JENSON, Professor of Religion, St. Olaf College

Contributors

ALVIN F. KIMEL, JR., Rector, St. Mark's Church, Highland, Maryland

ELIZABETH A. MORELLI, Associate Professor of Philosophy, Loyola Marymount University

DAVID A. SCOTT, William Meade Professor of Theology and Professor of Ethics, Virginia Theological Seminary

STEPHEN M. SMITH, Associate Professor of Systematic Theology and Ethics, Trinity Episcopal School for Ministry

JANET MARTIN SOSKICE, Lecturer in the Faculty of the Divinity School, Cambridge University, and Fellow of Jesus College

THOMAS F. TORRANCE, Professor of Christian Dogmatics Emeritus, University of Edinburgh

GEOFFREY WAINWRIGHT, Professor of Systematic Theology, Duke University

LESLIE ZEIGLER, Professor of Christian Theology Emerita, Bangor Theological Seminary

Introduction

A REVOLUTION is now taking place in the worship and discourse of English-speaking Christianity. Fads in theology come and go, of course, and rarely do they impact the parochial discourse directly and formatively. Not so, however, with the new feminist theology. Not only does the new thinking present a powerful critique of traditional theology and faith — as well as offering an attractive and, for many, compelling religious substitute in the name of Christ — but also it embodies this critique in very practical directives that alter the church's speech and prayer: the triune name is suppressed, prayer to the Father is asserted to be exclusive of women believers and therefore discountenanced, the appropriation of feminine images of God in worship and meditation is encouraged, and the use of the masculine pronoun for the deity is proscribed. This is one theological revolution that truly seeks to alter permanently the face and constitution of Christian faith.

Revolutions are exciting, energizing, inspiring, full of promise and hope. It is not surprising, therefore, that so many have eagerly enlisted in the feminist future. What is surprising, however, is the paucity of critical response from the theologians of the church. Despite the radicality of the feminist reconstructions of the doctrine of God in a rapidly increasing volume of theological work, and despite the dramatic changes both proposed and enacted in the church's liturgy, piety, and discourse, most theologians have simply either ignored the feminist arguments or accepted them with various degrees of enthusiasm and assent. This book seeks to remedy this situation, at least partially.

These essays attempt to do two things: first, to substantively and critically engage specific feminist thinkers, particularly (though not exclusively) in the areas of the doctrine of God and God-talk; and second, to offer constructive discussion and analysis of the crucial and often very complex theological issues. It is our hope that both dialogue and debate will be generated and sustained by these essays. Polemic, however, has often not been avoided, for the questions raised in the current controversy touch the heart of the Christian faith. When the gospel of Jesus Christ is at stake, passion also must enter into theology. This the feminist knows well.

What does it mean to be a feminist? If being a feminist means being convinced of the absolute equality and dignity of man and woman as created in the image of God, then each contributor to this volume is a feminist. But in current debate, theological feminism has moved far beyond such conviction and entered into a comprehensive critique and revision of orthodox belief, which, it is claimed, is fatally shaped by male sexism and used by the church for the exploitation and subjugation of women. God, Trinity, Christ — all must be rethought and reconceptualized in service to contemporary liberation. Accordingly, a new paradigm is presented. It is at this level that the theologians of this book enter into the fray. Serious questions are raised, criticisms are offered, and creative ways of thinking of the God of the gospel and of how he comes to speech in the mystery of triune being are explored.

The present contributors represent a wide range of ecclesiastical traditions — Anglican, Reformed, Lutheran, Catholic, Orthodox, Methodist, evangelical. All share a common commitment to the creedal fundamentals of Christian belief, yet the differences between them are manifest. These differences are evident both in their theological approaches and in their individual appraisals of feminism. All recognize that the issues involved are of vital importance to the life and mission of the church in fidelity to the gospel.

May this volume contribute to a deeper understanding of the wondrous and all-holy Father who has redeemed and reconciled woman and man through the atoning death and victorious resurrection of his Son, Jesus Christ, by the Holy Spirit of the coming kingdom.

Feast of the Holy Trinity   ALVIN F. KIMEL, JR.
26 May 1991

Exchanging God for "No Gods":
A Discussion of Female Language for God

ELIZABETH ACHTEMEIER

N O ASPECT of the feminist movement has affected the church's life more basically than has that movement's attempts to change the language used in speaking to or about God. Beginning with the introduction of the first volume of the National Council of Churches' *An Inclusive-Language Lectionary*[1] in 1983, inclusive language has steadily made its way into the Scriptures, prayers, liturgies, hymns, and publications of the mainline churches, largely through the instrumentality of those churches' denominational headquarters and often to the dismay of the laity in the pews.

The argument of the feminists is that women have been oppressed in the church since the second century and that the language of the church has fostered that oppression. For example, by the use of generic terms such as *man* and *mankind*, males have come to be seen as the definition of what it means to be human. And by the use of masculine titles and pronouns for God, maleness has been absolutized and males thereby given the right to rule over females. "Since God is male," Mary Daly says, "the male is God."[2]

1. *An Inclusive-Language Lectionary*, published for the Cooperative Publication Association by John Knox Press, Atlanta, Pilgrim Press, New York, and Westminster Press, Philadelphia.

2. Daly, "The Qualitative Leap Beyond Patriarchal Religion," *Quest* (Women and Spirituality) 1 (1974): 21.

A few portions of this article were first published in "Female Language for God: Should the Church Adopt It?" in *The Hermeneutical Quest: Essays in Honor of James Luther Mays on His Sixty-Fifth Birthday*, ed. Donald G. Miller (Allison Park, Pa.: Pickwick Publications, 1986), pp. 97-114. These portions are reprinted here with permission.

I

Therefore, claims Anne E. Carr, "God as father rules over the world, holy fathers rule over the church, clergy fathers over laity, males over females, husbands over wives and children, man over the created world."[3] Such a hierarchical worldview must be abolished, say the feminists, and one way to do that is by changing our language.

There can be no doubt that in many respects the women have a just cause. They have suffered discrimination in the church for centuries. They have been denied leadership roles and respect for their learning and persons. They have even been labeled by fundamentalist Southern Baptists as the source of sin in the world. They have been denied ordination by the Roman Catholic Church because they do not biologically "resemble Christ." That discrimination continues today, with the Bible misused as its instrument.

There also can be no doubt that such discrimination is a corruption and fundamental denial of the Christian gospel. The Scriptures clearly proclaim that both female and male are made in the image of God (Gen. 1:27), that husband and wife are to join flesh in a marital union of mutual helpfulness (Gen. 2:18), that the ancient enmity between the sexes and the subordination of women are a result of human sin (Gen. 3), that such sinful enmity and subordination have been overcome by the death and resurrection of Jesus Christ (Gal. 3:28), and that all women and men alike are called to equal discipleship in the service of their risen Lord. The Scriptures further show that our Lord consistently treated women as equals and that the New Testament churches could have women as their leaders. Thus, when one encounters those few instances in the New Testament in which women are made subject to the rule of men, as in 1 Corinthians 14, two of the Pastoral Letters, and the household codes, one must apply the Reformation's principle of letting the Scriptures interpret the Scripture. If that is done, it becomes clear that the subordination of women was historically limited to specific situations within some of the early house churches, and that the gospel of Jesus Christ is a ringing proclamation of freedom under God, for both females and males. For the church to claim or act otherwise is a denial of its gospel.

It therefore seems only fair for the feminists in the church to ask that the church's language about *human beings* be changed to include them, so that males no longer define humanity. The new 1990 edition

---

3. Carr, *Transforming Grace: Christian Tradition and Women's Experience* (San Francisco: Harper & Row, 1988), p. 51.

of the Revised Standard Version of the Bible has acceded to that request, and in it, generic English terms have been changed to reflect the meaning of the original texts. For example, John 12:32 now reads, "And I, when I am lifted up from the earth, will draw all people [rather than 'men'] to myself."

There is, however, a great difference between feminism as fairness and feminism as ideology, as Richard John Neuhaus has cogently pointed out,[4] and it is in relation to language *about God* that the feminists are most radically ideological. By attempting to change the biblical language used of the deity, the feminists have in reality exchanged the true God for those deities which are "no gods," as Jeremiah would put it (2:11).

The feminist claim is that all language about God is analogical and metaphorical, and that therefore it can be changed at will to overcome the church's patriarchalism and to foster women's liberation. Principally, therefore, the feminists seek to eliminate all masculine terminology used of God, either by supplementing it with feminine terminology or by using neuter or female images for the deity exclusively.

In speaking of God and Christ, some simply use "she" and "her."[5] For the Trinity of Father, Son, and Holy Spirit, others substitute *Creator, Liberator,* and *Comforter,*[6] and they avoid the excessive use of terms such as *Father, King,* and *Master* by often substituting *Yahweh* or *God* or *Abba.*[7] In *An Inclusive Language Lectionary,* the Bible's use of *Father* is changed to *Father (and Mother), Lord* to *Sovereign, King* to *Ruler* or *Monarch, Son of Man* to *Human One, Son of God* to *Child of God.* Rosemary Radford Ruether consistently calls her deity *Godless,*[8] while Rita Gross uses *God-She.*[9] Others apply feminine usage only to the Holy Spirit or avoid the

---

4. Neuhaus, "The Feminist Faith," *First Things: A Monthly Journal of Religion and Public Life* 2 (April 1990): 60.

5. See Elisabeth Schüssler Fiorenza, *In Memory of Her: A Feminist Reconstruction of Christian Origins* (New York: Crossroad, 1983), pp. 345, 347.

6. Letty M. Russell, *Human Liberation in a Feminist Perspective — A Theology* (Philadelphia: Westminster Press, 1974), p. 102.

7. Letty M. Russell, "Changing Language and the Church," in *The Liberating Word: A Guide to Non-sexist Interpretation of the Bible,* ed. Letty M. Russell (Philadelphia: Westminster Press, 1976), p. 92.

8. Ruether, *Sexism and God-Talk: Toward a Feminist Theology* (Boston: Beacon Press, 1983).

9. See Gross, "Female God Language in a Jewish Context," in *Womanspirit Rising: A Feminist Reader in Religion,* ed. Carol Christ and Judith Plaskow (San Francisco: Harper & Row, 1979), p. 173.

problem altogether by using impersonal terms for God such as *Wisdom, Glory, Holy One, Rock, Fire,* and *First and Last,* or neuter terms like *Liberator, Maker, Defender, Friend,* and *Nurturer.* Jesus is described as a male only in his earthly life, while he becomes Liberator, Redeemer, and Savior in his representation of the new humanity.[10]

Those who employ such changes in the biblical usage try to justify them by pointing to female imagery for God in the Bible or by claiming that the Catholic cult of Mary furnishes a tradition of female language and imagery in speaking of the divine. "If we do not mean that God is male when we use masculine pronouns and imagery," asks Rita Gross, "then why should there be any objections to using female imagery and pronouns as well?" She continues, "Female God language compels us to overcome the idolatrous equation of God with androcentric notions of humanity in a way that no other linguistic device can."[11]

Many things need to be said in reply. First, it is universally recognized by biblical scholars that the God of the Bible has no sexuality. Sexuality is a structure of creation (cf. Gen. 1–2), confined within the limits of the creation (cf. Matt. 22:30), and the God of the Bible is consistently pictured as totally other than all creation. This is what the Bible means when it says that God is "holy" — he is "set apart," totally other than anything he has made. "I am God and not man, the Holy One in your midst," he says in Hosea (11:9); "The Egyptians are men, and not God; and their horses are flesh, and not spirit" is Isaiah's word (31:3). "To whom then will you liken God, or what likeness compare with him?" asks the Second Isaiah (40:18). Thus, by insisting on female language for God, the feminists simply continue to emphasize the nonbiblical view that God does indeed have sexuality. In fact, some of them have misused the biblical concept of the *imago dei* to say that God must be female as well as male, since both sexes are made in God's image (Gen. 1:27). That is a total distortion of the biblical understanding of God, who is without sexual characteristics.

Second, as Roland Frye has amply demonstrated,[12] the few instances of feminine imagery for God in the Bible all take the form of a simile and not of a metaphor, and that distinction is crucial. A simile

10. Russell, "Changing Language and the Church," p. 93.
11. Gross, "Female God Language in a Jewish Context," pp. 170, 171-72.
12. Frye, "Language for God and Feminist Language: Problems and Principles" (Princeton: Center of Theological Inquiry, 1988).

compares one aspect of something to another. For example, in Isaiah 42:14, God will "cry out *like* a woman in travail," but only his *crying out* is being referred to; he is not being identified as a whole with the figure of a woman in childbirth. In metaphors, on the other hand, identity between the subject and the thing compared to it is assumed. God *is* Father, or Jesus *is* the Good Shepherd, or God *is* King. Thus the metaphor "carries a word or phrase far beyond its ordinary lexical meaning so as to provide a fuller and more direct understanding of the subject."[13] Language is stretched to its limit, beyond ordinary usage, to provide new understanding.

Third, the Bible uses masculine language for God because that is the language with which God has revealed himself. The biblical, Christian faith is a revealed religion. It claims no knowledge of God beyond the knowledge God has given of himself through his words and deeds in the histories of Israel and of Jesus Christ and his church. In fact, it is quite certain that human beings, by searching out God, cannot find him. Unless God reveals himself, he remains unknown to humanity. Unlike every other religion of the world, the Judeo-Christian faith (imitated by Islam) does not start with the phenomena of the world and deduce the nature of God from them; in this respect, the biblical religions are unique in history. Rather, the Judeo-Christian faith itself is the product of God's self-revelation within time and space to a chosen people, and apart from that self-revelation, biblical faith has no language for or experience of the divine. In short, only God can reveal himself.

But the God of the Bible has revealed himself. Contrary to those modern theologies (cf. that of Sallie McFague) which claim that God is the great Unknown and that therefore human beings must invent language for God that can then be changed at will, the God of the Bible has revealed himself in five principal metaphors as King, Father, Judge, Husband, and Master, and finally, decisively, as the God and Father of our Lord Jesus Christ. If we ask "What is the ontological nature of God?" we must reply "God is the Father of Jesus Christ." As Alvin Kimel explains,

> God is not just like a father; he is *the* Father. Jesus is not just like a son; he is *the* Son. The divine Fatherhood and Sonship are absolute, transcendent, and correlative. . . . The relationship between Christ Jesus and his Father, lived out in the conditions of first-century Palestine and eternally established in the resurrection and ascension of

13. Ibid., p. 18.

our Lord, belongs to the inner life of God. It constitutes the identity of the Almighty Creator . . . "Father" is not a metaphor imported by humanity onto the screen of eternity; it is a name and filial term of address *revealed* by God himself in the person of his Son. . . . No matter how other groups of human beings may choose to speak to the Deity, the matter is already decided for Christians, decided by God himself. To live in Christ in the triune being of the Godhead is to worship and adore the holy Transcendence whom Jesus knows as his Father.[14]

If one believes that Jesus Christ is the Word of God made flesh, the Son of God incarnate in time and space — a belief that feminists such as Elisabeth Schüssler Fiorenza and Rosemary Radford Ruether and a host of others would deny — then there is no contradiction that can be made to the particularity of God's self-revelation. God is not just any god, capable of being named according to human fancy. No, God is the one whom Jesus reveals as his Father.

The same particularity obtains in the Old Testament. Once again, God is not to be identified with just any god. For this reason, the central commandment in the Bible, first contained in Deuteronomy 6:4, begins with, "Hear, O Israel: The Lord our God is one Lord." That is, the God of Israel is not identical with the diffuse numina known to other peoples but is one particular God who has done particular things in particular times and places. Principally, he is "the Lord your God, who brought you out of the land of Egypt, out of the house of bondage" (Exod. 20:2 and throughout the Old Testament). If Israel asks who God is, the reply is that he is the God of the Exodus. And it is that God of the Exodus, then, whom Jesus also reveals to be his Father (cf. Mark 12:29-30). God defines himself in the Bible, through centuries of acting and speaking in the life of his covenant people, and it is only through that self-revelation, now handed down to us in the Scriptures, that we have any knowledge of him.

Surely several questions arise, however, and the first is this: Why does God reveal himself primarily in personal terms? If God has no sexuality, if he is Spirit (cf. John 4:24), then why does he not name himself through the media of impersonal metaphorical language? Why are not his primary designations those of Rock, Fire, Living Water, Bread, Way, Door,

---

14. Kimel, *A New Language for God? A Critique of Supplemental Liturgical Texts — Prayer Book Studies 30* (Shaker Heights, Ohio: Episcopalians United, 1990), pp. 11-12.

Refuge, Fortress, and other such metaphors that can be found throughout the Scriptures? Put another way, why does the Bible insist on those awkward anthropomorphisms for God, in which he is described as having hands and feet and mouth like a person, and which are finally brought to their ultimate anthropomorphism in the incarnation of Jesus Christ? Why a personal God when God transcends all human personality?

One answer is that a God named primarily Rock or Way or Door does not demand that we do anything. All of those impersonal metaphors for God in the Bible are encompassed within a principal revelation of God as supremely personal, because the God of the Bible meets us Person to person and asks from us the total commitment of our personalities: "You shall love the Lord your God with all your heart, and with all your soul, and with all your might" (Deut. 6:5); "If you love me, you will keep my commandments" (John 14:15). God asks of us primarily love in return for his love that was manifested in his dealings with us: "When Israel was a child, I loved him, and out of Egypt I called my son" (Hos. 11:1); "God so loved the world that he gave his only Son" (John 3:16). No impersonal designations of God, except they be explained by the Bible's personal names for him, can adequately express that gracious and demanding relationship of love with himself into which God woos and calls us.

More pressing for the feminists, however, is the question of why God reveals himself only in masculine terms. Elaine Pagels is quite correct when she states that "the absence of feminine symbolism of God marks Judaism, Christianity, and Islam in striking contrast to the world's other religious traditions, whether in Egypt, Babylonia, Greece and Rome, or Africa, Polynesia, India, and North America."[15] But why could a personal God not have revealed himself in feminine metaphors instead? God is never called "Mother" in the Bible and is never addressed or thought of as a female deity. That was unique in the ancient Near Eastern world; Israel was surrounded by peoples who worshiped female deities — Asherat and Anat, Nut and Isis, Tiamat and the Queen of Heaven, Demeter and Artemis. And such a masculinizing of the deity is still unique in our world.

The feminist argument is that the names for God in the Bible have been determined by the patriarchal cultures out of which the Bible arose, but that argument founders on the revelation in Jesus Christ, as we have seen. Feminists have a very difficult time with God the Father and God

15. Pagels, "What Became of God the Mother? Conflicting Images of God in Early Christianity," in *Womanspirit Rising*, p. 107.

the Son, although some of them hold that the feminine element is introduced by the Holy Spirit, even though the Spirit too proceeds from the Father and from the Son and is one with them. No, the Bible's language for God is masculine, a unique revelation of God in the world.

The basic reason for that designation of God is that the God of the Bible will not let himself be identified with his creation, and therefore human beings are to worship not the creation but the Creator (cf. Rom. 1:25). In the words of the Decalogue, we are not to worship "anything that is in heaven above, or that is in the earth beneath, or that is in the water under the earth; you shall not bow down to them or serve them" (Exod. 20:4-5; Deut. 5:8-9), because the God of the Bible is sharply distinguished from everything that he has made. To be sure, God works in his creation through the instruments of his Word and Spirit; he orders his creation and sustains it; he constantly cares for it; but he is never identified with it. And it is that holiness, that otherness, that transcendence of the Creator, which also distinguishes biblical religion from all others.

In most of the cultures of the world, deity and world are not differentiated. Rather, the divine is bound up with and revealed through the natural world. For example, in ancient Mesopotamia, the gods and goddesses were thought to emanate out of chaotic matter. And indeed, not only the Babylonians but also the Egyptians and Greeks and Romans saw in the manifestations of nature the life and activity of their deities. The expanse of the sky, the heat of the sun, the growth and death of vegetation, the fury of the storm — these were to those ancient peoples not impersonal happenings and objects but cosmic Thous which affected human life and demanded adjustment to them. Nature was alive for primitive peoples (as it still is for many today). Its changes were attributed to divine will, its conflicts to the struggles of opposing gods and goddesses. Its harmony was thought to be the result of the organization of the cosmic, divine state, as in Mesopotamian theology, or its harmony was said to stem from the genealogical relationships of the deities, as in Hesiod's *Theogony.* God and world were seen as one. Deity was believed to be revealed through all persons and things, and was therefore to be met through the phenomena of the natural world. In the worship of the biblical Canaanites, any natural object could be a medium of revelation — a stone pillar, a sacred grove, a stream — just as in the worship of Mesopotamia the heavenly bodies were thought to be deities (cf. King Josiah's destruction of such objects of pagan worship in 2 Kings 23:4-14).

It is precisely the introduction of female language for God that opens the door to such identification of God with the world, however. If God is portrayed in feminine language, the figures of carrying in the womb, of giving birth, and of suckling immediately come into play. For example, feminist Virginia Mollenkott writes of the God of Naomi in the book of Ruth as "the God with Breasts," "the undivided One God who births and breast-feeds the universe."[16] The United Church of Christ's Book of Worship prays, "You have brought us forth from the womb of your being." A feminine goddess has given birth to the world! But if the creation has issued forth from the body of the deity, it shares in deity's substance; deity is in, through, and under all things, and therefore everything is divine. Holding such a worldview, Mollenkott can say that "our milieu" is "divine,"[17] just as Zsuzsanna E. Budapest can go even further and write, "This is what the Goddess symbolizes — the divine within women and all that is female in the universe. . . . The responsibility you accept is that you are divine, and that you have power."[18] If God is identified with his creation, we finally make ourselves gods and goddesses — the ultimate and primeval sin, according to Genesis 3 and the rest of the Scriptures.

But we can never rightly understand ourselves and our place in the universe, the Bible tells us, until we realize that we are not gods and goddesses. Rather, we are creatures, wondrously and lovingly made by a sovereign Creator: "It is he that made us, and not we ourselves" (Ps. 100:3). The Bible will use no language which undermines that confession. It therefore eschews all feminine language for God that might open the door to such error, and it is rigorous in its opposition to every other religion and cultic practice that identifies creation with creator.

The principal fight of Deuteronomy, of the Deuteronomic History (Deuteronomy through 2 Kings), and of the prophets is with Canaanite baalism and with Mesopotamian astral worship, in which God has been identified with his world; the New Testament implicitly endorses the separation of creation and Creator by carefully stating that before there was the creation, there was the Word and the Word was God (John 1:1). Indeed, prophets and psalmists and the New Testament are quite certain that the world may pass away, but God will not pass away, because God and his world are not one (Pss. 46:1-2; 102:25-27; Isa. 51:6; 54:10; Mark 13:31 and parallels).

16. Mollenkott, *The Divine Feminine: The Biblical Image of God as Female* (New York: Crossroad, 1983), p. 58.

17. Ibid., p. 109.

18. Budapest, "Self-Blessing Ritual," in *Womanspirit Rising*, pp. 271-72.

No passage in Scripture more carefully preserves the understanding of God's otherness from his creation than does Genesis 1, a chapter that is the product of centuries of theological reflection. At first glance, it would seem that the priestly authors of Genesis 1 share the mythopoeic worldview of Mesopotamia, in which God is identified with his creation, because they borrow some of the language of that Mesopotamian view: God creates by bringing order into the primeval chaos, the great deep or *tehom,* which is the linguistic equivalent of the Babylonian Tiamat, the goddess of chaos. And the earth and the firmament are created from the chaos, as they are in the Babylonian story. But while the priestly writers use the language of their time, they carefully alter and demythologize it. In the Babylonian epic, the gods emanate out of the primeval chaos and therefore share common substance with the creation; in Genesis 1, God is above and beyond creation as its sovereign Lord. In the Babylonian story, the god Marduk must fight with the goddess of chaos, Tiamat; in Genesis, there is only one God, and he speaks to effortlessly bring about the universe. In the Babylonian account, creation takes place in the timeless realm of the divine; in the Bible, it is the beginning of the sacred history. In Babylonian theology, then, nature, which reflects the life of the divine, gives a cyclical pattern to human history — the cyclical pattern of its continual round of birth and life and death; in the Bible, the pattern for human history is linear, and both human beings and nature are subject to a time different from their own — namely, to God's time, to salvation history, which has a beginning and an end.

God, the biblical writers are saying, is in no way contained in or bound up with or dependent on or revealed through his creation. God creates the world outside of himself, by the instrument of his Word. Between God and his world stands the Word of God (cf. John 1:2), which always addresses the creation as an object of the divine speech (cf. Isa. 1:2; 40:22, 26; Mic. 6:2 et al.). The world does not emanate out of the being of God or contain some part of him within it. He has not implanted divinity within any part of the creation, not even in human beings, and therefore no created thing or person can be claimed to be divine.

The assurance and meaning that this biblical understanding of the Creator's relation to his creation give to faith, then, are profoundly important. First, because God is not bound up with his creation, that means that heaven and earth may pass away — we may blow the earth off its axis at the push of the nuclear button — but the eternal God is able to take those who love him into an everlasting fellowship with himself that does not pass away (cf. Ps. 102:25-27; Isa. 51:6; Mark 13:31 and parallels). In this nuclear age the person of biblical faith can therefore lead a life not of fear and anxiety but of joy and certain hope in God's eternal salvation (cf. Ps. 46:1-3).

Second, because God is not bound up with nature's cycle but stands above and beyond its spiral and subjects it to the linear time of his purpose (cf. Rom. 8:19-23; Isa. 11:6-9 et al.), the pattern for human life is no longer that of nature's endless round of becoming and passing away but becomes a joyful pilgrimage toward God's goal of his kingdom.

The feminists, who want to make Creator and creation one, should realize that there is no meaning to human life if it is patterned after and subjected to nature's round. As Ecclesiastes puts it, "Vanity of vanities! All is vanity. . . . A generation goes, and a generation comes, but the earth remains for ever. . . . What has been is what will be, and what has been done is what will be done; and there is nothing new under the sun" (1:2, 4, 9). Such a cyclical understanding of human history was the classical understanding until the time of Darwin, when it was seen that nature not only repeated itself but also evolved in newness. In many philosophies, the cycle of nature therefore came to be viewed as a spiral, to allow for the introduction of novelty. Nevertheless, nature's round remained the pattern for human life. That means, then, that a mother may painstakingly raise her children, who grow up and raise more children, who in turn grow up and raise their offspring, and each generation passes away in its time, ad infinitum. No goal is given to living. Each generation is born and suffers and dies, and human life does indeed become "a tale told by an idiot . . . signifying nothing."

Realizing that a cyclical understanding of human history results in meaninglessness, every nonbiblical religion and philosophy in the world has tried to escape that emptiness. In India and China, the goal of life is to escape the cycle of history into the timeless realm of Nirvana, a solution which implies that our everyday life has no meaning. In the philosophies of Plato and Aristotle, the escape from history is rational, and human beings take refuge from the circle of life by retreating into the realm of pure form. In modern philosophies, such as those of Nietzsche and Spengler, the only alternative is nobly to assert, if finally futilely, individual freedom. In Nietzsche, this leads to suicide, in Spengler to a form of fatalism. But whatever the escape sought, not one of these positions is positive, no one of them holding that the common life we live on this earth in time has any meaning.

Such too is the view of history in some forms of modern existentialism and in that branch of modern drama known as the theater of the absurd. In Beckett's play *Waiting for Godot,* for example, no action takes place because the message is that all action is meaningless. Life goes around in a circle and finally means nothing. History is an endless repetition of events, having no goal or purpose.

Such meaninglessness results from a theology that identifies God with his creation. And that identification almost automatically comes about when feminine language for God is used. Many feminists have argued that feminine language for God does not necessarily lead to the deity's identification with creation. But feminist writings themselves demonstrate that it does.

We have already seen such a demonstration from the writings of Virginia Mollenkott. It can perhaps most clearly be shown from the works of Rosemary Radford Ruether, who could be called the leading feminist writer in the United States today. Ruether wants to use female language for God, and therefore she names the divine God/ess. But Ruether, like all of the feminist writers, does not want her deity to rule over her: as I said at the beginning, feminists want to get rid of a hierarchical view in which God is their Lord. God for them must be not a Sovereign but a "friend" (Sallie McFague) or a "householder" (Letty Russell) or the power of love-in-relation (Isabel Carter Heyward, Dorothee Sölle). Ruether therefore defines her God/ess as the Primal Matrix, as "the great womb within which all things, gods and humans, sky and earth, human and nonhuman beings are generated" — an image, she rightly says, which survives in the metaphor of the divine as the Ground of Being[19] (cf. Tillich). But this is no mere image or metaphor for Ruether. This God/ess is divine reality: ". . . the empowering Matrix; She, in whom we live and move and have our being. . . . She comes; She is here."[20]

For Ruether, then, this God/ess is very much bound up with nature's life, and therefore in her book entitled *Women-Church* Ruether can write liturgies for worshiping groups of females that celebrate the cycles of the moon, the solstices and the seasons, as well as the cycles of menstruation and menopause and other changes in women's lives. We "reappropriate the hallowing of nature and cyclical time of ancient pre-Judeo-Christian traditions,"[21] she says, just as Sheila Collins, in her work, maintains that "the

19. Ruether, *Sexism and God-Talk,* pp. 48-49.
20. Ibid., p. 266.
21. Ruether, *Women-Church: Theology and Practice* (San Francisco: Harper & Row, 1985), p. 104.

exclusivity of the linear view of history dissolves. . . . The cyclical view of history becomes once again a possibility."[22] We "reclaim our true relationship with somatic reality, with body and earth," writes Ruether, "and with the Great Goddess that sustains our life in nature."[23] That is clearly a return to the worldview of Canaanite baalistic and Mesopotamian pagan theologies. Indeed, Ruether draws on the language of the latter. To celebrate menstruation, Ruether instructs the female in women-church to descend into a ritual bath, which "is seen as a descent into the primal sea [read 'Tiamat'] from which all things emerged in the original creation."[24]

The result is that Ruether and all those feminists who want to erase the distinction between God and his creation finally share with the most radical feminists, who have abandoned the Christian church and faith altogether, a view of divinity that is at home in modern witches' covens. Writes Starhawk, a self-proclaimed Wicca worshiper,

> There is no dichotomy between spirit and flesh, no split between Godhead and the world. The Goddess is manifest in the world; she brings life into being, is Nature, is flesh. Union is not sought outside the world in some heavenly sphere or through dissolution of the self into the void beyond the senses. Spiritual union is found in life, within nature, passion, sensuality — through being fully human, fully one's self.
>
> Our great symbol for the Goddess is the moon, whose three aspects reflect the three stages in women's lives and whose cycles of waxing and waning coincide with women's menstrual cycles. . . .
>
> The Goddess is also earth — Mother Earth, who sustains all growing things, who is the body, our bones and cells. She is air . . . fire . . . water . . . mare, cow, cat, owl, crane, flower, tree, apple, seed, lion, sow, stone, woman. She is found in the world around us, in the cycles and seasons of nature, and in mind, body, spirit, and the emotions within each of us. Thou art Goddess. I am Goddess. All that lives (and all that is, lives), all that serves life, is Goddess.[25]

Such statements serve as a vivid summary of the end result of a religion in which Creator and creation are undivided. And if female language for the deity is used, such beliefs are its logical outcome.

22. Collins, "Reflections on the Meaning of Herstory," in *Womanspirit Rising,* p. 70.

23. Ruether, *Women-Church,* p. 108.

24. Ibid., p. 219.

25. Starhawk, "Witchcraft and Women's Culture," in *Womanspirit Rising,* p. 263.

When such views are held, meaninglessness haunts human life. Perhaps that meaninglessness can be most poignantly illustrated by Ruether's views of death. There is no eternal life for those of faith in Ruether's female God/ess religion. Rather, the end she envisions for all of us and our communities is that we will simply end up as compost:

> In effect [at death], our existence ceases as individuated ego/organism and dissolves back into the cosmic matrix of matter/energy, from which new centers of individuation arise. It is this matrix, rather than our individuated centers of being, that is "everlasting," that subsists underneath the coming to be and passing away of individuated beings and even planetary worlds. Acceptance of death, then, is acceptance of the finitude of our individuated centers of being, but also our identification with the larger matrix as our total self that contains us all. . . . To the extent to which we have transcended egoism for relation to community, we can also accept death as the final relinquishment of individuated ego into the great matrix of being.[26]

Such a view finally means that there is no purpose for the creation of each individual human being, and that my life and yours in our communities have no eternal meaning beyond their brief and transitory appearances on this earth.

If God and creation are identified with one another, perhaps most disturbing of all is the feminists' claim to embody the deity within themselves — in other words, to be divine. "I found God in myself and I loved her fiercely," exults Carol Christ:[27] that is the logical result of a religion in which the deity is believed to be contained in all things and all persons, and feminists who hold such views then become a law unto themselves. Indeed, for feminists Dorothee Sölle and Isabel Carter Heyward, there is no such thing as original sin, and the "fall" of Genesis 3 is good, a liberation into knowledge and action and reliance on one's self.[28] "We do not have to sit around all year singing, with Luther, 'Did we in our own strength confide, our striving would be losing,'" writes Sölle. No, "we are strong;

26. Ruether, *Sexism and God-Talk*, pp. 257-58.
27. Christ, "Why Women Need the Goddess: Phenomenological, Psychological and Political Reflections," in *Womanspirit Rising*, p. 277.
28. See Sölle, *The Strength of the Weak: Towards a Christian Feminist Identity*, trans. Robert and Rita Kimber (Philadelphia: Westminster Press, 1984), pp. 126-29; and Heyward, *The Redemption of God: A Theology of Mutual Relation* (New York: University Press of America, 1982), pp. 150-52.

we can accomplish things."[29] According to Sölle, God is unnecessary: "To live, we do not need what has repeatedly been called 'God,' a power that intervenes, rescues, judges, and confirms. The most telling argument against our traditional God is not that he no longer exists or that he has drawn back within himself but that we no longer need him."[30]

God is in us, maintains Sölle, as our capacity to love. We are one with God in a mystical relation. We do not serve God; we manifest him:

> In the mystical tradition, there is no room for deferring to a higher power, for worshiping alien rule, and for denying our own strength. On the contrary, mystical texts often explicitly criticize the master-servant relationship. . . .
>
> Here, religion is a sense of unity with the whole, a sense of belonging, not of submitting. We do not honor God because of his power over us; we immerse ourselves in him, in his love. . . . He is, as Meister Eckhart says, the fundament, love, the depths, the sea. Symbols from nature are preferred where our relationship with God is not one of obedience but of unity, where we are not subject to the commands of some remote being that demands sacrifice and the relinquishing of the self, but rather where we are asked to become one with all of life.[31]

And so, for Sölle, because God is in us, all we need is love. That is the central idea in the Bible, she maintains:

> The tradition has added Christology and ecclesiology to it, the virgin birth, the resurrection and the ascension, the Trinity, original sin, and eternity. . . . I do not think we can restore this . . . house of language. I think we will have to abandon it in the condition it is in and build a new one on this simple foundation: All you need is love.[32]

To the contrary, however, in a world where human torture is the rule in most prisons, where a person on a subway platform in New York City can push a woman in front of an oncoming train "just for the hell of it," where little children in a nursery school can be tied up and sexually abused, where whole races can be uprooted or starved to death or burnt up in gas ovens, it must be said that Sölle's is a naive understanding indeed,

29. *The Strength of the Weak*, p. 158.
30. Ibid., p. 137.
31. Ibid., p. 102.
32. Ibid., pp. 133-34.

and that we do in fact need a Power greater than human evil — or, for that matter, a Power greater than even the highest human love and good, for it was the best religion and the best law that erected the cross on Golgotha. If there is not a God who is Lord over life, who "intervenes, rescues, judges, and confirms," and who has given his final judgment and won his decisive victory in the cross and resurrection of Jesus Christ, then human evil will always have the last word and there is no hope for this world. The feminists, believing themselves divine, think that by their own power they can restructure society, restore creation, and overcome suffering. But the tortured history of humanity testifies to what human beings do when they think they are a law unto themselves with no responsibility to God, and those feminists who are claiming that God is in them will equally fall victim to human sin.

The God of the Judeo-Christian biblical faith is holy God, the almighty Creator and Lord, totally other than everything and everyone he has made. We therefore cannot know and worship him unless he reveals himself to us. But with a love surpassing human understanding, he has revealed himself to us as the Holy One of Israel, who delivered her out of the house of bondage, and as the God and Father of our Lord Jesus Christ. In that revelation, now mediated for us through the Scriptures, he has offered to adopt us as his beloved children (cf. John 1:12; Gal. 4:4-7), to allow us to call him Father, *Abba* (cf. Rom. 8:14-17), and to know him as his Son Jesus Christ knows him. If in trust and obedience we accept that offering of himself to us, he promises to be with us all our lives long, to guide us in the paths of righteousness, to give us joy in the midst of the world's tribulation, to unite us in communities of love and peace with like-minded believers, to send us out to perform tasks that will give meaning to all our lives, and finally, at death, to receive us into his realm of eternal life and good that cannot pass away. For my part, I can imagine no reason ever to reject such a God or to exchange him for those deities of earth that are "no gods." Women suffer discrimination, yes; our world is full of all kinds of evil. But God is holy, the Father Almighty, Creator of heaven and earth, and by faith in him we shall always be more than conquerors, and nothing shall ever separate us from the love he has for us in Christ Jesus our Lord.

Language for God and Feminist Language: Problems and Principles

ROLAND M. FRYE

Different Understandings of Language and of God

LANGUAGE FOR God is not equivalent to the kinds of naming we use in ordinary speech. We say that "that which we call a rose by any other name would smell as sweet," and we recognize that ordinary names for creatures are subject to human custom, choice, and change. According to biblical religion, on the other hand, only God can name God. Distinctive Christian experiences and beliefs are expressed through distinctive language about God, and the changes in that language proposed by feminist theologians do not merely add a few unfamiliar words for God, as some would like to think, but in fact introduce beliefs about God that differ radically from those inherent in Christian faith, understanding, and Scripture. Briefly stated, that is the argument this essay will systematically expand.

None of my arguments against inclusive language for the deity entail rejecting the use of inclusive language for people, an entirely different issue that falls under the heading of adiaphora, or questions not central to faith. Furthermore, these arguments do not in any sense oppose equality for women in dignity, rights, and opportunities. Elizabeth Achtemeier has made that point in her fine essay entitled "Female Language for God: Should the Church Adopt It?" Achtemeier eloquently maintains that "the

---

Parts of this essay first appeared in "Language for God and Feminist Language: Problems and Principles" (Princeton, N.J.: Center of Theological Inquiry, 1988).

Christian gospel is a gospel of freedom and service, in Christ, for male and female alike," and she rightly declares that "as the church struggles with the issue of women's full equality — and struggle it must to insure that equality, if it wishes to live up to its Gospel — let it therefore divide the wheat from the tares in the demands women are making of it." I fully agree with such affirmations of full dignity and equal rights for women, and I also fully agree with Achtemeier's learned refutation of current efforts to introduce feminine language for God: "The church cannot and it must not accede to feminist demands that language about God be changed to feminine, for then the church will have lost that God in whom it truly lives and moves and has its being."[1]

Whereas Achtemeier judges feminist God-naming claims by reference to the authority of biblical and doctrinal tradition, feminist theologian Rosemary Radford Ruether reverses that approach and appraises the adequacy of biblical witness by reference to how well it supports feminist theology. Yet both writers express strikingly similar judgments of the possibility of finding biblical bases for feminist God-language. In Ruether's view, "Feminist theology must create a new textual base, a new canon. . . . Feminist theology cannot be done from the existing base of the Christian Bible."[2] With this assertion Achtemeier would agree.

In reviewing some of the recent efforts by feminist theologians to devise new liturgical language for addressing and referring to God, Susan Schnur is highly critical, but she declares, "I take issue not as a traitor at all, but out of loyalty to feminism." Having examined liturgical experiments within "Women-Church," she sadly finds too little interest in "manifestations of the sacred" or "any of the primary questions of liturgy." As she sees it, these feminist liturgies too often "have to do only with the *political.*" In such instances, Rabbi Schnur says, "politics is often the doctrine for which the liturgy is the vehicle (a dog wagged by a tail)."[3] Writing not on liturgy or theology but on women's history, Sara Pomeroy is widely recognized for her major scholarly contributions on women in the ancient world (and also for staunchly maintaining women's rights on

---

1. Achtemeier, "Female Language for God: Should the Church Adopt It?" in *The Hermeneutical Quest: Essays in Honor of James Luther Mays on his Sixty-fifth Birthday,* ed. Donald G. Miller (Allison Park, Pa.: Pickwick Publications, 1986), pp. 97, 109.

2. Ruether, *Womanguides: Readings Toward a Feminist Theology* (Boston: Beacon Press, 1985), p. ix.

3. Schnur, reviewing Rosemary Ruether's *Women-Church: Theology and Practice of Feminist Liturgical Communities,* in *New York Times Book Review,* 21 December 1986, p. 25.

her own university faculty); she has warned against the kind of history writing that subordinates "principles of historical investigation to feminist politics."[4]

Of at least equal concern is the subordination of thought to ideology; one might hope that we had already seen enough of that in our tragic century. Yet in this context the distinguished Diana Trilling deplores "the ideological excess we have come to associate with the women's movement,"[5] while Kenneth Minogue's seminal book on ideology cites feminist language theory as an example of ideology dominating evidence.[6] Of course, the women's movement need not be an ideological straitjacket, as many will testify, but it is necessary to protest when feminist politics and feminist ideology overpower critical judgment.

Proposals made by some feminist theologians to solve women's problems by changing the language for God are not true solutions at all but are distractors. Although *distractor* is not a very familiar word, it is highly pertinent here. As used by students of language and knowledge analysis, it identifies an answer that may look right but is not. Instead of providing a solution for a problem, it "distracts" those who are seeking solutions into accepting answers that do not work. The introduction of feminist-oriented language for God is such a distractor. Not only will it not resolve the issues to which it is addressed, but it violates the basic faith structures it purports only to modify.

Some of this will perhaps become clearer if we examine a feminist rallying cry coined in 1974 by Mary Daly: "Since God is male, the male is God."[7] The implied conclusion is that the liberation of women requires the emasculation of God. But Daly's slogan is full of errors, both of interpretation and of deduction. Ancient Greek and Roman gods such as Zeus showed that they were "male" in every sense, as the myths of their incessant sexual exploits demonstrate, but God the Father is not sexually male either in the Bible or in Christian doctrine. More will be said about grammatical gender and about figurative language for God in the Bible in the last three sections of this paper, but at this point we need to consider Daly's slogan.

4. Pomeroy, *New York Times Book Review,* 20 April 1986, p. 12.

5. Trilling was pleased to note that a recent book by Gloria Steinem "for the most part admirably avoids" that excess. See Trilling's review in *New York Times Book Review,* 21 December 1986, p. 23.

6. Minogue, *Alien Powers: The Pure Theory of Ideology* (New York: St. Martin's Press, 1985), p. 249.

7. Daly, "The Qualitative Leap Beyond Patriarchal Religion," *Quest* 1 (1974): 21.

"Since God is male" begins with an assumption that the mainstream of biblical religion has consistently denied. References to God as Father do not indicate male sexuality, either in the Bible or in the central Christian and Jewish traditions, although similar language did indicate divine sexuality (both male and female) in ancient pagan and Gnostic religions. Numbers 23:19 is typical in declaring that God is "not man," while Deuteronomy 4:15-16 details Moses' teaching about the sexual issue with unmistakable clarity: "Therefore take good heed to yourselves. Since you saw no form on the day that the Lord spoke to you at Horeb out of the midst of the fire, beware lest you act corruptly by making a graven image for yourselves, in the form of any figure, the likeness of male or female." After surveying the repeated biblical references to God as Father, Hans Küng writes that this fatherhood symbol "has no sexual implications and has nothing to do with religious paternalism."[8]

The church fathers spoke to the same effect: Athanasius, the great defender of trinitarian doctrine against the Arians, affirmed the nonsexual nature of God the Father and his begetting of Jesus as the incarnate Son: "In saying 'offspring,' we have no human thoughts, and though we know God to be Father we entertain no material ideas concerning him, but while we listen to these illustrations and terms, we think suitably of God, for he is not as man."[9] Hilary of Poitiers was equally explicit: repudiating "deities endowed with sex," he affirmed that "that which is Divine and eternal must be one without distinction of sex." In the same treatise he explained that we must not measure God's nature by the limitations of our own, "but gauge God's assertions concerning himself by the scale of his own glorious self-revelation."[10] That has been the position of Christians for centuries, and it can be summed up in the words of Dorothy Sayers: in doctrine and tradition, Christianity "sets its face against all sexual symbolism for the divine fertility," and "we do not suppose for one moment that God procreates children in the same manner as a human father and we are quite well aware that preachers who use the 'father' metaphor intend and expect no such perverse interpretation of their lan-

8. Küng, *On Being a Christian* (Garden City, N.Y.: Doubleday, 1976), p. 311.

9. Athanasius, *De Synodis*, 42, in *Athanasius: Select Writings and Letters,* in *Nicene and Post-Nicene Fathers of the Christian Church,* second series, vol. 4, ed. Philip Schaff (New York: Christian Literature Publishing Co., 1892), p. 472.

10. Hilary of Poitiers, *On the Trinity,* 1.4 and 18, in *Nicene and Post-Nicene Fathers of the Christian Church,* second series, vol. 9, ed. Henry Wace (New York: Christian Literature Publishing Co., 1899), pp. 41, 45.

guage."[11] The pervasive biblical references to God as Father do not teach that "God is male."

Neither do they teach that "the male is God." The claim of divine status for any human individual, group, or ideology is the originating sin from which all other sins derive. Regarding any individual, sex, class, race, nation, or party as God is blatant idolatry. Writing in the second century A.D., Theophilus defined the basic meaning the church has perennially found in the parabolic story of the Fall: "even then (Gen. 3:5) error was striving to disseminate a multitude of gods, saying, 'ye shall be as gods.'"[12] To act as though "the male is God" is not a logical outcome of biblical religion but a rejection of it.

Daly's slogan that "since God is male, the male is God" has exerted great influence. It also evidences the disparity between understandings of God in much feminist theology and in historic Christianity. Much the same thing will be found as we proceed to consider the distinctive Christian doctrine of the Trinity.

The Christian Godhead, Pro and Con

The New Testament church was committed to continuing the ancient traditions of Israel, and during the following centuries orthodox, catholic Christianity steadfastly rejected all heretical efforts to jettison the Old Testament. Early Christians were as committed as the Jews to monotheism, but their monotheism co-existed with and through experiences of the divine encountered as Father, Son, and Holy Spirit. Theologically their problem was to find language that would affirm and preserve both the oneness of deity and the threeness of divine presence they knew. It was not a simple problem. The perils of falling into one or another partial rejection of the faith were awesome. Under the circumstances, it would have been easy to settle for half-solutions and be left with either a sterile unitarianism or a stripped-down polytheism. Neither of these "solutions" would have solved anything, of course, and neither would have worked. Instead, the church continued to

11. Sayers, "The Image of God," in her *Christian Letters to a Post-Christian World* (Grand Rapids: William B. Eerdmans, 1969), pp. 100 and 102.

12. Theophilus, *To Autolycus*, 2.28, in *The Ante-Nicene Fathers*, vol. 2, ed. Alexander Roberts and James Donaldson (Buffalo: Christian Literature Publishing Co., 1885), p. 105. It would be good to trace the centrality of this understanding through the Christian centuries, but space does not allow me to do so here.

affirm both threeness and oneness, expressed in different ways in different times and places over a period of several centuries of thought, discussion, and debate, and eventually the church arrived at a lastingly satisfying theological "formula" for the triune God.

The formulation of the Christian doctrine of the Trinity is one of the most impressive intellectual achievements in human history, whatever else it may be. It involved analyses of at least equal sophistication to those of present-day astrophysics and physical theory, and it achieved coherence of theological meaning while preserving the divine mystery. Five or six centuries were required for the full development of this careful, nuanced, and balanced formulation to preserve and present theologically the three persons whom Christians encounter as divine, without falling into polytheism, but maintaining a single and undivided godhead: Father, Son, and Holy Spirit. In contrast, the effort to apply inclusive language to the Christian deity is no more than twenty years old. Feminist proposals for God-language thus bear the marks of hastiness more appropriate to political campaigning than to subtle and judicious theological analysis. Under the circumstances it would be neither right nor wise for the twentieth-century church to disrupt that trinitarian synthesis by superimposing upon it the unreconcilable God-language of feminism.

Some feminists wish to substitute such terms as *Creator, Liberator,* and *Comforter* for the three persons of Father, Son, and Holy Spirit in order to avoid "embarrassment" about the first two persons, perhaps unaware that the proposed terms are not synonymous with the trinitarian ones.[13] Others advocate "Father [and Mother]" in place of Father, or an alternation between them. Gail Ramshaw Schmidt proposes that in "liturgical prayer God the Father may and should be addressed as mother, providing that 'mother' be recognized as an epithet for God and not a divine name,"[14] but for most worshipers that would create vast confusion. Rita Gross uses the phrase "God-she" and holds that it "is appropriately used in every context in which any reference to God occurs."[15] Rosemary

---

13. See Geoffrey Wainwright's critique of such non-equivalent substitutions in his "A Language in Which We Speak to God," *Worship* 57 (1983): 319. See also his "Trinitarian Worship" in *The New Mercersburg Review,* Autumn 1986, pp. 3-11, and his critique of *An Inclusive-Language Lectionary* in *Biblical Theology Bulletin* 14 (1984): 28-30.

14. Schmidt, "Lutheran Liturgical Prayer and God as Mother," *Worship* 52 (November 1978): 517-18.

15. I do not see how this proposal can fit with either Jewish or Christian theology,

Ruether is comfortable with "God/ess" in referring to the deity.[16] Elisabeth Schüssler Fiorenza is partial to "Sophia-God" as placing Israel's God "in the language and *Gestalt* of the goddess."[17]

Some feminist advocates also object to references to Jesus as Son of God and Son of Man, proposing instead "Human Child" or "Child of God" and the elimination of the masculine pronouns "he" and "his," thereby reducing biblical particularity to generality. Thus the magnificent declaration of John 3:16-17 — "For God so loved the world that he gave his only Son, that whoever believes in him should not perish but have eternal life. For God sent the Son into the world, not to condemn the world, but that the world might be saved through him" — is recast in *An Inclusive-Language Lectionary* to read, "For God so loved the world that God gave God's only Child, that whoever believes in that Child should not perish but have eternal life. For God sent that Child into the world, not to condemn the world, but that through that Child the world might be saved."[18] Even worse than the plodding monotony of this rewriting of John 3 is its confusion of the original biblical clarity and directness, and its rejection of incarnate particularity.

Even worse than that is the explanation by the Inclusive-Language Committee that they changed biblical texts so that " 'God the Father and Mother' is used as a formal equivalent of 'the Father' or 'God the Father' " in their rendering of Scripture.[19] But the claim that "God the Father and Mother" is equivalent (formally or otherwise) to "God the Father" requires the use of a "double-speak" language such as George Orwell satirized in *1984.* Two examples will suffice. In John 4:23 of this lectionary, Jesus prophesied to the woman at the well in Samaria that "the true worshippers will worship [*God*] the [*Mother and*] Father in spirit and truth, for such are those whom God seeks as worshippers." Philippians 2:10-11 is altered to declare that at the name of Jesus every knee should bow "to the glory of God the Father [*and Mother*]."[20] Such "recasting" is in effect a rewriting of the biblical literature. It violates the integrity of a text. Even in secular

---

but see Rita M. Gross, "Female God Language in a Jewish Context," in *Womanspirit Rising,* ed. Carol P. Christ and Judith Plaskow (New York: Harper & Row, 1979), p. 173.

16. Ruether, *Sexism and God-Talk: Toward a Feminist Theology* (Boston: Beacon Press, 1983), p. 211 and passim.

17. Schüssler Fiorenza, *In Memory of Her: A Feminist Theological Reconstruction of Christian Origins* (New York: Crossroad, 1985), pp. 133-35.

18. *An Inclusive-Language Lectionary: Readings for Year A,* rev. ed. (Atlanta: John Knox Press; New York: Pilgrim Press; and Philadelphia: Westminster Press, 1986), p. 88.

19. Ibid., p. 269.

20. Ibid., pp. 92, 43.

literature, such violations are regarded by responsible students as the cardinal sin of literary criticism, interpretation, and translation.

Altering important literary texts and language to fit some ethical, political, or social purpose can be expected to do more unintended harm than intended good. Sometimes the results are merely ridiculous, as was the case with the first bowdlerized edition of Shakespeare. In the early years of the nineteenth century, the Reverend Thomas Bowdler was convinced that many expressions in the Bard's works could not be read "with propriety," and he proceeded to clean up the plays so that they could be read without offense or, as he put it, without raising "a blush of shame on the cheek of modesty." Bowdler's edition was not much of a contribution to literature, but it did result in adding a valuable new word to our vocabulary — the verb "to bowdlerize," which means to alter language to meet some desired social purpose. Easy as it is to laugh at in this case, bowdlerizing can have far more serious consequences, even though bowdlerizers always profess (and sincerely profess) the most exalted motives. When feminist advocates alter the biblical language for God, they are bowdlerizing the readings of Scripture and of Christian doctrine.

There is no evidence that such bowdlerizing of God-language will advance the cause of women. On the contrary, historical evidence indicates that the inclusion of feminine references and indeed of female divinities within polytheism did not result in improved status for women in the societies that revered those gods and goddesses, and there is no reason to think it would do so today. Noted historical scholar Samuel Terrien has observed that "the change to the metaphor of mother will not solve the problem which, for some women today, arises from the metaphor of father."[21]

What such changes can achieve is the confusion and even the disruption of the central Christian doctrine of the Trinity. "Inclusive" terms such as those proposed by feminist theologians are not only unreconciled with the judicious balances of trinitarian economy but obviously contradict them. When references are extended to include God the Mother and Father, we are already in a polytheistic world of quaternity, at the very least. The delicate and subtle distinctions that have allowed the presentation of three persons in a single monotheistic godhead are thus either confused or even disrupted and destroyed.[22]

---

21. Terrien, *Till the Heart Sings: A Biblical Theology of Manhood and Womanhood* (Philadelphia: Fortress Press, 1985), p. 210.

22. For a comprehensive general analysis, see Donald G. Bloesch, *The Battle for*

Whether or not feminist theologians recognize that feminist language for God disrupts the "trinity in unity," the fact remains that this is the result. What is more, the impression of the First Person is radically changed. Combined words such as *Father and Mother, Mother-Father, God-she,* and *he/she* suggest a grotesque hermaphrodite god or androgynous divinity. Rita Gross is quite candid about this, frankly advocating "imagery of bisexual androgynous deity."[23] This is not really a new religious option but revives Gnostic beliefs long ago condemned by Judaism and Christianity. I am reminded of the warning spoken in A.D. 380 by Gregory of Nazianzus against heretical attempts to introduce "the hermaphrodite god of Marcion [Marcus?] and Valentinus."[24]

The problems of feminist language arise not only from nouns but equally from pronouns. It is sometimes suggested that a solution lies in the evasion of pronouns altogether. Thus Gail Ramshaw Schmidt called upon us "to eliminate altogether . . . the expository use of pronouns referring to God," and Harold Oliver would go "beyond the feminist critique" (to echo his essay title) by dispensing with pronouns for God.[25] The avoidance of gendered pronouns for God may be possible in certain other languages, as I understand is the case in Korean, but such examples (though linguistically interesting) are not directly pertinent to the conduct of worship and theology in the Indo-European languages.

In English, the use of singular pronouns is restricted to masculine, feminine, and neuter. Furthermore, in English speech and writing, personhood and personality are conveyed by a choice of pronouns, and in our syntax and lexicon there is simply no means to convey this affirmation of person apart from choosing between the singular masculine and feminine pronouns. The elimination of pronouns would subvert the Christian belief in a personal God, just as the use of *he/she* variations would indicate a hermaphroditic deity.

Because biblical religion has consistently excluded sexual meaning

---

the *Trinity: The Debate Over Inclusive God-Language* (Ann Arbor: Servant Publications, 1985). See also the citations of Geoffrey Wainwright in note 13.

23. Gross, "Female God Language in a Jewish Context," p. 168.

24. Gregory of Nazianzus, "Fifth Theological Oration: On the Spirit," in *Christology of the Later Fathers,* ed. E. R. Hardy and C. C. Richardson (Philadelphia: Westminster Press, 1954), p. 198.

25. Schmidt, "De Divinis Nominibus: The Gender of God," *Worship* 56 (1982): p. 129; and Oliver, "Beyond the Feminist Critique," *Christian Century,* 1 May 1985, pp. 46-48.

from the "fatherhood" of God, thoughtful Christians have reason to be concerned when this traditionally nonsexual symbolism of God is being replaced or supplemented by explicitly feminist images, with the result that sexual emphasis is introduced in deity, where it has no place. One does not need to elaborate on extreme examples such as "the God with breasts" or "the empowering womb of the Great Mother goddess from which all creation emerges" to see this result. The campaign for feminine God-language even in its more restrained forms in effect replaces nonsexist metaphors with sexist metaphors, as Paul Minear has pointed out.[26] The result is a theological vocabulary compounded of pantheism, animism, and polytheism.

Many feminist theologians appear unaware of or undisturbed by such problems, but some leaders of the movement have candidly faced them. The influential Mary Daly describes "the significance of the women's revolution as anti-Christ and its import as anti-church," and she has left Christianity. Rosemary Ruether has not gone that far, but it is well to remember her statement that "feminist theology cannot be done from the existing base of the Christian Bible."[27] The importance of these two observations can scarcely be exaggerated.

Conflicting Approaches to History

One significant difference underlying contemporary debates about acceptable language for God concerns history and how it is to be understood. Feminist theology often defends the use of gender-inclusive language for the godhead by arguing that the vision of the biblical writers was bound by the patriarchal limits of their society and that they could not recognize the possibilities inherent in the idea of God as Mother or in affirming both the fatherhood and the motherhood of God. They thought of God as Father rather than as Mother because they were culturally conditioned or even controlled, and we are told that we in the twentieth century should correct those "errors." As a witty feminist friend once put it, "Those ancient Jews didn't know what they were missing." It is a plausible debating

26. Minear, "Changes in Metaphor Produce Changes in Thought," *Presbyterian Outlook*, 19-26 Dec. 1983.

27. Daly, *Beyond God the Father: Toward a Philosophy of Women's Liberation* (Boston: Beacon Press, 1973), p. 140; and Ruether, *Womanguides*, p. ix.

point, but it happens to be wrong. Far from being unable to conceive of worshiping female deities, the ancient Jewish and Christian authors of our Bible were more aware than we of the range and implications of polytheistic alternatives. They were surrounded and at many times almost engulfed by cults worshiping the Great Mother, along with other divinities of both sexes. Further, pagan societies in the ancient world who worshiped female deities were surely no less patriarchal than were the ancient Hebrews. The biblical authors were more familiar with the alternative than we are, and their awareness was both direct and existential.

Biblical scholar Elizabeth Achtemeier puts it this way: "It is not that the prophets were slaves to their patriarchal culture, as some feminists hold. And it is not that the prophets *could not* imagine God as female: they were surrounded by people who so imagined their deities. It is rather that the prophets, as well as the Deuteronomists and Priestly writers and Jesus and Paul, *would not* use such language, because they knew and had ample evidence from the religions surrounding them that female language for the deity results in a basic distortion of the nature of God and of his relation to his creation."[28] Conceptions of a feminine deity or deities have historically been false guides to religious truth, as Achtemeier cogently argues, and both historically and currently entail radically different views from those of Christianity on such a broad range of subjects as Creator and creation, nature and grace, time and history, sin and salvation, and revelation and Scripture. The great Martin Buber, whose understanding of the prophetic tradition has enriched all students of the Bible, found from his long reflection on the Canaanite threat to Israel in "the depths of the baalization of Yahweh" that the faith in Yahweh was undermined not so much from the *baalim* but "rather from the mother-goddesses."[29] The ancient goddess cults and other polytheistic religions did not by any means "liberate" women, but today we are being called to revive them in one form or another in order to provide a higher status for women. W. A. Visser 't Hooft comments on this anomaly: "The paradoxical element in this situation is that precisely when the great issue is the recognition of the full human dignity of women, there is a returning interest in those ancient religious systems, in which women were not fully regarded as persons."[30]

---

28. Achtemeier, "Female Language for God," p. 109; italics hers.
29. Buber, *The Prophetic Faith* (New York: Harper & Row, 1949), p. 121.
30. Visser 't Hooft, *The Fatherhood of God in an Age of Emancipation* (Philadelphia: Westminster Press, 1982), p. 132.

Carol Christ, who classifies herself as a radical feminist and whom Rosemary Ruether calls "a leading Goddess feminist," would doubtless disagree with Achtemeier, Buber, and Visser 't Hooft on most points, but nonetheless agrees with them on the question at issue here. As Christ puts it, the absence of female deities "in biblical religion is no mere oversight, nor can it be blamed on the cultural milieu in which the biblical canon was shaped. The active suppression of symbols of the goddess and God the Mother is at the heart of the process of the formation of the Hebrew and Christian Bibles."[31]

Biblical references to God as Father were not culturally imposed but were made in awareness of the alternatives, an awareness fuller and more immediate than our own. Such historical recognitions are disturbing to a number of feminist advocates and are often ignored. But history must be taken seriously, and such evidence simply must be faced. As Sara Pomeroy puts it, "The psychological advantage some women might gain from knowledge of a past in which women dominated men or were equal to them cannot, in the long run, justify the subordination of principles of historical investigation to feminist politics."[32]

That subordination of historical principles also appears in efforts to claim a broader foundation of biblical support for feminizing God-language than in fact exists. Several verses do compare God to a woman or a mother, and these should be properly considered within their immediate context and within the full context of Scripture. But the impression is often given that "there are many female images for God in the Scriptures," as the editors of *An Inclusive-Language Lectionary* put it, or that "many Old Testament writers" used maternal "metaphors" for God, as we read in *The Motherhood of God* (produced in a 1984 Scottish study panel), to cite only two examples.[33] These are not outright falsifications, but they

31. Christ, from her chapter "Symbols of Goddess and God in Feminist Theology," in *The Book of the Goddess Past and Present: An Introduction to Her Religion,* ed. Carl Olsen (New York: Crossroad, 1983), p. 249, with supporting cross-reference to her "Outsiders and Heretics," *Soundings* 61, no. 3.

32. Pomeroy, *New York Times Book Review,* 20 April 1986, p. 12.

33. *An Inclusive-Language Lectionary,* p. 269, and *The Motherhood of God: A Report by a Study Group Appointed by the Woman's Guild and the Panel on Doctrine on the Invitation of the General Assembly of the Church of Scotland,* ed. Alan E. Lewis (Edinburgh: Saint Andrew Press, 1984), p. 64. The Scottish report got a very hostile reception from the National Woman's Guild and was overwhelmingly rejected by the General Assembly. For brief reports on these two meetings, see the Church of Scotland magazine entitled *Life and Work,* the issues for June 1984 (p. 22) and July 1984 (p. 11), respectively.

are at least exaggerations. Part of the problem here involves interpretations of the feminine *Hōkmāh-Wisdom* personification, to which I shall turn in a later section when we examine rhetorical figures in the Bible, but let us now consider the other available examples.

Professor Mayer I. Gruber of Ben Gurion University in Israel has surveyed the Hebrew Scriptures for feminine references to deity and reports only four unequivocal feminine images for the deity, all in Second Isaiah (42:14; 45:10; 49:15; 66:13). In addition to these, he considers various arguments for other feminine allusions to God (including a few distantly gynomorphic etymologies), and he argues that it is incorrect to compare less palpable feminine references with these four verses. As he puts it, only "the anonymous prophet explicitly compares the Lord to a mother, while throughout the rest of the Hebrew Scriptures the Lord is explicitly compared to a father but not to a mother."[34] Although Gruber concentrates only on comparisons with human mothers, the addition of the few biblical comparisons of the deity to a mother bird do not significantly alter the picture. I shall consider these avian comparisons (including one by Jesus) when we come to consider figures of speech later in this essay. At this point, however, a simple recognition is in order: God is very rarely compared to a mother. And he is never *called* Mother or *addressed* as Mother in either Testament.

The opening centuries of our era saw a vigorous challenge to biblical monotheism from the Gnostic heresy. Here the issue of feminist theologies assumed great prominence, Gnosticism advocating female and hermaphroditic deities and remarkably ingenious pantheons in which Father, Son, and Holy Spirit might be included along with other divinities. Sometimes pairs or yokes or *syzygies* of male and female gods were sexually linked, while sometimes the connections appear to have been allegorical. The Gnostic movement did not develop a single nuclear conception of divinity and cannot be characterized by central doctrines, but its inclusion of active female and/or feminine beings is striking. When Elaine Pagels considers conflicting images of God posed by "early Christianity" in order to answer the question raised in her essay title, "What Became of God the Mother?" it is in the Gnostic movement that she finds the evidence of that goddess's

---

34. Gruber, "The Motherhood of God in Second Isaiah," *Revue Biblique*, Paris, 1983, p. 357. See also pp. 353-54 and pp. 351-59 passim. In citing Gruber, I follow his placing of Isaiah 66 as Second Isaiah, although that point may be questioned by some scholars. Another valuable analysis is John W. Miller, "Depatriarchalizing God in Biblical Interpretation: A Critique," *Catholic Biblical Quarterly* 48 (1986): 609-16.

continuing presence. Much of what Pagels finds is instructive for comparison with feminist theology, but a few brief examples will have to suffice. God is described not in trinitarian terms but "as a dyadic being who consists of both masculine and feminine elements," sometimes called "mother-father (matropater)." Prayers are offered to both the divine Father and the divine Mother — "Thee, Father," and "Thee, Mother." Much is made of Sophia, the Divine Wisdom, considered not according to Jewish and Christian teachings as a personified attribute of God but as an independent divinity or something of the kind. There are arrays of other "Powers" — masculine, feminine, and masculo-feminine, conceived as "bisexual Power."[35] Pagels offers a survey of such Gnostic conceptions, for which she shows considerable sympathy, and she even shows nostalgia for the loss of these inclusive views of divinity that orthodox Judaism and Christianity refused to accept. One can find in these Gnostic schemes much that is far closer to modern feminist theology than to any of the conceptions in the early church. Even on the unusual occasion when the church fathers used maternal comparisons or illustrations for God's concern and love, both content and context avoid any suggestion of Gnostic androgyny or of "matropater" theology.

For the medieval period, the acknowledged authority on the subject of female language for divinity is Caroline Walker Bynum, whose splendid historical study entitled *Jesus as Mother: Studies in the Spirituality of the High Middle Ages* has achieved wide and deserved recognition since its appearance in 1982. She does indeed find references to Jesus or to God as Mother among some Cistercians and several nuns or anchorites, as well as in a long prayer addressed to St. Paul by Anselm of Canterbury, but she frankly declares that "a handful of Cistercians does not typify the twelfth century, nor three nuns the thirteenth."[36] After completing her detailed analysis, she writes, "The theme of God's motherhood is a minor one in all the writers of the high Middle Ages except Julian of Norwich," and then comments about this theme: "Too long neglected or even repressed by editors and translators, it is perhaps now in danger of receiving more emphasis than it deserves."[37]

35. Pagels, "What Became of God the Mother? Conflicting Images of God in Early Christianity," *Signs: Journal of Women in Culture and Society* 2 (Winter 1976): 293-303, with direct citations from pp. 294 and 296-98.
36. Bynum, *Jesus as Mother: Studies in the Spirituality of the High Middle Ages* (Berkeley and Los Angeles: University of California Press, 1982), p. 3.
37. Ibid., p. 168.

Scripture, Authority, and Figurative Speech

In Christianity, scriptural authority is recognized as basic to the teaching and practice of the whole church. As a twentieth-century heir of the Reformed tradition, I do not always construe this authority in the same way as may a Roman Catholic theologian, or as did the great Reformers, but it operates for all of us.[38] Whatever doctrinal understanding particular churches accept, biblically oriented theologies recognize that it is impossible for unaided human beings to discover on our own the mysteries of God's being and will for us, however much it may be possible by observation and reflection (whether in humane or scientific studies) to recognize important elements of truth about humanity, society, and the created order.

Christianity of the patristic period knew, as G. L. Prestige put it, that God's "wisdom ranges further than human wisdom can compass, just as his power infinitely excels human creative capacity." That realization has been basic in Christian thought, Catholic and Protestant alike, and remains so. The church fathers recognized, as have their great theological successors in later centuries, that God has not revealed the totality of his nature as deity (which our human wisdom could not comprehend) but has revealed himself to our capacity in such ways "as human beings, themselves fettered to the flesh, are capable of hearing." According to Prestige, the foundation of early Christian faith was that God's gracious self-disclosure is effective for believers "to such extent as God can be discerned by man, and man's soul can, while yet in the body, discern God."[39] Thus what God has freely revealed to us is sufficient for our needs. So did the developing church of the first centuries see both the extent of God's providential self-disclosure and the limitations of human mind and language.

In a sustained attack upon Christianity, the second-century pagan philosopher Celsus contended that God "is not to be reached by word." Origen replied by citing a crucial distinction: God is indeed not revealed by the word that originates from us, but is revealed by his Word to us.

---

38. See, for example, the fifth and final version of the formulation on biblical authority of the Second Vatican Council: "The books of Scripture must be acknowledged as teaching firmly, faithfully, and without error that truth which God wanted put into the sacred writings for the sake of our salvation."

39. Prestige, quoted from his *God in Patristic Thought* (1936; reprint, London: SPCK, 1985), pp. 6, 8, 57.

And when Celsus declared that "he cannot be expressed by name," Origen replied that God can be expressed by the name he names himself in disclosing himself to us "in order to lead the hearer by the hand, as it were, and so enable him to comprehend something of God, so far as attainable by human nature."[40]

Hilary of Poitiers also focused the matter sharply: "What man cannot understand, God can be," he declared, and he warned us all that a person "must not measure the Divine nature by the limitations of his own. . . . For he is the best student who does not read his thoughts into the book, but lets it reveal its own; who draws from it its sense, and does not import his own into it."[41] These citations show how the church fathers understood God's self-disclosure to us: it was God's accommodation of his truth to our human capacity and need. The word *accommodation* is central here: God putting what we need to know "according to a mode" we can comprehend. As Calvin expressed it, God is "shown to us not as he is in himself, but as he is toward us."[42] Such attitudes toward scriptural authority have undergirded Christianity from the early church through the Reformation and into our time. They do not make the Bible into a paper idol, but they do receive it as an antidote against desperate ignorance and against presumptuous tampering.

The most dangerous kinds of tampering change biblical texts and language from what they say to what we prefer they should say. Plausible reasons may be advanced to justify such alterations, but nothing can excuse the tragic waste involved. Here I am not referring to an honest translation that can, for example, render the meaning of *anthropos* into English by *humanity* just as accurately as by *man*. Such translations are not my concern here; rather, I am concerned for the transposings of troublesome meanings into more "acceptable" ones. When we (whoever we may be) say of a biblical expression that we "have trouble with that language," we may merely be expressing our human limitations, but if we then proceed to change it to a more agreeable sense, we are subjecting the authority of Scripture to the authority of our tastes and biases. Efforts "to alter the thoughts, intention, and language of the Bible are a covert but nonetheless

40. Origen, *Against Celsus*, 6.65, in *The Ante-Nicene Fathers*, vol. 4, ed. Alexander Roberts and James Donaldson (Buffalo: Christian Literature Publishing Co., 1885), p. 603.

41. Hilary of Poitiers, *On the Trinity*, 3.1 and 1.18, pp. 62 and 45 in *Nicene and Post-Nicene Fathers of the Christian Church*, second series, vol. 9.

42. Calvin, *Institutes*, 1.10.2: *nobis describitur non quis sit apud se, sed qualis erga nos.*

destructive repudiation of the authority of the Bible over the church," as Paul S. Minear says about recommendations to change scriptural metaphors for God into the feminine gender. The problem, as he defines it, is that "when we change what the Bible does say to what we think it should say, it becomes a dummy for our own thought — and no dummy exercises authority over the ventriloquist."[43]

Thoughtful Christians and Jews recognize that biblical language about God is pervasively figurative, but that fact should not delude any of us into assuming that we can therefore change the biblical figures for others that we may prefer. The assumption that we can alter the *figurae* is not only historically and theologically false but equally false linguistically and literarily. The fundamental literary principle is that figures cannot be abandoned, symbols cannot be substituted, images cannot be altered without changing the meaning they convey.[44] That literary principle is even more pertinent to the Bible, where figurative expressions far more often operate as figures of thought than as ornamental figures of speech — or, to put it more directly, biblical figures of speech typically serve as figures of thought and understanding.

Scripture relies on figurative language for God not because such language is stylistically inviting but because it is the most effective mode for conveying God's self-disclosure, not because it is decorative but because it is necessary. God is not ordinary: if he were, we should not need for him to reveal himself to us. Augustine put the matter into sharp focus: "The super-eminence of the Godhead surpasses the power of customary speech."[45] Going beyond "the power of customary speech," Scripture employs figurative speech for God. If figures of speech are not understood, the biblical meanings will be misunderstood and unnecessary controversies

43. Minear, "Changes in Metaphor Produce Changes in Thought."

44. Broadly true as this principle is in reading texts, it is especially true in biblical texts, as contrasted, for example, with certain Greek philosophical readings of literary texts. Aristotle clearly regarded figurative language as ornamental, something used to add attraction to plain speech. One senses that Aristotle would have been happiest if language were totally plain and unadorned, and that he thought language most effective when it moved away from the figurative toward the literal and as close as possible to the mathematical. That position is understandable in terms of Aristotelian (and, in different ways, Platonic) philosophy, although even there it is wrong. But the significant point for us is the distance separating it from biblical conceptions of language.

45. Augustine, *On the Trinity,* 7.4.7, in *The Nicene and Post-Nicene Fathers of the Christian Church,* first series, vol. 3, ed. Philip Schaff (Buffalo: Christian Literature Publishing Co., 1887), p. 109.

will ensue. As Calvin put it, "disregarding the figure of speech, many superfluous contentions will arise."[46]

Our century suffers from a chronic, raging fever of misreading, and people often grossly misunderstand how figurative language operates. Where fundamentalists may insist upon a rigid literalism, their counterparts at the other extreme may assume that if a biblical expression does not literally and univocally represent the data to which it refers, then one figurative expression may work as well as another. These two approaches are mirror images of each other, two sides of the same coin, as I have argued elsewhere. Examples of feminist language for God fall into the second of these two errors.[47]

Because of the centrality of figurative language, it is necessary for us to analyze how it does and does not operate. Our concern will be with two points where advocacy for using feminine God-language has been based on misreading figurative speech: first are the biblical passages where Wisdom is made to speak, or is described and said to have done certain things, and second are the passages where God is compared to a mother. As for the first point, feminist theologians use the feminine gender of Wisdom in Hebrew and Greek to suggest something akin to a divine feminine apotheosis or hypostasis, whereas these passages should be read as examples of Hebrew personification. In the second place, the associations of God with motherhood typically come in similies, while the father associations typically operate through metaphor. In feminist interpretation, simile and metaphor are confused and even conflated so that a simile is assumed to do what a metaphor in fact is designed to do. In this way, occasional biblical comparisons of the divine to a mother are given the same force as if they were names or identifications. We shall consider these two confusions in order.

"Wisdom": Attribute Personified or Divinity Identified?

Sophia and *Hōkmāh,* the Greek and Hebrew words for wisdom, are in the feminine gender. To assume because of the feminine gender of *Sophia*-

---

46. Calvin, *Institutes,* 3.24.17.

47. For my "two sides of the coin" argument, see "Metaphors, Equations, and the Faith," *Theology Today* 37 (1980): 260-66. For my response to the pressing contemporary problem of rigid fundamentalist literalism as the first of these twin errors, see my book entitled *Is God a Creationist? The Religious Case Against Creation-Science* (New York: Charles Scribner's Sons, 1983).

Hōkmāh that these words refer to an actual female being is as dangerous an extrapolation as it would be to assume that abstract nouns in the masculine gender represented sexual males (in inflected languages, abstract nouns have genders that do not and cannot represent physical and biological distinctions of sex, as is also true for inanimate objects). A distinguished linguist has pointed out to me that in northern Europe the word for "sun" is feminine and the word for "moon" is masculine, whereas in southern Europe the opposite is so. That is one of the illogicalities of language which we must recognize: gender is not synonymous with sex.

In the Old Testament, wisdom is most commonly associated with prudence and know-how, but in Proverbs 8 it is the *Hōkmāh* of God that is presented as speaking. In traditional exegesis from the Tannaite rabbis and the church fathers into our own time, this representation has been interpreted not as an independent divine reality but as an instance of Hebrew personification, the rabbinic exegetes often viewing this Wisdom as personifying the Torah, and the Christian exegetes seeing it as dramatizing that attribute of God called wisdom, while rhetoricians took Proverbs 8 as a classic example of personification as a literary device.

In our own time, however, feminist theologians have often taken a radically different tack in which *Sophia-Hōkmāh* appears to have been elevated from a set of abstract divine attributes, characteristics, or qualities into a kind of feminine divinity, or alternatively seems to represent a kind of feminine divine hypostasis or person. The outlines of these interpretations are not always clear, to say the least, but at times we seem to be presented with an individual divinity strikingly like one of the ancient Egyptian or Near Eastern goddesses of Wisdom from a pagan pantheon. Space does not permit a full treatment of this theological development, so I shall illustrate by citing Elisabeth Schüssler Fiorenza's repeated references to the Hebrew's "gracious Sophia-God" and the "Sophia-God of Jesus." Whether by feminist apotheosis or by an inherent divine nature, *Sophia-Hōkmāh* is thus presented as a divine feminine being or hypostasis. As Schüssler Fiorenza puts it, "Divine Sophia is Israel's God in the language and *Gestalt* of the Goddess."[48] Here Schüssler Fiorenza and other feminist theologians are in line with Gnostic heresy, as when Ptolomaeus declared that the "celestial mother Sophia" bestowed the Logos upon Jesus at his baptism.[49] And so the old Gnostic pairing of feminine and masculine

48. Schüssler Fiorenza, *In Memory of Her,* pp. 132-35.
49. See Prestige, *God in Patristic Thought,* p. 130.

deities or *syzygies* is reintroduced, but those who do this often seem unaware of the polytheism inherent in this hypostatizing or apotheosizing, as the case may be. Furthermore, it is interesting that those who argue that *Sophia-Hōkmāh* is in some way a divine being are repeating a favorite Arian argument for the subordination of Son to Father by interpreting Jesus Christ as the incarnation not of God but of God's Wisdom.[50]

For the frequent biblical instances, we may find personification defined in the words of G. B. Caird: "Personification is a literary device whereby we treat as a person that which is recognized to be not a person."[51] Personification — of inanimate nature, of cities and peoples, of concepts such as love, jealousy, and death, and of attributes or marks of the divine presence — appear frequently in the Old Testament. Heinz Cassirer, Cornford, and other scholars have argued that personification often replaced mythical figures as polytheism receded before more rational attitudes. However that may be, skillfully employed personification can convey the power of mythical figures without implying mythical hypostases. R. B. Y. Scott, in his Anchor edition of Proverbs, holds that *Hōkmāh* is a "function or attribute" possessed within the deity, and that Wisdom is "neither instrument nor agent but the attribute displayed by Yahweh in creating," and again that it is "a divine attribute displayed in creative action, not an aspect of the divine reality having a quasi-independent identity."[52] On the other hand, those who argue for a divine feminine in Wisdom can easily fall into polytheism or at least the appearance of polytheism, whatever their intentions may be.

Mother Similes and Father Metaphors: Operative Distinctions

The Scriptures again and again use metaphor and naming to call God "Father"; occasionally they also compare him to a mother (whether avian or human) by the use of simile. The comparisons to a mother are very few in proportion to the identifications as "Father," but the significant differences here are not only a matter of keeping score. These significant

---

50. *The Anchor Bible: Proverbs, Ecclesiastes,* ed. R. B. Y. Scott (Garden City, N.Y.: Doubleday, 1965), p. 73. This is not to suggest that the Arians advocated inclusive language for divinity.

51. Caird, *Language and Imagery of the Bible* (Philadelphia: Westminster Press, 1980), p. 80.

52. *The Anchor Bible,* pp. 70-73.

differences are expressed through appropriate rhetorical and linguistic forms: the basic distinction lies between the operations of simile/comparing (mother) and metaphor/naming (father), and the meanings they convey.

Because *metaphor* is often used loosely as an approximate variant for *figures of speech* in general, there can be some confusion here. But there is a more precise and specialized sense in which the term *metaphor* is used that distinguishes it from the simile in terms of function and effects. Both involve some degree of resemblance or analogy between one "thing" and another, but the presentations differ markedly. The differences should be observed and evaluated in representative biblical texts: we need to appraise the function and effect of feminine similes for God as compared with masculine metaphors for God as found in the Bible. But first let us consider the meaning of the rhetorical terms.

Let us begin with the simple and straightforward definition given by a well-known nineteenth-century student of biblical rhetoric, E. W. Bullinger: "Simile differs from metaphor in that it merely states resemblance, while metaphor boldly transfers the representation," and again, "while the simile gently states that one thing is like or resembles another, the metaphor boldly and warmly declares that one thing is the other."[53] Recalling that such devices were used substantively and not ornamentally by the biblical writers (for whom figures of speech were typically figures of thought), let us now turn from definition to function.

I have chosen as examples of the different operations of simile and metaphor two instances of these figures, both referring to human mortality. The first, 2 Samuel 14:14, reads: "We must all die; we are like water spilt on the ground, which cannot be gathered up again" — an unmistakable example of illustrative simile. On the other hand, Genesis 3:19 provides a striking metaphor: "You are dust, and to dust you shall return." This

---

53. *Figures of Speech Used in the Bible*, 2nd ed., ed. E. W. Bullinger (1898; reprint, Grand Rapids: Baker Book House, 1968), pp. 727, 735. Bullinger was usually clear and correct on basic meanings and distinctions, and he was an immensely diligent cataloguer of examples, but he sometimes showed a lack of subtlety in his interpretations. Furthermore, he tended to ignore the fact that in certain periods different "terms of art" were applied to name such inherent distinctions as those between simile and metaphor, but for our purposes in this essay we have neither the need nor the time to trace these different terms. The distinctions Bullinger cites between simile and metaphor have provided the basic starting point for analyses in the time of the early Greek rhetoricians and into the modern period.

metaphor in Genesis identifies humankind with a physical element (dust) common to earth and recalls the creation from dust, while the simile in 2 Samuel compares human life to one physical element (water) and proceeds to indicate the nature of this particular likeness (human life, like literal water literally spilled, cannot be "gathered up again"). Obviously the two figures function in quite distinct ways, and it would misinterpret Scripture to say that humanity is water in the same sense that it is said to be dust. The dust metaphor resonates widely through the biblical and Christian traditions to contribute a very basic conception of human contingency.

For our concerns in this essay, such representative definitions and examples as I have cited (and others might have been used) are provided for early clarification, but what is more important is the actual functioning of relevant scriptural uses of language for God. Functionally, a metaphor is a rhetorical figure that carries words and phrases beyond their customary or lexical meanings in order to provide a fuller and more direct understanding of the subject. Simile, on the other hand, operates as a likening of words in their customary or "dictionary sense" in some particular way clarified or explained by the context. When metaphor operates with poetic power, it is "language at full stretch," to use a fine phrase coined by British critic Winifred Nowottny, and as she recognizes, it goes beyond or even contrary to the "dictionary meaning" to provide a fuller vision.[54] "The Lord is my Shepherd" is a fine example of metaphoric language at full stretch, where the dictionary meaning of *shepherd* is extended into new contexts and perceptions: as theologian Janet Martin Soskice observes, "It is characteristic of metaphor to be extendable."[55] That metaphor from the Twenty-third Psalm is taken up in John 10:11 as "I am the good shepherd," and also in Hebrews 13:20 in the apposition "Jesus, the great shepherd of the sheep." So "stretched," "the good shepherd" becomes a transparent equivalent to Jesus the Christ, in the sense that it recognizably identifies him, even functioning as a recognizable "naming" for him, even though he is never said to have literally herded sheep.

Jesus is also called the Lamb of God, and here we can again see how what I will call predicating metaphors operate. At least two stages

54. Nowottny, *The Language Poets Use* (London: Athlone Press, 1962), p. 85 and passim.
55. Soskice, *Metaphor and Religious Language* (Oxford: Clarendon Press, 1989), p. 94.

behind that "Lamb of God" identification is the animal lamb, and in the intermediate stage between the animal lamb and the Johannine phrase is the lamb of sacrifice, offered for sin and atonement according to the Pentateuchal code. By this metaphoric naming the Fourth Gospel reminds us of the small, harmless animal and also of the same animal sacrificed in the temple as a propitiation, but it goes beyond both to provide us with a new conception of the person of Jesus as the Lamb of God when John the Baptist calls him "the Lamb of God, who takes away the sin of the world" (John 1:29). Here we see a marvelous adaptation from zoomorphic to metamorphic use — and finally to the metaphoric naming and identifying use. Other adaptations may be found in the book of Revelation, in the war against the Lamb in which "the Lamb will conquer them" (17:14), and in references to the "throne of God and of the Lamb" (22:1-3 and other variants). In these ways the metaphoric predicating of "Lamb of God" becomes a transparent equivalent to Christ, whom it recognizably identifies.

A simile operates in a more restricted way. Instead of direct invocation or the straightforward grammatical subject-predicate-object relationship expressed or implied by metaphor, a simile draws a self-limiting comparison. An example may be found in Isaiah 42:13: "The Lord goes forth like a mighty man, like a man of war he stirs up his fury." The prophet is careful here not to identify the Lord with a war god, even a supreme war god. Instead, by a formal comparison God is said to "go forth" and "to stir up his fury" *like* a man of war.[56] In the line that follows, Deutero-Isaiah presents the Lord as speaking after a long silence, and once more the figure used is a simile: "now I will cry out like a woman in travail, I will gasp and pant"; the Lord compares himself specifically to a woman in the pangs of childbirth, but no more identifies himself as mother than as warrior. Again, in Isaiah 66:13, the Lord offers a reassuring maternal compassion: "As one whom his mother comforts, so I will comfort you; you shall be comforted in Jerusalem"; this is a deeply impressive and moving comparison. A simile or similitude does not posit a general association; rather, it posits an association applied to some particular sense within an encompassing lexical meaning. The similes comparing God to a mother illustrate some specified phase or facet of divine attitude or intent

56. Observe, in contrast, that Exodus 15:3 metaphorically asserts that "The Lord *is* a man of war," a statement basically different from the prophet's "The Lord is *like* a man of war" (both emphases added).

as defined in the simile's context, but they are not, and do not claim to be, a transparent equivalent to personal identity as are predicating metaphors such as "the good shepherd" and "the Lamb of God" and, even more broadly, God "the Father" and Christ "the Son."

Each of the two maternal similes just quoted from Second Isaiah first states a similarity between the Lord and a human mother and then illustrates that likeness (gasping and panting in travail or comforting her children) — both illustrating God's care for the children of Israel. These may be aptly called "illustrative similes," to apply Janet Martin Soskice's useful descriptive phrase.[57]

In addition to these comparisons of the Lord to human mothers, the Bible also provides illustrative comparisons of God to mother birds. Deuteronomy 32:11-12 lyrically describes God's care for Israel this way: "Like an eagle that stirs up its nest, that flutters over its young, spreading out its wings, catching them, bearing them on its pinions, the Lord alone did lead him." Similarly, Isaiah 31:5 declares, "Like birds hovering, so the Lord of hosts will protect Jerusalem; he will protect and deliver it, he will spare and rescue it."[58] A third and I think even more moving simile involving a mother bird comes in Jesus' lament in Matthew 23:37 and Luke 13:34, in which he speaks of his compassion for Jerusalem: "How often would I have gathered your children together as a hen gathers her brood under her wings, and you would not!" Whether these illustrative similes involve human or avian mothers, they movingly convey important aspects of God's concern for his people.

Whereas similes compare (as in the statement in Deuteronomy 32:11 that the Lord is "like an eagle that stirs up its nest, that flutters over its young"), metaphors directly predicate, identify, or name (as in the metaphoric predication of God in the sixth verse of the same chapter of Deuteronomy: "Is not he your father, who created you, who made you and established you?"). In metaphor, two "things," conceptions, or subjects are brought together in a predication that goes beyond or even counter to

---

57. Soskice, *Metaphor and Religious Language,* pp. 59-60.

58. As I have earlier noted (see p. 29 and note 34), Mayer I. Gruber does not include these avian comparisons along with the human comparisons of God to a mother that he considers unequivocal and apposite. I include them, but their significance should not be exaggerated. For example, the power of these similes to move us is lessened rather than enhanced when Virginia Mollenkott exuberantly twists the comparison into an identification by declaring that "God is our mother-eagle." See Mollenkott, *The Divine Feminine: The Biblical Imagery of God as Female* (New York: Crossroad, 1983), pp. 89-90.

customary, literal, or lexical meanings of the two parts, interanimating them to produce a new, overarching understanding. George Kennedy, who has helped us to see how important rhetorical devices are to reading and interpreting the New Testament, particularly cites the "I am" statements of Jesus — for example, "I am the bread of life," "I am the door," and "I am the vine, you are the branches."[59] Jesus' "I am the light of the world" provides a phrase that has become synonymous with him, as has "Behold, the Lamb of God." We hear all these metaphors as direct predications, while we avoid (as we should) a literalistic interpretation: the words *bread, door,* and *vine* and the phrases "light of the world" and "Lamb of God" are stretched beyond their ordinary uses to extend our understanding.

A more (probably even the most) structural scriptural use of metaphorical predicates comes in biblical references to God the Father and God the Son. In general usage, a metaphor is a designation that separates from others, but in the case of direct biblical references to the deity, metaphor typically separates from all others. Metaphors use "language at full stretch," going beyond the ordinary meanings so as to establish, with great boldness, a fuller representation (but not a reproduction) of their subjects. God as Father is not equivalent to any biological father; he is "our Father who is in heaven," the only almighty, all-loving, all-just, and all-wise Father. While teaching us to address God as "our Father," Jesus also taught us not to confuse any earthly father with the heavenly Father when he said in Matthew 23:9, "Call no man your father on earth, for you have one Father, who is in heaven."

Here it is also good to recall the perennial Christian understanding illustrated in the first section of this essay by the quotation from Athanasius that "in saying 'offspring' . . . we entertain no material ideas concerning him . . . [but] we think suitably of God, for he is not as man," and also by the quotation from Hilary of Poitiers that God the Father is "one without distinction of sex" and that we must not measure God's nature by the limitations of our own, "but gauge God's assertions concerning himself by the scale of his own glorious self-revelation." In our own century, Karl Barth has reaffirmed a continuing interpretation that "true and proper fatherhood resides in God, and from this Fatherhood of God what we know as fatherhood among us men is derived."[60] It is for this

---

59. Kennedy, *New Testament Interpretation through Rhetorical Criticism* (Chapel Hill: University of North Carolina Press, 1984), p. 26.

60. See notes 9 and 10 and Barth, *Dogmatics in Outline,* trans. G. T. Thomson (London: SCM Press, 1949), p. 43. See also Matt. 11:27 and Eph. 3:14-15.

reason that we do not regard God the Father as a magnification of the human fathers we know. We believe him to be our Father because of the teachings and example of his only Son, Jesus Christ, and because of the Scriptures witnessing to him.

So understood, the predicating metaphors "God the Father" and "the Son of God" become transparent equivalents to the divine reality, words by which the divine persons are called, addressed, recognized, or known. These expressions function as structural metaphors or foundational symbols and images, thereby forming the basis for the entire organism of belief, the vertebrate anatomy to which different parts of the living body of faith connect and through which they function. To ignore or deny such structural metaphors can cripple the whole body of theological meaning that they articulate. References to God as Father occur in every New Testament book with the sole exception of the brief epistle of 3 John. God is considered as Father about twenty times in the Old Testament and about 250 times in both Testaments.

Simile is the principal figure in the Scriptures by which God is related to feminine imagery. Virtually all of the indisputable figurative associations of the deity with a mother (whether human or bird) come in about half a dozen similes, not in metaphors, and that distinction is functional and fundamental. In simile two things are not predicated in such unity as we find in metaphor but are said to be similar in some way specified in the context of the developing comparison. Thus the Greek rhetorical term for simile, *homoeosis,* used the formative element *homoi* for likeness rather than *homo* for identification. Consequently, illustrative similes are not "extendable" in the ways that metaphors typically are. Whatever the biblical occasions on which God is compared to a mother, God is never *called* Mother or *addressed* in prayer as Mother in either Testament. The maternal association remains that of similitude or *homoeosis,* never that of appellation or of metaphor.

In a basic methodological sense, to introduce inclusive feminist language for the deity on the basis of *homoeosis* or simile is to replay the controversy between the Arian conception of divine similitude as *homoiousios* and the orthodox conception of *homoousios,* in which Arian "likeness" of Son to Father was pitted against orthodox identity of divine essence or substance in Father and Son, within the trinitarian unity. Whatever the intentions of individual Arians may have been, if they had won that battle they would have achieved the reduction of Christianity to the common level of the competing polytheistic cults of pagan culture.

Returning to our contemporary issues, what is at stake today is not just the wishes of any particular group of feminists but something far more basic. For the church to adopt inclusive feminist language for the deity would disrupt and destroy the careful, nuanced, and balanced formulations that for centuries have made it possible to proclaim the three persons — Father, Son, and Holy Spirit — whom Christians encounter as divine within a single and undivided godhead.

Radical feminist language for speaking of God involves major misreadings of language and of history and historical evidence. Such misuse of history and language cannot achieve desirable results. We cannot alleviate oppression among any segment of humanity by altering the language for the one sovereign God who revealed himself in Scripture and in the person of his only Son, who created us all, male and female, equally in his image and who calls us all to the dignity of his service and the strength of his redeeming love.

As Paul put it in Romans 8:15-16, "When we cry, 'Abba! Father!' it is the Spirit himself bearing witness with our spirit that we are children of God."

The Gender of God and
the Theology of Metaphor

GARRETT GREEN

THE CHRISTIAN community today finds itself embroiled in controversy about the language it uses to speak of God — in its prayer, its worship, its doctrine, and its theological discourse. Viewed from one angle, the issue of gendered language is only the latest in a long series of challenges that the church has faced since the emergence of an autonomous secular culture in Europe about three centuries ago. Like the challenges raised by Copernican astronomy to the church's official cosmology, by critical philosophy to its metaphysics, by scientific historiography to the authority of its scriptures, and by liberal and radical political theories to its social ethics — so the challenge raised by feminism today calls into question certain aspects of the church's belief and practice in light of the regnant secular faith in human autonomy. Perhaps the closest analogy in modern history is the theological controversy surrounding the abolition of slavery, in which the centuries-old Christian justification of slavery was for all practical purposes expunged from the tradition.[1] The undeniable fact that the powerful traditions of secular modernity have their roots in European Christianity contributes to the complexity of these issues, but it does not fundamentally alter the fact that the church throughout the modern period has faced a series of challenges

---

1. Jon D. Levenson discusses the appeals to the Bible, especially the Exodus narrative, made by both pro-slavery and abolitionist theologians in nineteenth-century America. Levenson argues that "both saw part of the picture — the part that provided biblical support for their own position — but failed to do justice to the remainder" ("Liberation Theology and the Exodus," *Reflections* [Yale Divinity School], Winter-Spring 1991, p. 5). Levenson's hermeneutical observations on this and other examples of social-political exegesis are instructive.

to its doctrine and authority from sources essentially external to its own norms and institutions. Viewing the issue of gender in Christian language — specifically, the masculine gender of God — against this background can help to place it in perspective and may even suggest useful analogies with attempts to resolve similar issues in the past.

There is another sense, however, in which feminist critique of Christian language raises more radical — that is, more deeply rooted — issues of Christian doctrine than other modern controversies. Not since ancient times, when the church first formulated its central dogmas in the face of challenges from the religions and philosophies of Greco-Roman culture, have basic Christian concepts been subjected to such scrutiny. Precisely those ancient teachings — the Nicene doctrine of the Trinity in particular — now face a challenge unlike any other in all the intervening centuries.

Despite the prominence of feminist themes in current theological discussion, theologians have not accorded the issue of gender-specific language for God the kind of sustained critical attention that it deserves. Because of the radical nature of the questions involved, failure to address them with theological rigor imperils the integrity of Christian teaching. Some theologians today, in a laudable effort to reverse the long legacy of Christian patriarchalism, are adopting uncritically a view of human language and imagination that is deeply flawed and, if left unchallenged, will do great damage to the coherence of Christian faith and doctrine. Moreover, it prevents theology from making constructive use of Scripture in the struggle to reform the sexual politics of the Christian community. Increasing numbers of Christians (not all of them theologians by any means) find themselves caught in a dilemma whose nature they only partially understand. On the one hand, they feel uncomfortable — even guilty — using biblical language with its masculine gender for God because so many voices are telling them that such language is "oppressive to women," or at the very least that "women can't relate to it." On the other hand, they sense the vacuousness of the abstract and impersonal alternatives and the artificiality of proposals to make the language of Christian prayer, liturgy, and Scripture either gender-neutral or gender-balanced. The way out of the dilemma, I propose, is to identify and criticize certain underlying principles — sometimes explicit, more often implicit, but almost never argued — on which proposals to alter the gendered language of Scripture are based. Only then will it become possible to identify and correct the real errors that have for so many centuries encouraged the subordination of women in the name of Christian doctrine.

45

In an effort to think through theologically the issue of the masculine gender of God, I want first to make explicit the principles implied by one influential type of feminist theology. My response will take two forms, one critical and one constructive: a critique of proposals to eliminate gendered language for God, followed by an attempt to articulate a sounder theological basis for the reform of Christian teaching and practice in response to the challenge of feminism. I will argue that a Christian theological appropriation of feminist concerns requires not the elimination of the masculine gender of God but its interpretation within the context of biblical narrative. This approach necessitates a rejection of traditional male-centered misreadings as well as an articulation of how the language of gender actually works in the Bible.

The Double Error of Genderless Theology

The thesis that God is beyond gender enjoys a certain common-sense plausibility that helps to explain why theological resistance to the neutralizing of Christian language about God has been so sporadic and ineffectual. Virtually no one wants to be associated with a position that seems to imply that God is male. The consequent abdication by theological moderates has left the field to the religious right, encouraging the impression that only biblical literalists and social reactionaries have a stake in defending the language of Scripture. This situation leaves a significant segment of the church (I am convinced that it comprises a majority of Christians today) in a dilemma in which they feel forced to choose between the authority of Scripture and the full humanity of women.

I want to propose a way out of the dilemma that requires us first to examine critically certain assumptions and presuppositions lying behind theological proposals to eliminate masculine language for God or to balance it with feminine terminology. For convenience, this position can be called the theology of the genderless God. It should be noted that both approaches (eliminating the masculine and juxtaposing the genders) proceed from the same premise: that masculine gender ought not to be predicated of God. Whether one responds by avoiding gendered language altogether or by relativizing it through use of the feminine is a secondary issue that I will not address because I am persuaded that their common premise is wrong.

The theology of the genderless God is doubly flawed. In the first place, it misunderstands the nature of the theological problem raised by feminist critique. At the root of the misunderstanding is an implicit acceptance of a projection theory of religion along with theological implications allegedly following from it. I will outline that theory of religion and its associated theology and will go on to examine what is currently its most popular form. This analysis will lead us to the other error of genderless theology: its appeal to a flawed theory of metaphor that compromises the normative function of Scripture for theology.

Role-Model Theology

Projection theories of religion can be traced back to Ludwig Feuerbach, who argued in *The Essence of Christianity* (1841) that "God is the mirror of man."[2] Feuerbach identified the "mystery of religion" in these terms: "Man . . . projects his being into objectivity, and then again makes himself an object to this projected image of himself thus converted into a subject."[3] Feuerbach's critique of religion was subsequently given a powerful sociopolitical twist by Karl Marx, and still later a psychoanalytic interpretation by Sigmund Freud.[4] Various forms of projection theory are widely held today by sociologists, anthropologists, psychologists, and philosophers of religion. One of the few defensible generalizations that can be made about the contemporary academic field of religious studies is that its practitioners typically assume the validity of some form of projection theory. Whatever the variations in detail (and some of them are very significant), there is widespread consensus that religion is the product of unconscious projection by individuals or societies, that human communities construct their gods as expressions of their personal and social values. All the early proponents of projection theory — Feuerbach, Marx, and Freud — understood it to be a refutation of Christianity in particular and of religion (at least traditional theistic religion) in general. As confi-

---

2. Feuerbach, *The Essence of Christianity,* trans. George Eliot (New York: Harper & Row, 1957), p. 63.

3. Ibid., pp. 29-30. Needless to say, feminists today would find the translator's rendering of *Mensch* (human being) as "Man" to be ironically appropriate — doubly ironic in view of the fact that the translator was one of the great female writers of the nineteenth century.

4. The classic texts are Marx's "Theses on Feuerbach" and Freud's tract entitled *The Future of an Illusion.*

dence in the positivist and evolutionary doctrine of science presupposed by these thinkers has declined over the past century, so has the automatic linkage between projection theory and atheism. Some recent scholars of religion, such as Peter Berger, have even argued that a "methodological atheism" in the study of religion is compatible with religious belief and theology.[5] More typically, theologians have taken a halfway position (it could be called a methodological agnosticism), maintaining that the socially constructed nature of human religion does not preclude the possibility that it may on occasion achieve a valid apprehension of divine reality. The resulting ambiguity has haunted modern theology since Schleiermacher: if theology describes not the metaphysical realm of the supernatural but human religious consciousness, how can it avoid the anthropological reduction proposed by Feuerbach and his heirs? The theology of the genderless God thus joins a long series of modern liberal theologies that take their departure from human experience and then find it difficult to justify their claim to be talking about God rather than humanity.

The axiom that religion is projection or social construction is not really theological but rather a pretheological assumption generally taken for granted by the proponents of a genderless God. But it is often assumed to entail a theological consequence — a position that I call role-model theology. The gist of the position is captured in Mary Daly's dictum that has become the quasi-official motto of much feminist theology: "If God is male, then the male is God."[6] Here's roughly how the logic of role-model theology goes. Since all religious communities construct their gods as expressions of their social values, a proper theology is one that expresses proper social values. Only such a theology is adequate to a proper religion — namely, one whose god is worthy of emulation by human beings. Since we moderns are committed to the full equality of the sexes, our theology must express that commitment; therefore, we should not speak of God in masculine terms (at least not unless they are balanced by feminine terms).

Role-model theology can be accommodated in a systematic theology to the extent that it does not come into conflict with other fundamental convictions. Thus it causes little difficulty for advocates of a

---

5. See Peter L. Berger, *The Sacred Canopy: Elements of a Sociological Theory of Religion* (Garden City, N.Y.: Doubleday, 1967). Berger wears his other, theological hat in *A Rumor of Angels: Modern Society and the Rediscovery of the Supernatural* (Garden City, N.Y.: Doubleday, 1969).

6. Daly, *Beyond God the Father: Toward a Philosophy of Women's Liberation* (Boston: Beacon Press, 1973), p. 19.

liberalism that treats Scripture "more as a resource than as an authority."[7] However, for those Christians who take orthodoxy seriously — especially the normative role of Scripture for doctrine — role-model theology leads to a dilemma. If the Bible is the touchstone of right doctrine, then theology must learn its doctrine of God from Scripture, not from the mores of secular culture — not even from egalitarian liberal-democratic culture. Rather surprisingly, therefore, the most radical feminist theologians escape the dilemma that confronts their more moderate colleagues. Theologians like Mary Daly and Carol Christ may be wrong in their claim that the traditions of Christian orthodoxy are sexist to the core, but they cannot be faulted for inconsistency. Believing as they do that Christianity is incompatible with the full humanity of women, they have abandoned it in favor of more promising sources of religious insight. *Christian* feminists are left in a more difficult position, wanting to claim allegiance to biblical traditions in some basic way while still rejecting the patterns of patriarchy seemingly woven into those traditions at nearly every point. Rosemary Radford Ruether, for example, argues on the one hand that "there are critical elements in Biblical theology that contradict" the sacralization of patriarchy so prominent in other parts of the biblical text.[8] On the other hand, she identifies the "critical principle of feminist theology" as the "promotion of the full humanity of women," without indicating the source or criterion of her anthropological doctrine of "full humanity."[9] The operative norm of her theology turns out to be the "revelatory experience" of women today,[10] before which all other authorities, including the Bible, must be called to account. Implicit throughout her argument is the assumption that the object of worship — what Ruether calls "God/ess" — functions as a role model for human beings.[11]

7. Charles M. Wood, "Hermeneutics and the Authority of Scripture," in *Scriptural Authority and Narrative Interpretation*, ed. Garrett Green (Philadelphia: Fortress Press, 1987), p. 6.

8. Ruether, *Sexism and God-Talk: Toward a Feminist Theology* (Boston: Beacon Press, 1983), p. 61.

9. Ibid., pp. 18-19.

10. Ibid., p. 13.

11. Joseph Epstein, in an amusing but pointed op-ed essay, calls into question the theory of role models (which he calls a "psychobabblish term") in human social interaction ("Say No to Role Models," *New York Times,* 23 April 1991). The doubts he raises about human role models apply *a fortiori* to alleged divine ones.

Blaming the Metaphor

The most sophisticated recent version of role-model theology generally goes under the name of metaphorical theology. Like all role-model theology, this position assumes that God must be conceived in a way worthy of emulation by human beings, and it sees the problem as essentially one of language — in particular, the metaphors, models, and images that people use to speak of God. As defined by Sallie McFague, its most influential practitioner, "Metaphorical theology . . . claims that in order to be faithful to the God of its tradition — the God on the side of life and its fulfillment — we must try out new pictures that will bring the reality of God's love into the imaginations of the women and men of today."[12] Traditional ways of speaking about God must be rejected because they contradict the divine nature, not because of anything they assert explicitly but because of the metaphors and images they employ. Although McFague no doubt has quarrels with some of the ideas affirmed by earlier theologians, it is to be noted that she directs her attack not against their ideas but against their metaphors. She rejects metaphors for God that are "patriarchal," "imperialistic," "triumphalist," and "monarchical," calling such imagery "oppressive" and "opposed to life, its continuation and fulfillment."[13]

This attack on biblical imagery is reminiscent of earlier battles, especially the controversy about demythologization unleashed by Rudolf Bultmann a half century ago; but there is an important difference. Earlier critics wanted to replace the images they attacked with more direct ways of expressing the text's meaning, whether with literal language in the case of rationalistic interpreters or with existentialist categories in the case of the Bultmannians. Metaphorical theology, on the other hand, proposes not a demythologizing but rather "a *remythologizing* of the relationship between God and the world."[14] Since theologians are, "as it were, painting a picture," McFague says, they presumably have the right to choose their own colors. And since "theology is *mostly* fiction," it should be free to change the story as needed to make its point. Accordingly, McFague proposes to replace the offending biblical metaphors with ones better

12. McFague, *Models of God: Theology for an Ecological, Nuclear Age* (Philadelphia: Fortress Press, 1987), p. xii.
13. Ibid., pp. ix-xi.
14. Ibid., p. xi; McFague's emphasis.

suited to our "ecological, nuclear age": God as mother, lover, and friend. So imagined, God can function as an appropriate role model for Christians committed to the proper social and political goals of feminism, environmentalism, and world peace.

The inherent weakness of role-model theology emerges with special clarity in the theory of metaphor employed by metaphorical theology. The proposal that biblical metaphors for God be replaced or supplemented by others assumes that one metaphor can substitute for another without loss or change of meaning. McFague, for example, is explicit that her three new divine "models" are intended to replace the trinitarian name of God in which Christians from the earliest times to the present have prayed, worshiped, and baptized.[15] The notion that metaphors are substitutable, however, runs afoul of recent theories of metaphor which stress the unique ability of metaphorical language to say what cannot be said in any other way. Surprisingly, McFague has been an articulate advocate of those theories. In her earlier book entitled *Metaphorical Theology* she presents a compelling argument for the "unsubstitutable" nature of metaphors. Against the long and influential tradition flowing from Aristotle, she demonstrates the superiority of the modern view — propounded by I. A. Richards, Max Black, and others — that sees metaphor "not as a trope but as the way language and, more basically, thought works."[16] The inconsistency between her own theory of metaphor and her theological proposals seems not to have been noticed either by her or by her critics: after arguing for unsubstitutability in *Metaphorical Theology,* she then argues for substituting metaphors in *Models of God.*

The contradiction originates in a social critique, one with close ties to projection theories of religion. This tendency, much in vogue in recent theory, theological and otherwise, could be called "blaming the metaphor." The thesis is that patriarchal and other abuses are the result of the metaphors by which we think, so that if we change our metaphors, we will change our thought and thus our behavior. For example, Gordon Kaufman credits McFague with showing us "how much our thinking has been unconsciously in the grip of metaphors that (however significant and appropriate they may have been in the historical situations in which they

---

15. Ibid., p. 181. Although acknowledging in a note that many theologians — including Karl Barth, Claude Welch, and Robert Jenson — insist that the trinitarian names allow no substitutes, McFague offers no refutation of their arguments (pp. 222-23, n. 1).

16. McFague, *Metaphorical Theology: Models of God in Religious Language* (Philadelphia: Fortress Press, 1982), p. 37.

arose and were effective) have now become not only misleading but dangerously destructive."[17] Kaufman does not explain how or why metaphors
that were once "effective" came to be so "dangerously destructive," but
his own metaphoric language about metaphors is revealing. They appear
as powerful and domineering tyrants, exercising a kind of thought control
over us (they have us "in their grip," but we don't know it because they
operate "unconsciously"). Such hostility toward the central images of
Christian tradition is widespread among theologians, especially those most
influenced by feminist critique. The root problem of patriarchalism, according to this account, is the paternal (and, more generally, masculine)
metaphors that pervade Christian language. The solution, then, appears
obvious: the offending metaphors must be rooted out, replaced by others
more in keeping with our own values and commitments.

But how, one may ask, did theologians come to conclude that
metaphors are to blame for the social and moral ills of Christianity? The key
lies in their prior commitment to role-model theology. If religion functions
by constructing divine models to be emulated by humans, a tradition that
imagines God as heavenly Father must surely serve to legitimate patriarchy:
"If God is male, then the male is God." But at this point a Christian
metaphorical theology finds itself caught up in contradiction. If metaphors
are uniquely informative — if they enable insights that are unobtainable
from any other source — then changing religious metaphors means changing religions. Furthermore, any religion that projects images of God that are
as destructive as metaphorical theology contends surely *deserves* to be replaced. Now the only way that the metaphorical theologian can escape the
implication that the religion itself — Christianity, in this case — is at fault
is to claim that Christians have some other, non-metaphorical information
about God against which to measure the adequacy of the metaphors. But
that is precisely the move precluded by modern metaphor theory, for it
returns to a view of metaphor as mere vehicle, a rhetorical ornament, an
optional means of expression that may in principle be replaced by another.
But this is, in fact, the view of metaphor employed by metaphorical theology,
whatever lip service it pays to the "unsubstitutable" character of metaphorical
language. At the heart of the theology that calls itself metaphorical is a failure
to take metaphor seriously: the metaphorical theologian already *knows* what
God is like from other — presumably non-metaphorical — experience and

17. Kaufman, review of *Models of God*, in *Religion & Intellectual Life* 5 (Spring
1988): 12.

merely makes use of metaphors as vehicles to express that experience. If one vehicle seems to convey the wrong message, it is exchanged for a more suitable one. This criterion becomes explicit in McFague's assertion that in speaking metaphorically "we are trying to think in an as-if fashion." But that is not the way metaphor works. Christians do not think of God *as if* he were a father; they address him as "our Father." McFague short-circuits the logic of metaphor by jumping from the valid observation that not all attributes of the metaphoric image are applicable to its meaning to the mistaken conclusion that metaphors are optional, that we can pick and choose our metaphors by asking "which one is better in our time."[18] One of the striking characteristics of living metaphoric speech (whether in poetry, religion, or science) is the accompanying conviction that it is the *only* adequate way to utter the intended meaning. This conviction is more powerful to the extent that a given metaphor is central to the text in which it appears. For the New Testament, and hence for the creeds and doctrines of the church, the metaphoric language of God the Father is very near the center. Thus Christians who confess that "God *is* our heavenly Father" will agree that "we think of God *as* Father" but not that "we think of God *as if* he were a father." The subtle but all-important difference between saying "as" and saying "as if" is the difference between truly metaphorical speech and speech that treats its metaphors as mere tropes or ornaments.[19] Theologically, it is the difference between taking Scripture seriously as divine disclosure and treating it as an optional resource for theological construction.

That some theologians now take for granted a theory of religion originally designed to expose the illusory nature of religious belief and the falsehood of Christian doctrine — that fact alone should be enough to provoke some critical questions about their theologies. Feuerbach, Marx, and Freud did not, after all, expose the dynamics of religious illusion in order to encourage theologians to update their illusions but rather to persuade modern people to give up religious belief altogether. Role-model theology wants to make use of their anti-religious critique (what Paul Ricoeur has dubbed the "hermeneutics of suspicion") to dissolve the images and metaphors of the tradition while exempting its own projections from the same fate. The theology of the genderless God arises from this halfway appropriation of projection theories of religion, one that does not

18. McFague, *Models of God*, p. 70.

19. For an elaboration of the distinction between *as if* and *as*, see my book entitled *Imagining God: Theology and the Religious Imagination* (San Francisco: Harper & Row, 1989), pp. 137-41.

take the critical force of those theories with sufficient seriousness and thus ends by repeating the error that the theories were designed to overcome: the divinizing of human values and institutions — in other words, the very kind of mistake made by patriarchal theology.

As paradoxical as it sounds, traditional patriarchalism and the theology of the genderless God share a common presupposition: that the function of divinity is to provide a model for humanity; that religion is the practice of conforming human behavior to a divine model. These most unlikely of allies, in other words, are both committed to role-model theology. They differ only on the question of what role is to be deified. Religious defenders of male privilege appeal to a masculine God in order to justify the authority of his male representatives on earth. Advocates of a genderless God prefer a divine model of sexual equality, whether in the form of an androgynous deity, a God/ess of ambivalent gender, or an impersonal divine principle beyond masculine or feminine. The usual response of theologians to the feminist critique of religious patriarchalism has been to insist that Christians must choose between these two alternatives: either the male God of patriarchy or the genderless God of feminism. But that is a devil's choice if ever there was one.

Toward a Truly Metaphorical Theology

The original temptation, according to the Genesis narrative, was the human urge to model oneself after God: "You will be like God," said the serpent (Gen. 3:5), who thus became the first role-model theologian. One of the deepest ironies of the creation story is that the very human creature who has just been formed in the divine image (Gen. 1:26-27) succumbs to the temptation to become "like God"! Evidently there is more than one way to be like God, and everything hangs on recognizing the difference. The crucial principle is that the logic of the *imago Dei* is not reversible. When God fashions us after his image, it is called creation; when we fashion God after our image, it is called idolatry. It is precisely this distinction that role-model theology misunderstands — in both its patriarchal and its genderless forms.

Here is the point at which to begin thinking theologically about the critical theories of religion stemming from Feuerbach. The way out of the dilemma posed by genderless theology begins with the recognition that we are being asked to choose between rival idolatries. There is a striking

54

similarity between the kinds of religion described by the critical projection theories and what Scripture and Christian doctrine call idolatry. Both seek to alert us to the alienating effects of humanly constructed models of divinity — the one in the name of human autonomy, the other in the name of divine autonomy. And both are right: idol worship threatens freedom, both human and divine. Christian theologians, however, must part company with the nineteenth-century projection theorists at the point where they absolutize their theories into omnicompetent explanations, and thus dismissals, of all religion. One of the strengths of Latin American liberation theology has been its theological appropriation of Marxist criticism of religion without drawing the orthodox Marxist conclusion that all religion is subject to such criticism. Theologians have employed Marxian insights into the ways in which ruling elites employ religion, including Christian religion, to legitimate their power while insisting that the gospel of Jesus Christ is on the side of liberation.[20] Similarly, in the twentieth century fruitful results have emerged repeatedly out of the confrontation of theologians with the religious critiques of Freud and Nietzsche — both of whom were as uncompromisingly hostile to Christian teaching as was Karl Marx. No more thoroughgoing rejection of "religion" is to be found, for example, than in the dogmatic theology of Karl Barth.[21]

A truly Christian theology, as Luther reminded the church of his day, must always be a theology of the cross. Theologians need that reminder again today as they think through the theological implications of the feminist challenge. The wrong kind of theology — Luther called it the theology of glory — wants to know God apart from the crucified Jesus. If role-model theology is subjected to this test, its root error becomes clear: by attempting to model human behavior after the image of God without regard to the image of God on the cross, this kind of theology wants to imitate the God of glory directly. Patriarchal theologians, for example, try to model themselves after God the Father as though he could be abstracted

20. One can appreciate this theoretical contribution while nevertheless wishing that those same theologians were equally critical of the legitimizing theories of the left. There is also a widespread tendency among liberation theologians to adopt the assumptions of role-model theology.

21. The classic discussion is in § 17 of the *Church Dogmatics,* but Barth's rejection of "religion" was a consistent theme from his earliest writings to the end of his career. Whether or not Barth was wise to identify the dynamics of religious idolatry so unqualifiedly with *religion* is a matter that theologians will have to ponder, especially in an age in which religious studies increasingly provide the context for theology.

from the crucified Son of God. The devotees of this theology want the privileges of divine fatherhood without its sacrifices; they want to share God's power but not his powerlessness.

Projectionist theories of religion can serve a useful *negative* function in Christian theology by exposing the dynamics of the universal human religious tendency toward idolatry. To take these theories as *positive* indicators of the content of Christian doctrine, however, would be to deny the fundamental affirmation of Christians throughout the ages that the gospel is God's own communication of himself to those who have ears to hear. Because God has chosen to reveal himself in the flesh as a fully human reality, we come to know him in the same way that we know other human agents: through his self-identification in the interaction of character and circumstance — in a word, narratively — as he is depicted in the words and images of faithful witnesses.[22] Such a story can, of course, be told only in a culturally embodied manner, and that means that it will reflect the customs and social patterns of the concrete human community in which it unfolds. The error of role-model theology is to confuse form with content: to assume that the cultural language of the story, rather than the narrative depiction of the protagonist, is the theologically normative content. I do not wish to minimize the difficulties of making the distinction; the attempt to do so, however, is as unavoidable as it is controversial.

Interpretation — the name for this process — is therefore the very lifeblood of theology, and a task which the Christian community cannot shirk or minimize without endangering the gospel it seeks to proclaim. Because the texts of Scripture are metaphorical, the theologian must assume an analogy between its story and ours — between what the text meant and what it means. But since the cross is the root metaphor of Christian interpretation, that analogy is never a direct one between human perfections and divine qualities.[23] The chief usefulness of the hermeneutics

---

22. See Hans W. Frei, *The Identity of Jesus Christ: The Hermeneutical Bases of Dogmatic Theology* (Philadelphia: Fortress Press, 1975), esp. chaps. 4 and 9.

23. Robert W. Jenson relates this hermeneutical principle explicitly to the issues of gender and religious projection: "The assumption that it is a deprivation not to address God in one's very own gender is a case of humankind's general religious assumption of direct analogy from human perfections to divine qualities. In the faith of the Bible, this direct line is, for our salvation, broken. Indeed, Christianity's entire soteriological message can be put so: God's self-identification with the Crucified One frees us from having to find God by projection of our own perfections" (*The Triune Identity* [Philadelphia: Fortress Press, 1982], p. 16).

of suspicion is precisely to expose such direct analogy to critique. The actual analogies of the Bible — shocking to the sensibilities of role-model theology — can employ as metaphors for divine activity the most trivial, base, or terrible features of earthly reality: a thief (1 Thess. 5:2), vomiting (Jonah 2:10), a corrupt judge (Luke 18:2-8), a poisonous snake (Amos 9:3). Robert Jenson points out that "the gospel is free to take its analogies sometimes from human perfections and sometimes from human imperfections, depending on theological need. Sometimes it takes them from death and sin, by no means thereby ranking these above life and virtue." And he suggests that we view the metaphor of fatherhood against this ambiguous background.[24]

In other words, a theology that aims at being both consistently metaphorical and authentically scriptural must reject both role-model theology and the substitutional theory of metaphor. It may employ the variations of projection theory, like other critical theories, as aids in Christian self-criticism and the Christian critique of culture, as long as the theories remain subject to properly theological criteria. Its negative task will be the critique of all idolatry — that is, of every attempt to construct models of God out of human religious, moral, or cultural experience. But it will undertake this critical task in the service of the far more important constructive task of exploring and elaborating the biblical paradigm so that its meaning and implications can be heard in the present. Metaphors in theology, as in the natural sciences, are neither ornamental nor optional. A defensible metaphorical theology must therefore begin by acknowledging the normative status of the biblical paradigm and its constituent metaphors and images for Christian thought, teaching, and practice. Christians are people who acknowledge and seek to live by the vision of reality embodied paradigmatically in the canon of the Old and New Testaments. Faith, understood as the human response to the self-revelation of God in the imagination of the prophets and apostles, has no other access to God by which it might judge the adequacy of biblical metaphors. Accordingly, it understands its task to be not the construction of a new paradigm that better expresses our contemporary sensibilities (that would be idolatry) but rather the interpretation of the metaphorical matrix of Scripture in order to bring it more clearly into relation with life in the world today.

24. Ibid.

The Kenotic Masculinity of God

Since the advent of modernity Christian theologians have had to wrestle repeatedly with the "scandal of particularity," the seemingly indissoluble link between Christian truth claims and certain concrete specifics of history, culture, and person. Modern thinkers have been scandalized by Christian particularity because of its apparent arbitrariness and resistance to universalizing generalities. From the Deists of the seventeenth and eighteenth centuries to proponents of interreligious dialogue today, the calls have not ceased for Christians to give up their stubborn allegiance to historically and culturally specific particulars in the name of religious harmony and universal truth. But the Christian community has been right to resist pressures to interpret its confession as one symbolic expression of a more abstract and general religious truth. The odd presence of Pontius Pilate in the creed (the only mortal so included other than the Virgin Mary and the incarnate Christ) is a constant reminder that Christian faith has to do centrally not with religious and moral generalities but with decisive historical particulars.

Theologians today who would never dream, for example, of revising liturgies to play down the Jewishness of the central symbols of Christian faith are nevertheless eager to disguise the masculinity of the same symbolism, even in the case of the incarnate Christ. Why is it that those who do not balk at a New Testament that accepts slavery as part of the social order and employs it metaphorically are embarrassed to pray "our Father"? The reasons, of course, have to do with topics of currently pressing social and political concern. Yet the same offensive particularity clings to Scripture and doctrine whether one focuses on class, gender, or ethnicity. And in all such cases the temptation to abandon the awkward particularity of the Bible in favor of an abstract conception of deity must be resisted. Christian faith means having one's imagination grasped by the story of God and the world as told by the prophets and apostles and proclaimed by the Christian community throughout the ages. Why that story rather than another is a question for which the theologian has no answer — except the one implicit in the narrative itself: that *this* story is not just another figment of the imagination but God's own story; in short, that this story is *true*. The challenge of feminist critique is one more reminder that Christians know God only in this stubbornly particular way, by imagining him as the One whose identity is depicted in the narrative of Israel and the church. Since that depiction is thoroughly metaphorical,

God's identity is mediated to us in these quite specific images — which, like all true metaphors, convey a meaning that is inseparable from their particularity and cannot therefore be replaced either by literal paraphrase or by different metaphors. Theology, as the intellectual response to the God of this quite particular narrative, is not properly in the business of rewriting the story or designing divine models with an eye to their suitability to contemporary sensibilities. Rather, the job of the theologian is to interpret the story, to say what it means in terms that can be understood by people of the theologian's own generation.

At this point it is appropriate to turn once again to the pressing demands of feminist critique for a theological hearing. What does the predominantly masculine grammar of the biblical God mean to us who live not in a traditional patriarchal society but in one increasingly committed to the equality of the sexes on all levels and to a much greater flexibility of gender roles than has ever been known in the past?

The most valuable contribution of feminist theology has been to cast a new and critical light on traditional ways in which the metaphor of divine fatherhood has been misused to legitimate patriarchal institutions and practices. The appropriate response to this critique is not to reject the metaphor, as proposed by role-model theology, but rather to correct the distortions of male-centered misreadings. This critical contribution of feminism opens the way for us to reread the biblical texts with new eyes in order to discover how patriarchal metaphors actually function in their scriptural context.

One of the failings of metaphorical theology has been its tendency to treat metaphors atomistically, as though they were independent units of thought, each containing an intrinsic meaning. The irony of this approach is that it misses the metaphoric nature of the metaphor; it makes the mistake of literalism by focusing attention on the image itself (the "vehicle," in the terminology of I. A. Richards) rather than the subject matter that the metaphor wants to illumine (the "tenor"). An interpreter, for example, may be so taken by the masculinity of the metaphor "Father" as to miss its point, which may depart from, or even invert, the common meaning of the word as used non-metaphorically. When Christians call God "Father," it is always shorthand for "the Father of our Lord Jesus Christ." In other words, Christians are not referring generally to God as *a* father but rather are addressing him in solidarity with Jesus as "*our* Father." The meaning of the metaphor is accordingly to be sought in the story of the one whom Jesus calls Father.

If we attend to that story, we discover a protagonist very different from the authoritarian patriarch exalted by androcentric tradition and vilified by feminist critique. *This* God does not jealously hoard his power. As husband he does not beat his unfaithful wife but cries out with the pain of a jilted lover and redoubles his efforts to win her back (Hos. 2).[25] As Father he "did not spare his own Son but gave him up for us all" (Rom. 8:32). As Son he did not claim the prerogatives of power and lord it over his subjects but "emptied himself, taking the form of a servant. . . . He humbled himself and became obedient unto death, even death on a cross" (Phil. 2:7-8). As Spirit he incorporates us into the mystical body of Christ, in whom "there is neither slave nor free, there is neither male nor female" (Gal. 3:28). As king he does not isolate himself in heavenly splendor but wills to dwell with his people, to "wipe away every tear from their eyes" and to deliver them from all that oppresses them, even from death itself (Rev. 21:4).

Anyone who claims that masculine metaphors such as these are "oppressive to women" is interpreting them out of context, treating them as isolated units of meaning rather than integral elements of a living narrative. The theological cure for such abstract thinking is re-immersion in the concrete text of Scripture, in all its bewildering and liberating particularity. In its concentration on isolated metaphors, contemporary

---

25. Brian Wren picks precisely this imagery from Hosea as "an example of a God-metaphor ripe for change" (*What Language Shall I Borrow? God-Talk in Worship: A Male Response to Feminist Theology* [New York: Crossroad, 1990], p. 109). Because social and cultural mores change, Wren reasons, metaphors must change to keep up with the times. "When I realize that I live in a society in which men subordinate women and that God does not intend this or wish it to continue," he comments, "Hosea's imagery presents problems." The patriarchal assumptions of the text "give a distorted model for relationships between women and men." But Wren's problem is the reflection of his application of role-model theology to the text. The scriptural point of the text is not to provide us with a model of sexual relationships, distorted or otherwise. Rather, the prophet is talking about *God*. That he does so in the language of his own culture goes without saying (what other language might we expect him to use?). Understood in the prophet's context (and that's what it means to understand a text), his metaphor proclaims the love of God. Wren is correct that this metaphorical language will be misunderstood if taken naively — that is, without regard to its historical context. That is why Christian faith, based as it is on a historical revelation, must continually *interpret* the proclamation of Scripture: that is the job of theologians and preachers. To suggest as Wren does that we abandon the text because its cultural assumptions are foreign to us would lead, if applied consistently, to the abandonment of the Bible itself. The properly theological response to Hosea's text is not to *blame* the metaphor but to *interpret* it.

feminist hermeneutics (together with much of liberation theology generally) has often overlooked the dramatic dialectics of power and weakness in the biblical narrative. To say without qualification or irony that God favors the weak and poor is to invite a fundamental misreading of the dynamics of the story.[26] God's choosing of the scattered tribes of Israel to be his people presupposes that he is Creator of all nature and Lord of all history; without the latter assertion, the theological point of the former is lost. The one who forgives sin is the same one who establishes the law and rules with justice; that is precisely what gives his forgiveness its poignancy and its meaning. The God who goes into exile with his people is the same God who uses his people's enemies as instruments for their chastisement. The Crucified Man is himself the Messiah who comes to deliver Israel. Jesus' obedience unto death is the act of the very one who is Lord of life. The self-emptying of God presupposes his fullness; his weakness presupposes his strength; his "femininity" presupposes his "masculinity."

To tinker with the pronouns or alter the metaphors of such a narrative is to risk losing or seriously distorting its meaning.[27] One of the lessons of the modern theory of metaphor, ignored by metaphorical theology, is that true metaphors are open-ended, constantly yielding up new meaning to those who live by them faithfully and attend to their nuances in changing situations. Any theology that thinks it knows in advance what biblical metaphors will mean has not paid attention either to modern theories of metaphor or to the history of interpretation. To treat the Bible as Holy Scripture, as the place where one expects again and again to hear the living voice of God, is the characteristic stance of the Christian community and the special responsibility of its theologians. Part of that responsibility is refusing to foreclose on the meaning of the text in advance, wrestling with it as with a divine messenger until it blesses us at last. If it sometimes seems more like our enemy than our deliverer, we are at least in the company of Job, of Jeremiah, and of Jesus, all of whom we know through that very text.

26. Jon Levenson demonstrates how such distortion has taken place in the use of the Exodus story by liberation theologians ("Liberation Theology and the Exodus," esp. pp. 7-9).

27. It is a fact worth pondering that the politically correct revisers of Scripture, liturgy, and hymns do not ordinarily propose similar improvements (for example) to Shakespeare. Why is it that the literary classics of culture are treated with greater respect for their integrity than the Bible? Aesthetic considerations are surely not definitive for theological hermeneutics, but any interpretation that ignores them should be treated with suspicion.

Too many theologians and church leaders, misled by the popularity of role-model theology and the stridency of political pressure groups inside and outside the churches, have jumped to premature and simplistic conclusions about the meaning of the metaphorical language of Scripture, liturgy, and doctrine. A more nuanced reading of the sources reveals a subtler and more complex picture than the prevailing ideology would lead us to believe. It is noteworthy that in a Bible whose cultural setting is so thoroughly patriarchal one never encounters an explicit appeal to the masculinity of God for any purpose whatever. Even in the history of doctrine one is hard-pressed to find such appeals. On the contrary, all major Christian bodies have long held (in the words of the Anglican Thirty-Nine Articles) that "there is but one living and true God, everlasting, *without body, parts, or passions.*" That misogynists and powerful males in church and society have taken scriptural authorization of their views for granted is obvious; that their assumptions are justifiable on the basis of the texts is doubtful. Once again, the precedent of slavery is instructive. The fact that Christian slaveholders for centuries appealed to Scripture for support did not prevent Christians in the modern period from concluding that they had been wrong — nor did it lead them to reject the powerful metaphorical language of master and slave in the Bible.

But the more important reason for retaining the masculine grammar of God is positive and constructive. In view of the ironic dialectics of power in the Bible, a change in gender would obscure precisely that aspect of the biblical message most needed in an age sensitized by feminist and liberationist critiques: the ironic reversal of power — including masculine power. Susanne Heine points out that gender is crucial to the meaning of Jesus' vicarious representation. "A woman," she writes, "could not represent the humiliated because she herself is already where these people are. [Vicarious] representation involves the voluntary renunciation of power and privileges."[28] An image of a suffering female would not challenge the powers of this world because she would merely be one more victim. The point is nevertheless uttered by a female voice in Mary's triumphant response to the announcement of her Son's advent: "He has put down the mighty from their thrones, and exalted those of low degree"

---

28. Heine, *Matriarchs, Goddesses, and Images of God: A Critique of a Feminist Theology,* trans. John Bowden (Minneapolis: Augsburg, 1989), p. 138. I have emended the translation to bring out the fact that Heine's term *Stellvertretung* refers explicitly to *vicarious* representation.

(Luke 1:52). To the extent that the problem is "masculine," one might argue, the solution must be expressed in masculine terms. God himself — the Mighty One of Israel, the heavenly King, the God of the Fathers — sends his Son and heir to be the scapegoat, the Victim. Far from justifying male dominance, this symbolism calls it under judgment. In the words of Paul, "God chose what is low and despised in the world, even things that are not, to bring to nothing things that are, so that no human being might boast in the presence of God" (1 Cor. 1:28-29). But such language is not an undialectical celebration of weakness, for Paul also insists that "the weakness of God is stronger than men" (v. 25b).

Feminist theologians seem generally to have missed the irony of biblical patriarchy. But it is even more obvious that it has been missed by patriarchs through the ages, who have humorlessly and unimaginatively adopted the patriarchy of Scripture as a "model." Instead of repeating their error by inventing new models, theologians today would do better to borrow a page from the religion of black slaves by discovering the liberating power of the Bible against its misuse by its self-appointed spokesmen.[29] Just as words have definitions but no meaning until they are used by people speaking in sentences, so the specifics of culture — the Jewish man Jesus, or the Roman practice of capital punishment by crucifixion — have no meaning apart from the narrative of which they are constituents. More specifically, they have no *theological* meaning apart from their scriptural context. They do have other kinds of meaning — historical and sociological, for example. So we can discover from biblical texts that first-century Judea was a patriarchal society (a cultural-historical fact), but this fact has no theological meaning in itself. That meaning emerges from the use to which the cultural particular is put in the biblical narrative. The metaphor of language is not arbitrary, nor does it originate with contemporary philosophical predilections, for Christians have called Jesus the *Word* of God from the start: "these last days he has spoken to us by a Son" (Heb. 1:2). In order rightly to understand the message of any text, we must rid ourselves of inappropriate connotations associated with the vocabulary employed and attend to the text itself. This is all the more necessary in the case of the Bible, which, when read as *Scripture,* sets the context for our understanding of God, the world, and ourselves.

In the face of the feminist challenge, Christian theologians need to

---

29. See Albert J. Raboteau, *Slave Religion: The "Invisible Institution" in the Antebellum South* (New York: Oxford University Press, 1978), esp. chap. 6.

insist on a subtle but decisive distinction: God is not male, yet the appropriate language in which to describe, address, and worship him is nevertheless masculine.[30] Such masculinity is one grammatical aspect of the paradigmatic biblical narrative through which he has disclosed himself to Israel and the church. Read in context, however, this masculinity turns out to be "kenotic," an aspect of the divine self-emptying[31] by which God divests himself of all majesty, dominion, and power in order to overcome the powers (masculine and otherwise) of this world. Those whose imaginations are captured by this story will continue to receive it, in all its scandalous particularity, as the gift of God. For it enables them to do what would otherwise be impossible: to know, to love, and to praise the one true God, Father, Son, and Holy Spirit, in human — and that can only mean in culturally particular — language.

30. Anthropologists distinguish between *sex,* a biological characteristic, and *gender,* its cultural elaboration. An instructive example of how the distinction can be used to shed light on the universal social subordination of women to men is the influential article by Sherry B. Ortner entitled "Is Female to Male as Nature Is to Culture?" in *Woman, Culture, and Society,* ed. Michelle Zimbalist Rosaldo and Louise Lamphere (Stanford, Calif.: Stanford University Press, 1974), pp. 67-87. I am here using the qualifier *male* as a sexual (natural) term and *masculine* as the corresponding gender (cultural) term. The difference is too often ignored in contemporary theological writing.

31. The New Testament term is *kenosis;* cf. Phil. 2:7.

Proteus and Procrustes:
A Study in the Dialectic of Language
in Disagreement with Sallie McFague

COLIN GUNTON

Language, Projection, and Discovery

THE POSSIBILITIES, as they say, are infinite. One of the features of the study of language and especially of metaphor today is that language is being shown to be (almost) infinitely flexible. Metaphor signals the protean capacities of language, its bendability into almost any shape, and it is that aspect on which Sallie McFague draws in her theological development of the possibilities in her book entitled *Metaphorical Theology*.[1] On her account, metaphor consists in both the assertion and the denial of a proposition, so that possibilities of meaning lying within the tension between the two become innumerable. It must be noted, however, that such a width of possibility involves a corresponding danger, and it is a danger of loss of control. If it is true, for example, that Jesus' death is metaphorically a sacrifice, and so both is and is not a sacrifice, as I have argued elsewhere, there is some need, if anything significant is to be said, to spell out in what respects it is and is not.[2] The importance of this point can be signaled in advance, though its significance must be explored later. The claim that the subject of a metaphorical predication both is and is not what is asserted of it cannot be stretched so far that it involves a license to say anything, for that is either to have ceased to speak the truth or to

---

1. McFague, *Metaphorical Theology: Models of God in Religious Language* (London: SCM Press, 1983). See also *Models of God: Theology for an Ecological, Nuclear Age* (London: SCM Press, 1987).
2. See my book entitled *The Actuality of Atonement: A Study of Metaphor, Rationality and the Christian Tradition* (Grand Rapids: William B. Eerdmans, 1988), pp. 120-28.

have done no more than project upon reality the patterns of our fragmented experience. As I shall hope to show, it does not follow from saying that if God is only metaphorically — and so both is and is not — Father, he is also justifiably said to be mother.

The perils of too protean a view of the possibilities of language are twofold: the peril of projection and the peril of a weakening of criterion and control. First, I shall treat the matter of projectionism and its implications for language and theology. By projection I mean an understanding of the function of descriptive language as not so much describing the world as projecting upon it patterns of interpretation — "perspectives." Professor McFague's theory of metaphor has much of projectionism about it: "We are not dealing, on the one hand, with 'reality as it is' and, on the other hand, with views of it," she says, "but *solely with the latter*."[3] How does she reach this position? It is not much of an exaggeration to say that her view of language is systematically ambiguous when it comes to the employment of metaphor and model in science, but becomes heavily projectionist when it comes to theology. Let us look at the two spheres one by one.

In the matter of science, there are in *Metaphorical Theology* passages which suggest the author's belief that language is capable of in some way or other describing or representing aspects of what the world really is rather than simply imposing external or subjective patterns of meaning upon it — a critical realist rather than a projectionist view of language. Thus Professor McFague makes some use of theories of science which talk of discovery and teach that models are "a genuine but *partial reflection of its reality*."[4] But side by side with this critical realism there are signs that other forces are at work — what might be called naive idealism. McFague frequently refers to the fact that we *construct* our world through metaphor, and on at least one occasion she speaks of our being in a world that we *create*.[5] The root of the equivocation between realism and idealism comes to light when she speaks of metaphor as making the unintelligible intelligible. By this does she mean that by metaphor we make intelligible that which is *intrinsically and essentially* unintelligible, or that we make (more) intelligible that which was previously unintelligible? Because of the systematic ambiguity that pervades the discussion, it is difficult to say. But if we are to continue to hold that science involves discovery, does it not

---

3. McFague, *Metaphorical Theology*, p. 134, my italics.
4. Ibid., p. 99, McFague's italics.
5. Ibid., pp. 15-16, 78.

require at least some form of knowledge of what actually is, however inadequately that is expressed in our language?

Theologically, much hangs upon the distinction between projectionism or constructivism and critical realism, for underlying it is the question of God. In theology, are we concerned with the articulation of the intrinsic intelligibility of the God who makes himself known in specific forms of relatedness to us, or with a much less definite matter of naming God through certain experiences that we take to be formative? It is not difficult to find evidence of projectionism in McFague's doctrine of God nor too great a caricature of her position to say that as one age projected certain features of patriarchal experience upon eternity, we must now right the balance by a corresponding projection of maternal imagery.

One should not, however, be too immediately dismissive of the proposals for two reasons, historical and systematic. Historically, the Christian tradition has not been free from projectionism in its treatment of the doctrine of God, even though McFague's use of the illustration of God as an old man with a beard grossly exaggerates what she calls the literalism of the tradition.[6] There have been theologies in which doctrines of the Fatherhood of God appear to result more from an ideology of fatherhood than from revelation. Some may find this to be the case of nineteenth-century theologies like that of Adolf Harnack, placing as they do the Fatherhood of God at the center while denying the trinitarian controls without which it does become projection. More generally, a case can also be made that the Christian tradition has propounded what has come to be called a "monotheist" concept of God (or should perhaps better be called a concept with unitarian tendencies), in which abstract and impersonal being has displaced personal communion at the heart of reality. These are matters to which I will return later in the essay. The main point to be made here, however, is that the discovery of mistakes in the past does not justify the making of similar mistakes, even though they are made in an attempted correction of balance. The questions remain: what language may we use of God, what are we doing when we use it, and what are our criteria of usage?

The systematic reason for taking seriously Professor McFague's contentions concerns the relation of theology to its past. McFague is aware of the problems of continuity. Certain changes of model in effect bring about a different religion.[7] The question to be put to her, as in the matter

6. Ibid., p. 97.
7. Ibid., p. 109.

67

of the relation of language and reality, is whether the balance is tipped so far in one direction that she emerges saying the opposite of the tradition and so subverting the gospel by propounding an essentially different faith. For the moment we can gladly concede that a merely defensive and conservative theology has never been true to the eschatological dynamic of the faith. We know in part, and therefore any theological formulation is revisable in the light of new truth breaking forth from the Word of God. We can gladly concede also that in this respect, Procrustes is as great a danger as Proteus. But even here we must ask whether it is the traditionalist or the modernist who is being procrustean, for the two are in point of fact extremes that amount to the same thing — equal and opposite sides of the same problem. The procrustean will force everything into a given form of language or thought; the protean will find reality so diverse that anything — or nothing (in the end it is the same thing) — can be said of it. The suspicion of McFague is that her protean conception of language is but a mask for the programmatic forcing of the gospel into the language of the latest modern fad: procrusteanism by the back door. The question here is similar: where is truth, and how is it to be discerned?

The Question of Criteria

The greatest Christian theology has always emerged through engagement with questions thrown up by contemporary culture. Irenaeus, perhaps the greatest theologian of creation of the Christian tradition, hammered out a conception of the goodness of the material universe in a dialectical engagement between a theology of the incarnation and the world-denying philosophies of his opponents. Similarly, it is to be hoped that a more adequate theology of man and woman together embodying the image of God in Christ will emerge from engagement with many gnosticisms that face us in our day. There is continuity in the challenges the faith faces, too, and the question of continuity and change brings us to the second of the two pitfalls of too protean a view of language: a loss of criteriological control. The fact that language is (almost) infinitely protean should not be allowed to obscure the fact that there are definite limits on what may, truthfully, be said.

The limits on the sayable are, again, both historical and systematic. First, our place in history places definite limits on what we are able to accomplish. The contingency of all worldly being does not imply that it is absolutely open. The famous remark about the capacity for a longer view of things for those who stand on giants' shoulders reminds us that the past is an essential matrix for what can be said in the present. There can be no absolute revolution in thought any more than there can be an absolute revolution in politics. There could be no language of relativity theory without the language of Isaac Newton and James Clerk Maxwell, because there would be no matrix in which the new conceptuality could be formed. Here Michael Polanyi's point is essential: that without indwelling in a tradition, nothing, and certainly nothing new, can be said at all. To deny the past is to lose a hold on reality, the threat to all forms of post-Enlightenment theology, and particularly that which would deny in the name of a modern ideology the main thrust of Christian thought. Professor McFague is aware of this; the question to be put to her is whether as a matter of fact she has behaved as though it is not true and has in fact recommended a religion that is continuous not with historic Christianity but with its subversion.

This brings us to the systematic contention: that taking the past seriously is one important control on projectionism. In that respect, the constraints of history are one form of what must serve as the chief criterion and control: reality. This means at least that we must take seriously the concept of truth, and not merely the truth of our relation to reality but the truth of the reality to which we claim to be related. That language — especially metaphorical language — which enables us to express something of the reality of things is true; that which fails to do so is false. I am not here suggesting that questions of truth are easy to resolve; they manifestly are not. Rather, I am suggesting that the logic of the concept of truth requires us to ask the question about which of our assertions are true and which are not. This is particularly important in questions of the nature of God, for it is here that projectionism is always the danger. In that respect, if not correct in all of his arguments, Karl Barth was right about natural theology. I am reminded of a remark made some time ago by Professor D. Z. Phillips in a discussion. Commenting on a book of essays by a group of celebrated individuals entitled *The God I Want,* he said that he could not imagine a sillier enterprise: "It is not the God I want, but the God you are damn well going to get."

The issue becomes clearer when we realize that theories of language are inextricably bound up with theories of reality, and that between McFague's thesis and the one being argued here is a dispute about the nature of reality — of the being of God, the nature of the world, and human life and thought within it. All centers on the matter of how we see person and world to be related. Let us first examine the matter of relationality, one of the fashionable words of modern theology. Describing the loss of the once all-pervasive belief in the sacramentality of the universe, McFague claims that the lost view "depends upon a belief that everything is connected." However, she tells us, this does not now hold: "In our time . . . there is skepticism concerning the unity of all that is. . . . Our time is characterized by disunity, by skepticism that anything is related to anything else, and by secularity."[8] One can leave to the sociologists the highly questionable assertion that our time is characterized by secularity. But what of the belief that "we" are skeptical of the claim that everything is related to everything else? McFague appears to be operating with a dualism between human historicity and existentiality on the one hand, and the world of scientific discovery on the other.

The reason is that if we look at recent scientific discovery, we see that quite the opposite of what she says is the case. The metaphysical implications of relativity theory and its successors are most concretely revealed by the famous illustration of chaos theory: that the fluttering of a butterfly's wings over Peking can later affect the behavior of storm systems over New York. That one illustration is symbolic of a general truth: that what we call the universe is a network of particularities in dynamic inter-relation. The universe is indeed contingent and marked by richness and plurality, but through all that — by means of it — it is a unity. The relatedness of everything is no support for a relativist theory of knowledge; quite the reverse. We live, as Professor McFague holds, in a relational universe. Whence then the skepticism that anything is related to anything else? It can only come from a dualistic view that in some way makes an absolute or near-absolute distinction between the unity-in-relatedness of reality and the apparently irreducible and incurable pluralism of the human response to it. McFague's effective renunciation of the concept of the unity of being is the gateway to an absolutely protean view of language which at the same time entails a relativist view of truth. We can say what we like so long as it expresses our "relation" to that of which we have no true knowledge.

The systematic weakness of *Metaphorical Theology* and its successor is the inadequacy — indeed, almost absence — of the author's concept of revelation. The vague employment of the idea of Jesus as parable (Why

8. Ibid., p. 6.

not as savior? Is that too authoritarian and "patriarchal"?) and of the kingdom as root metaphor masks a concerted attempt to minimize the centrality of divine action, the decisive self-relating of *God* to lost humankind in Christ, in favor of an almost exclusive concentration on *our* relatedness to a God who has no shape other than that which our language happens, from time to time, to confer upon him. (Or should we say "it," in view of McFague's assertion that "God is not a 'person' or 'personal' "?[9]) All the weight is thrown upon the subject of experience and none to speak of upon the eternal God who, by coming in Christ to the lost world *in person* to restore its directedness to perfection, makes known both himself and his love for his fallen world. Here the parallels between science and theology are of immense relevance. If in the former there is discovery, the laying open of what was not before known or understood, it is only because the world presents itself to be known *as what it is and not another thing*. Science, too, depends upon a kind of doctrine of revelation, as art depends upon a kind of doctrine of inspiration. Unless it is true that there is revelation in some sense — that there is a way in which the world offers itself to be known — there can be no discovery, no avoidance of the nightmarish possibility of solipsism.

Corresponding to the ontological dualism that underlies McFague's theology is a dualism in her theory of language. It is this which enables her both to parody traditional trinitarian theology and to erect after the destruction of a straw man an equally strawy reconstruction, and it involves a major error in the theory of language. At the heart of the modern rediscovery of metaphor is the recognition that the difference between the literal and the metaphorical is a matter of usage, not reference. Literal usage is that which reflects the principal way in which a word or expression is used at the time when it is described as literal; metaphorical usage is that which represents some kind of transfer of meaning. This means that the particular use of a word can be metaphorical yesterday, literal today, and metaphorical again tomorrow. An example is the word *muscle*. When first introduced into anatomical language, *muscle* was metaphorical: derived from the Latin *musculus,* meaning "little mouse," it was a way of describing — presumably because of a likeness of shape — a feature of animal anatomy. Now, of course, *muscle* has a literal meaning: the fact that a muscle both is and is not a little mouse is not now in the mind of users of the language. A further interesting and very relevant point is that

9. Ibid., p. 128.

71

new metaphors are now derivable from this literal use: for example, an editor might ask an author whose first draft she has considered to put more muscle into his argument. A word is used, as a metaphor, to refer. It then comes in time to refer literally to the same phenomenon, after which it takes on new metaphorical meaning when transferred to new reference.

In total contrast to this, Professor McFague's argument depends upon a distinction not between ways in which words are used but between ways in which they are related to their objects of reference. While there may at times be suggestions of another view, the determinative conception with which she works is between literal language as "picturing" and metaphorical language as being in some way more allusive and indirect. She is thus able to suggest that those who claim that God is *really* Father are in some sense using language "idolatrously" because they believe that it pictures God directly. Her tendentious appeal to paintings that render God as an old man with a beard enables her to dismiss traditional trinitarian language as, in effect, *mere* metaphor and to posit its supplementation by or replacement with the language of motherhood as being of equal validity and appropriateness. But her procedure traduces the Christian tradition. First, orthodox Christian theology has never held that the word *Father* pictures God or that it implies that God is of the male gender. Quite the reverse: the apophatic tradition has always insisted that all the connotations of the finite usage must be thought away if we are really to be speaking not of some projection but of God. Second, the mainstream tradition, beginning with Ephesians 3, has not held that talk of the Fatherhood of God involves the projection of patterns of human fatherhood upon God. Quite the reverse: Barth is here representative of the tradition in saying that the doctrine of the Fatherhood of God derives from the fact that he is the Father of Jesus Christ, and that this is *revelatory* of the character of true human fatherhood.[10]

The interesting development here is that it becomes in this case difficult to decide where is literal speech, where metaphor. We saw that in the case of the word *muscle,* the anatomical usage, once a metaphor, has in the course of time come to be the literal use and now is able to spawn metaphors from itself. But we have before us more than an interesting anatomical term. In view of the determinative theological role of

---

10. Barth, *Church Dogmatics,* 4 vols., ed. Thomas F. Torrance, trans. Geoffrey W. Bromiley (Edinburgh: T. & T. Clark, 1936-1969), I/1:386ff.

the word *Father* as articulating something of the character of the God to whom we are brought by Jesus and the Spirit, it might appear that we have in it a basic analogy in the sense of a term through which the very nature of being is made known. In that respect, it is an analogy from above: an analogy of revelation making known what it is in which true fatherhood consists. In that sense, God is literally Father, as the one who provides both the origin and the true instantiation of fatherhood. But, paradoxically, such literality has to be understood with the help of the theory of metaphor, for it is clear that this Fatherhood has nothing to do with masculinity or the mechanics of sexual reproduction.

By contrast, McFague's trading upon a mistaken conception of the distinction between the literal and the metaphorical generates an unbalanced view of the relation between language and reality. The stages of argument are basically as follows:

1. We interpret our world metaphorically.
2. Metaphor, in contrast to literal language, does not attempt to picture reality directly.
3. Therefore, metaphor is a form of indirect characterization of a kind that *does not really speak of reality at all.*

Accordingly, the way is open to project onto the deity any forms of relationality of which we happen to approve. Against this combination of the protean and the procrustean, the discovery that the distinction between the literal and the metaphorical is a matter of convention and current usage enables us to free ourselves from the dualism of the directly picturing and the indirectly projectionist. Rather, all language refers indirectly, in the sense that although it may sometimes use pictorial forms of expression, it does not picture in the "old man with a beard" sense. A reading of the *Philosophical Investigations* should be enough to disabuse anyone of that fallacy. Any language, metaphorical or literal, may succeed or may fail *in different degrees* in expressing the nature of reality. The question here is not whether the word happens in any instance to be used metaphorically or literally, but whether it succeeds in being true to the world or the God to whom it seeks to be faithful.

The example of *muscle* is a case in point. In all the cases, the question at issue is whether the usages enable us to understand anatomy and the construction of persuasive arguments; it has nothing to do with picturing at all. The clinching blow is struck when we consider those

73

examples in McFague's own language of picturing. The odd thing is that it is the metaphorical usage, not the literal usage, which pictures when it is first employed as a means to understand the unknown. By being pictured as a little mouse, the anatomical object becomes knowable. Once the usage becomes literal, there is no picturing at all, absolutely none, except in the odd case of a consciously archaizing and classically educated anatomist. That is the reverse of McFague's view, which is that to believe that God is really Father is to succumb to a gross picture. On the contrary, it can now be argued that it may well be that God is *really* Father but in no sense is *pictured* as a father. The key to that matter, as in all uses of metaphor, is to be found in what it means to address God as Father, and in whether we are right to do so.

Metaphor and Trinitarian Language

Why is all this so important? In the first place, it means that we cannot be as cavalier as McFague and others with similar views appear to be about the tradition. If we are to avoid the kind of projectionism into which she has fallen, then we must ask again: What legitimates the theological use of one word rather than another? Here I begin with an affirmation: Christianity stands or falls through the confession of Jesus as Lord, as the concrete and saving presence of the eternal God to lost human time. Any weakening of that, as in McFague's use of the vague idea that Jesus is a parable of God, runs the risk of so emptying the doctrine of God of christological content that it is open to being filled with any content that happens to meet the approval of the moment or to be the fashion of the time — the flavor of the month, so to speak. As it stands, that may appear to be simply authoritarian assertion. Let me compound the offense. Christianity is necessarily "patriarchal" in the sense that it concerns the realization in time of the eschatological rule of God the Father over the creation.

Is that authoritarian? Yes, in the sense that we cannot alter the facts; it is, I believe, "the God we are going to get." As I pointed out earlier, language may not be absolutely protean if we are to respect the constraints of reality. Clearly, there is, as has already been apparent, a straightforward difference in ontology between that of this essay and that implied in McFague's theology. It is not that one is relational and the other "static," "substantialist," and the rest of the misleading epithets. At stake is rather a difference in the form that relationality takes. My contention is that the prior relation is that in which God the creator and redeemer so relates himself to the world that particular patterns of finite relationality are constituted. It is only as the finite responds appropriately to the creator's self-relatedness that it fulfills that which it was created to be. The constructivist option suggests that almost any response is appropriate if it enables us to construct our world to our own satisfaction. That way, I believe, lies the far greater authoritarianism of a relativism that will accept nothing as true except itself.

But, more important, the approach is not authoritarian in the most important sense of the term. Here we can agree with Professor McFague that there is a problem. There has taken place in the Christian church a patriarchalism that is not that of the Father of our Lord Jesus Christ. Where we disagree is in the program for its transformation. Let me begin by explaining why I believe that Professor McFague's program in fact achieves the opposite of what she intends. The root of the matter is to be found in her denial of the real personhood of God. If God is not personal but is one on whom we project gender *ad libitum,* we are of all creatures the most miserable, for it means that the world is not a place in which humans may live, love, and flourish. There is here an absolute choice to be made: between such a world and one in which personal values are ultimately swallowed in meaninglessness. The logic of such a choice cannot be spelled out here, though I have attempted it, with the help of Coleridge and others, elsewhere and must ask for indulgence for abbreviation here.[11] The basis of such a view is to be found in the argument that only a trinitarian form of belief, in which the divinity that shapes our ends is a communion of persons in relation, is a sufficient guarantee against a theology in which the many — particular persons — are submerged in the impersonal One.

The perils of the subordination of personal values to totalitarian unity are nowhere better illustrated than in the advocacy of the motherhood of God. It must be made clear at the outset that no doubt is being cast on the notion that the concept of mother and the concept of father equally imply personhood. Quite the reverse: in their everyday employment, the concepts of both fatherhood and motherhood are terms descriptive of personal relation. Rather, what is at stake is the direction in which the logic of the disputed metaphors takes us or is likely to take us. The

11. See my book entitled *The Promise of Trinitarian Theology* (Edinburgh: T. & T. Clark, 1991), chap. 2.

problem comes when some of the connotations of motherhood are projected onto infinity. As a matter of fact, as the history of religion and of
some of the excesses of feminist religion demonstrate, the logic of the
female deity is a logic of pantheism. That logic has been spelled out often
enough elsewhere, as has the fact that the Old Testament prophets decisively rejected the deities of their opponents in the name of human
flourishing.[12] You cannot have the language without paying its ontological
price. The reason is both patent and trinitarian. To be a person, one must
be constituted in one's particular otherness. This is the point of all that
talk of relations: only in a process of mutual and reciprocal giving and
receiving are we truly personal and so truly what we are created to be. All
forms of pantheism, however, deny the reality both of otherness and of
relation, for they ultimately render particularity and distinction unreal.
Here we have a case of a change of metaphor which, far from supplementing or correcting the excesses of another, alters things so much
that the Christian faith is translated into something entirely different.

That said, we must return to the positive question of the way in
which an orthodox trinitarian theology establishes personal values — and
that includes those of men and women in relation — rather than denying
them. Christianity is a religion depending on authority in the sense that
its realization of salvation — and so the constitution of true personhood
— is embodied in a community of worship and belief centered on the
Jesus of Scripture. But because salvation is mediated by Jesus, the one who
was crucified — and that is a means virtually ignored by McFague — it
has what W. A. Whitehouse has called an authority of grace.[13] That is a
way of speaking of an authority not only personally exercised but also
exercised as the self-giving at once of the Father and of the incarnate Son.
The pattern of divine-human action realized in Jesus of Nazareth is personal also in the sense that it recognizes the otherness and individuality
of those toward whom it is exercised. There, and not in flirting with
immanence and pantheism, is the key to structures of personal life in
which the uniqueness and yet interrelatedness of persons is recognized and
reinforced.

In the light of this pattern of relationality set up by and around

12. See, for example, Roland Frye, "Language for God and Feminist Language:
Problems and Principles," *Scottish Journal of Theology* 41 (1988): 441-69.
13. Whitehouse, *Creation, Science and Theology: Essays in Response to Karl Barth*
(Grand Rapids: William B. Eerdmans, 1981), p. 142.

the crucified Jesus, the inadequacy of the idea of Jesus as parable becomes clear as an essentially reductionist and noetic rather than soteriological conception. As such, it opens up too much space between his reality and our interpretation — *a vacuum* — which the protean and procrustean tendencies of fashionable language rush to fill. Jesus is not the parable of a general relationality but the realization through the Spirit of a *particular* relation to the one he called Father. Can we project mother language upon God without smothering this particular relationality? That is the question. If we contrast that possibility with another suggested by McFague, that of God as friend, we can see the differences.[14] Despite the danger of sentimentality involved in the conception of God as friend, there can be no doubt that it has a positive relation to the biblical narration of the Jesus history in a way that mother language does not, and equally is unlikely to collapse into pantheism. To repeat, this is a question not of biblicism but of the kind of world that is articulated by the essentially opposing theologies with which we are faced here.

Christianity's Patriarchalism

When it is realized that patriarchy and its cognates are terms employed metaphorically, we shall realize that Christianity, according to Professor McFague's own canon, both is and is not patriarchal. Of course, Christianity is not, or should not be, patriarchal in the sense that it validates an ideology according to which all dominion and authority should be exercised by men. That it has been and in some places still is patriarchal in that sense is a ground for repentance and change. Insofar as the alleged maleness of God or the actual maleness of Jesus has been used as the basis for arguments excluding women from playing a full part in the ministry of the church, there has been, I believe, a denial of the gospel. But it is a denial of the *gospel,* not of some supposed inherent human or female rights. Once we go down that latter road, there is no end to the confusion.

But Christianity is patriarchal in the metaphorical sense that it has at its center the rule of "the Father, from whom every family in heaven and on earth is named" (Eph. 3:14-15). The question we have to face is asked by moving beyond conditioned reflexes about male domination and inquiring instead about the nature of the Father's rule and the way in

14. McFague, *Models of God,* chap. 6.

which it is exercised. The fatherhood of God has nothing to do with maleness but has to do with patterns of relationality revealed and realized in Jesus. According to the main thrust of the New Testament, it would appear that the rule of the Father is exercised by Jesus and realized by the Holy Spirit. When Irenaeus affirmed that the Son and the Spirit were the two hands of God the Father, he made the point that it is by them that the rule of God the Father is realized in the world. If we maintain his balance, we shall see that the patriarchy of God the Father is anything but that anathematized by the feminists.

Let us see how things fall out when we examine the patriarchy of God as it is trinitarianly realized in the matter of the relations of men and women, and let us do so by beginning with the theology of the image of God. Karl Barth has done great service to theology by calling attention to the fact that in Genesis the image is linked with the affirmation of the male-female polarity.[15] As a matter of fact, I agree neither with Barth's overdependence upon the epistle to the Ephesians in the articulation of the matter nor with his tendency to construe it in relative abstraction from the question of the *dominium terrae,* the other essential component of a theology of the human image of God. But what he has done is the service of breaking the bondage of locating the image of God in reason, a tendency that has encouraged both a false patriarchy and a false notion of the human dominion of the earth. Barth has enabled us to see that the constitution of right relations between men and women is at the center of the Christian gospel.

As the agent of the rule of the Father, Jesus Christ is, as Paul's relocation of the language of image implies, the one who is the true image and likeness of God. He is therefore the one who, by bringing both man and woman into redemptive relation with the Father, restores their relation with one another. That is the clear meaning of such texts as Galatians 3:28: In Christ there is no male nor female. It is not that the distinction ceases to be real but that it is no longer to be seen as constitutive of human alienation. Just as, according to Romans 1, disorderly sexual relations are the first symptoms of human sin, so their reconstitution in Christ is among the first signs of what it is to be in renewed relationship through Christ to God the Father. To repeat the matter in other words: to be conformed to the image of Christ means to be placed in a structure of relations with God the Father in which the most decisive — and divisive — of all relations of human beings with others encounters redemption and renewal.

15. Barth, *Church Dogmatics,* III/1:184ff.

I am making no suggestion here that the church has in the past made a great success of being the institution in which the sexes are reconciled in their differences. Nor do I believe that there is anything automatic about the process of reconciliation. It is here that we come to the second hand of God the Father, the Holy Spirit; by his agency in relating people to the Father through Christ, the rule of God is realized. The Spirit, as is often now remarked, is to be understood as the eschatological agency of God, the way by which the conditions of the age to come are realized in the midst of time and space. And there is one aspect of his work in particular that is again very much a feature of recent theology. The Spirit is the agent of community, for where through Christ he brings both men and women into relation with the Father, there is realized the community of the last days.

In the light of the foregoing argument, it must be said that the moral objection to some forms of feminism (and here I am not speaking of the feminism of Professor McFague but of more radical and militant forms) is that they endanger the essence of community by their encouragement of divisiveness between the sexes, and the accompanying price we are having to pay is to be seen in a breakdown of civility in both society and, God forbid, the church. It is a version of the revolutionary fallacy of which our world has seen too much: that one may remake human relations not by patient rebuilding but by warfare or destruction. But it demands an even more catastrophic theological price. There is no evidence that community will be better achieved by projecting feminine characteristics upon the deity. On the contrary, by a destruction of a trinitarian theology of community, human community is threatened at its very basis.

The basis of community, as we learn from the theology of the Trinity, is otherness in relation. Both are crucial. First, the matter of otherness reminds us that the male-female polarity, as the prime expression of human imaging of God, is of immense importance. Just as both men and women are what they are only by virtue of the otherness of one to the other, so it is with the relations of God and world. The matter of the Fatherhood of God is a matter not of maleness but of ontological discontinuity: of otherness. Second, however, we may not affirm God's otherness without affirming also that it is a being which is realized only in community, in relatedness. That is the core of the metaphor of God's Fatherhood. If this is not at the basis of our theology, then the only alternative is pantheism, which by destroying both otherness and relation destroys also human autonomy and freedom.

The outcome of all this is that metaphors are not freewheeling constructions but language which exacts its corresponding ontological and moral price. Either they allow us to indwell the gospel and the world, or they set up patterns of alienation that tear us apart from our God, our brothers and sisters, and our world. That is why we are here faced with a choice that must be made: between the gospel and a "different gospel" which is no gospel at all.

Can a Feminist Call God "Father"?

JANET MARTIN SOSKICE

L ET ME DISTINGUISH the question I wish to address in this paper from two others that do not directly concern me here. The first is in fact this misguided question: Must feminists *always* call God "father"? It is misguided because there is no basis, theological or philosophical, for insisting that the feminist or anyone else should use one divine title exclusively. In the Jewish and Christian traditions, God has always had many names — One, rock, king, judge, vine-keeper — and will continue to do so. The second question, not a misguided one, is this: Is it expedient for feminists and those sympathetic to them to call God "father" in writings, prayers, and liturgies where continuing to use this title may mask an imbalance in our ideas about God? This is an important question with practical and theoretical ramifications, but it is not the one I wish to consider here. My more radical question hovers around the question of expedience but is separable from it. It is this: Can a feminist be at home in a religion where "father" is a central divine title, if not necessarily in current usage, then certainly in the foundational texts and the subsequent history to which these have given rise? Is the fatherhood language central to this religion, and, if so, does it not bind Christianity fast to an unacceptable patriarchal religion that the feminist must reject? The question "Can a feminist call God 'father'?" thus resolves into two others: Can the "father" language be eradicated from text and tradition? And can a feminist live with Christianity if it cannot be eradicated?

This essay also appears in another collection entitled *Women's Voices in Religion,* ed. Teresa Elwes (London: HarperCollins, 1992). It is reprinted here with permission.

So just what is in a name? What hangs or doesn't hang on a particular notation? If we "designate" the same subject in a different way, are we saying anything different? Ludwig Wittgenstein struggled with these questions as he tried to escape from the rigid and unworkable theory of language that he put forward in his early work, the *Tractatus*. In the pages of the *Blue and Brown Books* Wittgenstein becomes more sensitive than ever he was in the earlier work to the ambiguities of natural language. He puzzles over the capacity of a notation to affect understanding and even perception. He imagines someone who wants to divide England in a way different from the customary divisions, who objects to convention. "The *real* Devonshire is this," the objector says. But he is answered, "What you want is only a new notation and by a new notation no facts of geography are changed." But is this really so? Does the new notation change nothing? "It is true," Wittgenstein adds, ". . . that we may be irresistibly attracted or repelled by a notation."[1]

What difference does a new notation make? Why are we irresistibly drawn or repelled? Why does one metaphor or set of metaphors seem to fit the situation exactly, and another not? And what happens when a set of metaphors ceases to attract and begins to repel? In any religion where God is conceived of as radically transcendent, it is arguable that all the language used of God will be metaphorical or at least figurative. This means that a change in preferred metaphor or notation is always a theoretical possibility; and, indeed, Christian religious language, like that of any other religious tradition, is a mobile thing, responsive to the needs and perceptions of religious adherents. For the most part, however, shifts in guiding metaphors take place slowly and are largely unnoticed. Describing the Christian as a "slave of Christ" or "slave of God," metaphors that enjoyed some popularity in the Pauline epistles and early church, are now scarcely used (despite their biblical warrant) by contemporary Christians who have little understanding of or sympathy with the institution of slavery and the figures of speech it generates. The abandonment or neglect of this metaphor was not forced; it just happened. Students of the history of metaphor can see other metaphors wax and wane.

But at certain points in religious history one sees abrupt changes of imagery, a sudden revulsion to accustomed metaphors and preference for new or different ones. A dramatic instance today is the controversy surrounding the metaphor "God as father." The immediate cause for

---

1. Wittgenstein, *The Blue and Brown Books* (Oxford: Basil Blackwell, 1958), p. 57.

complaint is the growing number of women (and men) who find sex-exclusive language in the liturgy and, by extension, the tradition's almost exclusively male language for God both alienating and offensive. Given the universal and egalitarian nature of Christian faith, they say, we can no longer utter the creedal phrases "for us men and for our salvation" or "almighty and most merciful Father." This language must go.

At first glance this problem may appear open to a simple resolution: like industry, government, and other institutions, the churches could simply shift over to sex-inclusive language (e.g., "for us and for our salvation") and complement the male images for God with a sprinkling of female images taken from biblical text and tradition (e.g., Jesus' description of himself as a hen gathering her chicks or Anselm's address of Christ as "mother"). This achieves an initial plausibility because on one fundamental point agreement can be reached by all concerned. It is this: God is not a human being and *a fortiori* not a *male* human being. God is not a male and God is not literally "father." For classical theologians like Aquinas, "father" and "king" are metaphorical divine titles because they imply limitation. Aquinas restricts what can literally be said of God to a few, bare predicates   the so-called perfection terms: One, Being, Good, and so on. These terms, which to his mind do not involve limitation, can be predicated literally of God, even though we may not know what their full significance would be in the Godhead. Aquinas, like most of Christian orthodoxy, would have difficulty with the idea that the naming of God as father is more than figurative speech. Indeed, the insistence that God really "is" father occurs within Christian heresy. Certain Arians insisted that the Bible does not speak symbolically of God and thus that God *is* the father and Christ *is* the son. From this followed the heretical conclusion that the son, Christ, must have been non-existent before begotten. The consensus is, then, that calling God "father" is a metaphor, however central.

Now optimistic, or perhaps naive, egalitarian reformers have seemingly supposed that to admit that all language about God is figurative would lead readily to the supplementation or even replacement of the male language of Godhood by female alternatives. But this easy resolution has proved unacceptable to conservatives and revisionists alike. Why so?

While it may be that, at the level of pure theological theory, God is not male, at the level of ideology God is or has been male in the Jewish and Christian religions. At this point we find unexpected agreement between religious conservatives and radical feminists — both agree that the God of Christianity is untransposably male — and it is for this reason that the conservatives insist that no change to the church's language is possible, and that some feminists leave the churches and become "post-Christian" feminists.

The case for those, whether conservative or radical, who say the Christian God is untransposably male is a strong one. It is beyond doubt on a strictly textual basis that God in the Old Testament is stylized as a masculine God and that the few feminine images of God (as a nursing mother or a nesting eagle) are always subservient to the guiding masculine images. With the Christian New Testament comes the added force that Jesus' preferred title for God is "father." Jesus always uses this title to invoke God in prayer. He also teaches his disciples to pray "Our father." Over and against feminist sensibilities, then, is set dominical command. But what of those feminists who find they do not wish to abandon either Christian faith or feminist principles, who are convinced as Christians of the full dignity of men and women, and who believe that the Christian message must be consonant with this dignity? Let us look more closely at our dilemma.

Putting things bluntly, as Mary Daly does, it is this: "If God is male, then the male is God."[2] If God is seen as male, then woman is not fully in the image of God. This conclusion is not a new one; in fact, it was reached by a number of (male) theologians of the early church — women are not fully in the image of God. Often cited in this context was 1 Corinthians 1:7: "For a man ought not to cover his head, since he is the image and glory of God; but woman is the glory of man." This text was understood by some of the "fathers" to imply that women somehow *were not* in the image of God. This conclusion, remote from most contemporary Christian intuitions, was reached by a combination of a certain sensitivity to the metaphorical nature of biblical texts and a set of cultural assumptions about "female nature." The "fathers" realized that the "image" in question was not a physical image, for God does not have a body. Rather, they concluded, it was by virtue of man's capacity for freedom, rationality, and dominion that he was "in God's image." But these features — rationality, freedom, and dominion — were precisely those which, according to the consensus of classical antiquity, women lacked. In a line that can be traced from Plato and Aristotle right through Philo, Origen, Augustine, and up to the debates surrounding women's suffrage of our own modern time, women have been held to be deficient in reason and

2. Daly, *Beyond God the Father: Toward a Philosophy of Women's Liberation* (Boston: Beacon Press, 1973), p. 19.

naturally subordinate, and the marriage relationship to be one of natural ruler to natural subject. It is not surprising that many of the "fathers" thought women were not fully in the image of God. At the turn of the fourth century Chrysostom said, "Then why is the man said to be in the 'image of God' and the woman not? Because 'image' has rather to do with authority, and this only the man has; the woman has it no longer."[3]

Ambrosiaster, writing about the same time, reversed the normal order of argument that went from religious conviction to civic status by arguing from the civic status of women to conclusions about their religious status as *imago Dei:* "For how can it be said of woman that she is in the image of God when she is demonstrably subject to male dominion and has no authority? For she can neither teach nor be a witness in a court nor take an oath nor be a judge."[4] By such circular reasoning women and other non-dominant groups have ever been kept in their places.

If God is styled as male, then the female is that which is "not God." In the Catholic tradition female titles are reserved for the church, the soul, nature, and Mary.[5] Often the female is associated with negative features or features that play a negative role in a set of balanced pairs. Thus in patristic literature a tendency emerges to characterize the female as carnal, emotional, and creaturely, as opposed to the male, which is spiritual, impassible, and divine. In his allegorical interpretation of Genesis, the Jewish neo-Platonist Philo says that the woman, Eve, represents the sense perception which leads the man, Adam (who symbolizes reason), to fall. Furthermore, the supposed "natural" subordination of woman to man, as natural subject to natural ruler, was taken by many of the "fathers" to be the paradigm of other kinds of divinely imposed subordination. So Chrysostom again: "For since equality of honour does many times lead to fightings, He hath made many governments and forms of subjection; as that, for instance, of man and wife, that of son and father, that of old men and young, that of bond and free, that of ruler and ruled, that of master and disciple."[6]

3. Chrysostom, cited in Elizabeth E. Clark, *Women in the Early Church* (Wilmington, Del.: Michael Glazier, 1983), p. 35.

4. Ambrosiaster, cited in Arlene Swidler, "The Image of Woman in a Father-Oriented Religion," in *God as Father?* ed. J.-B. Metz and E. Schillebeeckx, Concilium (Edinburgh: T. & T. Clark, 1981), p. 75.

5. Rosemary Ruether, "The Female Nature of God: A Problem in Contemporary Religious Life," in *God as Father?* p. 63.

6. John Chrysostom, *Homily XXIII.*

It should be clear from this by no means exhaustive discussion that what disturbs feminist theologians is not simply that God has been styled as male in the tradition, but that God is styled as male in particular ways and especially has been styled as powerful, dominant, and implacable. This is the feminists' real objection to the rhetoric of patriarchy: not just that it subordinates women but that it also gives divine justification to a hierarchical reading of the world invariably conceived in terms of powerful/ powerless, superior/inferior, active/passive, male/female. One is reminded of the anti-Calvinist remark of the Chevalier Ramsey, a Scottish contemporary of David Hume: "The grosser pagans contented themselves with divinizing lust, incest, and adultery; but the predestination doctors have divinized cruelty, wrath, fury, vengeance, and all the blackest vices."[7]

It is this image of God as distant and controlling that the feminist theologian Sallie McFague finds so unsatisfactory. The primary metaphors in the tradition are hierarchical and dualistic. To speak of God as king, ruler, lord is to portray God as so omnipotent and other from God's creatures as to make reciprocity and love between God and humankind an impossibility. She suggests that even the one metaphor that might have permitted more mutuality, "God as father," has been compromised by its consistent association with omnipotence, as in "almighty Father."[8]

Here, then, is the feminist objection — much broader than the simple objection that the language of Bible and church excludes women, and reaching right into the "fatherland" of the Christian tradition. The mere complementing of male images with attendant female ones is clearly not enough. As Rosemary Ruether says, "We cannot simply add the 'mothering' to the 'fathering' God, while preserving the same hierarchical patterns of male activity and female passivity. To vindicate the 'feminine' in this form is merely to make God the sanctioner of patriarchy in a new form."[9] Similarly, tinkering with the language of the liturgy, changing "he" to "he and she," may be a cosmetic change which, from the feminist's point of view, conceals a more profound and idolatrous tendency to pray to a male God. After Foucault and Ricoeur, we can no longer think the interrelation of ideology and language so simple or so easily unraveled.

There is little consensus, however, even among feminists, about

7. Ramsey, cited in *David Hume: Dialogues Concerning Natural Religion,* ed. Norman Kemp-Smith (Indianapolis: Bobbs-Merrill, 1947), p. 10.

8. McFague, *Models of God: Theology for an Ecological, Nuclear Age* (Philadelphia: Fortress Press, 1987), pp. 18-19.

9. Ruether, "The Female Nature of God," p. 66.

how such problems should or even could be resolved. One might replace the "father/son" symbols with symbols from nature,[10] but this would diminish the personal element that others like McFague feel to be essential. One could speak of God as "Mother-Daughter-Spirit," but this language finds no home among the texts from which Christianity takes rise, and is perhaps also open to hierarchical reading. One could speak, as Mary Daly prefers to do, of God as "Be-ing" (Daly refuses now to use even the word "God"), but this abstract language runs the risk of making God even more remote, a tendency McFague deplores. Moreover, it could be argued that any of these strategies, if employed not to complement but to actually *replace* the Christian language of "God as father," would result in the institution of a new religion, that the language of "fatherhood" is too deeply rooted in the Christian texts and the religion itself too intimately tied to those texts. Accordingly, the best course for the feminist who could not accept the language of "divine fatherhood" would be not to tinker with models of God but to abandon Christianity, a step from which post-Christian feminists have not shrunk. And as for feminists who find they cannot abandon Christianity? Must we accept all the apparatus of patriarchal religion if we accept the language of God's fatherhood? Is there not another way, a way by which the language of divine fatherhood may be detached from the male idol of patriarchal religion? This is what I would like now to explore.

I am encouraged in this project by an article of Paul Ricoeur's entitled "Fatherhood: From Phantasm to Symbol." One of his central theses is that the "father figure is not a well-known figure whose meaning is invariable and which we can pursue in its avatars, its disappearance and return under diverse masks; it is a problematic figure, incomplete and in suspense. It is a *designation* that is susceptible of traversing a diversity of semantic levels."[11] Ricoeur applies his arguments to three fields: psychoanalysis (Freud), the phenomenology of spirit (Hegel), and the philosophy of religion. It is the treatment of this last that most concerns us here.

In discussing the "dialectic of divine fatherhood," Ricoeur takes as his discussion partner not the theologian but the exegete. He has

10. Dorothee Sölle, "Paternalistic Religion as Experienced by Women," in *God as Father?* p. 73.

11. Ricoeur, "Fatherhood: From Phantasm to Symbol," in *The Conflict of Interpretations: Essays in Hermeneutics,* ed. D. Ihde (Evanston: Northwestern University Press, 1974), p. 468.

interesting reasons for doing so. Exegesis, as opposed to theology, remains at the level of "religious representation" and does not carry the "refinements" of later theory.[12] Exegesis, the study of the texts, is concerned with the progression of representation in these texts and, in this case, with the development of the figure of the "father." Furthermore, exegesis "invites us not to separate the figures of God from the forms of discourse in which these figures occur."[13] The particular kind of discourse, whether saga, myth, prophecy, hymn, or psalm, is important because the designation of God differs according to the manner in which he is designated — whether God is described as agent, or spoken on behalf of, or invoked in prayer.

Turning to the Old Testament, Ricoeur draws attention to a remarkable aspect of the texts themselves — the qualitative insignificance of the divine title "father" in the Old Testament. Ricoeur's observation may be usefully complemented by some research by Robert Hamerton-Kelly, who notes that whereas God is described as "father" over 170 times by Jesus in the New Testament, and is never invoked in prayer by any other title, God is designated "father" only *11 times* in the entire Old Testament and is never invoked as such in prayer.[14] Instead, in the early narratives (or sagas) of the book of Exodus, God is described as "the God of *our* fathers" (my emphasis). The connection certainly exists between God and patriarchy and Israelite family life of this time, for just as families are headed by fathers, so fathers are headed by leaders of clan or tribe who ultimately are responsible to God. But still it remains that God is not "father" but "God of our fathers," and the difference is significant. Hamerton-Kelly argues that this Mosaic strand in the Old Testament identifies the "God of our fathers" through the narrative and by means of historical association "rather than the mythological schemes of the Ancient Near East in which the gods are imagined to be the 'biological' fathers of human beings. . . . Mosaism replaces creation by a mythical procreation with creation by the mysterious Word of God. . . . Fatherhood is strictly a symbol or metaphor for God's relationship to his people."[15] Ricoeur, too, speaks of the remarkable "reservation" on the part of the Hebrew people. The main name relation of God to the people in

---

12. "Representation" in this (Hegelian) sense Ricoeur defines as "the shaped (figuree) form of the self-manifestation of the absolute" ("Fatherhood," p. 481).

13. Ibid., p. 482.

14. Hamerton-Kelly, "God the Father in the Bible and in the Experience of Jesus," in *God as Father?* pp. 98, 96.

15. Ibid., p. 97.

Exodus is covenant and not kinship — it is, at best, the adoption of Israel and not their biological generation by God. God is *not* described as "father"; the people of Israel are *not* true "sons." The prime name of God in Exodus is that given to Moses from the burning bush, I AM THAT I AM, a connotation, Ricoeur says, without designation. Indeed, it is a "name" that casts itself in the face of all names of God. In Exodus "the revelation of the name is the dissolution of all anthropomorphisms, of all figures and figurations, including that of the father. The name against the idol."[16] The God of Israel is defined, then, over and against father gods, gods who beget the world; and paradoxically, it is this abolition of the biological father God that makes non-idolatrous, metaphorical "father language" about God possible. By means of a number of other designations (liberator, lawgiver, the bearer of name without image) space is created where God may be called father. Movement may then take place to the designation of God *as* father, which occurs in the prophets, to declaration *of* the father, and finally the invocation *to* God as father, complete only with the Lord's Prayer in the New Testament.[17]

The prophets are of particular importance to Ricoeur, for they announce the exhaustion of Israel's history and look to the future kingdom of God. It is here that the father figure is declared and recognized, and it is a figure of futurity and hope, a hope for a relation that is to be. Ricoeur cites the extraordinary passage in Jeremiah (3:19-20) where God speaks to his "faithless children" thus:

> . . . I thought you would call me, My Father, and would not turn from following me.
> Surely, as a faithless wife leaves her husband, so have you been faithless to me, O house of Israel.

In this "mutual contamination" of kinship metaphor, where God is both father and spouse to Israel, Ricoeur sees the "shell of literality" broken and the symbol liberated: "A father who is a spouse is no longer a progenitor (begetter), nor is he anymore an enemy to his sons; love, solicitude, and pity carry him beyond domination and severity."[18] As Ricoeur has insisted, the father figure is not an "invariable figure" but problematic, incomplete, even shocking.

16. Ricoeur, "Fatherhood," p. 486.
17. Ibid., p. 487.
18. Ibid., p. 489.

Within the Christian writings that make up the New Testament a further shock occurs. The modest 11 designations of God as father in the Old Testament contrast sharply with the 170 times Jesus designates God as father in the very much shorter New Testament. Even more remarkable is the fact that Jesus uses the domestic title of "father," *abba,* when invoking God. This title in all probability is the designation used by Jesus himself. Moreover, it would seem a designation central to his eschatology. According to Hamerton-Kelly, the "intimacy and accessibility of Almighty God is the essence of Jesus' 'good news.' God is not distant, aloof, not anti-human, not angry, sullen and withdrawn: God draws near, very near; God is with us."[19] Already, then, we see the turning of the symbol: the God who is "not father" in Exodus becomes father and spouse in the prophetic literature and is revealed in the intimacy of the address of *"abba"* in books of the New Testament.[20]

According to Ricoeur, the audacity of addressing God as *abba* breaks the "reserve to which the whole Bible testifies. . . . The audacity is possible because a new time has begun." And Ricoeur goes on, "Far, therefore, from the addressing of God as father being easy, along the lines of a relapse into archaism, it is rare, difficult, and audacious, because it is prophetic, directed toward fulfilment rather than toward origins. It does not look backward toward a great ancestor, but forward, in the direction of a new intimacy on the model of the knowledge of the son."[21]

On a Christian reading of the scriptural texts, this movement from phantasm to symbol, the retreat from the language of physical generation to that of a word of designation (I AM THAT I AM), is completed by the audacious address of the son. To use Ricoeur's terms, it is only with the true son that one can have the true father, for "father" is a dependent title: "There is a father because there is a family, and not the reverse."[22]

---

19. Hamerton-Kelly, "God the Father in the Bible and in the Experience of Jesus," p. 100.

20. The degree of intimacy implied by the title *abba* has recently been questioned, but even if it is not equivalent to the modern "daddy," the argument above holds. As James Barr points out, it still belongs to "the familiar and colloquial register of language." Nor need it be of crucial significance whether Jesus was first to address God as *abba.* That he addressed God so at all would still be an eschatological marker. See James Barr, "Abba Isn't 'Daddy,' " *Journal of Theological Studies* 39 (1988): 28-47.

21. Ricoeur, "Fatherhood," pp. 490-91.

22. Ibid., p. 479. In discussing the explicitly Christian reading of texts, including texts of the Hebrew Bible, Ricoeur is not thereby saying the Christian reading is the only or the best reading of them. Obviously Jews read the same texts quite differently, and without the Christian teleology.

It is the son as first-born among the children of God who, in this sense, makes God "father." And it is in the son's death that this distinctive fatherhood is finally established, for the death of the son is also in some sense the death of the father who is one with the son.[23] This death of God Ricoeur sees in Hegelian terms as the "death of a separated transcendence." One is left not without God but without the separated God.

It remains to be seen whether this archaeology of symbols will bring any solace to the Christian feminist. Superficially the language of fatherhood is in place more firmly than ever, for in Ricoeur's scheme it is this "achieved language of fatherhood," reached first by rejection of divine paternity in the Mosaic narrative, then the designation of the prophets, and the address and invocation in the New Testament, which finally colludes in its own destruction and opens the way for a non-patriarchal religion of hope. Furthermore, it seems superficially to blow a wide hole in simple versions of the "Jesus, the Good Feminist" argument, where Jesus is styled as inheriting a religion with a dreaded "father God" and transforming it through a personal regard for women. This might be no bad thing, since Jewish feminists rightly caution their Christian colleagues against achieving a "clean" Christianity by painting Judaism in dark colors. The real point, however, is that religions are not patriarchal simply by virtue of styling their deities as "fathers" but rather by underwriting social patterns that privilege men over women. This could be the case in a religion that used no personal stylizations for God of any form.

But what real choices does the Christian feminist have? The least problematic, as I have said, is to reject Christianity altogether. If, on the other hand, one stays within Christianity, one must come to terms with those sections of its texts and those parts of its tradition where the symbolism is ineradicably masculine. Undoubtedly the new language of liturgy and devotion will be more inclusive and less masculine than that of the tradition. Some Christian communities may and perhaps must elect not to use "father" as a divine title, given the pain it can cause. In the long run one is faced with Jesus himself, God incarnate in Christian orthodoxy, whose physical masculinity cannot be gainsaid. Of course, it is open to Christians now, as always since antiquity, to deny the divinity of Christ; but this option, while resolving some feminist difficulties, creates many others. Apart from the rupture with trinitarian orthodoxy, it is not clear that one is any better off honoring Jesus as a male demi-God or supreme

23. Ibid., p. 497.

91

holy prophet. Indeed, I think this is worse. Better, again, to leave Christianity altogether.

The other possibility that we have only begun to explore is that while the paternal imagery remains in place in the historic literature at least, it be seen not as a figure "well-known" and "invariable" but, as Ricoeur suggests, as an incomplete figure that traverses a number of semantic levels. It is not a model there from eternity (the patriarchal father) but a mobile symbol the sense of which develops through the Hebrew Bible, and which for Christians takes on a different sense in the books of the New Testament, where "father" is known from the sisters and brothers in Christ to whom God stands as *abba,* father.[24]

Jürgen Moltmann has argued that the name "Father" for God has two backgrounds, one in patriarchy, the "Universal Father" and "dreaded Lord God" (here the term is used metaphorically), and the other where God, literally, is father of the "first-born" son.[25] It is the second sense that must be decisive for Christianity. "The patriarchal ordering of the world — God the Father, Holy Father, father of the country, father of the family — is a monotheistic ordering, not a trinitarian one," says Moltmann.[26] The father of Jesus, on the other hand, both *begets* and *gives birth* to his son and through him to the *twice-born* family of God. Moltmann offers this comment:

24. I should emphasize that the use of "father" as a messianic title in the New Testament does not oblige one to give a central role to the title in contemporary religious practice, especially in situations where its use might convey the opposite of hope and promise. It is one messianic title among many and needs to be understood in its literary and historical context, but even so understood it may need to be used with caution. Those who do not see why the "father" title should be problematic for women might well read the chilling indictment by Susan Brooks Thistlethwaite in her book entitled *Sex, Race, and God* (New York: Crossroads, 1989). Writing on the basis of her work with battered and sexually abused women, Thistlethwaite recognizes that the original intent of the "father" title was not to justify violence against women, but she offers this comment: "For me, in my work with these survivors, it does not fundamentally matter. The entire history of Western abuse of children, particularly of girl children by fathers, stands between us and those texts; and no amount of ahistoricism can change that fact" (p. 114). Thistlethwaite also notes, however, that black Christian feminists in America do not have the same difficulty with "father" language as do white feminists and that a certain amount of toleration is needed with regard to preferred divine titles.

25. Moltmann, "The Motherly Father: Is Trinitarian Patripassianism Replacing Theological Patriarchalism?" in *God as Father?* p. 51. I have some difficulties with Moltmann's ascription of literal usage to the second, but this is not to the point here.

26. Ibid., p. 52.

A father who both *begets* and *gives birth* to his son is no mere male father. He is a motherly father. He can no longer be defined as single-sexed and male, but becomes bisexual or transexual. He is the *motherly Father* of his *only-born Son,* and at the same time the *fatherly Father* of his *only begotten Son.* It was at this very point that the orthodox dogmatic tradition made its most daring affirmations. According to the Council of Toledo of 675 "we must believe that the Son was not made out of nothing, nor out of some substance or other, but from the womb of the Father *(de utero Patris),* that is that he was begotten or born *(genitus vel natus)* from the father's own being." Whatever this declaration may be supposed to be saying about the gynaecology of the Father, these bisexual affirmations imply a radical denial of patriarchal monotheism.[27]

While feminists may be dissatisfied with Moltmann's strategy of ascribing to the "father" the motherly attributes, this passage makes the ambiguity of the classical symbolism obvious.

We can move things in a more radically orthodox direction by drawing on an unexpected source: Julia Kristeva's recent book entitled *In the Beginning Was Love: Psychoanalysis and Faith.* A Lacanian analyst (of a sort) and French feminist (of a sort), Kristeva begins her discussion with Freud's observation that the foundation of his cure is "Our God Logos." She continues to describe her own perception of the psychoanalytic task as one of making word and flesh meet, making the word become flesh in a discourse of love directed to an "impossible other." She develops her comments with an analysis of the Apostles' Creed, noting that in the Genesis narratives God creates by making separate. Separation is the mark of God's presence: the separation of light from dark, of heaven from earth, of sea from dry land, of male from female. And this dividing and separating reaches a climax in the Christian story with the crucifixion, the desertion of Christ on the cross and the cry of dereliction. To add a theological gloss to Kristeva's point, this supreme moment of creation/separation is the separation of God from God. Yet it is because one is deserted, Kristeva suggests, that one may achieve ecstasy in completion and reunion with the father, who, she adds, is "himself a substitution for the mother."[28] If her reading is correct, the symbolic weight of this Christian narrative

27. Ibid., p. 53.
28. Kristeva, *In the Beginning Was Love: Psychoanalysis and Faith,* trans. Arthur Goldhammer (New York/Guilford: Columbia University Press, 1987), p. 32.

re-establishes a fusion with the Other, who is both maternal and paternal: "So God created man in his own image, in the image of God he created him; male and female he created them" (Gen. 1:27). It is difficult to know quite what to make of this psychoanalytic approach, but in the future we might at least hesitate before stating too didactically which religious symbols are male symbols and which are female.

It is easier, if only slightly, to chart the history of symbols than to predict their future. Does the "father God" have a future? If Christianity has a future, then the answer is probably "yes." But it would be reasonable for a dispassionate student of religions to wonder whether Christianity will survive the rapid changes taking place — around the world, not just in the privileged West — in women's self-understanding. In my opinion, Christianity now faces a serious challenge, and one that addresses core metaphors, narratives, and ideologies (like Ricoeur, I find these three are closely related). It may be that Christianity will not meet the challenge or will linger on as a pleasing anachronism distant from the life of the cultures it inhabits. You may well think we are watching yet another stage in the death throes of a dinosaur. On the other hand, I, like Ricoeur, find the heart of religion in hope. The Christian religion with its complex metaphorical structures has shown before its remarkable resilience and capacity to make a vital response to new circumstances. It will be interesting to watch how it does so now.

"The Father, He . . ."

ROBERT W. JENSON

I.

IT IS USUALLY thought that current churchly conflicts over "inclusive" redoing of liturgical texts, biblical translations, and homiletical and pedagogical diction are familial if sometimes bitter disputes within a shared faith. The conflicts are provoked by a campaign to replace "Father, Son, and Spirit" with allegedly equivalent formulas in ritual acts, hymns, and prayers, to replace the pronominal structure of biblical and homiletical narrative with "God . . . God . . . God . . ." and with such coinages as "Godself," and to handle all descriptive language about God as coinable and so disposable "metaphor." The campaign is widely successful yet not very obviously well founded by historical, exegetical, or sociological scholarship.[1] It would therefore seem to invite active refutation. But those who disapprove it are usually commended to abide the reconstructions as necessary adjustments or, at worst, manifestations of an aberration that will pass in due course.

For opponents of the "inclusivist"[2] enterprise to accept such advice

1. The truth of this observation is not impugned by the truly enormous body of writing produced in the last years *within* the enterprise of "feminist analysis," "feminist theology," and so on. Rarely has the intellectual world known so quickly developing a scholasticism.

2. It should not be but probably is necessary to say explicitly that I approve feminism as the drive for political and economic equality. In the church and other religious circles, however, the word "feminist" has been appropriated for a very specific ideological-religious program, and I use it here in the sense such feminists have given it.

95

is, in my judgment, an error fatally dangerous for the church. The current attack upon the received linguistic structure of Christianity is not an inner-Christian dispute; it is occasioned by the invasion of an antagonistic religious discourse and represents a true crisis of the faith that cannot be dealt with by compromise.

Indeed, one may fear that the current crisis, where it is in progress, is equaled in the previous history of the faith only by the gnostic crisis of the second and third centuries[3] and by the crisis of vulgar Enlightenment at the hinge of the eighteenth and nineteenth centuries.[4] If one historical event could fully repeat another, one might even say that the "inclusivist" crisis is a simultaneous rerun of the two, joined into one by recapitulation also of the causal relation between them.

A deep general likeness has often been observed between late Western modernity and the declining Mediterranean antiquity that produced gnosticism.[5] Now as then, cosmopolitan economic and social structures have undone the local and regional polities in which finite individuals can belong responsibly to their world. Now as then, continual military and ecological destruction has battered the possibility of hope for this world. Now as then, an "Enlightenment" that consists in the dominance of a merely critical form of intelligence and in — ironically — a sadly *un*critical general interpretation of the cosmos by mechanistic metaphor has undone the bonds of natural community and left a swarm of individual moral atoms. Now as then, a bewildering welter of religious possibilities imposes simultaneously a desperate need to mitigate religious particularities and severe difficulty in committing to any actual religion at all. The sum and heart of the matter is this: now as then, the fundamental religious experience is of sheer separation between God and world.

That God has become distant from us is of course a stereotypical late-modern lament. It is impossible, however, not to hear in it a certain note of satisfaction. For if God is indeed hopelessly distant, then he is at

---

3. The great study from which to learn of this, and so to much of which I will refer in my discussion, remains that of Hans Jonas, *Gnosis und spätantiker Geist,* 2 vols. (Göttingen: Vandenhoeck & Ruprecht, 1954).

4. For analysis of the nature of this crisis, I refer to portions of my own contribution to a joint volume: Robert W. Jenson, "The Christian Doctrine of God," in *Keeping the Faith: Essays to Mark the Centenary of Lux Mundi* (Philadelphia: Fortress Press, 1988), pp. 25-53.

5. If "post-modernity" is to be anything other than the decadence — or perhaps fulfillment? — of modernity, its time is clearly yet to come.

least off our backs, then the millennial campaign of *liberum arbitrium* ("free choice") to clear for each human creature a space in which he/she can be sovereign has at last succeeded. Adam's and Eve's agreement with the serpent in the need to exercise *liberum arbitrium* would have been more satisfying had their God not been given to showing up in their garden and walking about in it.

And if we nevertheless still wish to be in some way religious, to cultivate "transcendence" or something along those lines, a tolerably ineffable God is the kind to have. The total apocalyptic silence of God a la Nietzsche is perhaps not, after all, what most of us want. Instructions in properly "inclusive" language recently issued by the central authorities of my own denomination capture the tone of still-permitted religion perfectly: what we may have and seek to communicate is "glimpses of the divine." A God close up is likely to afflict us with his own particular reality, but we do like to peek at divinity from a safe metaphysical distance. From sufficient remove, we need have indeed only "glimpses" that we can connect according to our needs, projecting thereby whatever "image" of divinity will provide appropriate "love" or "empowerment" or "nurture" or whatever, without intruding its/his/her own definitions of such services.

The conflict is over words: "Father," "Son," "he." Accommodating church folk are likely to say that the conflict must therefore be at least partly about "just words," which merely shows how deeply we all are implicated in the disorder. For of course, within Christianity words are never "just" words. The Christian God *is* his own word, and all churchly words are either the actuality of God's word and so the presence of God himself, or the means by which we combat his presence.

On the other side, the matter is subtler and more ironic. Insofar as the reconstructors wish for whatever reason to remain in the church and so are interested in persuasion, they must argue that the changes they demand can be made without altering the faith's substance. Yet they are generally more aware than are their opponents of the ontologically constitutive place of words; it is precisely this awareness that moves them to their campaign. In what follows, it may become clear how these positions are not in fact contrary.

The conflict between gnosticism and biblical faith has always been over the ontological position of the word. For Judaism and Christianity, God's *Logos* is God's personal address to us; in that there is the Word, it is established that the meeting between God and us is not a showing and a peering through a haze of metaphysical distance but an exchange between persons who appear as such precisely in that they find themselves able to engage in mutual discourse. God talks to us and solicits an answer; just so we are persons together in community. For gnosticism ancient and modern, *per contra,* the *Logos* is an "image" that *substitutes* for God's presence with us, an emanation by which, although God itself (the only possible English grammatical gender in this context) remains the "unknown god," a channel is established between God's realm and ours, along which glimpses can be obtained. For Christianity — and Judaism! — the Word is "of one being with the Father," is simply God's own being as self-communicated; for gnosticism, all words are one ontological step down from the "real" God, an alienation of God to accommodate our need.

In what follows I will consider two chief matters of the conflict, two questions on which the linguistic spirits of Christianity and invading gnosticism divide. The one matter (discussed in the following section) is the function of pronouns: Can, for example, "God sent *God's* Son" (never mind here the gender of "Son") be truly a reconstructed version of "God sent *his* son"? The other matter (discussed in section III) is the replaceability or irreplaceability of certain phrases — most notably, of course, "Father, Son, and Holy Spirit."

II.

Surely, many accommodating church folk have thought, if hearing God referred to by "he," "him," "himself," and so on offends some, we may and then should eschew the practice. We do, after all, want to be all things to all whomevers. Where one would previously have used a pronoun in reading Scripture or in homiletical or pedagogical discourse, we will now repeat "God" or in reflexive contexts use "Godself" or similar coinages. Those with little acquaintance of Judaism sometimes propose to assuage the monotony with "Jahweh."

In reply to this, it is often and correctly pointed out that "God" is a common name, and that therefore such sentences as "God sent God's Son" do not establish that the referent of the second "God" is the same as the referent of the first, or to which divinity this "Son" is then related. The sentence could, so far as its grammar shows, be the report of a typical polytheistic transaction. In the case of such usages as "God emptied Godself," objectors may explicitly warn of gnosticism, pointing out that what the form of the sentence intrinsically suggests is that "Godself" is a second entity ontologically after God, very much in the style, say, of Valentinus.

At this point in the typical exchange, the pronoun-avoiders reply that they are using "God" as a proper name,[6] and that even if this sense is not strictly supported by general usage, it can be relied upon in the community of the church. But neither will this move work. If someone says, "Joan sent Joan's son," this sentence does not in fact establish that the son sent is the son of the person named by the first occurrence of "Joan." For of course, there may be and usually are many bearers of the same "proper" name.[7] Where the initial instance of a proper name has in the semantic context effected a successful identification, its later repetition in place of a pronoun positively suggests that two different persons are referred to. The repetition of "God," precisely in a context where this is heard as a proper name, must still most naturally belong to a polytheistic discourse.

It is at this juncture that suddenly the real question comes out of hiding. For the rejoinder is "But of course *this* name, proper or otherwise, has in fact only one bearer; there is only one God. In the community whose speech is in question, everyone knows that." And indeed, whether "God" functions as a common name or a proper name, it has only one bearer; and in the Christian community this is indeed supposed to be known. But *how* are we to know it? That, I suggest, is the real matter at issue.

In the gospel and in the Scripture, the uniqueness of God is *narratively* established. That the *numen* who spoke to Moses from the burning bush was not a new divine emergent or heretofore sidelined godlet was determined by the narrative telling that he was "the God of . . . Abraham, the God of Isaac, and the God of Jacob." It was unlimited repetition of this sort of narration that established in the course of Israel's religious history that there are *no* divine acts not done by the same one who rescued Israel from Egypt, no deities not personally identical with the Lord of the Exodus — that is, that he is the one and only God. Although the religious and literary history is complex, the logic is simple: the narrative begins with a name or identifying description of God, "The Lord did . . ."; then the narrative is extended with "and he had done . . . , and he had

6. In the everyday sense, not in the perhaps unexemplified technical-philosophical sense.

7. I have stolen this direct way of making the point from an intervention by my colleague at St. Olaf College, Prof. Bruce Marshall, in an actual debate of this sort.

done . . . , and then he did . . . , and then he did . . . ," until there are no godly deeds not specified as the deeds of the one originally identified agent. The so-called historical books of the Hebrew Scripture are in fact but one long narrative determination of the Lord's unicity and uniqueness.

But this way of knowing that there is only one God depends on pronominal reference, on starting the story with a common or proper name or an identifying description and then continuously identifying the agent of each new event by unambiguous reference back to that name or description. How, for New Testament example, could a Paul bereft of pronouns have said what he had to say in Romans 1:1-3: ". . . the gospel of God which he promised beforehand through his prophets . . . , the gospel concerning his Son. . . ."?

I do not, of course, maintain that where God's unicity and uniqueness *are* established, narrative of his deeds cannot sometimes and in specific rhetorical forms proceed by repetition of "God" — as gloriously in the first chapter of Genesis. But if the pronominal structure of normal narrative is generally suppressed, then even though narrative may be about one and the same person and be known to be so, the narrative itself can no longer provide this information. The fact of God's uniqueness must be *otherwise* known. *How then?* Since the oneness of God is a determining factor of his being, this other procedure will decisively determine which and what sort of God is actually worshiped.

If God's uniqueness is not established by exhaustive narrative, there is only one other way in which it has been or can be known. This is what Luther called "the theology of glory," and it is the procedure of standard religion and the permanent alternative to faith's procedure. Its deep intrusion into Christian theology is old, repeated, and disastrous, particularly, perhaps, in the Latin church.[8] In many ways, "feminist theology" merely consummates an ancient flaw of mainline theology.

In the usual, "glorious" way of being religious, we begin with experience of this world, of its goods and of the fragility and insufficiency of those goods. That is, we begin with the polytheistic suggestion,[9] with a multiplicity of goods, each of which raises the hope of its own secure and sufficient Ground. Each of the thereby posited divinities is then a

8. On this point I refer to a work of my own: Robert W. Jenson, *The Triune Identity* (Philadelphia: Fortress Press, 1982), pp. 114-38.

9. I do not wish thereby to take any position on the question of whether religious *history* begins with a monotheistic "revelation."

"one" over against its "many" temporal reflections — there is only one Mars but many victories, one Aphrodite but many loves, and so on. It is the suggestion contained in this structure of religious projection itself which more than anything else eventually prompts the further projection of a unitary "deity" to be the one Ground of the many divinities — of, to continue with the example of our own culture, the one deity "whom men call Zeus."

The biblical God's unique self-identity as God is established by his history on a narrative line parallel to the temporal line of our history — he is precisely the *triune* God, the God whose being is constituted in the action between Jesus and the one he called "Father" and their future in the Spirit. This line, if I may put it so, cuts across the "vertical" line between God and creatures so that the narrative is at once of God's history and ours, is a narrative precisely of divine-human history. Quite differently, the unique self-identity of the one God of standard religion is established by the upward convergence of an ontological pyramid, on a line vertical to our history and parallel to the relation between God and his emanations,[10] and is known by our ascent of that pyramid. These two ontologies are mutually exclusive, as are the deities whose uniqueness they determine and the cults of those deities.

On this matter it remains only to make this note: what gnosticism does is to make the religious pyramid itself the true object of religious devotion. Thus current "metaphor theology" is unwilling to worship the deity specified by any one set of metaphors; its deity is specified in the *process* by which ever-new metaphors transcend one another. And therewith we are brought to the second matter of this essay.

III.

A.

Churchly conflict has been centered on a particular few bits of language: "Father, Son, and Holy Spirit" in its use as the Christian name for God,

---

10. On this, see the quite remarkable article by Christopher B. Kaiser, "The Ontological Trinity in the Context of Historical Religions," *Scottish Journal of Theology* 29 (1976): 301-10. See also the more general development in Jenson, *The Triune Identity*, pp. 21-102.

a few resultant phrases within trinitarian theology, "Father" by itself as a term of address in prayer, and, less vigorously, a selection of words such as "Lord" or "King." This language is said to prohibit full participation by women in the life of the church, and it is proposed to substitute for the triune name various formulas such as "Creator, Redeemer, and Sanctifier"[11] or "Parent, Child, and Paraclete"; to substitute the more abstractly stated formulas, about "hypostases" and "processions," of technical trinitarian discourse; to substitute "Father/Mother" or wholly non-filial terms of address for "Father"; and to substitute various gender-neutral or feminine-gendered substitutes for "Lord" and the like.

Both the objection to the traditional language and the assertion that it can be replaced rest on classification of "Father," "Lord," and so forth as metaphorical or otherwise tropic when used of God. In the following I will restrict my discussion to "Father," since the triune name and the Lord's Prayer are the heart of the conflict, and because the position taken here will in large part determine the position to be taken at most other points.

Addressing God as "Father" is said to oppress and exclude women because of the act of metaphorical projection in which it allegedly occurs. All language, it is said, is inadequate to specify God; therefore, all language about God must be metaphorical.[12] It is not so much said as supposed without question that *we* coin the metaphors. It is further said that the metaphors which a community then actually comes to use for God project onto eternity the structure of values operative in that community; since God is the good, our metaphorical projection begins with our most deeply controlling supposed goods. Thus "patriarchal" communities will use "Father," "King," and similarly gendered metaphors for their God or gods. Finally, it is said that a religion constituted by male metaphors both reveals the patriarchal structure of the community whose religion it is and enforces and legitimizes that structure.

Whether or not this account is phenomenologically accurate in the case of other religions and whether or not it reveals the *truth* of any religion

11. It is to the side of my discussion here, but perhaps nevertheless useful again to make this note: where phrases of this general form are used as more than comment on "Father, Son, and Holy Spirit," they teach the most primitive (in both senses) of all trinitarian heresies, "modalism."

12. There are other tropes than metaphor, of course. Classification of God language under some of these would in fact make a better argument for the reconstructivist case — but that by the by.

at all are matters I must again leave to the side. For it is in any case easily shown that the *church's* use of "Father" in the triune name and generally in prayer to the Christian God is not a metaphor or any other kind of trope. This does not mean that the church's discourse about or for God does not also contain a rich variety of metaphor, as does the discourse of the Bible. God is indeed also *like* a father, as he is like a mother — and like a rock, a hurricane, and a whisper. Moreover, of course, the address the church makes to God by using "Father" straightforwardly may be unfounded and in that case blasphemous gibberish, but that is a wholly other question.

The deepest origin of and continuing reason for the Christian address of God as "Father" and the "Father/Son" pairing within the triune name is the instruction Jesus gave his disciples when they asked their master how to pray. In the Lord's Prayer he taught them, little is original over against previous Jewish prayer, except its address to God. "Share my relation to God," said Jesus. "Approach him as I do, with 'Father'; pray *with* me, I who am the Son." From that day to this, Christian prayer has notoriously been to the Father, with the Son, in their Spirit.[13]

Jesus called upon God as "Father." How does that work? If I call upon a parent and do so by uttering "father," I perform a speech act that is of its own and perfectly straightforward sort: "father" is an individuating term of address. It would be quite meaningless even to ask whether "father" in this context could be a metaphor or other trope.[14]

Next it is vital to notice this: nothing changes if I am adopted. An adoptive child's address to his/her father is no whit more a trope than if he/she were the result of this parent's inseminating. The meaning and function of "father" as a term of address clearly does not depend upon the character of its basis in events. And indeed, we cannot claim to know what all possible ontic grounds for the existence of the father-son relation may be unless we claim to know not only many created facts we in fact do not know and never will, but also the inner possibilities of God. This ignorance does not render ineffable the relational reality posited in the use of "father" as a term of address. Thus there is no linguistic reason why, when Jesus called God "Father," this must have been a trope, even though the first

13. It will be noted that my discussion in this essay does not much allude to the Spirit. In this, it reflects the general situation of Western theology, in which the present conflict occurs. It may well be that Western weakness in the doctrine of the Spirit is the deepest ground of Western weakness for gnosticism.

14. Unless, to be sure, we wish to rob the word "metaphor" of any import by decreeing that all speech is metaphorical. But then the "feminist" program is undone utterly.

Person of the Christian God indeed neither inseminates nor is inseminated, nor yet has — according to dogmatic decision — adopted Jesus.[15] Nor then is there any linguistic reason why, when we at Jesus' behest join him in calling God "Father," when we address God as adoptive siblings of the Son, this must be a trope.

It is probably also necessary to point out that there is no metaphor merely in the male grammatical gender of "father." A child calling to "mother" is simply choosing the term of address that will fetch the parent wanted, and for a child to call a parent by the inappropriate address is not a metaphor but a mere misfire. That Jesus addressed God as "Father" was in the same way a matter of using the term of filial address that would in fact pick out the God upon whom he intended to call. Of the possible individuating terms of filial address, "father" rather than "mother" was required, because Jesus' God was the God of Israel. Israel could not, for reasons given in every step of its history with God and still as compelling for Israel as ever, address the Lord as "mother,"[16] this being the appropriated address to the principal deity alternative, then as now, to the Lord: the god/ess of fertility religion.

That Jesus called on God with "father" rather than with "mother" is a fact about the historic person Jesus that we can no more change by decree than we can decree that he was not Jewish, or a wandering rabbi, or unpopular with the Sanhedrin. Since the church's address of God is authorized only as repetition of Jesus' address, this fact about him is determinative for the church. Some of us, to be sure, may not wish to worship the God of Israel, and throughout Christian history, groups have left the church on one sort or other of that account. The church itself has been damaged by such departures only when they were later rather than sooner.

The immediate observation is only that there are no linguistic reasons why Jesus' address of God as "Father" must have been a trope. There may of course be metaphysical reasons why it nevertheless in fact was one. Whether it was or not is then a material theological question. And it is the question upon which Christianity finally separated itself completely from the gnostic impulse, the question upon which the one catholic church defined itself as the church it has been.[17] For the entire

15. It is in fact a contention of most traditional theology that the ontic character of "begets" in "the Father begets the Son" is God's permanent secret.

16. See, for example, Gerhard von Rad, *Theologie des alten Testaments,* 2 vols. (Munich: C. Kaiser, 1957-1965), 1:24ff.

17. On this, see the monumental history by R. P. C. Hanson, *The Search for the Christian Doctrine of God: The Arian Controversy, 318-381* (Edinburgh: T. & T. Clark, 1988).

joint contention of the variously "Arian" or mediating parties in the great struggle of the fourth century can be summarized thus: "Jesus is the Son of the Father" is a trope. And the entire contention of the Nicene party can be summarized thus: "Jesus is the Son of the Father" is not a trope.

It is surely possible to address God as "Father" — or refuse to do so — using "Father" as a trope. But it is not possible to do so as a faithful member of the Christian church, at least if the phrase "the Christian church" is to be used in any historically honest way. Those who maintain that Jesus' and our address of God as "Father" has to be tropic maintain that the church's fundamental creedal decision at Nicea and Constantinople was precisely false. Any who wish to maintain this are at liberty to do so. But they should do it as avowed opponents of the church, not as alleged reformers thereof.[18] The matter at this point is merely one of truth in advertising.

The church does not, of course, use "Father" exclusively as a term of address. But when "Father" is used in the rhetorical third person, as in a preacher's "The Father loves you," this occurs by way of the appearance of "Father" in the triune name. And in the triune name, "Father" occurs solely to evoke Jesus' address of God; the Father in "Father, Son, and Holy Spirit" is called "Father" precisely and only as the Father of the next-named Son, and not by application of a general appellation for God, metaphorical or otherwise. The very ability of the triune name to be a name is given by its invocation of Jesus' specific relation to and address of God. "Father" in the church's discourse, at whatever juncture, always means "the one whom Jesus called Father."

Thus far my result is still mostly negative in its force. "Inclusivist" reasons for wishing to replace the triune name and closely related masculine-gendered language, and "inclusivist" reasons for holding this language to be replaceable, are false. Use of this language excludes only such persons as choose that it shall. Those who insist that such language must be what it claims not to be — metaphor — and themselves then use or refuse to use it so, will in consequence indeed be oppressed by it.[19] It remains to be seen that the inherited language is in fact irreplaceable.

18. And the best thinkers and scholars of "feminist" or "womanist" theology/religion now do just that.

19. Intrinsically, moreover, the persons who in this way oppress themselves can as well be men as women, since the impulse to project deity from the virtue of the opposite sex, in whom precisely what one lacks is made up, is plainly as much a possibility — and if anything historically predominant — as is what one might call same-sex religiosity.

B.

The place to begin is with an astonishment. The church's attempt to address God with straightforward terms of address and its claim to know invocations to which he responds as I do to "Robert" and to possess other bits of language like "The Father begets the Son," which likewise cognitively touch his personal being, may of course be deluded. But if they are not, then something universe-shaking is afoot. For nothing could be more amazing than that we should have such language.

Who could speak in this way? Who could except as gibberish say, "O God, Father, Son, and Holy Spirit, we worship you, we adore you, we magnify you"? Or thereupon refer to him among one another? Who could discourse with and about God as a member of their community? Only, surely, the saints around the throne, in the kingdom of God. If such speech is possible for creatures, then it is possible only for creatures who have been, as Eastern Christianity has put it, "deified." Thus Thomas Aquinas, no eschatological eccentric, taught that our ability to "theologize" rests on participation in the knowledge which "the blessed" have,[20] in anticipation of the knowledge we *will* have when we join them.[21]

If "Father, Son, and Spirit" truly is a name of God, then the sounding of this name — with all the others which, so far as we know, he has — is a distinctive event of what is to happen around the throne, and if we here and now dare sound it, we thereby claim somehow to share in that gathering, to speak, as the worship of the church in fact has it, "with . . . all the company of heaven." If God may be seen in such great visions as those that the seer John claims to show us, of the throne and the Lamb or of the fires or of the City, it can only be the saints themselves whose eyes are transformed to such vision, with the seer permitted momentarily to join them behind the veil of the future; our icons and rhetoric must either be *mis*representations or be a *mimesis* guided by their sight rather than by our own. It is throughout eternity that we will be initiated into the pattern of the life among the divine Three; if we are now able to shape our liturgy by the "begetting" and "sending" constitutive of that life, it can only be that we are permitted to trace a life not yet of this world.

---

20. Aquinas, *Summa theologiae,* I,1,2. On this and following invocations of Thomas generally, see Robert W. Jenson, *The Knowledge of Things Hoped For* (New York: Oxford University Press, 1969), pp. 58-89.

21. Aquinas, *Summa theologiae,* II-II, 171-74.

Just those bits of language that make the worship and theology of the church possible at all, bits of language that are proper to the triune God's personal being and constitute the base of the trinitarian identification of God, can be ours only in anticipation of the utterance around the throne. And therefore such bits of language must share certain characteristics of those more-than-linguistic signs we in the West call "sacraments," most notably in this context their irreplaceability, their sheer weight and density as things that mean.

All words — all "signs," in the language that St. Augustine created for Western sacramentology[22] — are in themselves, of course, *things:* they are articulated sounds, marks on paper, cups of wine, hand-touches on the head. In Augustinian language, they are *res* (plural), "somethings." It was Augustine's phenomenological observation, taken up by the Western church's theology, that signs can, with respect to their actuality as somethings, be divided into two sorts: those fully linguistic signs whose sheer antecedent being as *res* can, once the sign has been stipulated, be replaced, and those of which this is not true.

A sign that belongs to a proper language, constituted by knowable semantic and syntactic rules, can be replaced in the language by some other sound or mark, following the same semantic rules by which the sign was specified in the first place. But we are not in a position to do this with such signs as the bath of baptism. We are not able to create a different ceremony of initiation — say, the giving of a particular lifelong haircut — and declare that this will now mean what baptism has meant. The reason is that we possess no semantic rules to control the translation.

The Supper's loaf and baptism's bath cannot be replaced because we cannot know the rules by which they were "instituted" — that is, given force as signs. We can know that they *are* signs, and even take them as signs into our discourse, with *its* rules. Indeed, we can even after the fact sometimes work out how these signs are apt to their purpose — why, for example, bread and cup are apt to mean the crucified Messiah. But we do not know the rules of these signs' home language; we do not know why God says "I am with you" by bread and cup instead of by some other signs. For us, the givenness of the loaf and the bath can be nothing but historical contingencies to which we are bound as we are bound to the contingencies of God's choice of Israel from the nations or of Mary from

22. On this whole matter, see Johannes Betz, *Eucharistie in der Schrift und Patristik,* vol. 4, fasc. 4a of *Handbuch der Dogmengeschichte* (Freiburg: Herder, 1979), pp. 150ff.

the maidens of Israel or of Jesus from Mary's many possible children. Accordingly, we are not able to translate cup and bath into true equivalents; the *res* themselves are inseparable from their meaning.

The language by whose rules bread and cup and bath are instituted can only be the language of God and his saints. It is the language of a community to which we now belong only across the line of death and new creation; our possession now of some of its signs is mysterious in the strict sense. For it is identical with the identity across death and resurrection of the sinner that I was with the saint that I will be. And the same must be true of the dense signs of primary trinitarian talk.

The saints in heaven may know God so well as to make new names for him to suit their love; perhaps they do it instant by instant. But we have membership in their company only across death and resurrection. How do we know any names for God? Or that "The Father begets the Son" is a meaningful and true sentence? Only if he lets us overhear, across the border of our own non-being and new being, the conversation of heaven. Only — which is to say exactly the same thing — if the continuing theological attention of the church, in which such phrases on rare occasions appear, is indeed "guided by the Spirit." And why he and his saints let us overhear one name instead of another, one phrase instead of another, we do not know at all.

Thomas Aquinas distinguished sharply between metaphorical language about God,[23] which he knew to be rich and useful, and that "analogical" language about God which founds our discourse about God and in which we anticipate the discourse of saints. What makes the latter language precisely analogical, and therefore *neither* metaphorical nor a claim to know God as we cannot know him, is that on the one hand a word like "good" truly fits God first and straightforwardly and only thereupon and derivatively sometimes fits creatures, but that on the other hand the rules by which *we* know how to apply the word learned to creatures are not the rules by which it applies to God.[24] If there is a metaphorically projective use here, it is such a word's use for *us!*

---

23. Aquinas, *Summa theologiae*, I,13,3.

24. Ibid.: *"Quantum igitur ad id quod significant huiusmodi nomina, proprie competunt Deo. . . . Quantum vero ad modum significandi, non proprie dicuntur de Deo; habent enim modum significandi qui creaturis competit."* See Jenson, *The Knowledge of Things Hoped For,* pp. 74-79. My argument in this essay differs from Thomas's in that he principally considers the language — "being," "good," and so on — by which he specifies the one being of God, and I principally consider sheerly given phrases of trinitarian discourse.

The clashing linguistic spirits share a true intuition. Both Christianity and gnostic religion know that God is beyond our manipulation, by language or by any other means. Both know that therefore all true speech about God must be "apophatic," must deny the rules by which we wield the language spoken. The difference between Christianity and the gnostic spirit is then simple and straightforward: for the latter, apophaticism means that *we* have continuously to *make up* language in which to speak of God, since all speech fails as soon as it is used; for Christianity, apophaticism means that we are *given* language that is *immune* to our manipulating, that is "sacramental" in its density.

IV.

For the church, the question of *faithfulness* is always posed and decisive. Other religions can perhaps be relaxed about the question of God's identity, about the question of which God they in fact worship, and whether it is the same one they once set out to worship. For the gods of the religions are accommodating on this point and meld easily into one another. But the church's God is the *jealous* God of Israel, the God whose primary saving mandate is "You shall have no other gods." It is precisely the soteriological peculiarity of the God of Scripture to insist on his peculiarity. The great question of the church's theological self-critique is always, at the last, Are we faithful to the one and only God?

In a certain strict sense, it can be said that this decision is at risk in *every* theological confusion or dispute. But that strictness is not, of course, the strictness of actual discourse. For the most part, the clashes of "theologies" are indeed familial disputes within a faith defined by speech beyond their reconstructing.[25] But sometimes things get beyond that, or even start out so.

25. Thus Hanson, writing a history of what is usually called the "Arian controversy," rightly wrote instead on the "search" for the Christian doctrine of God, as the title of his book indicates (see n. 17). At least at the beginning, there was nobody involved except believers afflicted by "cognitive dissonance." Thus all parties acknowledged the authority of the baptismal name for God — "Father, Son, and Holy Spirit" — however much difficulty they may have variously had in accommodating it within their constructs.

Naming the One Who Is above Us

GERHARD O. FORDE

T HE FOUNDATIONAL BELIEF upon which this essay is built is the scriptural assertion that God was in Christ reconciling the world unto himself (2 Cor. 5:19). That is to be understood in an exclusivist sense: apart from Christ, we are not reconciled to God. Furthermore, all human attempts to effect such reconciliation are futile and ultimately counterproductive. God can come to speech as *God for us* only as speaking — ultimately preaching — of Christ. Reconciling God-talk is that inspired and mandated by Christ.

We need to be reminded of this devastatingly simple but profoundly inescapable truth today because we live at the tag end of a theologically decadent age that has sought its salvation by ignoring it. Since at least the time of the Enlightenment, the age has attempted to correct St. Paul's message to the Corinthians by assuming that God was in the mind of the theologian or philosopher reconciling the world to himself. So it has persistently been opined that what we really need are better explanations of God, less offensive definitions of the divine "essence," or, in these latter days, better names, metaphors, or parables. The aim of such intellectual effort has been to construct thought and speech about God which removes that which is threatening or unpleasant to us, does away with such unpleasant realities as divine law and wrath, and exonerates the divine from complicity in evil, tragedy, and oppression.

Willy-nilly, we fall into the same trap as the gnostics of old. Unable to reconcile ourselves to the world actually at hand, we attempt, so to speak, to think our way out of it. Like the gnostics — or even Mary Baker Eddy, of more recent vintage — we assume that our problems are primarily "in the mind," a matter, perhaps, of mistaken metaphysics. We are ostensibly estranged in an alien place, the true gnosis being forgotten or out of reach, and we grope for correct formulas. We try to disassociate ourselves and our projected gods from the actual and messy world in which we live. If we are oppressed by certain language about God, we seem to think that all we need to do is change it and that we actually accomplish something thereby. We seem to think that in our God-language we are free to construct a metaphysical "heaven" according to our liking. We fall for the Marxist idea that speech is just a front for ideology and thus most often the fruit of conspiracy. So it is to be overcome by appropriate changes. Americans, says George Steiner, think they can democratize eternity.[1] If there is something we don't like — even about God — we think we can just vote it out. We are, it would seem, more seduced by the power of positive thinking than we would like to admit. All we need to do about God is think positively! God is in the human mind reconciling the world unto himself. If we can just manage to get through to the right gnosis, to think appropriately positive thoughts about God, we'll be home free! So we think.

But why then did God go to all the bother to be in Christ to reconcile the world unto himself? Why the suffering, agony, and death on the cross? As St. Anselm already put it, why should the Almighty have to "stoop to such lowly things" or "do anything which such great labor"?[2] If all that was needed was a name change, couldn't God have found some more simple and perhaps impressive way to announce it? All God needs, it would seem, is better public relations — a new ad agency, perhaps.

Theology can be thankful to the feminist movement for at least bringing this problem unmistakably to our attention. But what I wish to contend here is that most of our struggles about the naming of God fail to grasp or reflect the deep complexities of the problem. We have finally and correctly learned, I expect, that names are important — especially when purporting to speak of God. We have also perceived that names and titles can be used by the privileged to oppress and subjugate. But what we have apparently not learned very well yet is that changing names to suit our fancy accomplishes little or nothing. The changes are for the most part merely cosmetic. At best, the effect lasts for a time, but then the

---

1. Steiner, *Real Presences* (Chicago: University of Chicago Press, 1989), p. 33.

2. St. Anselm, "Why God Became Man," in *A Scholastic Miscellany: Anselm to Ockham,* ed. and trans. Eugene R. Fairweather, vol. 10 in the Library of Christian Classics (Philadelphia: Westminster Press, 1956), p. 110.

makeup wears off and the so-named God turns out, if anything, to be as bad as or even sometimes worse than before.

An example from recent history demonstrates how this can happen. Post-Enlightenment theologians increasingly found traditional trinitarian theology too metaphysical and heteronomous and so moved to change the language. Jesus, it was maintained, did not claim to be the divine Son of God but was rather a religious genius who taught such sublime truths as the coming of the kingdom of God, the Fatherhood of God, the infinite value of the human soul, the higher righteousness, and the commandment of love.[3] God, in other words, was disengaged from the exclusive trinitarian relation in which the Father and the Son mutually determine and define each other and was now to be described and named under the general and abstract rubric of "fatherhood" — apparently by analogy to human fatherhood. According to Adolf Harnack, in his famous "summa" of liberal views at the turn of the century, this understanding of the matter is supposed to present the truly "restful" elements in Jesus' message and show us that the gospel is not heteronomous (i.e., not a "positive" religion containing statutory or particularistic elements) but is *religion itself.*[4] Now, however, just a century later, it has apparently turned against us. Fatherhood understood by analogy to human fathers and thus separated from specific and exclusive relation to the revelation in the Son turns out to be as much bane as blessing, especially for many women. The attempt to reconcile us to God by changing the language is only cosmetic. The supposedly benign and "restful" idea of the "fatherhood" of God turns out to have sharp teeth.

But that fact ought also to stand as a warning that merely shifting to "motherhood" or like abstractions is not likely to fare any better. If fatherhood bespeaks male dominance and control, motherhood can likewise promote female devices for dominance and control. Shuffling names, attributes, and virtues about does not get at the real problem posed by our attempts to bring God to speech. For the truth is that all *our* attempts must necessarily fail — and the secret is precisely in the failure. Our speech about God is at best only half-true. But it is not neutral half-truth. For half-truths about God are deadly. Indeed, they become monstrous lies when they claim to hold out solutions to our problem.

3. Harnack, *What Is Christianity?* trans. Thomas Bailey Saunders (New York: Harper & Brothers, 1957), pp. 51, 65.

4. Ibid., p. 63.

They are not the solution but the problem. Our speech is like that of the chief priests and scribes, the Sanhedrin and Pilate. Like the law (indeed, as law) it drives us to crucify Christ. And it is only in our failure — the death and resurrection of this man — that we are reconciled to God. When Pilate was asked to change the naming of the crucified one to make it less offensive, he answered, "What I have written, I have written!" The names are etched in the stone of history: "Jesus of Nazareth, King of the Jews." But now we are getting ahead of ourselves. We must look more closely at the problem of bringing God to speech.

The Hidden God

What we need to do today perhaps more than ever is to be aware of the way speech about God actually works. It has long been a basic tenet of Protestant theology that apart from the revelation in Jesus Christ, God is hidden, and that the hidden God is ultimately a God of wrath. But we do not, I think, grasp the full gravity of such assertions. The problem is not merely — as we may indeed admit — that our language is inadequate to the task of predicating God and that we are not appropriately sensitized to that fact. Were that the case, we could simply join the loud protest against those who make extravagant claims for univocal God-language — either biblical or traditional — and insist on appropriately modest analogical and metaphorical claims. Indeed, there seems to be a general sentiment abroad in the theological world that we can heave a collective sigh of relief now that we have discovered or rediscovered the metaphorical nature of our God-language. Talk of God has at last, supposedly, been rescued from absolutist claims elevating it to the level of divine speech and returned safely to the confines of our speech, where we can bring it under some control again. It is, after all, "only metaphorical." If we don't like the metaphors, we can change them. Thus do we comfort ourselves in our banality.

The hiddenness of God does not mean that God is so transcendent as to be out of the range of our speech. Rather, the hiddenness refers to the fact that God lies in wait for us in our attempts to speak of him. The real problem for us is in the way speaking of God actually works. As Luther would say, the Spirit is in the *use,* not in the object as such.[5] Hiddenness

5. Luther, "That These Words of Christ, 'This is my Body,' etc., Still Stand Firm Against the Fanatics," *LW* 37:92.

means not that God is "far off" but rather that he actively hides from us in inescapable presence and so will not be caught or used by us. God, as the Latin has it, is *absconditus,* "the absconder," the one who wills not to be seen by us in his "naked majesty."

This means that apart from Christ, God can come to speech only as the God of wrath, one who is against sinners. We may protest this fact, but there is nothing, really, that we can do about it. We may try to *construct* a god who is for us, but it can't work. We simply cannot preside over that which is above us. We think to dispose over the metaphysical or eternal realm, but God will not have it. The example cited previously about what happens to speech about the Fatherhood of God illustrates the fact. Whatever *we* wish to say about God on our own will simply turn against us. Developing speech that seeks to make a god amenable to our projected hopes and dreams is no different from making a god of wood or stone or bronze: it is simply idolatry, and it is born of unbelief. And idols all have one thing in common: they do not have anything to say. So we must figure out what to say and do for them; one might say we have to furnish speech for them. In a way they are indeed gods — what Luther called "masks" of God, and thus terrifying enough. But they don't say or do anything; they just make demands on us in their silence. They can only be law, not gospel. And ultimately they will destroy us.

That the hidden God lies in wait for us in our speech is rather obvious from a moment's reflection on our ordinary attempts to bring God to speech. To name God adequately we have to stretch and project our language to "trap" God, so to speak. But since we don't know who or what we're talking about, we have to set as big a trap as possible. Perhaps the most prominent way of doing this was the so-called *via negativia,* the way of negation. Since God is not what we are, God can be spoken of by negating human attributions. We are finite; God is *in*-finite. We are mutable; God is *im*-mutable. We are mortal; God is *im*-mortal. We are passible; God is *im*-passible. We are limited; God is *un*-limited. And so on. Or God is spoken of in terms of superlatives: God is *omni*-potent, *omni*-present, *omni*-scient. Or we might say that God is the highest of — indeed, higher than — all imaginable virtues, the *summum bonum,* absolute truth, beauty, and wisdom. God is at the outermost limit of our speech — and beyond: God is "that than which no higher can be thought." All of that is at least formally true. But what does such speech ultimately do to us or for us? The fact is that it kills us. It is the end of us. The divine wrath finds us out in the end. God, defined by negation or superlatives, turns out, quite consequently, to be the negation of everything human. The point is that if God is indeed all those things — immutable, impassible, omnipotent, and all the other omni's, what then is left for us? We are left simply crying out in protest, "We aren't puppets, are we? Don't we have something to say or do about our destiny?" And secretly — or of late, more openly — it must be our project to get rid of such a God.

So the hidden God lies in wait for us in our speech. Twist and turn as we will, we cannot escape the divine wrath. We may, of course, attempt some of the more common devices of the day to redefine God more to our liking — fit God out with a new set of attributes, perhaps. We may, for example, use the tactic of theological erasure or amnesia. We may try to remove the threatening attributes by ourselves.

We may, for instance, simply try to deny that God has anything to do with wrath and insist that God is just pure love, love, love, and nothing but love. So we erase all references to wrath, law, and things unpleasant from our books and our memories. But this is simply the tactic of antinomianism transferred to language about God.[6] One seeks to whisk the problem out of sight by removing the words. It doesn't work. The reality remains even if the words are removed. As Luther put it, it is a drama played in an empty theater.[7] Even if one says that God is just love — *der liebe Gott* spoken of so disparagingly by Karl Barth and others in our time — such love becomes an abstraction and simply turns on us as well. If God is love, what is the matter with us? Why are we so unloving? Wrath cannot be erased; it can only be conquered. A divine love that is not actually a conquering of wrath for us is simply an abstraction and so finally an accusation. Like the *summum bonum* and similar "highest beings," such a god is simply the highest imaginable human virtue and so cannot but be, finally, law and wrath. Love, to be actual love, cannot be an abstraction. If the lover announces to the beloved, "I am love," that is hardly very enlightening or encouraging. Especially in the case of God, love has to be the verb in a trinitarian sentence if it is to be something other than a threat: "God so [exactly so and not otherwise!] loved the world, that he gave his only begotten Son . . ." (John 3:16, KJV); God shows his love for us "in that while we were yet sinners Christ died for us" (Rom. 5:8).

6. For further elaboration of this point, see my article entitled "Fake Theology," *Dialog* 22 (Fall 1983): 246-51.
7. Luther, "Quinta disputatio . . . contra Antinomos," *WA* 39, 1, 355:39-40.

The same problems appear when contemporary theologians try to repair the divine reputation by introducing simplistic notions of the suffering of God. The idea that God is not impassible but supposedly passible and somehow participates in or is even enriched by our sufferings is no automatic theological boon. It can lead merely to a kind of "misery loves company" theology. As Ronald Goetz puts it, the idea that God is enriched by our suffering is little better than the "bathos of the sentimental butcher who weeps after each slaughter."[8] In the attempt to give God nicer or more advantageous names, we only make matters worse and more threatening. If God is enriched by suffering, perhaps now at last we know the reason for eternal torment! Like love, suffering cannot be applied to God as an abstraction but can only be part of a trinitarian sentence: God overcomes suffering for us in his crucified and risen Son. Where we merely tinker with the language and shuffle attributes about, matters just get worse. That is the way the language works, and that is the way the hidden God lies in wait for us in our attempts to speak of that which is above us. We can neither find nor escape the hidden God.

Luther repeatedly referred to this peculiar circumstance vis-à-vis God in terms of the concept of the "masks" *(larvae)* of God.[9] This is an intriguing and, I think, theologically more fruitful way of thinking about how our God-language actually works — indeed, about our relationship to God in general as fallen beings. The idea that God is masked in this age, no doubt especially in our language, and that we are unable to tear the mask from God's face captures more accurately our actual predicament over against God. The idea of the "mask" encompasses both the idea that God is not absent and the idea that he can in no way be presumed upon. God as masked is present but does not submit to our manipulation. Where we try yet another name apart from Christ, we only fashion another mask — usually worse. All such attempts encounter only wrath. Indeed, the Latin term *larva* does not mean only "mask" but also "demon" or "ghost." Thus Luther could even say that apart from what happens in Christ, God and Satan tend to merge in confusing fashion.[10] Were we to regard our naming of God in terms of this understanding of masks and the way they

8. Goetz, "The Suffering God: The Rise of a New Orthodoxy," *Christian Century*, 16 April 1986, p. 388.

9. See, for example, Luther's "Lectures on Galatians, 1535," *LW* 26:95, 96, 104, 170, 256, 263, 284, 298, 321, 323, 324.

10. See Gerhard Ebeling, *Luther: An Introduction to His Thought*, trans. R. A. Wilson (Philadelphia: Fortress Press, 1970), pp. 235-37.

work, we would, I would hope, be much more sensitive to the demonic possibilities in our own speech about God and much less inclined to optimism about our own linguistic innovations.

All of which is to say that in our speaking of and ultimately for God, we should be aware that the true art of the theologian is to learn — as the Reformers insisted — to speak an entirely new kind of God-talk: gospel-talk. But gospel-talk arises only out of the actual conquest of law-talk in the death and resurrection of Christ. Gospel-talk arises out of the trinitarian narrative alone. "Christ is the end of the law, that every one who has faith may be justified" (Rom. 10:4). The true task of theology, therefore, is to be aware of the way the language works and how to use it. Theology is not the art of erasing unpleasantnesses but the art of an ever-renewed speech that conquers sin, death, and the devil. Theologians are supposed to distinguish between law-talk and gospel-talk and have some idea of how they work and how to get from one to the other. They are supposed to know how to speak not just ABOUT God but FOR God.

The Revealed God

To sum up, when left to ourselves, we are not very good at naming God. We manage only to arrive at abstractions that choke and kill us. So God must undertake to make a name for himself, to do the reconciling by himself. So there was a man named Jesus, sent from God, who came among us and named God "my Father" — indeed, even *"the* Father" — and invited us to pray with him to this God as "our Father." We should not imagine that this naming of God was received either with approval or with great joy. Quite the contrary. Of the Gospels, John sets forth most profoundly what is involved in the problem of naming God. It is pointed out that Jesus' compatriots sought to kill him "because he not only broke the sabbath but also called God his own Father, making himself equal with God" (5:18). And in the end, to put the matter directly, he was killed for calling God his Father: "We have a law, and by that law he ought to die, because he has made himself the Son of God" (19:7). But he was raised from the dead. The Father vindicated him, establishing his authority as the Son. What is established thereby is the specific and intimate relation between the Father and the Son. The Father can be understood only in terms of the relation to the Son: God is the Father of Jesus Christ. As we read in John, "No one has ever seen God; the only Son, who is in the bosom of the Father, he has made him known" (1:18). The Son, in turn, is the perfect revelation of the Father. The Son can do and does "only what he sees the Father doing" (5:19). That is, God is not to be named in analogy to human fathers, not in terms of abstractions like "fatherhood," but only in relation to Jesus Christ. The name God acquires for himself is strictly and exclusively "the Father of Jesus Christ," and one can rightly call God "Father" only as one is properly related to the Son (8:41-44). Indeed, in Matthew's Gospel we are exhorted to use the designation "Father" exclusively for God: "Call no man your father on earth, for you have one Father, who is in heaven" (23:9). Whatever difficulties we have with the name can be resolved only in the light of the relation between the Father and the Son. God was in Christ reconciling the world to himself, not in our minds or in our linguistic innovations.

But is it not possible to substitute other less offensive names or metaphors? This is the question that hangs over us today. I have already attempted to show in the preceding discussion of the hidden God that it is ultimately a futile exercise. Now, however, we have the fact of the revealed God to take into account. Accordingly, a number of things must be added to the picture.

First of all, we have to do with revelation in time, through historical particularity. We have to do with a Jew in first-century Palestine who called God his Father and who has invited us to pray on his warrant (in his name) to God as our Father. This man was raised from the dead by "the Father." We need no longer "trouble deaf heaven with our bootless cries." We have been given an address for our pleas. That, at the outset, is the most important fact we have constantly to bear in mind. Nothing can or need change that now. There is no exhaustively necessary reason we can cite to show why Jesus should have used this language. The fact is simply that he did. If Jesus had called God "the Mother" or "the Great Spirit" or any number of other things, we would no doubt be obligated to that. But he didn't. It is as with the Lord's Supper. There is no reason, ontological or symbolical or otherwise, why one must use bread and wine outside of the historical fact that that is what Jesus used, and so must we — unless, of course, we want to do it in forgetfulness of him. To assume, as many have and many still do, that we can proceed by analogy and say that the elements can be changed in order better to counter current objections, moral and otherwise, is to deny the historical particularity of the gospel and to turn it into an abstraction.

Second, the texts themselves yield some data that should not be ignored. The New Testament identifies God as Father 261 times. By contrast, for instance, God is referred to as "creator" or "creating" in some fashion only 14 times. Of course, this is not to say that the New Testament does not believe in God as creator. It is to say, however, that that is not the distinctive burden of its message. Indeed — and thirdly — the fact that God is so consistently referred to as the Father of Jesus Christ rather than just as creator is no doubt intentional. It is intended to counter prevailing views in Hebrew Wisdom literature (e.g., Proverbs, Ben Sirach, Wisdom of Solomon) which maintained that the creator is known through the Torah.[11] In other words, the battle about whether to name God "creator" or "Father" was joined at the outset. "The law was given through Moses; grace and truth came through Jesus Christ" (John 1:17). That God is "creator" no one disputes, but that is something of a mixed blessing. That God is the Father of Jesus Christ is good news.

So in the end it all comes down to a matter of the gospel. The one who is above us is simply an intractable problem for us. We cannot penetrate or remove the threatening masks behind which God absconds. But in the person of Jesus in his historical particularity, God is revealed. He dies for us. If we are antipathetic toward God, God bears it all in Jesus. God goes out of the way for us, refuses finally to be a God of wrath for us. But this is possible only in the concrete historical person of Jesus. It is only in him that we are reconciled to God. Only in him do we find God the true Father of us all. This is not a general truth. Jesus does not propose better names for God accessible to all and sundry. For Jesus not only dies but also is the death of us — the death of the old being who cannot speak the truth about God. To be found in him is to die to all else so that one might live to God. Thus the historical particularity belongs to the essence of the gospel. The gospel is that the God with whom we endlessly contend dies for us. That can only happen concretely, historically. But if God dies, we die as well. And then our hope is in Jesus, who was raised by the one whom he called "my Father" and invited us to call "our Father." This historical particularity means simply that we have no other chance, and, indeed, that we need no other. And only if that is so for us have we encountered the one who is truly above us.

11. My colleague Donald Juel has advanced this thesis in an article entitled "I Believe in God: A Johannine Perspective," soon to be published in *Horizons*.

The Christian Apprehension
of God the Father

THOMAS F. TORRANCE

"ALL THINGS have been delivered unto me by my Father; and no one knows the Son except the Father, and no one knows the Father except the Son and anyone to whom the Son chooses to reveal him" (Matt. 11:27; Luke 10:22). In that teaching of the Lord Jesus mediated through the gospels of St. Matthew and St. Luke, the early church learned that the mutual relation between the Father and the Son belongs to the innermost core of the gospel, and they discerned in it the basic principle upon which the Christian apprehension of God rests. No one can know God except God, and so no one can know God except through God — that is, only through sharing in some way in the knowledge which God has of himself. This is what has been made possible for us through the incarnation of God's Son and his mediation to us of the Spirit of the Father and of the Son, through whom we may enter into communion with God and learn to know him through himself in accordance with his own eternal nature as Father, Son, and Holy Spirit.[1]

Hence it became indubitably clear to Christians from the beginning that knowledge of God is initiated by God himself and actualized through God himself. Our knowledge of God the Father Almighty does not and cannot arise apart from his gracious activity in making himself known and in revealing himself to us in accordance with his own incomparable nature

---

1. Consult my account of the teaching of Irenaeus, especially in "The Deposit of Faith," *Scottish Journal of Theology* 36 (1983): 8ff.; and my book entitled *The Trinitarian Faith: The Evangelical Theology of the Ancient Catholic Church* (Edinburgh: T. & T. Clark, 1988), pp. 54-55.

as God. Knowledge of God is impossible on any ground other than that which God himself is, for as God is of himself alone, so he is known through himself alone. Thus when we know God, we know him only on the free ground of his own being who reveals himself, names himself, and proves himself in his act of revelation, and who confronts us with none other than himself in that act of revelation. This is not a revelation that can be detached from God, for what God reveals is not something of himself but his very self: he is himself the objective content and reality of his revelation. What God the Father is in his self-revelation through the Son and in the Spirit he is in himself, and what he is in himself he is in his revelation. It is impossible for us, therefore, to seek to know God apart from his revelation, or to try to go behind that revelation to what God is in himself, for there is no God apart from his revelation. The only God there is and the only God that is known is the God who is clothed with his revelation and who is who he is in all his activity toward us. We may know who God is only because *God* reveals *himself* through *himself,* in a triadic movement of self-communication whereby he announces himself to us and names himself as *Father, Son, and Holy Spirit.* This is not a revelation simply of different modes of being that God transiently assumes in his activity toward us, but a revelation of what he really is in his own eternal nature apart from us. God *is* Father, Son, and Holy Spirit. The trinitarian content and the trinitarian structure of God's self-revelation are one. There is no other God than this God who has revealed himself in this way, and there is no other way for us to conceive of the one being of God in accordance with his divine nature except as Father, Son, and Holy Spirit.

Divine and Human Fatherhood

How can we human beings think of God as Father in view of the fact that the Fatherhood of God must be as different from human fatherhood as God the Creator is from the human creature? Karl Barth once asked about our human thinking and knowing of God: "How do we come to think by means of our thinking, that which we cannot think at all by this means?"[2] The problem behind such questions has to do with the utter

---

2. Barth, *Church Dogmatics,* II/1, ed. Thomas F. Torrance, trans. Geoffrey W. Bromiley (Edinburgh: T. & T. Clark, 1957), p. 220.

incongruence between God and man, and in particular the incongruence between God as he is known and man as the knower. The answer to the question, as we have just seen, is that to which the New Testament and the early church direct us: we come to our knowledge of God by the grace of God, whose self-revelation has assumed incarnate form within our visible, tangible world in space and time. We human beings may know God only as he enters into actual relation with us as human beings and reveals himself to us within the range of our human knowing and within the frame of our human speech in this world. This would not be possible for us apart from the *Word* of God become flesh in Jesus Christ, for in him God addresses us in such a way as to create in us the ability to hear him beyond any creaturely capacity we may have in ourselves. Nor would it be possible for us apart from the *Spirit* of God, for God through his Spirit graciously makes himself present to us within the littleness and lowliness of our creaturely existence and sustains us from below in relation to himself, thereby opening our hearts and minds toward him and enabling us to receive his Word and understand his self-revelation.[3] There is thus a two-way movement in the realizing of divine revelation: from God to us and from us to God. It is only within the circle of that movement that we may apprehend something of what divine Fatherhood and human fatherhood are in their relation to one another and in their distinction from one another.

Our understanding of this reciprocity between God and humankind derives not from any kind of *a priori* reasoning but from the actual knowledge of God that God has historically mediated to humankind through the election of Israel and the incarnation of his Word in the midst of Israel. It was through his covenant-partnership with the people of Israel that God brought his Word and Spirit to bear upon the innermost existence and being of this people, thereby molding and shaping them religiously and conceptually to be the earthly-historical partner of divine revelation and the chosen instrument of his ultimate self-revealing and self-giving to humankind. Then in the fullness of time that covenant-partnership of God with Israel was brought to its culmination with the advent of Jesus Christ, the promised Messiah in whom, as God himself become man, God's self-revelation to humankind was brought to its decisive fulfillment in the world. Through the reconciliation of human-

---

3. See Barth, *Church Dogmatics*, I/1 (rev.), ed. Thomas F. Torrance, trans. Geoffrey W. Bromiley (Edinburgh: T. & T. Clark, 1975), pp. 450-51, 472.

kind with God in the life, death, and resurrection of Jesus Christ, and through the gift of his Holy Spirit, God made himself present to his people in a new way in profoundly intimate and personal relations, thereby achieving and grounding his self-revelation in the reception, understanding, and fellowship of a community of faith, the reconstituted partner of divine revelation in history. Thus in the saving economy of God's love there was brought into being a new form of God's covenant-partnership with his people in the church as the Body of Christ, entrusted with the Word of God and commissioned to bear witness to the unique self-revelation of God to humankind as Father, Son, and Holy Spirit. The very existence and continuity of the church are thus inseparably bound up with the triune self-revealing and self-naming of God sealed upon it and all its constituent members in holy baptism.

It is with this knowledge of God mediated to us in history through the Scriptures of the Old and New Testaments that we may now participate in the two-way movement from God to humankind and from humankind to God and thus continue to be in dialogue with him. Within that circle of divine address and human response we come to understand something of both the nature of God's revealing activity and the mode of his revealing address to human beings. God does not hold himself aloof from us but establishes a reciprocal relation with us — indeed, a community of reciprocity between humankind and himself, within which he continues to speak to us and make himself known. Within that two-way relation it is *we* who are given to know God, but in such a way that there takes place a reversal in our knowing relation under the commanding act of God in making himself known to us. Hence, although we cannot cut off our knowledge of God from our knowing of him, nevertheless in our knowing of God we know that it is through God's knowing of us that we are enabled to know him, that our knowing of God is included within the circle of mutual knowing which he freely establishes with us. Thus our knowing of God rests not on a center in ourselves but on a center in God, not on the ground of our own being but on the free ground of God's being. Our ability to know him is grounded not in some capacity of our own but in the activity of God in opening himself to our knowing and in actually making himself known to us through his Word. It arises from and rests in the inherent openness and readiness of God toward us, but is realized and sustained in us through the presence of his Spirit. As man was brought into being by God out of nothing and cannot exist apart from being continually sustained by God through the creative activity of his Word and Spirit, so he can know nothing of God apart from

God and without being sustained by God through his self-revealing activity in Word and Spirit.

Our knowing of God takes place, then, within the two-way movement in which his revealing of himself and our knowing of him in that self-revelation are interlocked. The Word that God addresses to us in his self-revealing is Word that eternally inheres in God, Word that God himself is, so that the content of God's revelation is God himself. On the other hand, God addresses that Word to us human beings in such a form and in such a way that we may hear and understand it without ceasing to be human beings and without having to go outside of ourselves. In and through entering into relation with us, God creates within us as human beings the capacity to hear and know him. He thereby establishes and upholds a *human co-efficient* in the knowing relationship, and really makes us partners with himself in this two-way relationship. Thus the act of God's self-revealing to us takes our human speaking, hearing, and knowing into its concrete realization within God's personal interrelation with us, and so there is necessarily included within it an *anthropomorphic* component.[4] It cannot be stressed too much that this is not an anthropomorphic element which is generated by any independent act of knowing or conceiving of God on our part, but one that arises in the self-determination of God's being toward us, in his creating us for fellowship with himself, in his establishing personal relations between us and himself, and in his making himself known to us within those relations. As such, the anthropomorphic component is to be understood not in terms of some cultural inheritance from the past that we may replace as we choose, but in terms of what God himself has adapted and defined in his unique self-revealing to us. It is not, therefore, something defined by what we human beings are of ourselves and projected by us onto God in our conceiving of him.

Anthropomorphism in theological thought and speech is not to be understood except in the light of the biblical teaching that God has created man for fellowship with himself in such a way that despite the utter *difference* between them, man — by which term I mean both male and female human beings — is made after the likeness and the image of God.[5] This means not

4. Cf. Martin Buber, *The Eclipse of God* (New York: Harper Torchbooks, 1957), pp. 14-15.
5. As the Latin Bible rightly renders it, man was created *"ad imaginem Dei."* This is what Athanasius called "the grace that God gave him" (*Con. Gentes,* 2) or "the grace according to the image" (*De Inc.,* 7).

that the image of God inheres in man's nature, but that it is a *donum superadditum,* a gift wholly contingent upon the free grace of God. Hence it does not mean that man is the offspring of the divine nature or that through his own human nature he can somehow reflect God's nature; it means only that man is specifically destined by grace to live in faithful response to the movement and purpose of God's love toward him as his creaturely partner. The Creator/creature relationship in being and knowing between God and man cannot be reversed. Accordingly, far from God being conceived in the image of man, man is to be conceived as formed after the image of God. It is this biblical *theomorphism,* understood in this irreversible way, that must be taken into account in assessing the place of any anthropomorphism in our thinking and speaking of God, for since God has made man after his own image, all authentic knowledge of God by man is grounded in and points back to God's relation to man.[6] That is to say, man's knowledge of God arises by way of response to God's initiative in addressing man and in revealing himself to man. In thus establishing fellowship with his human creature, God posits and sustains not only the God-manward relation between them but the man-Godward relation as well, although in such a way that any independent man-Godward relation, any self-projection of the human into God — *eritis sicut Deus* — is ruled out, and yet also in such a way that a real man-Godward relation is given an integral place in the Creator/creature relationship between God and man, and thus also an inevitable anthropomorphic element in the way man is bound to know and speak of God.

Expressed otherwise, God's self-revelation to man incorporates into itself as part of its concrete movement a human co-efficient through which it realizes itself in man and "earths" God's revealing of himself in man's actual knowing of God. While in this mediation of revelation God takes up into his self-revelation anthropomorphic elements, he remains transcendent over them, and at the same time he shines through them all and makes himself known in spite of all unlikeness and incompatibility between man and his Creator. This paradoxical nature of divine revelation in which all anthropomorphic elements are governed by divine theomorphic activity characterizes the mediation of God's self-revelation to humankind in and through his long historical dialogue with Israel, which is embodied in the Old Testament Scriptures. They

6. Cf. Oliver C. Quick, *Doctrines of the Creed: Their Basis in Scripture and Their Meaning To-day* (London: Collins, 1947), pp. 29ff.

are full of the most startling anthropomorphisms and dramatic images in the language used to speak of God — as in the frequent reference of biblical writers to the hands, ears, mouth, heart, or even bowels of God — language that gives vivid expression to the intensely personal relation of God in love and judgment toward human beings. Nevertheless, throughout the Old Testament there is a persistent attack upon all naturalizing of religion in the worship of Baalim and Ashtaroth, with its heathen projection of male and female gender into Deity. Hence the Word of God is steadily addressed to Israel through the prophets in such a way as to denounce all images of God conceived by the human heart, whether conceptual or physical, as forms of idolatry. On the one hand, God's covenant with Israel disciplined the mind and soul of Israel as the earthly-historical partner of his self-revelation to humankind in order to constitute it the unique matrix within which the Word of God was to become incarnate. On the other hand, however, throughout that long dialogue between God and Israel, the self-revelation of God shone through all the anthropomorphic forms of thought and speech used by God as the transparent medium of that revelation. God remained transcendent over all "earthing" of his self-revelation in Israel and its embodiment in the Scriptures of the Old Testament, for God is not man's fellow creature, nor is he inherently anthropomorphic. Hence the Word of God mediated in and through the Old Testament makes clear that, just as God is the eternal I AM WHO I AM, so in his self-revelation he is he who infinitely surpasses all our conceiving or naming of him and is known only as he who names himself to humankind: I AM WHO I AM.

This is the self-revelation of God to humankind that has been fulfilled and established once and for all in the incarnation, when the Word of God became man within the structures of our human interpersonal relations, and when the appropriate, divinely adapted anthropomorphic element in our relation to God was anchored in the divine-human person of Christ, and was thus anchored in God. Jesus Christ the Word of God become flesh in space and time is identical with God's self-revelation in such a singular way that there is no alternative revelation of God and there can be none.

In him the divine and the human have united with one another so that in Jesus we human beings may know the transcendent God as he has condescended to be with us and to speak to us within the same sphere of reality to which we belong. In Jesus we encounter the very EGO EIMI of

God, so that in him we are summoned to know God in accordance with the way in which he has actually objectified himself for us in our human existence and communicated himself within the structure and modes of our human knowing and speaking. However, this does not give us leave simply to read our human characteristics back into God or to confine knowledge of him within our human subjectivities. Quite the reverse is the case, for in his self-revelation God makes them point to himself altogether beyond what they are in themselves — and so they are in no sense descriptive of God.

Thus in the incarnation it becomes clear that the ineradicable element of anthropomorphism in God's revealing of himself and our human knowing of him is the obverse of the sublimity and transcendence of God, and as such is not rejected by God but taken up into himself in Christ. The incarnation tells us that in his utter difference and complete otherness God does not hold himself aloof from man but turns himself toward man, and that it is only as such that he gives himself to be known — that is, on the ground of his divine self-adaptation to our humanity, which also adapts and lifts up our humanity into communion with God. Here we see the epistemological inversion taking place in our knowing of God, for in Jesus Christ it is we who are required to be adapted to him, so that we have to renounce ourselves and take up our cross if we are to follow him and know God in and through him. It is in this way that the estranged human self is reconciled to God and the damaged person of man is healed and re-created in communion with God, and that the immense distance between knowing man and Holy God gives place to a cognitive union with God in love. The human subject is established before God by the outgoing of the divine love to him, while he on his part is brought to respect the objectivity of God as he learns to love him and know him for his own sake.

Two points here need to be stressed.

In the first place, we cannot talk about knowledge of God without taking into account the fact that it is we human beings who know him, and that our knowing of him is humanly conditioned. As we have already seen, there is inevitably involved here an ineradicable anthropomorphic element to which we cannot shut our eyes, and which we cannot do without if *we* are to know God. It may be noted, however, that something like this applies in a real way to all human knowledge, for knowledge of anything by a human subject, insofar as it is *his* knowledge, is limited by the fact that his knowing is inescapably a part of it, and thus limited at its very root, which it cannot transcend without ceasing altogether — no human knowledge, as modern science has taught us so clearly, will ever be in a position to pass beyond the interplay between the human knower and what he seeks to know. How much more is that the case between the human knower and God! In his revelation God condescends to our ignorance and littleness and accommodates himself to our knowing in order to lift us up into communion with himself through reconciling and adapting us in conformity to himself; but all this is the adaptation of human modes of knowing to God, in which God used the anthropomorphic factor in realizing within us knowledge of himself. Since God has purposely created and formed man for partnership and fellowship with himself, there is no genuine reciprocity between them without the inclusion of a distinctly anthropomorphic ingredient, even though God is not inherently anthropomorphic. Apart from real encounter of this kind between man and God, God can be for man no more than an abstraction, a negative borderline concept empty of living content. As H. R. Mackintosh once wrote, "What the conception of God may become when once the life-blood of anthropomorphism has been drained out, we see in the God of Mohammed. The Deity pictured in the Koran is 'like the desert, monotonous and barren, an unfigured surface, an unresponsive immensity.' "[7]

In the second place, this recognition of an unavoidable anthropomorphic factor does not absolve the human knower from the need for self-critical and self-corrective processes through which his thinking and speaking of God are pruned of inappropriate anthropomorphisms and illegitimate subjective features. It is the conflict that arises in his knowledge between the pure humanity of Christ and his own humanity that exposes the self-centeredness of the human subject, calls into question every attempt to impose himself upon the object, and thus serves to restrain and control his subjectivity. This is why in theological science we must develop corrective devices with which to check the objectivity of our knowledge and the ontological reference of its conceptual content in order to obstruct the intrusion into our trains of thought of any distorting images and extraneous analogies projected out of our own self-analysis and self-understanding onto God. A faithful knowing of God will certainly recognize that the subject of the human knower cannot be kept out of its process, and so far from eliminating the

7. Mackintosh, *The Christian Apprehension of God,* 4th ed. (1934), p. 111.

anthropomorphic factor altogether, theological science seeks to let the apprehension of the human knower be adapted to its divine object and be controlled by it. In this event, modes of thought and speech about God that have arisen under the impact of his self-revelation must be of a spiritual kind appropriate to the transcendent nature of God, who as Spirit cannot be conceived or represented in visual or sensual images. That is why, in line with the teaching of the Hebrew Scriptures, theologians in the early church held that all images properly used in speech and thought of God refer to him away from themselves *without imaging him*.[8] This does not mean that we must cut all images out of our theological speaking and thinking of God, but it means that we must use them only in a "see-through" way and *not* in any mimetic or descriptive way of God. Thus used, theological forms of thought and speech, far from eclipsing knowledge of the transcendent God, become transparent media or open analogies through which the truth of God may disclose itself to us and through which the Word of God himself may sound through to us and be heard by us, and not some word of ours that we project into God's mouth.

It is in this way that we are surely to think of "father" and "son," as terms which divine revelation uses, and terms consequently which Christian theology is bound to use, about God. It is only in Jesus Christ, the one offspring of God's nature, that we may know God in accordance with who he really is in his divine nature. Thus it is only with the use of "father" and "son" as they are appropriated by God and adapted by God for his unique and specific self-revelation to us through Jesus Christ, his incarnate Son, that we may think of him, speak of him, and worship him aright. As such, the concepts of fatherhood and sonship do not derive from any analogy or inherent likeness between the creature and the Creator. They are laid hold of by divine revelation and are made to point back away altogether from their creaturely and human use to their creative source in the transcendent nature of God, who is eternally Father in himself, apart from and altogether antecedent to any relation with us. In and through Jesus Christ his Son, God is also our Father, but he is so because he is by nature Father in himself, as eternal Father of the eternal Son. Since man is created after the image of God, all fatherly relations within humanity derive from and point to the unique, aboriginal, and transcendent Fatherhood of God. Accordingly, human fatherhood may

8. See, for example, Gregory Nazianzen, *Orations*, 28.12ff.; 29.2; 31.7, 33.

not be used as a standard by which to judge divine Fatherhood, for there is strictly no comparison between human fatherhood and divine Fatherhood any more than there is between human being and divine Being. On the contrary, it is according to the uncreated Fatherhood of God that all creaturely fatherhood is to be understood, and not the other way round, even though in his unique self-revelation as Father, God uses the creaturely term for fatherhood to bring us to know him in encounter with his transcendent Fatherhood. As Karl Barth once wrote, "If we call God Father, it is because he is Father in reality. And the relation between God's Fatherhood and fatherhood among men reverses itself: we do not call God Father because we know what that is; on the contrary, because we know God's Fatherhood we afterwards understand what human fatherhood truly is. The divine truth precedes and grounds the human truth. 'For this reason I bow my knees before the Father from whom every fatherhood in heaven and earth is named.'"[9] The fact that "God is Spirit" (John 4:24) and "the Father of spirits" (Heb. 12:9) means that we must think of the Fatherhood of God and the relation of human fatherhood to it in an altogether *spiritual* and *imageless* way, and thus without ever reading back descriptively into God the creaturely content or finite imagery of human fatherhood. We recall that in the Ten Commandments the Word of God categorically forbade the making of any image or likeness of God (Exod. 20:4; Deut. 4:15-18; 5:8).

The Centrality of the Father-Son Relation

In the Scriptures of the Old Testament, the power and compassion of God toward his people are frequently described in colorful figurative language reflecting qualities characteristic of the parental authority and care of a human father or mother, but without conceptions of human fatherhood or motherhood being read back into the nature of God. The designation of God as "Father," which is not very frequent, is used mostly to speak of the special covenant relation of God to Israel, in which he regarded Israel as his "first-born son": "Thus says the Lord, Israel is my son, my first-born" (Exod. 4:22); "I called my son out of Egypt" (Hos. 11:1; cf. 1:10). A

---

9. Barth, *The Faith of the Church: A Commentary on the Apostles' Creed according to Calvin's Catechism*, trans. Gabriel Vahanian (New York: Meridian Books, 1958), p. 14. The biblical reference is to Ephesians 3:14-15.

general conception of God as Father and Creator of all humankind is not wanting. "Have we not all one Father?" asks Malachi. "Has not one God created us?" (2:10). As found in the Old Testament, however, "Father" is not a proper name for God but is like the other designations of God which, as Calvin pointed out, are all strictly "titles" or "epithets"; the exception is "Yahweh," the one ineffable substantive name with which God expresses his own self-existent being.[10] It is rather the conception of *sonship,* applied to Israel as a whole or to one or another of its divinely recognized representatives, as in the concept of the servant-son *(ben-bayith)* in the Second Isaiah, which has central significance in the fulfillment of divine revelation and redemption through Israel.

When we turn to the Scriptures of the New Testament, we find a radical deepening of the Old Testament doctrine of God, for "Father" is now revealed to be more than an epithet — it is the personal name of God in which the form and content of his self-revelation as Father through Jesus Christ his Son are inseparable. Jesus Christ gathers up the whole filial relation of Israel to God enacted in the history and worship of Israel, embodies it in himself, and fulfills the vicarious role of the anointed servant-son *in his own incarnate life and mission,* all in such a way that the concepts of sonship and fatherhood are brought together to express the unique inseparable relation between Jesus Christ and God the Father. The notion of the general Fatherhood of God as the Creator of humankind and the Provider for his human children is far from wanting, as we see in the prayer "our Father," which Jesus puts into our mouths, but this is not a conception of divine Fatherhood analogically built upon the basis of human fatherhood. Thus Jesus himself says, "Call no man your father on earth, for you have one Father, who is in heaven" (Matt. 23:9); and St. Paul tells us that it is from God that "every fatherhood in heaven and on earth is named" (Eph. 3:15). That is to say, the meaning of the word "father" as applied to God derives wholly from God himself. What is now predominant throughout the New Testament is the revelation of God as the Father of Jesus Christ and of Jesus Christ as the only begotten Son of the Father. It is the exclusive unbroken relation between the incarnate Son and God the Father that is absolutely normative for our knowledge of God, for it is precisely in Jesus Christ his Son that God is our Father, and

---

10. Calvin, *Institutes,* 1.13.9-11. Calvin points out that the designation *Kyrios* applied both to Christ and to the Holy Spirit in the New Testament is the equivalent of the Hebrew *Yahweh.*

so there is no way for us to come to the Father except through him. In the Old Testament God may sometimes be known as Father, but in the New Testament it is the Father who is known as God. And "Father" is now the name of God that we are to hallow, as our Lord Jesus taught us: "Our *Father* who art in heaven, *hallowed* be your *name*."

Of crucial importance here, as the Nicene theologians saw so clearly, is the ontological bond between Christ and God, the oneness in being and agency between the incarnate Son and the Father. What God the Father is toward us in Jesus Christ he is antecedently, inherently, and eternally in himself, and what he is antecedently, inherently, and eternally in himself he is toward us in Jesus Christ his incarnate Son. Fatherhood and Sonship are no longer merely unavoidable anthropomorphic components in the dialogue between God and man, for the hypostatic union between divine and human natures in Jesus Christ means that while they are not to be confused with one another, they cannot be separated from one another but belong intrinsically together. In and through the incarnation the manward activity of God and the Godward activity of man have become one in Jesus Christ, the one Mediator between God and man, who thereafter constitutes the one ultimate ground upon which all authentic encounter or personal dialogue between God and man and man and God may take place, and upon which authentic knowledge of God the Father as he really is in his own being is mediated to humankind.

Let us reflect on the point made by the great Athanasius in the following sentence: "It would be more godly and true (or accurate) to signify God from the Son and call him Father, than to name God from his works alone and call him Unoriginate."[11] In this statement Athanasius was defending the centrality accorded by the Council of Nicea to the Father-Son relation and its primacy over the Creator-creature relation. He had in mind the scientific principle that true or accurate knowledge of anything must be strictly in accordance with its nature, for it is the nature of the reality we seek to know that prescribes for us the specific way in which we are to know it and the specific way in which it is to be demonstrated. This scientific approach applies even more forcefully to God than to creaturely realities, for there is no likeness between the eternal being of God and the being of creaturely things. God may be known as God only

---

11. Athanasius, *Against the Arians*, 1.14; *Defence of the Nicene Decrees*, 31. Consult my discussion of this in *The Trinitarian Faith*, pp. 40ff.

out of himself and according to his divine nature. To know God strictly in accordance with his nature — that is, in a godly way — is both devout and scientific. That is why true and accurate knowledge of God is gained only through his Son, who is begotten of God's own nature, rather than through what God has created out of nothing and given a reality of its own in complete difference from his divine nature. When we think and speak of God merely from the perspective of the Creator-creature relation, therefore, we can do so only in vague, general, and negative terms, at the infinite distance of the creature from the Creator where we cannot know God as he is in himself or in accordance with his divine nature. In such an approach the only "content" we can put into what we claim to be knowledge of God is inevitably derived from knowledge of creaturely realities or devised through our own imagination and falsely projected onto God. That would be, Athanasius argued, a mythological way of thinking from a center in ourselves and governed by our own human nature, rather than a theological way of thinking from a center in God and governed by his divine nature. Moreover, if we try to reach knowledge of God in this way from some point outside of God, we cannot operate with any point in God by reference to which we can test or control our conception of him; we are inevitably thrown back upon ourselves and our own confused self-understanding. Even if we relate God negatively to what we are in ourselves, we are nevertheless unable to escape from using ourselves as some sort of measure for what we think and say of God. That kind of approach, together with the ways of thinking it involves, is precisely what has been set aside by God in his self-revelation as Father through the incarnation of his only begotten Son in Jesus Christ: "No one has ever seen God, but the only begotten Son who belongs to the heart of the Father has made him known" (John 1:18).

Two further considerations are called for.

First, if we human beings are really to have knowledge of God, we require a point of access to him which is both in God himself and in our creaturely existence — that is, we need a bridge across the infinite distance between God and ourselves which is grounded both in God and in man. That is precisely what we are given through the incarnation of God's Word and Son in Jesus Christ, the one Mediator between God and man. In him the God-manward movement and the man-Godward movement of divine revelation to humankind are consummated and perfectly united in one indivisible person who is both God of God and man of man. When God makes himself known to us in that unique way, he does so within the conditions of space and time to which we human beings belong and within the bounds of what we human beings may apprehend. At the same time, the knowledge of himself that God thus mediates to us is from a center in his own divine being where all our human thinking and speaking of him may be governed and tested in accordance with his divine nature. When we know God as Father through the Son, therefore, our knowledge of him in the Son is grounded in the very being of God and is determined by his own divine nature. Everything then depends on the unbroken relation in being and act between Jesus Christ and God. That is the very point which the Nicene Creed secured in the faith of the church in its central statement that the incarnate Son is of one being with God the Father.

Second, the fact that Jesus Christ the incarnate Son of the Father is God as well as man means that his Sonship is divine as well as human. His human sonship and his divine Sonship are inseparable from one another and are the obverse of one another. It is precisely as such, in his divine nature, that the incarnate Son of God is the unique revelation of God as Father. Precisely in being revealed in his own nature as the Son, Jesus Christ reveals the nature of the Father, not just by teaching us what God is like but by being what he was and is, the unique offspring of the divine nature, the only begotten Son of the Father incarnate in human life. This means that the Fatherhood of the Father and the Sonship of the Son are what they are in their coinherent relation to one another. Thus belief in God as Father is inseparably bound up with belief in Jesus Christ his Son, for Jesus Christ as Son not only images the divine nature but also embodies the divine nature in himself. Whatever is said of the Father is said of the Son except Fatherhood, and whatever is said of the Son is said of the Father except Sonship.

It is at this point also that we may discern the crucial significance of the Nicene assertion of the oneness in being between the incarnate Son and God the Father, instead of the assertion of a likeness in being between them. In point of fact, it was held, Jesus Christ could only be really like God in being if he were actually of one and the same being with him. What was at stake in the Nicene Council was the supreme truth of the deity of Christ and thus the identity between the content of God's revelation in Jesus Christ and God himself. Hence by the *homoousion* the Nicene Council affirmed a relation of identity in Jesus Christ between the image and the reality of his divine Sonship, and thus between the image of the divine Fatherhood reflected in his Sonship and its eternal reality in God.

If there is no ontological relation between Jesus Christ and the Father, if Jesus Christ is not himself very God of very God but ultimately only a creature, then what he images of God and what God really is are ultimately quite disparate, and what the gospel says of Jesus as "the Son of God" can be understood only in some kind of symbolic way. If Jesus Christ is not really God manifest in the flesh, then, of course, the very substance falls out of the gospel, and the forgiveness of sins that he mediates and his atoning sacrifice will have no ultimate divine validity. Our immediate concern here is with what it would involve for our understanding of God the Father if Jesus Christ were not of one being with him but were only tangentially related to him, and if therefore the image of God that Jesus exhibited in his Sonship were detached from the being of God. In that event we could not know his Father as God or God as Father or really know God as he is in his nature, for if the Father were bereft of his Son, all that would be left would be some kind of black hole from which there could be no emission of light! That is indeed just how Athanasius regarded the Arian conception of a God eternally bereft of his Word or Son, as an "infertile desert" or an "empty hole."[12] It cannot be stated firmly enough that the doctrine of the Fatherhood of God stands or falls with belief in the deity of Jesus Christ, his only begotten Son, and thus with the inseparable relation between the form and content of God's self-revelation in and through the Lord Jesus Christ.

The perfection of this union once and for all in being and agency between the *incarnate* Son and God the Father raises serious questions for us. What are we to think of the incarnational assumption of our human nature into union with the divine nature in Jesus Christ, and thus into the very life of God himself? We have already discussed the fact that there are and cannot but be *anthropomorphic* ingredients in the two-way relation which God establishes with us human beings. Now, however, we have to reckon with the fact that in Jesus Christ, *God* has not just come into man but come *as Man*.[13] This means that, in the indissoluble oneness between God and man in the person of his incarnate Son, God has once and for all incorporated *anthropic* ingredients into his self-revelation in Christ — that is, ingredients that cannot be treated as merely figurative, for they are integral to the Word of God *become* flesh, to the humanity which God

---

12. Athanasius, *Against the Arians*, 2.2; *Defence of the Nicene Decrees*, 15. See *The Trinitarian Faith*, pp. 133-34.

13. Thus Athanasius — see *The Trinitarian Faith*, pp. 150-51.

has laid hold of and *forever* taken up into himself in Christ, and therefore to what God eternally *is* toward us and for us. This means that it is utterly — indeed, divinely — impossible for us to probe behind the revelation with which God has once and for all clothed himself in Jesus Christ, or ever to set it aside in trying to think or speak of God apart from or outside of what he is in Jesus Christ, for in him God and man are now indissolubly and eternally one. We cannot go behind the incarnation, for there is in fact no God behind the back of Jesus Christ, and no God apart from his own self-revelation. However, the serious questions still press upon us. How far may we trace back into God what the eternal Son actually became in his incarnation within the structures of space and time? In what sense may we read into God what the Son of God assumed from us in our lowly human and creaturely being and existence in order to be one with us and reconcile us to the Father? Several things may be said in answer.

First, even though there is no God behind the back of Jesus Christ, and no possibility of our conceiving of him apart from his actual self-revelation in Jesus Christ, nevertheless the very God whom we know in and through Jesus Christ we know to be infinitely beyond what we can ever conceive of him. We apprehend him, but we cannot comprehend him. Only God can comprehend himself, and only God can name himself — hence his unique self-revelation and ineffable self-naming to us as *Yahweh, I am who I am, I shall be who I shall be.* What God ultimately is in the essence of his eternal being we cannot know, but we are given by God to know *who* he is. This takes us into the doctrine of the Holy Trinity, but here, where we are concerned with the centrality of the Father-Son relation, it should be pointed out that the indissoluble relation between the incarnate Son and God the Father cannot but mean that Fatherhood and Sonship belong to the eternal, unchangeable being of God. There is no Father without the Son, and there is no Son without the Father — Fatherhood and Sonship are equally ultimate in the eternal being of the Godhead. God is Father in himself in his own eternal nature as Father of the eternal Son. Accordingly, there is no possibility of stripping God of his Fatherhood or of his Sonship, for there is no God but he who has made himself known to us as the Father and the Son. Here, then, in the revelation of the divine Fatherhood and Sonship there are authentically anthropic elements which are ineradicable from the reality that God is in the self-determination of his own being, and not just anthropomorphic elements that cannot be avoided in God's dialogue with human beings. If we cannot think past all anthropomorphic components in God's interrelation with human beings without breaking off dialogue with God, for he has put the seal of his decisive self-revelation upon them, how much less can we think past the anthropic elements that inhere through the incarnation in God's being without lapsing into some form of agnosticism or even atheism? We cannot think or speak of God except in the forms of thought and speech which he has elected to use in the unique mediation of his Word to humankind through the people of Israel and through the exclusive personal incarnation of that same Word in the Lord Jesus Christ, for there is no other God than this God who has actually made himself known in this specific way as the God and Father of Jesus Christ, his only begotten Son. Hence our thinking and speaking of God, if they are to be true to him, must be in accordance with the actual forms of thought and speech prescribed for us by the nature and movement of God's specific self-revelation to humankind given through Israel and fulfilled in Jesus Christ.

Second, this does not absolve us from critical discernment of what we may read back from the incarnation into God and what we may not read back into him. Consider, for instance, the kind of sonship we know on earth, which is that of a son who is the son and grandson of other sons and who is himself the father of a son and the grandfather of another. That kind of sonship we cannot read back into God, for we cannot project the creaturely relations inherent in human sonship into the Creator. Nor, of course, can we read gender back into God, for gender belongs to creatures only. This is a point where our knowing of God suffers a radical inversion as our creaturely and human modes of thought are called into question and turned around. Our knowing of God is grounded in his knowing of us, and our understanding of the Fatherhood of God, who is who he is as Father of the Son, is of the one Fatherhood from which all other fatherhood is named. When we speak of God as Father, therefore, we are not using the term "Father" in a transferred, improper, or inadequate sense; we are using it in its completely proper sense, which is determined by the intrinsic Fatherhood of God himself. God alone is truly and ultimately Father — all other fatherhood is a reflection of his. When we say *"God is,"* the "is" is very different from any other kind of "is." It is an "is" that is appropriate to the nature of God, an "is" that is defined by his nature. And when we say "God is love," the love that God is is different from any other kind of love. As St. John says, "Herein is love, not that we loved God, but that he loved us, and sent his Son to be a propitiation for our sins, and not for our sins only, but for the sins of the whole world" (1 John 4:10). Likewise, when we hear that "God *is* Father," the "is" is unlike any other "is," for it is defined solely by the revealed nature of God; it is in that unique sense that the Fatherhood of God is to be understood. God is *Father* in an utterly singular and normative way, and it is only on that basis that we may say that the Father of our Lord Jesus Christ is God.

Third, because *God is Light*, the relation of the incarnate Son to the Father was described by the Nicene Creed not only as "God of God" but also as "Light of Light." Athanasius tells us that this expression "Light of Light" was specifically inserted into the creed at Nicea in order to help elucidate the biblical statement that the Son is "the express image of the Father's hypostasis" (Heb. 1:3). The intention behind it was also to guard the understanding of the relation of the only begotten Son to the Father from any distorting intrusion of material forms of thought and speech commonly used to speak of physical generation.[14] As himself Light, Christ "images" the Father in a quite unique and ineffable way as the radiance of the Father's glory — that is, in an *imageless* way. It is the same idea that is found in Athanasius's striking statement that, while the Son is the "Image of Godhead," the Spirit is "the Image of the Son."[15] The significance of this may be discerned in the fact that the Spirit himself is *imageless*. This implies that it must be in a wholly spiritual and imageless way that we are to think of the interrelations between the Father and the Son. It is by linking together in our minds the unique imaging of the Father by the Son and the unique imaging of the Son by the Spirit that we are enabled to refer such images as we have away from our human relationships to the Godhead in a spiritual and not in a material or creaturely way. And that principle must be allowed to govern the answers to the serious questions raised previously.

Here, then, we must also take fully into account the doctrine of the Holy Spirit. Because *God is Spirit*, the relation of the incarnate Son to the Father is to be understood, like the relation of the Holy Spirit to the Father, in an essentially *spiritual* way. As Calvin pointed out, the truth that God is Spirit applies not just to the person of the Holy Spirit but to the whole spiritual nature and being of God.[16] The three divine persons have one and the same spiritual being, so that we cannot but think of the

---

14. See Athanasius, *Against the Arians*, 1.9.

15. Athanasius, *Against the Arians*, 3.6, 10; *Letters to Serapion on the Holy Spirit*, 1.19ff.

16. Calvin, *Institutes*, 1.13.19f., 24.

consubstantial relation of the incarnate Son to the Father in the same spiritual way in which we are bound to think of the consubstantial relation of the Holy Spirit to the Father. It is through putting these consubstantial relations of the Son and the Spirit together that we are enabled to discern how we may read what God is toward us in Jesus Christ back into what he is antecedently and inherently in himself in a way that is appropriate to his spiritual nature, and to discern at the same time also something of what it is not spiritually appropriate to read back from the incarnate condition of the Son in Jesus Christ into the eternal being of God the Father. What must be allowed to govern our thought here is the point mentioned previously — that the Spirit is himself imageless. Accordingly, the linguistic and conceptual images we human beings are bound to use in speaking of God must be allowed to refer to him without imaging him, or, expressed otherwise, to refer to him in such a way that the self-revealing reality of God shines *formlessly* through the images which arise in his self-revealing interrelations with us.[17]

This imageless way of knowing and thinking of God, in whose Light we see light, is something like what we are now accustomed to in our scientific understanding of the orderly universe. Light itself is invisible, but we may see what is lit up by light and interpret it through the information with which light signals are laden in their mathematical properties as they shine through to us. Thus, instead of trying to explain the invisible in terms of the visible, we seek to explain the visible by reference to the invisible, but in that procedure we have learned to operate with critical devices to prevent us from reading our optical images back into the intrinsic structure of the universe. This is where we need the lenses of the Old Testament Scriptures, and indeed Jewish eyes, if we are properly to apprehend the mystery of Jesus Christ as the Son of God incarnate in the midst of Israel, and see the face of the Father in the face of Jesus Christ.

The Triune Name of God

By its very nature, divine revelation is essentially singular and once and for all, because there cannot be a multiplicity of revelations any more than

---

17. Cf. Gregory the Theologian, *Orations*, 24.4; 28.12ff.; 29.2, 8; 30.17; 31.7, 13; 37.7, 33; 38.12ff., etc. And see *The Trinitarian Faith*, pp. 69ff., 120ff., 134, 194-95, 207, 212-13.

there can be a multiplicity of Gods. That is the exclusive nature of God's self-revelation mediated to us in the Holy Scriptures: "I am the Lord your God. . . . You shall have no other gods before me" (Exod. 20:2-3; Deut. 5:6-7). By their nature the Holy Scriptures, given by divine inspiration, cannot be revised, let alone rewritten. In them God has set his seal upon his self-naming as Father, Son, and Holy Spirit, and thereby set his seal upon the language we are bound to use in praying to him and speaking of him. The triune name of God thus has an essential place in our knowledge, experience, and worship of God. We may not, therefore, bypass God's self-naming. The one way that God has thus chosen in making himself known to us as Father, Son, and Holy Spirit and addressing us in human language specifically adapted to his self-revelation as the Father, the Son, and the Holy Spirit sets aside any ways of speaking about him that we may devise and choose for ourselves.

The self-revelation of God as Father, Son, and Holy Spirit made exclusively through Jesus Christ is one in which content and form are inseparable. God is himself the content and reality of his revelation — accordingly, there can be no other revelation, for there is no other God. There is no separation between what God is and what he reveals of himself, so that the form of that revelation is to be understood only out of its substance and dynamic structure. Thus "Father," "Son," and "Holy Spirit" are essential to the informational content of revelation and are not just metaphorical ways of speaking of God derived from Jewish culture; for they are rooted in and determined by what God is inherently in himself, and are thus not detachable or changeable representations or images of God. In Jesus Christ, God has imaged himself and named himself once and for all over against all our erroneous images and designations of him. He cannot be known aright apart from his own self-imaging or self-naming in Jesus Christ, for there is no God apart from him, and no knowledge of God behind the back of his self-revelation. As John Calvin once wrote, unless we grasp knowledge of God as he has designated himself and offered himself for our contemplation in three persons, only the bare name of God, empty of his reality, flaps about in our brains.[18] The doctrine of the Holy Trinity — Father, Son, and Holy Spirit — belongs to the essential core of God's self-revelation in accordance with what he is in himself in his divine nature. To depart from that means that we want to think of God from a center outside of God, apart from him, and thus from a center

18. Calvin, *Institutes*, 1.13.2.

in our own selves and through the devising of our human imagination. In that case, we cannot but operate with a heathen anthropocentric idea of "God," a "God" fashioned in the image of human being — that is, some kind of mythological representation which we adopt in place of the unique and exclusive self-revelation of God as the Father of the Lord Jesus Christ.

We cannot forget that the trinitarian formula — Father, Son, and Holy Spirit — gives expression to God's *personal self-revelation,* one in which what he is toward us in the persons of the Father, the Son, and the Holy Spirit, he is inherently and eternally in himself, three persons in one divine being. Any other formula such as "Creator, Redeemer, and Sustainer," while a true expression as far as it goes of God's external acts toward us in creating, redeeming, and sustaining us, does not express what God eternally and personally is in himself — three persons who mutually contain and indwell one another — but only something of what he is toward us. However, detached from what God is in himself as Father, Son, and Holy Spirit, the terms *Creator, Redeemer,* and *Sustainer* are primarily correlated with what we are, so their meaning for us is reduced to little more than symbolic expressions of an in-turned religious consciousness. As such they cannot stand for the objective reality of God's triune self-revelation or give expression to its intrinsically personal and personalizing substance. In fact, far from referring to the three persons of the blessed Trinity, the formula "Creator, Redeemer, and Sustainer" by itself does no more than give expression to a unitarian conception of God characterized by three different names, modes, or operations. Moreover, the impossibility of "Creator, Redeemer, and Sustainer" being a substitute for "Father, Son, and Holy Spirit" is apparent from the fact that there can be no coinherent or perichoretic relation between Creator, Redeemer, and Sustainer, for that would imply that God creates, redeems, and sustains himself! The effect of that would be to identify God's functional relations toward the creaturely world with the intrinsic interrelations of his divine being, which would amount to a very gross form of anthropomorphism. There is, in fact, no authentic trinitarian formula other than the one grounded in the mutual and coinherent relations immanent in the eternal being of God and arising out of God's unique triadic revelation of himself through himself, as Father, Son, and Holy Spirit, which conveys the truth of God's intrinsically *personal, interpersonal,* and *personalizing* being. Thus, apart from the doctrine of God as Father, Son, and Holy Spirit — "three persons, one being" — our conception of God quickly degenerates into an impersonal or nonpersonal one, or becomes merely the personification and deification of our own desires and ideals.

Moreover, it should be pointed out that to alter the trinitarian formula of Father, Son, and Holy Spirit would be to suggest that the Lord Jesus Christ was mistaken and indeed quite wrong in teaching us to hallow the name of the "Father" and to believe in himself as the "Son" of the Father. And would it not be sin against the Holy Spirit, who, in being sent to us from the Father through the Son, cries "Abba, Father" in our hearts, echoing within them the prayer of the Son to the Father? Any person or any church that departs from the centrality of the Father-Son relation in faith and worship thereby rejects the particularity and finality of God's self-revelation in the Lord Jesus Christ and puts in question any claim to be authentically Christian. At the same time, departing from the centrality of the Father-Son relation would have the effect of undermining the validity of holy baptism in the name of the Father, the Son, and the Holy Spirit, and thus of disrupting the oneness and integrity of the church.

The Christian understanding of the doctrine of the Trinity stands or falls with the singularity and concrete particularity of God's self-revelation in Jesus Christ, his incarnate Son. In the incarnation that revelation took a concretely particular and once-and-for-all form in which the self-revealing and self-giving movement of God toward humankind was actualized in our world of space and time in an unrepeatable event with definite space-time coordinates. That decisive intersection of the eternal and the spatio-temporal in Jesus Christ was a unique event both for God and for humankind which can no more be undone than God can dismantle the incarnation or repudiate the sacrifice of his dear Son on the cross. In the incarnate life, death, and resurrection of Jesus Christ, God has given himself to humankind in a singular act on which he does not go back — he has committed himself to union with humankind and committed humankind to union with himself in an utterly final and irrevocable way. That astonishing *singularity* in the gospel was challenged by hellenizing thinkers in the early centuries of the Christian era, for they could only think "scientifically" of the Christian religion if it belonged to a universal class of religions — the singularity of Jesus Christ and of his cross was sheer folly to the Greek mind. It is precisely the same issue that the church faces today in objections to the centrality of the Father-Son relation at the heart of God's once-and-for-all self-revelation in Christ. The singularity of Jesus Christ and God's one comprehensive self-revelation in and through him is steadily under attack today in the lapse from definitely Christian theology into what is called "religious studies," in which Christianity is robbed of its uniqueness through being subjected to interpretation in terms of timeless universal religious ideas. That is the cultural climate within which the unique nature and ultimate sanctity of the Father-Son relation are being challenged. That is to say, behind attempts to change the traditional trinitarian formula lies a strange return to Enlightenment rationalism and relativism. It is quite otherwise in the scientific world of today, for the concept of "singularity," discarded as offensive by the Enlightenment, has bounced back with immense force and now plays an absolutely pivotal role in our understanding of the whole cosmos and all processes within it. It is thus not surprising that many scientists now react in a very different way to the Christian emphasis upon the uniqueness and centrality of the incarnation. Moreover, they want to understand the kind of onto-relations that are enshrined in the Christian doctrine of the Trinity, for they find that its presentation of the inner relations of the triune God, in which the three "map" to the one and the one to the three, has something very important to teach them that they need in their own fields of thought — for example, in quantum theory!

The urgent call to the church today is to repent of its wayward substitution of the word of man for the Word of God, and to put back into the center of its life and mission faithful proclamation of Jesus Christ as the one *Lord* and *Savior of humankind.* The church, including its theological colleges, seminaries, ministers, and theologians, needs to learn again how to be *unashamedly biblical and evangelical* — otherwise it is bound to become submerged in waves of sociocultural secularization in which the souls of men, women, and children are easily and quickly drowned.

Apophatic Theology and the Naming of God in Eastern Orthodox Tradition

THOMAS HOPKO

CONFUSION EXISTS about how Christians can hold that God is beyond creaturely comprehension and yet is most properly named Father, Son, and Holy Spirit. Some thinkers attribute the apparent contradiction to muddled thinking and the tyranny of custom. Certain feminist thinkers go further in identifying the allegedly indefensible doctrine as the creation of men (mainly white and Western) to insure male power in church and society through the use of masculine titles for God. These thinkers call for an apophatic qualification of all words and concepts applied to Divinity because they consider all divine names and images to be metaphors derived from human experience. In their view, the names of Father and Son are especially in need of emendation, if not outright elimination, because they are considered to be male-serving metaphors produced by an oppressive patriarchal culture whose structures and institutions they are intended to establish and secure.[1]

My intention is not to dialogue with those of other views, certainly not with feminist thinkers.[2] My purpose is rather to explain how the relation between apophatic theology and the naming of God is understood in Eastern Orthodox theology and worship.[3] My hope is that Christians

1. See the feminist theological writings of Mary Daly, Rosemary Radford Ruether, Anne Carr, Sallie McFague, Elisabeth Schüssler Fiorenza, Patricia Wilson-Kastner, et al.
2. I say this because theological dialogue requires common suppositions rooted in common experience. Discussion between Orthodox Christians and feminist thinkers must begin with issues of spiritual and ecclesial experience before there can be meaningful dialogue on theological questions.
3. On this issue, see Vladimir Lossky, *The Mystical Theology of the Eastern Church*

disposed to defend the traditional trinitarian names will be helped by what follows, and that others may at least receive an idea about how one theological tradition combines the traditionally Christian naming of God with the equally Christian conviction that God's being is beyond all categories of creaturely comprehension and expression.

The Personal God

God is known by Christians as the I AM who lives, speaks, and acts. Christian scriptures witness to God's personal activity in the world. The question naturally arose for Christians about how the God of Abraham, Isaac, and Jacob, the one who spoke face-to-face with Moses as with a friend, is to be understood in relation to Jesus Christ, God's unique Son and Word incarnate in human form; and about how God and his Son relate to the Holy Spirit, who spoke by the prophets, anointed Jesus in his messianic ministry, and continues to inspire and empower the church in its witness and worship as the personal pledge of God's kingdom until it comes in power with Christ's parousia at the end of the ages.

In attempting to summarize what is now regarded as dogma in the Orthodox Church, I cannot emphasize too strongly that the one God of faith is the God of Israel confessed by Christians to be the Father of Jesus. When the Nicene Creed confesses belief "in one God, the Father almighty, the creator of heaven and earth and of all things visible and invisible," the one God confessed is not the Holy Trinity. Neither is it the divine being or "divinity-in-general." It is the person of God the Father. This point is crucial to the Orthodox experience and conceptualization of God. St. Gregory of Nazianzen made the point most simply when he said that there is one God because there is one Father, "one God because of the *monarchia*."[4]

(Crestwood, N.Y.: St. Vladimir's Seminary Press, 1976); Vladimir Lossky, *The Vision of God* (Crestwood, N.Y.: St. Vladimir's Seminary Press, 1983); John Zizioulas, *Being as Communion: Studies in Personhood and the Church* (Crestwood N.Y.: St. Vladimir's Seminary Press, 1985); and Deborah Malacky Belonick, "Revelation and Metaphors: The Significance of the Trinitarian Names, Father, Son and Holy Spirit," *Union Seminary Quarterly Review* 40 (1985): 31-42. For an introduction to Eastern Orthodoxy generally, see Kallistos Ware, *The Orthodox Way* (Crestwood, N.Y.: St. Vladimir's Seminary Press, 1986); and Serge Bulgakov, *The Orthodox Church,* rev. translation (Crestwood, N.Y.: St. Vladimir's Seminary Press, 1988).

4. Gregory of Nazianzen, *Oration on Holy Baptism,* Oration 40.41. See also Basil, *On the Holy Spirit,* 18.45.

Properly speaking, God the Father is the one God *(O Theos)*. The Father is God not simply when the term *God* is used as a predicate nominative — as, for example, when we say that the Holy Spirit is *God* in a manner similar to the way in which we would say that Adam is *man*. When the word *God* is used as a proper name, the Father is God, and God is the Father. This, virtually without exception, is the usage of the church's scriptures, creeds, and liturgies. It is certainly the usage of the Bible.

Although God's only Son, incarnate as Jesus of Nazareth, is called "God" in St. John's gospel, both as the Word that was "in the beginning" and as the risen Christ (John 1:1; 20:28), the term *God* is generally not used to refer to Jesus in the Bible. It is never used to refer to the Holy Spirit.[5] Both Christ and the Spirit, however, are referred to as *Lord* in the church's apostolic scriptures and in the creedal statements derived from them. Argument may even be made that the term *Lord* (Kyrios/Adonai), the Septuagint word for YHWH, is a more emphatic divine title in the sacred writings than the word *God* (Elohim/Theos). In any case, this raises the issue about the proper understanding and articulation of the relationship between God the Father, Jesus Christ the incarnate Son and Word, and the Holy Spirit.

The solution to this question was worked out in the tradition of the Orthodox Church through the theological (and ontological and linguistic) distinction made between *hypostasis* and *ousias,* usually translated respectively as *person* and *essence* (or being, nature, substance). This formulation, which became normative for Eastern Orthodox trinitarian doctrine and worship, is crucial to our attempt to understand how the trinitarian names relate to apophatic theology.

Person and Essence

The formulation of the trinitarian dogma begins with the experience of the three distinct subjects — Jesus, God, and the Spirit — and not with an abstract conception of "deity" and/or "unity." It is grounded in the conviction that God is the Father because he has with himself his divine Son and Word, who became the man Jesus in his human birth from the Virgin Mary, and that God also always has with himself his Holy Spirit,

---

5. Gregory of Nazianzen boasts that he boldly calls the Holy Spirit *God,* and justifies, in his funeral oration, his friend Basil's careful refusal to do so. See *On the Holy Spirit,* 10; *Panegyric on St. Basil,* Oration 63.68-69.

who eternally proceeds from the Father and abides in the Son. God the Father and the Logos/Son and the Holy Spirit are divine with one and the same divinity, the Son from the Father by way of "generation" and the Spirit from the Father by way of "procession." But the three are not *personally* the one God. The one God *personally* is the Father, of whom are the Son and the Spirit.

The word *hypostasis* came to designate personal uniqueness. It articulated the experience that *who* God the Father is is not *who* God's Son and Word is, who is not *who* the Holy Spirit is. The word *hypostasis* affirmed that the Father, Son, and Holy Spirit are three distinctly existing and acting subjects *(hypokeimena)* of divine being, action, and life, each subsisting in his own right, uncompromisingly existing as *three* in who they are and how they act in their identical divinity.

The word *ousia,* or essence (being, substance, or nature), came to designate *what* a person (or even a thing) is, not in the specificity of its particular existence but in the generality of its being. In this view, no essence exists except as "enhypostasized" concretely as a uniquely distinct "mode of existence" *(tropos hyparxeos).* This metaphysical insight, born from the need to articulate the theological experience of the Holy Trinity, came to be formulated with linguistic, logical, and theological precision by the Cappadocian Fathers following the doctrinal witness of St. Athanasius. It represents a teaching that, according to orthodoxy, avoids the error of unipersonal monotheism (which we might perhaps more accurately call uni-individual-istic "monad-theism"), which makes God the metaphysical archetype of the self-centered individual, while also excluding all varieties of henotheism and polytheism. St. Basil of Caesarea put it this way:

> If any one says that Father, Son, and Holy Spirit are the same, and suppose one thing under several names, and one hypostasis described in three persons *[prosopa],* I rank such as belonging to the faction of the Jews. Similarly, if any one says that the Son is in essence unlike the Father, or degrades the Holy Spirit into a creature, I anathematize him and say that he is coming near to the heathen error.[6]

Basil explains his thought further in a letter to his brother St. Gregory of Nyssa, a letter that some scholars attribute to Gregory himself.

---

6. Basil, *To the Ascetics,* Letter 226.4. See also *On the Holy Spirit,* 18.47; *To Amphilochius,* Letter 236.6. In addition, see Gregory of Nazianzen, *On the Theophany,* Oration 38.8.

It contains the same teaching that Gregory develops in his famous *Letter to Ablabius: On 'Not Three Gods.'*

> Suppose that two or more are set together, as, for instance, Paul, Sylvanus, and Timothy, and that an inquiry is made into the essence or substance of humanity. No one will give one definition of essence or substance of humanity. No one will give one definition of essence or substance in the case of Paul, a second in that of Sylvanus, and a third in that of Timothy; but the same words which have been employed in setting forth the essence or substance of Paul will apply to the others also. Those who are described by the same definition of essence or substance are of the same essence or substance *(homoousios)*. When the enquirer has learned what is common, and turns his attention to the differentiating properties whereby one is distinguished from another, the definition by which each is known will no longer tally in all particulars with the definition of another, even though in some points it is found to agree.
>
> My statement, then, is this. That which is spoken of in a special and peculiar manner is indicated by the name of the *hypostasis*. Suppose we say "a man." The indefinite meaning of the word strikes a certain vague sense upon the ears. The nature is indicated, but what subsists and is specially and peculiarly indicated by the name is not made plain. Suppose we say "Paul." We set forth, by what is indicated by the name, the nature subsisting *[ephestosan]*.
>
> . . . It is customary in Scripture to make a distinction of this kind. . . . Transfer, then, to the divine dogmas the same standard of difference which you recognize in the case both of essence and of hypostasis in human affairs, and you will not go wrong.[7]

This same teaching is found in the theology of St. Gregory of Nazianzen:

> This I commit unto you this day; with this I will baptize you and make you grow. This I give you to share, and to defend all your life, the one Godhead and Power, found in the Three in Unity, and comprising the Three distinctly, . . . the infinite conjunction of Three Infinite Ones, each God when considered in Himself . . . the Three one God when contemplated together; each God because of the one

7. Basil, *To His Brother Gregory,* Letter 38.2. See also Gregory of Nazianzen, *On the Holy Spirit,* Oration 30.19.

essence *(to homousion)*; one God because of the *monarchia*. No sooner do I conceive of the One than I am illumined by the splendor of the Three; no sooner do I distinguish the Three than I am carried back to the One.[8]

For to us there is but one God, the Father, of whom are all things; and the one Lord Jesus Christ, by whom are all things; and the one Holy Spirit, in whom are all things; yet these words — of, by, in, whom — do not denote a difference of essence . . . but they characterize the hypostases of an essence which is one and unconfused.[9]

The Supraessence of God

The radical difference between God and everything else that exists by God's power and will enters into human thought and speech not when the term *essence* is used "abstractly" or "schematically" to denote what a being is (e.g., the Holy Spirit is God, and Adam is man), but when it is used to indicate the *content* of a particular being or class of beings. When the term *essence* is used in this way, the Orthodox theological tradition claims that God's being or nature is unlike all others because everyone and everything besides God is God's creature. This does not simply mean that God's essence is different from all other natures in the sense that God is not man, like man is not angel. It means rather that God is unlike everything else that exists besides himself in such a way that the very term *nature* or *essence* cannot be applied to God as a category in exactly the same way in which it is used in relation to creatures. In this sense, it can be said that relative to God the term *essence* (or being, substance, nature) is understood as indicative of something totally unlike anything and everything else that exists because it is God's nature to be this way because of who and what God is.

When it comes to *content,* therefore, and not merely to *form,* when it comes to what God is *in fact* and not merely to what God is as *a category of reality,* Orthodox theology insists that God's being is radically different from all other beings. God is different as the only being that eternally and necessarily exists. God is different as the maker of everything that exists besides himself and his Word and his Spirit, who are "of one essence"

8. Gregory of Nazianzen, *Oration on Holy Baptism,* Oration 40.41.
9. Gregory of Nazianzen, *Oration on the Holy Lights,* Oration 39.12.

(homoousios) with him. God is different in that the Father alone, with his Son and his Spirit, is and has the fullness of being and life in contradistinction to everything else that is partial and incomplete. And God exists in his divinity in a manner absolutely incomprehensible to creaturely minds.

The being and life of the Holy Trinity admits of no opposites or contraries to itself. Nonbeing and becoming are not the opposites of God as "supreme being." Nonbeing is the opposite of created being, which because it is not divine is always in a process of becoming. The Trinity's being is fully actualized, and that in a manner befitting God alone. In this sense, therefore, the divinity of the Father, Word/Son, and Spirit is said to be *beyond being* in regard to the content of God's divine nature and activity, which is totally different from that of creatures.

In Orthodox theological tradition the word *supraessential* (or supranatural, suprasubstantial, beyond-being) has been coined as the technical term to express this conviction. The term, *hyperousios* in Greek, indicates that the *essence* of God understood formally is *supraessential* when understood ontologically. It means that God's being, abstractly or schematically considered, is to be beyond all categories of being, nonbeing, and becoming when God's essence is considered in terms of its metaphysical content and reality.

This position is defended by faith and spiritual experience as well as by reason and logic. God's essence is known by living experience to be beyond all creaturely categories of expression. And this is considered reasonable and logical if God is really God and not simply the "perfect" or "preeminent" or "supreme" form of the being and nature of creatures who are not God. This conviction is affirmed in Orthodox liturgical worship, in which God is addressed in the following way:

> O Lord our God, Thy power is incomparable, Thy glory is incomprehensible, Thy mercy is immeasurable, Thy love for man is inexpressible.[10]

> . . . . For Thou art God ineffable, inconceivable, invisible, incomprehensible, ever-existing and eternally the same; Thou, and Thine only-begotten Son and Thy Holy Spirit. . . .
>
> For holy art Thou, and all holy, Thou and Thine only begotten Son and Thy Holy Spirit; holy art Thou and all holy, and magnificent is Thy glory.[11]

10. *Divine Liturgy of St. John Chrysostom,* Prayer of the First Antiphon.
11. *Divine Liturgy of St. John Chrysostom,* Eucharistic Anaphora. See also the eucharistic canon of the Liturgy of St. Basil the Great.

Examples of this view of God the Father, Son, and Holy Spirit and this way of speaking about God's being and action abound in the writings of the church fathers. I will give just a few examples.

Athanasius and Gregory of Nyssa

In his treatise entitled *Against the Heathen,* St. Athanasius says that God is by nature incomprehensibly beyond all created existence:

> For God, being good and loving to mankind, and caring for the souls made by Him — since He is by nature invisible and incomprehensible, having His being beyond all created existence, for which reason the race of mankind was likely to miss the way to the knowledge of Him, since they are made out of nothing while He is unmade — for this cause God by His own Word [who is incarnate as Jesus Christ] gave the universe the order it has. . . .
>
> . . . Who then is this [God], but the Father of Christ, most holy and above all created being . . . ?[12]

St. Athanasius' teaching that God is in essence above and beyond all nature and being is developed with greater clarity by the Cappadocian Fathers. This is especially true when it concerns God's self-manifesting actions in the world through his consubstantial Son and Word incarnate as Jesus and through his divine Spirit. The examples that follow from St. Gregory of Nyssa's writings can be multiplied by identical teachings of St. Basil and St. Gregory of Nazianzen.

In *On the Beatitudes,* St. Gregory gives this explanation of the divine nature:

> Now the divine nature, as it is in Itself according to its essence, transcends every act of comprehensive knowledge, and it cannot be approached or attained by our speculation. Man has never discovered a faculty to comprehend the incomprehensible; nor have we ever been able to devise an intellectual technique for grasping the inconceivable.[13]

12. Athanasius, *Against the Heathen,* 3.35.1 and 3.40.2.
13. Gregory of Nyssa, *On the Beatitudes,* Homily 6 (see *From Glory to Glory: Texts from Gregory of Nyssa's Mystical Writing,* trans. and ed. Herbert Musurillo [New York: Charles Scribner's Sons, 1961], pp. 98-101).

By way of example, St. Gregory refers to Abraham, who "passed through all the reasoning that is possible to human nature about the divine attributes" and, "after he purified his mind of all such concepts," came to know "the incomprehensible Godhead" as the one who "completely transcends any knowable symbol" yet is still known by faith in the multiplicity of his divine operations.[14] He refers as well to Moses, who "enters into the hidden, invisible sanctuary of the knowledge of God" yet does not remain there because he is "led to penetrate the realm where God exists." In that "realm," which, according to Gregory, means the "invisibility and incomprehensibility of God," Moses "still begs God to give him more." Moses is refused, and that very refusal is itself a revelation from God, who speaks and acts, fulfilling Moses' desire "by the very fact that it remains unfulfilled," for God really shows himself to Moses, and Moses really comes to see and to know him — not as God is in himself, however, which cannot be known, but by being led by God.

In Gregory's mystical theology, Moses follows God as God leads him. He "does not see God face to face, but merely looks at his back." This "back side" (*LXX: ta opiso*) of God that Moses sees symbolizes God's manifestation to his creatures in his divine energies (cf. Exod. 33:23). The "face of God" that creatures cannot behold is God's essentially hidden "supraessence" which remains everlastingly concealed, not because God does not want to reveal it but because it cannot be known.[15]

Gregory theologizes in this same way in commentaries on the biblical psalms and canticles. David the psalm-writer, who was "lifted out of himself" by the Holy Spirit, "glimpsed . . . God's infinite and incomprehensible beauty." He saw, Gregory declares, "as much as a mortal can see," and his only just and accurate response was to cry out that "every man is a liar" (Ps. 116:11). Man is a liar because "anyone who attempts to portray that ineffable light in language" — a light really seen and experienced, a light genuinely manifested and authentically known — "is truly a liar, not because of any abhorrence of the truth, but merely because of the infirmity of his explanation."[16]

---

14. Gregory of Nyssa, *Answer to Eunomius' Second Book*. (See *From Glory to Glory*, pp. 119-22, where the reference is incorrectly made to *Against Eunomius*, book 12.)
15. Gregory of Nyssa, *The Life of Moses* (see *From Glory to Glory*, pp. 142-52, or *The Life of Moses*, trans. Abraham J. Malherbe and Everett Ferguson, Classics of Western Spirituality series [New York: Paulist Press, 1978]; see also Cistercian Studies, no. 31 [Kalamazoo, Mich.: Cistercian Publications, n.d.]).
16. Gregory of Nyssa, *On Virginity* (see *From Glory to Glory*, p. 105).

In speaking this way, Gregory makes the double affirmation that will become classical in Orthodox tradition. God is absolutely unknown in his innermost being, but he manifests himself personally through his powers and works in the world of his making. Human minds cannot grasp God even in his workings, and human speech cannot fully express the experience. But the revelation is real, and the conceptions and expressions about it are true. In commenting on the book of Ecclesiastes, Gregory sums up the teaching in this way:

> The great men have spoken not of God but rather of His works, saying: . . . *to the magnificence of the glory of His holiness there is no end.* Ah, the wonder of it! Why does the sacred text fear to approach the glory of the divine mystery, so that it has not even expressed any of those effects which are outside His limit, judging it rash even to express this in a concept; rather it merely marvels at the vision of the *magnificence of His glory.* But once again he is unable to see the substance of this glory; he is merely in amazement at the glory of His holiness. He is far from being concerned with the exact nature of God's essence; he has not the power to show admiration for the least of God's manifestations; for he does not admire God's *holiness,* nor even the *glory of His holiness,* but merely attempts to admire the *magnificence of the glory of His holiness,* and even here his powers fail. . . .
>
> Thus in speaking of God, when there is question of His essence, then it is the *time to keep silence.* When, however, it is a question of His operation, a knowledge of which can come down even to us, that is the time to speak of His omnipotence by telling of His works and explaining His deeds, and to use words to this extent.[17]

St. Gregory's reference to the "magnificence of the glory of God's holiness" is particularly significant because, as we have seen, the divine liturgy attributed to St. John Chrysostom that is regularly used in the Orthodox Church employs this expression in its eucharistic prayer. After the people sing the thrice-holy hymn central to the Christian eucharist, the celebrant in the Orthodox Church continues to pray:

> With these blessed powers, O Master who lovest mankind, we also cry aloud and say: Holy art Thou, and all-holy, Thou and Thine only-begotten Son and Thy Holy Spirit! Holy art Thou, and all-holy,

17. Gregory of Nyssa, *Commentary on Ecclesiastes,* Homily 7 (see *From Glory to Glory,* pp. 128-29).

153

and magnificent is Thy glory! Who has so loved Thy word as to give Thine only-begotten Son that whoever believes in Him should not perish, but have everlasting life.[18]

The Dionysian Conceptualization

In Orthodox Christian tradition no one is "more apophatic" than the anonymous author known as Dionysius the Areopagite. This mysterious mystical theologian affirms unequivocally that the "supraessential Godhead" which "is unutterable and nameless" is most properly to be praised by "denying it every manner of attribute."[19] This is known by experience, when God reveals himself to creatures through divine self-manifestation:

> Now concerning this hidden supraessential Godhead we must not dare, as I have said, to speak, or even to form any conception thereof, except those things which are divinely revealed to us from the holy scriptures. For as it has lovingly taught us in the scriptures concerning itself that the understanding and contemplation of its actual nature [are] not accessible to any being; for such knowledge is supraessentially exalted above all. . . .
>
> Not that the Good One is wholly incommunicable to anything; nay, rather, while dwelling alone by itself, and having here firmly fixed its supraessential ray, it lovingly reveals itself by illuminations corresponding to each separate creature's powers, and thus draws upwards holy minds to such contemplation, communion and resemblance *[theoria, koinonia, homoiosis]* of itself as they can attain.[20]

The point which the Dionysian author is making here is that there are, in fact, two aspects to the supraessential God. There is the aspect of unqualified otherness, hiddenness, and unknowability, and the aspect of God's self-revelation in everything which exists to such an extent that literally every name of every thing can in a sense be applied to God, not only things spiritual (such as spirit, mind, goodness, and love) but even things physical (such as light, fire, water, and rock). In the Dionysian view,

18. *Divine Liturgy of St. John Chrysostom,* Eucharistic Prayer.
19. Dionysius the Areopagite, *On the Divine Names,* 1.5 (see *Dionysius the Areopagite,* trans. C. E. Rolt [Naperville, Ill.: Allenson, 1920], pp. 59, 50).
20. Dionysius the Areopagite, *Mystical Theology,* 1 (see *Dionysius the Areopagite,* p. 191).

God is both totally other *and* perfect exemplar. But for this anonymous theologian there can be doubt which names and titles are most "adequate to the Godhead":

> Now in the former Treatises [i.e., *The Divine Names*] the course of the argument, as it came down from the highest to the lowest categories, embraced an ever-widening number of conceptions which increased at each state of the descent, but in the present treatise it mounts upwards from below towards the category of transcendence, and in proportion to its ascent it contracts its terminology, and when the whole ascent is passed it will be wholly dumb, being at last wholly united to Him Whom words cannot describe. . . .
>
> We therefore maintain that the universal Cause transcending all things is neither impersonal nor lifeless, nor irrational nor without understanding; in short that it is not a material body, and therefore does not possess outward shape or intelligible form, or quality or quantity, or solid weight, nor has it any local existence which can be perceived by sight or touch; nor does it suffer any vexation of disorder through the disturbance of earthly passions, or any feebleness through the tyranny of material chances, or any want of light; nor any change, or decay, or division, or deprivation, or ebb or flow, or anything else which the senses can perceive. None of these things can be either identified with it or attributed to it.[21]

Such a passage may appear to be saying that when God is so described, it follows that what is not specifically negated in God is thereby positively affirmed, and that in a supremely eminent way. What we find in the pseudo-Areopagite, however, is not this at all. For instead of denying the opposite of what is affirmed of Divinity and affirming the opposite of what is denied, the author negates the "oppositions" as well. Because of the importance of this point for our present purposes, I will quote him again at some length:

> Once more, ascending yet higher, we maintain that it (i.e. Divinity) is not soul, or mind, or endowed with the faculty of imagination, conjecture, reason or understanding; nor is it any act of reason or understanding; nor can it be described by the reason or perceived by the understanding since it is not number, or order, or greatness, or

21. Dionysius the Areopagite, *Mystical Theology*, 3, 4 (see *Dionysius the Areopagite*, pp. 198-99).

littleness, or equality, or inequality, and since it is not immovable nor in motion, or at rest, and has no power and is not power or light, and does not live, and is not life; nor is it personal essence, or eternity, or time; nor can it be grasped by the understanding, since it is not knowledge or truth; nor is it kingship, or wisdom; nor is it one, nor is it unity, nor is it Godhead or goodness; nor is it a Spirit, as we understand the term, since it is not sonship or fatherhood; nor is it any other thing such as we or any other being can have knowledge of; nor does it belong to the category of non-existence or to that of existence; nor do existent beings know it as it actually is . . . nor can the reason attain to it to name it or know it; nor is it darkness nor is it light, or error, or truth; nor can any affirmation or negation apply to it; for while applying affirmations or negations to those orders of being that come next to it, we apply not unto it either affirmation or negation, inasmuch as it transcends all affirmation by being the perfect and unique Cause of all things, and transcends all negation by the pre-eminence of its simple and absolute nature — free from every limitation and beyond them all.[22]

This is the very limit of human expression about God that can be attained. It expresses an apophatic theology beyond affirmation *and* negation — a supreme apophaticism which passes even beyond all negations. Yet the "nameless God" whose supraessential supradivinity includes all names and none is still addressed in prayer by this most apophatic of all church fathers as *Trinity: Trias! Hyperousie! Hyperthee! Hyperagathe!*[23]

For the mysterious Dionysius, the supraessential, supradivine, supragood Divinity whose nature is beyond all names and includes them all is God the Father with his only begotten Son and Word and his most holy Spirit.

Supraessential Trinity

St. Maximus the Confessor (d. 662) developed the Cappadocian and pseudo-Dionysian doctrine of God and integrated it into the church's teaching about Jesus Christ as truly God and truly man, with the fullness of

22. Dionysius the Areopagite, *Mystical Theology,* 5 (see *Dionysius the Areopagite,* pp. 200-201).

23. Dionysius the Areopagite, *Mystical Theology,* 1.

both natures and operations enhypostasized in the one person of the incarnate Word. St. Simeon the New Theologian (d. 1022) reaffirmed the teaching, with emphasis on the personal activity of the Holy Spirit. St. Gregory Palamas (d. 1359) gave the doctrine a further elaboration, witnessing particularly to the real distinction between God's supraessence and his divine actions and energies, by which God personally reveals himself in creation through his Son and Spirit. And countless dogmatic hymns *(dogmatika)* and Trinity hymns *(triadika)* originating in these centuries and still sung in Orthodox liturgical worship can also be presented as testimony to this theological vision which St. John of Damascus (d. 749), himself a hymnographer, had already summarized in the church's first doctrinal synthesis presented as a "complete exposition" of the Orthodox faith:[24]

> The Deity being incomprehensible is also assuredly nameless. Therefore since we know not His essence, let us not seek for a name for His essence. . . . Inasmuch, then, as He is incomprehensible, He is also unnameable. But inasmuch as He is the cause of all and contains in Himself the reasons and causes of all that is, He receives names drawn from all that is, even from opposites: for example, He is called light and darkness, water and fire: in order that we may know that these are not of His essence but that He is supraessential and unnameable; but inasmuch as He is the cause of all, He receives names from all His effects.
>
> Wherefore, of the divine names, some have a negative signification, and indicate that He is supraessential. . . . Some again have an affirmative signification, as indicating that He is the cause of all things. . . . So He is spoken of as Being and Essence. . . . [And] He is called reason and rational, wisdom and wise, intellect and intellectual, life and living, power and powerful. . . . These, then, are the affirmations and the negations, but the sweetest names are a combination of both: for example, the supraessential Essence, the Godhead that is more than God, the Beginning that is above beginning, and the like.
>
> . . . And these names are common to the whole Godhead, whether affirmative or negative. And they are also used of each of the hypostases of the Holy Trinity in the very same and identical way and with their

24. See, for example, Maximus the Confessor, *Centuries on Love* and *Centuries on Theology;* Simeon the New Theologian, *Theological and Practical Chapters* and *Hymns on Divine Love;* and Gregory Palamas, *Triads in Defense of the Holy Hesychasts.* For liturgical examples, see the Trinity Hymns *(Triadika)* at Matins in the Lenten Triodion; also the Anaphora of the Liturgy of St. Basil the Great and the Kneeling Prayers at Pentecost Vespers.

full significance. For when I think of one of the hypostases, I recognize it to be perfect God and perfect essence; but when I combine and reckon the three together, I know one perfect God.[25]

Orthodox theological and liturgical texts unanimously affirm the conviction that the three divine hypostases of the Godhead, with their proper names of Father, Son, and Holy Spirit, are not subject to apophatic qualification as are all metaphysical properties and metaphorical images attributed to God's essence. In this tradition, God's nature can be referred to with all possible names, images, and attributes that exist in the created order — abstract and concrete, positive and negative, spiritual and physical, masculine and feminine, animate and inanimate — because the divine nature is the metaphysical source and exemplar of everything created. This is already clearly witnessed in the Bible, the primary source of Orthodox theology and worship.

Everything that can possibly exist in creaturely form actually exists within the Godhead of the Father, Son, and Holy Spirit in a transcendently supraeminent, incomprehensibly divine manner. This is known because God has revealed it to creatures by way of his divine actions and operations in and by which creatures become "partakers of the divine nature" through personal communion with God the Father, Son, and Holy Spirit in God's self-disclosure within creation (cf. 2 Pet. 1:4). Or, to put it another, perhaps somewhat more accurate way, creatures know this through their personal communion with God the Father through his divine Son and Word incarnate as Jesus Christ, by the Holy Spirit who proceeds from the Father and rests in the Son.[26]

In this theological vision and articulation, the hypostases of Father, Son, and Holy Spirit are never transcended and/or negated. They cannot be because hypostases are not emanations or manifestations of essence (or supraessence) but are rather subjects of the essence (or supraessence) that makes them what they are. How the essence (or supraessence) is actually enhypostasized in each person is unique to each hypostasis, which is always a specific "mode of existence" *(tropos hyparxeos)* of the essence (or supraessence) that it shares in common with other persons of the same essence (or supraessence).

25. John of Damascus, *On the Orthodox Faith*, 1.12.
26. See John 15:26; see also Pentecost Vespers hymns that quote Gregory of Nazianzen, *On Pentecost*, Oration 41.9; and John of Damascus, *On the Orthodox Faith*, 1.8 and 13.

In the case of God, the divine essence, which is supraessential in content, is enhypostasized in three distinct and unique modes *(tropoi)* of divine existence that are personally named Father, Son, and Holy Spirit. The church fathers rarely elaborate on the significance of the names of the three divine hypostases of the suprasubstantial Trinity except to say that they are given by God and belong to him in a uniquely divine manner. On one level, they are incomprehensible to human understanding, but on another level, through the divine operations, they make God personally known, available to creaturely communion, contemplation, and imitation.[27]

Ephesians 3:14-19 reads as follows:

> For this reason I bow my knees before the Father, from whom every fatherhood *[patria]* in heaven and on earth is named, that according to the riches of his glory he may grant you to be strengthened with might through his Spirit in the inner man, and that Christ may dwell in your hearts through faith; that you, being rooted and grounded in love, may have power to comprehend with all the saints what is the breadth and length and height and depth, and to know the love of Christ which surpasses knowledge, that you may be filled with all the fulness of God.

Even the mysterious Dionysius, the least overtly trinitarian of the church fathers, refers to this sentence (attributed to the apostle Paul) with his affirmation that all fatherhood in heaven and on earth "exists and draws its name" from the first hypostasis of the Trinity, the only true God, the Father of Jesus. In this he represents the tradition which consistently testifies that this is so because God has made human beings in his image and is not made by human beings in theirs.[28]

Yet God's *essence* cannot be identified with fatherhood or sonship or spirithood, or with any positive or negative attribute of divinity such as goodness or wisdom or peace or power. Still less can the supradivine essence be identified with any of the metaphors applied to it from creaturely existence, such as God being likened to a rock or a mother, or to light or fire. But the nature of God — capable of any number of names

---

27. E.g., John of Damascus, *On the Orthodox Faith*, 1.8.

28. Dionysius the Areopagite, *On the Divine Names*, 1.4. See also Ephesians 3:15; in addition, see Athanasius, *Against the Arians*, 1.7.23; and John of Damascus, *On the Orthodox Faith*, 1.8.

and symbols and images and titles, and capable, strictly speaking, of none of them because Divinity in itself is beyond them all — is still that of the Father, Son, and Holy Spirit, each of whom enhypostasizes the same incomprehensible divinity in his uniquely and distinctly personal way.[29]

In this perspective God is said to be essentially beyond being, divinity, paternity, sonship, spirithood, goodness, wisdom, power, and so on. But God is never said to be hypostatically beyond Father, Son, and Holy Spirit. For God is supraessential and even nonessential. But God is not suprahypostatic or nonhypostatic, suprapersonal or nonpersonal.

The names of Father, Son, and Holy Spirit for the three divine hypostases are never changed or emended. They cannot be, because they contain, actualize, and reveal an interpersonal union *(henosis)* and communion *(koinonia)* of trihypostatic divine being and life that is of critical significance for those to, for, and with whom the Holy Trinity acts in the dispensation of creation, redemption, sanctification, and deification. While the Orthodox tradition insists that the trinitarian names are to be understood in a manner strictly proper to God, it also testifies, as has been already indicated, that these names have a certain revelatory and exemplary significance for human being and life. Exactly what the tradition considers this significance to be in regard to our being made in God's image and likeness, and that particularly as male and female, remains to be fully explained. The naming of God was a question that concerned previous generations primarily in controversies with Gnostics, who introduced sexuality into the Godhead, and Arians and Eunomians, who denied the eternal Fatherhood of God in timeless relation to his consubstantial Son. There is little said about the application of the hypostatic names to human being and life. On the basis of what is witnessed in the tradition, however, it seems reasonable to hold that the names of Father, Son, and Holy Spirit possess a crucial and profound theological and spiritual significance for human beings made in God's image and likeness as men and women. This significance is to be found in the manner of God's interrelation with creatures in his Son and Spirit.

The familial and conjugal imagery and symbolism of Christian

---

29. The pronoun "his" bears theological significance in the *oikonomia* of the Father and Son because of the personal activity of these hypostases, the second of whom has become man as Jesus. In languages other than English we might call the Spirit "she" (Hebrew/Old Syriac) or "it" (Greek). In Slavonic languages the word *Trinity* is feminine, requiring the pronoun "she." In regard to *theologia,* however, no significance can be given to the gender of the trinitarian names. See Gregory of Nazianzen, *On the Holy Spirit,* 30.7.

scripture and liturgy that discloses and describes God's communion with creatures is inextricably bound up with the names and actions of the three divine persons. By contemplating, participating in, and imitating the saving activity of the Father, Son, and Holy Spirit in the *oikonomia* of creation, salvation, and deification, human persons can discover what it means for them to be men and women, fathers and mothers, husbands and wives, sons and daughters, brothers and sisters in the image and likeness of God the Father revealed through Christ the Son in the Holy Spirit, who makes creation to be God's bride, the wife of the Lamb, and whose presence in the church is already the anticipatory pledge *(arrabon)* of the "Jerusalem above," which is "free" and is "our mother" (Gal. 4:26).[30]

Orthodox Christians refuse to emend the trinitarian names of Father and Son and Holy Spirit apophatically because the "nameless God" has personally revealed himself to them as Father through the person of Jesus Christ the Son, by the person of the Holy Spirit. Therefore, these trinitarian names remain for Christians uniquely appropriate for worship, contemplation, communion, and imitation of the Holy One, who, with his Son and Spirit, is absolutely beyond all that creatures can know, think, and say, but who has revealed himself to us with these names for our salvation.

30. Some modern Orthodox theologians (e.g., Bulgakov, Florensky, Lossky, Evdokimoff, Schmemann, Verhovskoy, and Meyendorff) see a certain connection between the Holy Spirit and the feminine, particularly as the Holy Spirit acts in creation, Israel, the church, and the Virgin Mary. They describe this connection tentatively and in different ways. I hope to treat this subject in a book I am now preparing on God and gender in Orthodox tradition.

Knowing and Naming the Triune God:
The Grammar of Trinitarian Confession

J. A. DiNOIA, O.P.

"**O** ABYSS! O eternal Godhead! O deep sea!" exclaims St. Catherine of Siena in the prayer to the Trinity that concludes *The Dialogue:* "What more could you have given me than the gift of your very self?"[1] In St. Catherine's eloquent prayer, the awestruck Christian heart cries out in praise of the great mystery of the gift of the triune God's very self through the grace of Christ. The mystery defies expression but invites wonder, worship, and love. Although no words can exhaust it, the final test for the adequacy of any words that dare to name this mystery is that they be true to its reality.

This essay considers some recent suggestions for revisions in the Christian community's manner of speaking of the triune God who abides with that community in grace. One measure for assessing the Christian aptness of these proposals is furnished by the reality of the gift itself. Do the proposed ways of speaking permit the full reality of this gift to come to expression?

I

As Christians have understood it, to affirm the presence of God's "very self" in grace is to affirm the personal presence of the Blessed Trinity. Christ himself promised this: "Anyone who loves me will be true to my word,

---

1. Catherine of Siena, *The Dialogue,* trans. Suzanne Noffke, O.P., *The Classics of Western Spirituality* (New York: Paulist Press, 1980), p. 365.

and my Father will love him; we will come to him and make our dwelling with him" (John 14:23). In the central action of the great narrative that recounts God's divine engagement with humankind, the presence promised by Christ is enacted and achieved. For in the person of the Word, God is united with human nature, and through his suffering, death, and glory, human beings are reconciled with the triune God, "for through him we both have access in one Spirit to the Father" (Eph. 2:18). Indeed, it could be said that the whole economy of salvation is directed by God to nothing less than the incorporation of created persons into personal communion with the uncreated Trinity.[2]

How such a communion can come about St. Catherine intimates elsewhere in her prayer: "O eternal Trinity, fire and abyss of charity . . . by the light of understanding within your light I have tasted and seen your depth . . . and the beauty of your creation. Then, when I considered myself in you, I saw that I am your image. You have gifted me with power from yourself, eternal Father, and my understanding with your wisdom — such wisdom as is proper to your only-begotten Son; and the Holy Spirit, who proceeds from you and your Son, has given me a will, and so I am able to love."[3] The triune God so transforms and empowers human capacities as to become known and loved in his inner being as Father, Son, and Holy Spirit. The gift of the triune God's "very self" entails not an intensification of the divine presence but a transformation of human personal and social existence. For how could it be possible for the God who actively sustains all things in existence to become "more" present to his creatures? Divine indwelling supersedes divine omnipresence, so to speak, because in grace the triune God occasions and enables human engagement with the personal Father, Son, and Holy Spirit.

Indeed, as St. Catherine's prayer suggests, this engagement itself possesses a trinitarian structure. Aquinas makes a similar point. The knowledge of the triune God given in grace partakes of the Son's knowledge, and

2. See recent discussions of the doctrine of the Trinity: Karl Rahner, *The Trinity,* trans. Joseph Donceel (New York: Herder & Herder, 1970); William J. Hill, *The Three-Personed God* (Washington: Catholic University of America Press, 1982); Robert W. Jenson, *The Triune Identity* (Philadelphia: Fortress Press, 1982); Walter Kasper, *The God of Jesus Christ,* trans. Matthew J. O'Connell (New York: Crossroad, 1984); and Eberhard Jüngel, *God as the Mystery of the World,* trans. Darrell L. Guder (Grand Rapids: William B. Eerdmans, 1983). For the history of the doctrine, see Bertrand de Margerie, *The Christian Trinity in History,* trans. Edmund J. Fortman (Still River, Mass.: St. Bede's Publications, 1981).

3. Catherine of Siena, *The Dialogue,* p. 365.

hence, through the Spirit, it is the sort of knowledge that breaks forth into love.[4] The gift of God's very self thus entails the incorporation of human persons into the inner life of the Father, Son, and Holy Spirit. In an important way, the structure of this incorporation replicates the mutual relations of the persons of the Trinity. Christ's sonship is the principle of our coming to life in grace — our adoption — as sons and daughters who can with Christ speak the name of the Father in the power of the Spirit: "God sent forth his Son . . . so that we might receive adoption as sons. And because you are sons, God has sent the Spirit of his Son into our hearts, crying, 'Abba! Father!'" (Gal. 4:4-6). Moreover, Christ's sonship is also the principle of a reconciled and restored human community, as his own prayer makes clear: "Holy Father, keep them in your name, which you have given me, that they may be one, even as we are one" (John 17:11).

"What more could you have given me than the gift of your very self?" Scripture, creeds, liturgy, sacramental rites, catechesis, preaching, theological tradition — all, like St. Catherine's prayer, are suffused with faith in the reality of the gift of God's very self in grace. As embodied in Christian utterance and practice, this faith defines the context for any consideration of the knowability and speakability of the trinitarian mystery.

The triune identity of the God who gives us his very self is knowable, strictly speaking, only through revelation. But even though the mystery is known, it permanently eludes human comprehension. Thus St. Catherine sounds another traditional theme when she prays, "You, eternal Trinity, are a deep sea: The more I enter you, the more I discover, and the more I discover, the more I seek you."[5] The mystery of the presence of the three-personed God to human knowledge and love in grace is inexhaustible and in that sense never fully comprehensible or expressible. To be sure, faith is the source of our knowledge of this mystery. But since its object is the transcendent God, this knowledge can never be complete or comprehensive.

It follows that, along with understanding, language itself falters before this mystery. The challenge to speak appropriately of this mystery has confronted the Christian community and its theologians in every generation. For the unknowable and unspeakable mystery at the heart of the Christian narrative and the life it fosters are found to be renderable in human utterance if for no other reason than to give voice to the truth of God's nearness. Just as God is the first teacher of trinitarian truth, so also

---

4. Aquinas, *Summa theologiae* 1a.43, 5 ad 2um.
5. Catherine of Siena, *The Dialogue*, p. 364.

is it God who provides the first lesson in trinitarian grammar: "When we cry, 'Abba! Father!' it is the Spirit himself bearing witness with our spirit that we are children of God" (Rom. 8:15-16). Or as Christ's promise in a different context has it, "When they deliver you up, do not be anxious how you are to speak or what you are to say; for what you are to say will be given to you in that hour; for it is not you who speak, but the Spirit of your Father speaking through you" (Matt. 10:19-20). The speakability of the otherwise unspeakable mystery of the triune God presupposes the gift of God's very self and depends on resources that come with that gift. It is a possibility rooted in the very presence whose reality faith affirms, a presence that supersedes the limitations of human understanding and utterance in the face of the radically transcendent creator. The Christian aptness of proposed forms of speech about the triune God must be measured at least by this criterion: Can these proposed forms of speech do justice to the reality of the gift of God's very self?

II

Over the past two decades a number of theologians have argued that standard forms of Christian speech about the triune God enshrine masculinist conceptions of God.[6] These conceptions are said to affect women adversely in at least two ways. First, they legitimate patterns of male domination and patriarchy in the church and in society at large. Second, they make it difficult if not impossible for women to relate to the divine in a way that is religiously meaningful.

---

6. For readers unfamiliar with this literature, a good start can be made with Ann Loades, "Feminist Theology," in *The Modern Theologians*, vol. 2, ed. David F. Ford (Oxford: Basil Blackwell, 1989), pp. 233-52. Indispensable for understanding the case for the proposed reformulations of traditional trinitarian language are the following works: Mary Daly, *The Church and the Second Sex* (San Francisco: Harper & Row, 1975); Rosemary Radford Ruether, *Sexism and God-Talk* (Boston: Beacon Press, 1982); Elisabeth Schüssler Fiorenza, *In Memory of Her* (New York: Crossroad, 1985); Sallie McFague, *Models of God* (Philadelphia: Fortress Press, 1987); and Anne E. Carr, *Transforming Grace* (San Francisco: Harper & Row, 1987). The Viennese feminist theologian Susanne Heine has mounted a vigorous critique of standard feminist theology in two works: *Women and Early Christianity,* trans. John Bowden (Minneapolis: Augsburg, 1987), and *Matriarchs, Goddesses, and Images of God,* trans. John Bowden (Minneapolis: Augsburg, 1989). A helpful analysis of general feminist theory is found in Jean Bethke Elshtain, *Public Man, Private Woman* (Princeton: Princeton University Press, 1981).

Would it not be desirable to reformulate language about the triune God so that it would better reflect our diverse experiences of God? Some have argued not only that it would be advantageous to do so but also that it is necessary to do so in order to redress actual harms done to women which came to be legitimated and reinforced by androcentric language about God. Furthermore, it is hoped that such reformulation would foster the equality and liberation of women. To be sure, since the offending linguistic practices are embedded in the scriptural, liturgical, doctrinal, and theological traditions of all Christian communities, the proposed reformulation would affect all aspects of Christian public discourse. In fact, proposals in this vein have already given rise to provisional biblical and liturgical texts, primarily for use in public worship.[7]

Among the proposed reformulations, the following are prominent. With respect to customary trinitarian language, the names of the first and second persons of the Trinity — "Father" and "Son" — and the manner of conceiving their relationship are singled out as instances of androcentrism. It is proposed that names like "Creator," "Redeemer," and "Sanctifier" (and variants) be adopted to replace "Father," "Son," and "Holy Spirit." Some suggest that "Father/Mother" or "Mother" replace "Father" in references both to God and to the first person, and that the traditional "Word" or newly proposed "Child" replace "Son" in references to the second person. Others propose that the Holy Spirit be considered feminine and be referred to by feminine personal pronouns (*she* and *her*). Others eschew all gendered pronouns when referring to God and suggest the repetition of the word *God* in place of *he, him,* and *his,* and the substitution of *Godself* for *himself.*

Some have further argued that classical Christian theism enshrines androcentric conceptions in the divine attributes (in particular: simplicity, immutability, eternity, omniscience, and omnipotence) in that they project the ideal of a distant, detached, and omnicompetent male. This conception is seen to be in need of amplification or replacement by one in which female attributes of relationality and engagement figure.[8] This proposal

7. See, for example, *The New Companion to the Breviary* (Indianapolis: Carmelite Monastery, 1988).

8. This issue will not be considered in this paper. See discussions of the matter in, for example, Carr, *Transforming Grace*, p. 145, and notably in an influential essay by Elizabeth A. Johnson, "The Incomprehensibility of God and the Image of God Male and Female," *Theological Studies* 45 (1984): 441-65. Two recent philosophical discussions of the divine nature, while critical of classical theism at various points, do not take up the feminist critique: Edward R. Wierenga, *The Nature of God* (Ithaca: Cornell University Press,

ventures beyond the field of linguistic practice and advances a more nearly theological agenda.

Some authors, while agreeing that Christian talk about God is androcentric, nonetheless judge the proposed reformulations to be implausible and unenforceable. The view that Christian talk and conceptions of God are incorrigibly masculinist furnishes for some the grounds for departing from the Christian community to newly formed post-Christian feminist communities or simply to a personally shaped post-Christian religiosity.[9] Some of these propose some form of goddess religion.[10]

Still, reformist as distinguished from post-Christian feminists continue to press for the desired reformulation of Christian linguistic practices, often arguing that such reformulation serves not only the cause of women's equality but also that of negative theology. Some reformists contend that exclusively androcentric conceptions of and language for God can become idolatrous.[11] In order to safeguard the incomprehensibility and ineffability of the transcendent, such language must be complemented by categories and terms derived from women's experience.

1989), and Christopher Hughes, *On a Complex Theory of a Simple God* (Ithaca: Cornell University Press, 1989). A passage from a work by Anglican Carter Heyward entitled *The Redemption of God* (Washington: University Press of America, 1982), will perhaps convey some idea of the feminist critique of traditional conceptions of God: "It is in the nature of our idol to be intolerant of ambiguity. His first and only love is Himself. He is an impassible unflappable character who represents the headship of a universal family in which men are best and women least. He is the keeper of an ethical scorecard on which 'reason' gets good marks and 'relation' fails. He is a master plan-maker who maps out and, by remote control, directs our journeys before we have learned to walk. His narcissism is unquenchable. He demands that he be loved. The cold deity is the legitimating construct of the patriarchal desire to dominate and control the world. He is the eternal King, the Chairman of the board, the President of the institution, the Guru of the youth, the Husband of the wife, the General of the army, the Judge of the court, the Master of the universe, the Father of the church. He is our superior, never our friend. He is a rapist, never a lover, of women and of anyone else beneath Him. He is the first and final *icon of evil* in history" (p. 156).

9. A powerfully argued case for post-Christian feminism is Daphne Hampson, *Theology and Feminism* (Oxford: Basil Blackwell, 1990). This book is indispensable reading.

10. See Ruether, *Sexism and God-Talk*.

11. For the frequently reiterated charge that the traditional conception of God is idolatrous, see the influential article by Gail Ramshaw Schmidt, "*De Divinis Nominibus:* The Gender of God," *Worship* 56 (1982): 117-21. See also Sallie McFague, *Metaphorical Theology* (Philadelphia: Fortress Press, 1982), pp. 147-48; and Carr, *Transforming Grace,* pp. 138, 140-41. See the illuminating discussion of this issue in Garrett Green, *Imagining God* (San Francisco: Harper & Row, 1989), pp. 91-97.

Is the customary trinitarian language of the Christian community revisable in the ways proposed by reformist feminist theologians? Some critics say no.[12] But on the assumption that the cause is a good one — that is to say, promotes the equality and dignity of women — let us entertain the reformist (as distinct from post-Christian) proposals as potentially appropriate revisions of Christian linguistic practices.[13] In order to assess these proposals, let us consider them in the light of the grammar of Christian patterns of discourse about the triune God, particularly as these patterns are meant to secure the reality of the faith in the presence of God in grace and the incorporation of human persons into the life of the Trinity. Although some critics argue that these revisions compromise central Christian beliefs about the triune God, let us assume here that the reformist case presses not for a radical revision of Christian doctrine but simply for the reformulation of Christian language.[14] Some of the proposed reformulations have a basis in tradition, while others are more clearly innovative. In defense of the innovations, reformists argue that the Christian tradition has shown itself to be remarkably pliable and flexible in its appropriation of new ways of speaking and thinking when these seem suited to new circumstances. Why not adopt some of the revisions suggested? Don't the experiences reported by some women (and men) imply the advent of a new opportunity for creative evolution in the linguistic practices of the community? If the commonly proposed reformulations can do justice to the central convictions of the Christian faith about the triune God's gift of his very self, then at least on this score they would appear to be Christianly apt.

12. Important nonfeminist critiques of feminist theology are Donald G. Bloesch, *The Battle for the Trinity* (Ann Arbor: Servant Publications, 1985), and William Oddie, *What Will Happen to God?* (San Francisco: Ignatius Press, 1988).

13. Typical descriptions of the goal of feminist theology are, for example, "promoting the human dignity of women" (Johnson, "The Incomprehensibility of God," p. 442) and "the equality of women and men" (Hampson, *Theology and Feminism,* p. 87).

14. Since feminist theology presents a variety of positions, this generous presumption will not be verified in all cases. Thus, for example, the post-Christian feminist Daphne Hampson doubts whether the Christian feminist Sallie McFague is a theist (see *Theology and Feminism,* pp. 158-60). And throughout *What Will Happen to God?* William Oddie contends that the feminist agenda is universally a radical one.

III

Consider first the suggestion that the names "Creator," "Redeemer," and "Sanctifier" (or "Sustainer") be substituted for "Father," "Son," and "Holy Spirit." A variant of this proposal is the triad "God, Christ, and Spirit."

In favor of such a substitution are two main considerations. First, it eliminates in one stroke the masculinist associations of the terms *father* and *son,* along with the male conception of the processions and relations between the first and second persons of the Trinity. Second, the substitution employs terms that are unimpeachably traditional. "Creator," "Redeemer," and "Sanctifier" occur widely in the characteristic discourse of the Christian community as equivalents for "Father," "Son," and "Holy Spirit," both individually and triadically.[15] These factors explain the increasing appeal of this proposal. Some worshiping communities, persuaded of the legitimacy of the reformist case, have adopted the proposed triad as an apt substitution for the classical doxology and occasionally also as a substitute for the classical baptismal formula.

Critics of this reformulation can appeal to several considerations. For some, the substitution of "Creator," "Redeemer," and "Sanctifier" (and its variants) for "Father," "Son," and "Holy Spirit" in classical liturgical settings is precluded on the grounds that such revision of traditional forms of worship is simply inappropriate. Traditional forms should not be tampered with.[16] At this point, reformists can respond that previous generations of Christians neither recognized nor acknowledged that women were oppressed. Awareness of this situation today makes it difficult for women and many men to participate in worship whose language canonizes and protects the androcentrism now in retreat in most sectors of society. Reformists contend that the understandable reluctance to alter hallowed texts and formulas must yield to the just demand for inclusive forms of language for God.

Opponents of the proposed substitution appeal not only to the non-optional status of the traditional language but also to doctrinal and theological considerations. There are two important objections of this kind.

According to the first objection, the terms "Creator," "Redeemer,"

---

15. See Bloesch, *The Battle for the Trinity,* pp. 50-55.

16. See Roland M. Frye, "Language for God and Feminist Language: Problems and Principles," *Scottish Journal of Theology* 41 (1988): 446.

and "Sanctifier" are not in fact, as alleged by reformists, equivalent to "Father," "Son," and "Holy Spirit." For one thing, "Father," "Son," and "Holy Spirit" are personal names, while "Creator," "Redeemer," and "Sanctifier" are functional terms.[17] What is more, the names "Father," "Son," and "Holy Spirit" are unsubstitutable self-descriptions of the persons of the Trinity.[18] These are the names by which God has chosen to be known. In intimate relationships with other persons, we usually refer to them by their names, not by the functions they perform, and we respect their preferences in matters of nicknames, and so on. Since the only knowledge we possess of the triune God comes from Scripture, it follows that the names of the Father, Son, and Holy Spirit are non-optional in a strong sense. This defense of traditional trinitarian language appeals not simply to the authority of Scripture but also to the scripturally and narrationally warranted self-description of the triune God.

A second important objection suggests that the proposed substitution is crypto-modalist in its implication that the triadic structure of the economy of salvation — represented by the threefold actions of creation, redemption, and sanctification — exhibits nothing of the internal life of the triune God. Characteristic of modalism in its historic and implicit forms is the conception of an internally undifferentiated deity who appears in the forms of Father, Son, and Spirit respectively in order to create, redeem, and sanctify humankind. Thus, precisely as replacements for "Father," "Son," and "Spirit," the terms "Creator," "Redeemer," and "Sanctifier" possess unexpungeably modalist implications.[19] Advocates of the substitution insist that a revision of Christian public utterance that does not exclude women is compatible with the profession of orthodox trinitarian belief and indeed necessary for it in present circumstances. It is at this point that such variants as "God, Christ, and Spirit" or "Source, Word, and Spirit" are advanced to correct the modalist implications of "Creator, Redeemer, and Sanctifier."

Beyond simply reiterating the case in favor of some version of the proposed substitution, reformists can pursue two lines of counterargument at this juncture. One reformist response might be that, as products of a patriarchal and male-dominated culture, the Scriptures themselves are

---

17. For a careful and thoroughly informed theological critique of reformist proposals, see Jenson, *The Triune Identity*, chap. 1.

18. See Bloesch, *The Battle for the Trinity*, p. 50.

19. Ibid.

susceptible of critique and revision. But this line of counterargument ventures perilously close to a post-Christian rather than a strictly reformist position and poses issues that lie beyond the scope of the present essay.[20] A second line of counterargument appeals to the incomprehensibility of God and the inadequacy of all human talk about him. This reformist response will be considered in the next section of this essay.

But the arguments so far considered both for and against the substitution of "Creator," "Redeemer," and "Sanctifier" for "Father," "Son," and "Holy Spirit" do not directly address the issue of the adequacy of the proposed formulation when measured against the reality of the triune God's self-gift.

In order to apply this measure, let's consider a useful distinction between essential and personal terms in the grammar of trinitarian confession.[21] Essential terms are those that identify all that is common to the three persons of the Trinity, while personal terms are those that identify what is proper to each of the persons. Thus, to move directly to the matter at hand, terms that identify relations of the created order to the Trinity function as essential names for God, while terms that identify the relations of the trinitarian persons to each other serve as personal names for them. "Creator," "Redeemer," and "Sanctifier" are each instances of essential names because they identify the agential interaction of the triune God with the creaturely order. On the other hand, "Father," "Son," and "Holy Spirit" are personal names that refer precisely to the relations of the persons with each other.

What is at stake doctrinally in this distinction? Since the three persons are equally God, eternally subsisting within the divine being, no causal or agential interaction is possible between them. By definition, the causal activity of the triune God has the creaturely as its object. In creation, redemption, and sanctification, the triune God functions as the agent of created outcomes in the created order. The persons of the Trinity exercise agency not with respect to each other but only with respect to the creaturely realm. The suggestion that terms denoting agential interactions — for

---

20. The issue of the authority of Scripture in feminist theology is a complex one. See the essays in *Interpretation* 42 (1988): 3-57.

21. This discussion is dependent on a reading of the grammar of trinitarian confession provided by Aquinas in *Summa theologiae* 1a.32-42. My reading of these questions is informed throughout by T. C. O'Brien's remarkable commentary as presented in his notes and appendices in the Blackfriars edition of St. Thomas Aquinas, *Summa Theologiae*, vol. 7 (New York: McGraw-Hill, 1976).

example, "Creator," "Redeemer," and "Sanctifier" — could appropriately name the persons in relation to each other would be inescapably subordinationist because it would introduce a hierarchy of causality into the Trinity. An agential understanding of the processions of generation and spiration entails a subordinationist account of the being of the Son and the Spirit. To avoid this pitfall, a sophisticated grammar of trinitarian confession evolved in the historic Christian mainstream that safeguarded the truth of the eternity of the processions and the complete absence of differentiation in being in the Father, Son, and Holy Spirit. Even the personal names "Father" and "Son" have to be understood analogously (as we shall see subsequently), to correct for the connotations of superiority and subordination in creaturely fatherhood and sonship.

It follows that essential names are not equivalent to personal names and are applied to the persons only according to the linguistic rule of "appropriation." This rule — implicit in Christian linguistic practice — allows that terms denoting the common being and agency of the triune God with respect to the created order are ascribed to one or another of the three persons according to their affinity with the personal properties or the missions of the persons. Thus, Father, Son, and Holy Spirit can be named, respectively, "Creator," "Redeemer," and "Sanctifier" by appropriation of the common activities of creation to the Father (unbegotten), of redemption to the Son (because of the visible mission of the incarnation), and of sanctification to the Holy Spirit (by virtue of the invisible mission of the indwelling). In the characteristic discourse of the Christian community, there are other examples of such appropriations of essential names to the three persons.

It is clear, then, that the terms of the triad "Creator, Redeemer, and Sanctifier" cannot serve as personal names for the Trinity. Similar considerations apply to such variants as "God, Christ, and Spirit" and "Source [or Ground], Word, and Spirit." The terms "Spirit" and "Word" are proper names and hence unobjectionable. But since each of the three persons can be called "God," the name specifies nothing proper to the first person. In this combination, however, its application in the post-Nicene church to the first person entails a subordinationist conception of the second and third persons. "Christ" names the incarnate divine hypostasis of the second person in human nature but fails to name the Son in relation to the Father and the Spirit. The difficulty with the use of terms like "Source" or "Ground" for the first person is that such terms have agential connotations. The use of an essential name for any one of the three persons in combination with personal names for the other two entails subordinationism in suggesting either inequality in divinity or a causal interaction between them.

These considerations supply an important test for the suitability of "Creator," "Redeemer," and "Sanctifier" (and variants) as substitutes for "Father," "Son," and "Holy Spirit." The preceding analysis demonstrates that the proposed substitutes fail to be equivalent for or interchangeable with "Father," "Son," and "Holy Spirit." Moreover, the grammar of trinitarian confession implies something profound about the Christian life in God's conception of it. Names that apply specifically only to the inner life of God — names, in other words, that belong properly only on the lips of the Father, Son, and Holy Spirit speaking to each other — are given to be spoken by creatures. That human beings are invited to adopt God's own names and to share God's own life is the goal of the trinitarian action of creation, redemption, and sanctification. Our employment of the triad "Creator, Redeemer, and Sanctifier" identifies our reception of the benefits of this action; our employment of the names "Father," "Son," and "Holy Spirit" signifies our recognition and enjoyment of these benefits. Surely, no considerations — no matter how compelling — can justify a preference for terms that identify the effects of divine agency over names that identify the divine relations themselves. Accordingly, it is clear that, as substitutes for "Father, Son, and Holy Spirit," the triads like "Creator, Redeemer, and Sanctifier" fail to do justice to the full reality of the presence of the triune God and of our incorporation in grace into the inner-trinitarian life.

IV

At this juncture, proponents of the reformulation of customary trinitarian language could mount a potentially strong counterargument. Granted — reformists might argue — that the triad "Creator, Redeemer, and Sanctifier" is vulnerable in that it replaces personal names with essential terms. In this way the triad fails to identify relations internal to the Trinity and names external relations instead. Perhaps other alternatives to the androcentric "Father, Son, and Holy Spirit" could be found that avoid the confusion entailed by the employment of triads like the preceding one. "Father/Mother, Child, and Spirit" is one candidate that comes to mind.

But, more seriously, the defense of traditional trinitarian language advanced in the preceding section seems to have fallen under the spell of literalism. Is it an implication of this defense that the first person is literally Father and the second person literally Son? If so, then haven't the rules of negative theology been violated? Divine reality cannot be captured by human concepts or identified with human expressions. If God is incomprehensible, then there can be no literal description of the inner life of the Trinity nor a set of non-optional proper names for the trinitarian relations.[22]

Reformists appeal to the incomprehensibility and ineffability of God in order to relativize the prevailing androcentric conventions in language about the triune God. If God is incomprehensible and all claims to knowledge and forms of utterance about him radically inadequate, then the masculinist set of conventions is in no way privileged. Furthermore, reformists argue, a plurality of divine names will be more successful than a narrowly defined set at referring to the God who is beyond human comprehension and expression. Divine attributes and names that draw upon women's experience can correct deficiencies in conceptions of God that draw exclusively upon men's experience. Since reformists can lay claim to the tradition of negative theology, their program of reformulating customary trinitarian language has relevance for the entire community, not just for its women members.[23] The literalism of the defense of traditional trinitarian language in the preceding section of this essay effectively blocks the path to needed revision of trinitarian language, a path that advocates of such revision feel justified in identifying with the objectives of the classical *via negativa*.

The reformist case against literalism also draws strength from a variety of theories of the semantic force of Christian language. Prominent among these is the view that this language is to be understood as metaphorical and expressive of experiences of the transcendent. This combination of experiential with metaphorical theology provides the prevailing theoretical justification for the negative theology fundamental to the reformist case in most of its current versions.[24]

The metaphorical/experiential argument for revision of traditional trinitarian language runs roughly as follows. Religious language refers primarily to our experience of the divine being. In itself, the divine being is utterly transcendent and unknowable. It is knowable only on the basis

22. "The Incomprehensibility of God and the Image of God Male and Female" by Elizabeth Johnson is fundamental for most feminist discussions of this issue.
23. Ibid.
24. The representative and influential sources for this argument are the already cited works of Sallie McFague.

of the impact it makes on human religious consciousness. The adequacy of religious language must be assessed at least in part by its capacity to express the experience of the divine. Since no literal forms of speech can capture its meaning and truth, only nonliteral (chiefly metaphorical) language is suited to the symbolization of this range of experience.

Feminist theory supplies the additional premise that women's experience is distinctive in ways that can be specified (despite disagreements among feminists about the content of this specification). In order to be meaningful and true, Christian speech about God must express women's experience as well as men's. But traditional trinitarian language is thoroughly biased in favor of men's experience. Such language must therefore be corrected for its androcentric bias if it is to continue to refer successfully to God in present circumstances. Since God is in any case incomprehensible and ineffable, it follows that such language will adequately express our experience of him only insofar as it is morally inclusive — insofar, that is, as it redresses the harms done to women by the hegemony of androcentric language and thinking, and encourages the reform of social structures massively legitimated by this language in the past. Apparently literal forms of speech embedded in the tradition can be reconstrued to possess a metaphorical force. In addition, if this goal is to be achieved, new metaphors must be developed and fielded for Christian use. This broad theological project must be preceded by revisions of the public discourse of the Christian community so that it reflects the appropriateness of language that ascribes to the triune God feminine as well as masculine names and traits.

We can make headway in grasping the force of this argument if we consider two examples of assertions about God that occur in the customary discourse of the Christian community: "God is the rock who saves us" and "God is faithful." Compare these assertions about God with the following statements: "Kristen is a rock" and "Kristen is faithful." These utterances pick out a trait of Kristen's character. One employs the term *rock* to suggest Kristen's solidity and constancy; the other uses the term *faithful* in its primary meaning to ascribe to Kristen the quality in question. It is not controversial to distinguish the two remarks about Kristen by noting that the first is an instance of metaphorical utterance and the second an instance of literal utterance. The reformist argument sketched in the preceding paragraphs implies that the distinction between metaphorical and literal utterances, while applicable to ordinary speech, is inapplicable to Christian speech.

But if this is the outcome of the claim that all religious speech is metaphorical in character, then the reformist case — at least insofar as it depends on this claim — seems implausible as an account of Christian discourse about God. Users of Christian discourse have at their disposal and in fact employ speech that has the form both of literal utterance and of nonliteral utterance.[25] The reformist case just outlined is implausible in requiring that all apparently literal speech about God be reconstrued as nonliteral and, in particular, metaphorical speech.

In noting the at least prima facie distinction between literal and metaphorical speech in Christian discourse about God, there is no question here of preferring literal speech to metaphorical speech. It is inconceivable to imagine that Christians could dispense with the one or the other. Rather, the point is to try to account for the one without reducing it to an instance of the other. There is reason to think that one test of the adequacy of theories about Christian discourse (as well as of the discourse of other religious communities) would lie in their capacity to field nonreductionist accounts of this discourse in all its variety and peculiarity.

It would be a mistake to draw the distinction between literal speech and metaphorical speech as if the former were "reality-depicting" or referential while the latter were not. Substantial affirmative predications about God can have either metaphorical or literal form. In common versions of the reformist case (such as that outlined here), metaphorical utterances are contrasted with literal utterances in a way that conflates "literalism" with "realism." This conflation results in part from premises drawn from experiential theology about the force of religious utterances. As noted previously, experiential theology holds that religious discourse refers to human experience of the transcendent (partially knowable and expressible) but fails to refer to the transcendent in itself (unknowable and inexpressible). A thorough examination of these premises would take us far afield of the chief burden of the reformist case.[26] The possibility that metaphorical

25. In *Metaphor and Religious Language* (Oxford: Clarendon Press, 1985), Janet Martin Soskice defines metaphor as "that figure of speech whereby we speak about one thing in terms which are seen to be suggestive of another" (p. 15). At the level of complete utterances, metaphor is a form of nonliteral speech (along with allegory, parable, and so on) and is contrasted with literal or "accustomed" speech, in which terms are used according to their primary meanings (p. 69). Soskice's important work is crucial to sorting out the issues discussed in this section.

26. For a discussion of these issues, see my essay entitled "Philosophical Theology in the Perspective of Religious Diversity," *Theological Studies* 49 (1988): 408-16.

speech about God can be no less "reality-depicting" than literal speech about him is not directly at issue here.[27] Because of the reformist deployment of the claim that all religious language is metaphorical, what is needed here is a defense of the possibility of literal speech about God.

Granted the difficulty of speaking about the transcendent realm and the healthy determination to avoid bald rationalism in this area, Christian traditions of theological inquiry have sought to account for the force of utterances about God that have the form of literal speech. There are good reasons for trying to make sense of these utterances. Even traditions with a strong preference for negative theology have wanted to avert sheer agnosticism in their accounts of discourse about God.[28] As posed for us by the reformist case, the issue is this: Can a nonreductionist account of literal utterances like "God is faithful" be consistent with an affirmation of the radical incomprehensibility and ineffability of God? The answer to this question will have important consequences for the shape of trinitarian language and its expression of God's self-gift.

But a defense of the possibility of literal speech about God seems to commit us to the implausible claim that some kinship obtains between the statements "Kristen is faithful" and "God is faithful." We think we know what it means to ascribe faithfulness to Kristen: we know what faithfulness means, and we know what it means for persons to possess or lack this trait. But we have no way of knowing what being faithful is for God. It may turn out that the kinship between the two statements is no more than grammatical. In their endeavor to avoid a rationalistic account of Christian talk about God, some have arrived at precisely this conclusion. They have argued that the term *faithful* possesses no more the same meaning when applied to God and Kristen than does a homonym like *bark* when applied to the covering of a tree and the sound a dog makes. In each case the terms are identical, but the things to which they refer are

27. For the term "reality-depicting" and for a realistic account of metaphor, see Janet Martin Soskice, "Theological Realism," in *The Rationality of Religious Belief*, ed. William J. Abraham and Steven Holtzer (Oxford: Clarendon Press, 1987), pp. 105-19; see also her *Metaphor and Religious Language*, passim.

28. I have gained much in my understanding of the issue of the divine incomprehensibility and other issues considered in this essay from the monumental two-volume dissertation of Gregory P. Rocca, *Analogy as Judgment and Faith in God's Incomprehensibility: A Study in the Theological Epistemology of Thomas Aquinas* (Ann Arbor: University Microfilms, 1989). See his article entitled "The Distinction between *Res Significata* and *Modus Significandi* in Aquinas's Theological Epistemology," *The Thomist* 55 (1991): 173-97.

utterly disparate. Christian talk about God employs terms like *faithful* and *good* but with unknown meanings. Other thinkers have understandably judged this account of Christian discourse as leaning too far in the direction of agnosticism. They have suggested that the meaning of the term *faithful* is identical whether it is applied to Kristen or to God. But when applied to God such terms single out perfections that exist in God to a supereminent degree.

A shorthand characterization for these alternative accounts of the kinship between literal utterances about God and those about Kristen goes like this: rationalist views take *faithful* to apply univocally to God and Kristen, while agnostic views take it to apply equivocally. But can the literal force of statements like "God is faithful" be understood in a way that avoids agnosticism on the one hand and rationalism on the other?

It may be helpful at this point to call upon a distinction that Aquinas found useful in sorting out these issues and advancing his own proposal for construing such statements in Christian discourse.[29] Drawing on the earlier work of grammarians, he distinguished three elements in utterances: the *res significata* (that to which reference is being made — e.g., a quality in Kristen), the *ratio nominis* (the concept by which this quality is specified — e.g., faithfulness), and the *modus significandi* (the grammatical form of the utterance, in this case a predication). According to this account, what makes a predication equivocal is that the *ratio nominis* of, for example, the homonym *bark* is different when it is applied to dogs than when it is applied to trees. What makes a predication univocal is that the *ratio nominis* of, say, the term *faithful* is the same whether it is applied to Kristen or to Jack. Sometimes, however, the terms we use cannot be classified in either of these ways. For instance, in the statements "Chocolate is good" and "Kristen is good," the *ratio nominis* of *good* applies to both subjects in some sense. Goodness in human beings is different from goodness in sweets, but it is perfectly appropriate to use *good* to cover both instances. This example helps us to see that univocal and equivocal predications do not exhaust the range of literal utterances. Terms like *good* resist classification within these alternatives. Such terms support analogous predications because in their various legitimate uses the *ratio nominis* is both the same and different with respect to the various *res significata* to which such predications apply.

---

29. Aquinas, *Summa theologiae* 1a.13. See also Rocca, *Analogy as Judgment and Faith in God's Incomprehensibility*, pp. 616-41.

Aquinas thought that this point was an important one for understanding a certain class of statements about God that have the form of literal utterances and ascribe some positive attribute to him, like "God is faithful" and "God is good." He thought that theories which explained these statements by reconstruing them as negative statements that deny limitations in God (like "God is unchangeable") or relative statements that affirm the outcome of his agency (like "God is the cause of goodness") were implausible in a way similar to theories which reconstrue them as nonliteral or metaphorical. Suppose that, like the term *good* when it is used to describe people and chocolate (and many other things as well), certain terms of perfection are predicated of God in an analogous way. In this case, one could say, to return to the example of goodness, that when we assert that "God is good," the *res significata* is the supreme reality of goodness as it exists in God identical with his very being, even though the *ratio nominis* is based on our ordinary uses of the term for the things familiar to us through our experience. On this account the crucial insight of negative theology is preserved at two points. First, the *ratio nominis* derives from the created order and in no way functions as a conceptualization of God's being. For this reason, such predicates are employed analogously rather than univocally or equivocally in assertions about divine being and activity. Second, the *modus significandi* of Christian talk about God — although taking the grammatical form of predications of attributes in the created order — could never capture the way in which such attributes exist in God. We have no way of specifying linguistically (indeed, we have no way of knowing) how God, who is sheer existence, can be said truly to be good, faithful, and so on without seeming to ascribe qualities to him in a way that implies potentiality and composition. To insist that the *modus significandi* of such predications of God differs from predications of created beings is to provide a linguistic rule that continually corrects for implications of our way of speaking that can never be true of God.

These remarks open the way to distinguishing literal from metaphorical predications in Christian discourse about God.[30] Terms of perfection have a literal but analogous sense in predications about God in that the perfections they ascribe are found supereminently in God, who

30. As Soskice states clearly in *Metaphor and Religious Language,* analogy is a type of literal speech: "The categories of univocal, equivocal and analogical are different in kind from that of metaphor. Thus, when we speak of God as infinite, perfect, or transcendent, we speak analogically of God . . . but not, as some have suggested, in a flagrantly pictorial or metaphorical way" (p. 66).

is their cause in creatures. Such terms have a nonunivocal sense in that their *ratio nominis* derives from creaturely concepts and in that their *modus significandi* is more appropriate to creatures than to God. Some terms of perfection can function in literal predications about God because their meaning is separable from their creaturely embodiments. Nothing prevents the literal ascription of such attributes as goodness, faithfulness, wisdom, and mercy to God because the meaning of these attributes does not entail the limitations characteristic of such perfections when they exist in the created order. Hence it can be said that predications of such attributes are more true of God than of creatures, even though we have neither a concept of divine goodness nor a way of signifying the goodness of God. Terms used literally of God apply primarily to him and secondarily to creatures. Recognition that the *modus significandi* differs with respect to predications about God corrects for any creaturely limitations associated with such terms. Thus, for example, in the assertion "God is the Creator, Redeemer, and Sanctifier," the fact that the divine agency produced temporal effects does not entail change or temporality in God. We correct for such limitations by noting that, while this assertion is literally true of God, we cannot specify this truth without using temporal categories.

Other terms (some of which are terms of perfection) function in metaphorical predications because the meaning of these terms is logically inseparable from their creaturely embodiments. The following assertions are examples of metaphorical predications (though nonetheless clearly reality-depicting): "God is angry," "God stretched out his mighty arm to save us," "God is a rock." Having an arm or being a rock are things attributed to God metaphorically because they entail the possession of bodily being, while anger entails bodiliness and emotions. Terms used metaphorically of God apply primarily to creatures and secondarily to God. The classification of such predications as metaphorical is a logical remark. There is no suggestion that such expressions are "merely" metaphorical or that they should always be "translated" into literal speech (although there might be occasions when this would be appropriate).

This nonreductionist account can specify the logical force of some of the different forms of utterance available to users of Christian discourse. To distinguish metaphorical from literal forms of predication and to defend the possibility that customary trinitarian language contains literal forms of speech is not to fall under the spell of an unwarranted literalism, as prominent versions of the reformist case imply. Rather, this account shows that a vigorous realism about the trinitarian presence in grace does not contravene the tradition's equally vigorous insistence on the incomprehensibility and ineffability of God.

V

We are now in a position to consider a second widely advocated revision of language about the triune God: the substitution of "Father/Mother" or "Mother" for the name "Father." There are two main arguments for this revision. The first is that here is the crucial instance where patriarchy is canonized and where it must be eradicated. The exaltation of fatherhood in God constitutes the chief legitimation of patriarchal patterns that have been oppressive of women and supportive of their exclusion from equal participation in the church and in society at large. This nearly metaphysical foundation for conceptions of female inferiority must at all costs be shaken and toppled. Christian women who feel the urgency of this objective have come to be persuaded that unless God can be called "Mother" it will be impossible for them to continue to participate in good conscience in the life of the Christian community.[31]

The second set of considerations favoring the use of "Mother" has a basis in the tradition itself. On this view of the matter, to call God "Mother" exploits resources furnished by strands in the tradition in which feminine traits are attributed to God. While it is admitted that the Bible never calls God "Mother," it describes him in terms of feminine and maternal characteristics. In addition, mystical literature is replete with feminine characterizations of the deity.[32]

This widely debated proposal has provoked objections from feminists and their critics as well. Some feminist authors argue that the attribution of feminine characteristics to God simply confirms the androcentric conceit of a superior male divinity who can with ease encompass feminine as well as masculine traits.[33] Others have argued that calling God "Mother" and attributing feminine traits to him reinforces the very stereotyping of women that feminists deplore.[34] Some feminists share with their critics doubts about a fundamental premise in the reformist case for calling God "Mother." There

31. See Carr, *Transforming Grace*, p. 141.
32. See the discussion in Hampson, *Theology and Feminism*, pp. 92-96; see also Johnson, "The Incomprehensibility of God," p. 462.
33. See Hampson, *Theology and Feminism*, p. 94.
34. See Heine, *Matriarchs*, p. 28.

is no evidence that societies in whose religions goddesses were prominent had a social structure any less patriarchal than those with male deities.[35] Still, while some feminists advocate a goddess religion either on the periphery of Christianity or in self-consciously post-Christian communities, others regard this suggestion as uninviting and alien, particularly if it involves the selective and artificial reconstruction of extinct polytheistic religions (whether ancient Egyptian, Mesopotamian, or Hellenistic, or combinations of these).[36] Some feminists argue that, while it might be desirable for God to be reconceived in feminine terms, such a reconceptualization would involve so profound a transformation of traditional Christianity as to be unworkable. It may well be thought that the incidence in the Bible of feminine imagery for God hardly supplies the basis for the conception of a feminine God in Christianity.[37] This admission might be a reason to develop another religion — not necessarily a goddess religion, but rather one in which the deity is not conceived in personal terms at all.[38]

In this connection, it is recognized that if the deity is thought to be personal, then talk about it cannot be gender-neutral or, for that matter, double-gendered. Some feminists view as muddled the suggestion that God be called "Father/Mother" in that it is impossible to visualize anything being both in any meaningful way, short of an unacceptable introduction of androgyny into the divine being. It is hard to see how any human could identify or pick out so utterly alien a being.[39] Some nonfeminist critics of the proposal under consideration voice the same objection and argue further that the language "Father/Mother" introduces a range of sexual images into the Christian conception of the deity that the Bible and the tradition scrupulously resisted.[40] There is plenty of evidence of a deliberate avoidance of such conceptions in the formative periods of Israel's faith when the community sought to distinguish itself from surrounding religious conceptions. The language "Father/Mother" seems to reintroduce

---

35. See Heine, *Matriarchs*, especially chap. 3, and Elshtain, *Public Man, Private Woman*, pp. 212-15.

36. See Heine, *Matriarchs*, pp. 44-48, and Hampson, *Theology and Feminism*, pp. 157-58.

37. See Hampson, *Theology and Feminism*, especially chaps. 3 and 5.

38. Hampson adopts this position in *Theology and Feminism*; see especially chap. 5.

39. See Heine, *Matriarchs*, chap. 1.

40. See Elizabeth Achtemeier, "Female Language for God: Should the Church Adopt It?" in *The Hermeneutical Quest*, ed. Donald G. Miller (Allison Park, Pa.: Pickwick Publications, 1986), pp. 97-114.

conceptions decisively rejected a long time ago. This consideration also bears on the proposal to refer to the Holy Spirit as "She." Whatever advantages such usage may seem to have from the feminist perspective, it introduces gender differentiation into speech about God and, in effect, sexual differentiation into the divine being. In addition, it is argued that "Father/Mother" and similar locutions in effect replace a trinitarian with a quaternitarian conception of God.[41]

The case against the substitution of "Mother" or "Father/Mother" for "Father" in talking about God and about the first person of the Trinity seems a strong one. But considerations suggested by the grammar of trinitarian confession can render this case decisive — particularly when viewed in the perspective of the divine invitation to created persons to enjoy the inner life of the Trinity.

It is possible to distinguish three senses in which the term *father* can be applied to God: metaphorically to the triune God, by appropriation to the first person, and literally and properly to the first person.[42] The third sense is absolutely crucial to Christian forms of speech that do justice to the reality of our incorporation in grace into the inner-trinitarian life.

In the first place, the term *father* can be used to refer to the triune God. In this way of speaking, the attribution of fatherhood to God is metaphorical. First, the term *Father* is meant to suggest the creator or personal principle of all that exists. Since fathers play an important role in the generation of their children, we use the term *father* as a metaphor for productions of various sorts, as when we say that someone has fathered an idea or an institution. On this basis, we can say that the triune God is the Father of the created order. While this is not a uniquely Christian way of speaking about God, there is plenty of biblical warrant for it. The suggestion is that God's creative agency in regard to the human race is describable in terms that evoke the intimacy, concern, attention, and engagement of a good father. Second, the term *Father* is metaphorical in reference to God in that its meaning entails the limitations of human fatherhood. Generation of progeny requires both a father and a mother and suggests sexual differentiation and engagement. For this reason, the metaphorical naming of the

41. See Frye, "Language for God and Feminist Language," p. 449.

42. See O'Brien's commentary in the Blackfriars edition of *Summa Theologiae*, pp. 239-51. See also Alvin F. Kimel, Jr., "The Holy Trinity Meets Ashtoreth: A Critique of the Episcopal 'Inclusive' Liturgies," *Anglican Theological Review* 21 (1989): 26. John W. Miller offers a defense of the name "Father" from the perspective of developmental psychology in *Biblical Faith and Fathering* (New York: Paulist Press, 1989).

triune God as "father" does not absolutely exclude the metaphorical naming of God as "mother." As we noted previously, the difficulties posed by such usage and the lack of unqualified biblical support for it rule out the simple substitution of the name "Mother" for "Father" in the public discourse of the community when the triune God is mentioned. But there seems to be no reason why private devotion and prayer might not afford scope for such usage — though not, as I shall argue subsequently, as a substitute name for the first person of the Trinity.

In addition to the metaphorical predications of the triune God as Father, the rule of appropriation permits the first person of the Trinity to be named "Father" just as he can be named "Creator." The personal property of unbegottenness provides the basis for such appropriation. As we saw earlier, an activity common to the three persons can be attributed by appropriation to the first person without implying that he acts independently of the other two when acting externally. Viewed as an essential term denoting the agential interaction of the triune God with creaturely reality, the name "Father" can be appropriated to the first person.

In its third use, the term *Father* serves as the preferred personal name of the first person of the Trinity. As we saw earlier, personal names of God are those that refer not to the agential interaction of the triune God with creatures but to the internal relations of the persons. They refer to what is true in God independent of the existence of creaturely reality and describe the intimate, eternal reality of the three persons. These personal names are inaccessible to creatures except by virtue of the divine revelation and the invitation to communion that this revelation entails.

The personal names "Father" and "Son" describe a familial intimacy of a particularly intense form. According to the Scriptures as they are read in the church, the "comings forth" *in* God are distinct from the coming forth of things *from* God. The trinitarian processions do not involve creation or causation of any kind, but they give rise to real relative opposition in God. The theological tradition has been challenged to the utmost of human reflective powers to show how this mystery can be understood, but there can be no way of gaining access to it except as invited and occasioned by the triune God. Thus we know that the first person is the Father because the Son calls him by that name; it is the Son's personal way of speaking of the Father. The same is true of the name of the Spirit. These names do not originate in our experience of God and his agency in the world, as do many of the essential names we use to speak of God. We have no basis for naming the persons of the Trinity by their proper names except their own "usage." Insofar as we become intimates of the Trinity by grace, we can learn to use these names as well. Since we have no uninvited basis for naming the persons, we have no grounds to prefer other terms to these personal names for the Trinity. These names are proper because they identify nonagential relations internal to the Trinity itself. The exclusive warrant for their aptness lies in Christ's revelation of the inner-trinitarian life. This consideration supports a decisive case against the substitution of the name "Mother" for "Father" when speaking of the first person of the Trinity.

This consideration is connected with the very structure of the revelation of the nearness and presence of God and what it promises for us. Christ is the son by "nature," and we are sons and daughters by adoption. What this means is that we are invited by the triune God to enter into the most intimate possible relation with the three persons, in that we are entitled to call the first person by the same name by which the Son calls him, by that proper, private, family name that is the Son's divine prerogative. In a treatise on the Lord's Prayer, St. Cyprian wrote, "Let us pray as God our master has taught us. To ask the Father in words his Son has given us, to let him hear the prayer of Christ ringing in his ears, is to make our prayer one of friendship, a family prayer. Let the Father recognize the words of his Son. Let the Son who lives in our hearts be also on our lips."[43] God's entire salvific initiative is seen to be the full and perfect incorporation of human beings into the life of the triune God. The adoptive filiation of human beings — their participation in the life of the Trinity in grace — is grounded in the natural filiation of the Son.

A final comment is in order concerning two further proposed revisions of traditional trinitarian language. Although the substitution of "Child" for "Son" cannot be positively excluded, it should be noted that it blurs rather than enhances the personal reality suggested by the relationship of son to father. At the same time, it carries a connotation of immaturity that the name "Son" does not.[44] Similarly, a string of impersonal or suprapersonal terms for God — "Heavenly Parent, Source, Eternal Spirit, Ground of Being" — while not thoroughly objectionable, strike one as inadequate. In terms of the analysis offered earlier, as substitutes for the metaphorical name "Father" as applied to the triune God, these

43. A passage assigned for the Readings on Tuesday during the first week of Lent in *The Liturgy of the Hours,* vol. 2 (New York: Catholic Book Publishing Co., 1976), p. 105.
44. See Bloesch, *The Battle for the Trinity,* p. 46.

expressions miss the very point of using "father" in this sense. They replace the connotations of the personal engagement of God with an impersonal, more nearly deistic conception of the Supreme Being. To be sure, as has been noted, some feminists admit that an impersonal conception of the deity is preferable to a masculine one and more plausible than a feminine one — an idea that seems to point the way toward post-Christian forms of feminist religiosity. It is hard to see how it is possible to remain true to the Christian conviction about God's nearness and presence to us if personal categories for speaking about this mystery are abandoned. To speak of God in impersonal or suprapersonal terms constitutes not a revision of Christianity but an alternative to it. In this connection one is reminded of St. Paul's rebuke to the Galatians: "Formerly, when you did not know God, you were in bondage to beings that by nature are no gods; but now that you have come to know God, or rather to be known by God, how can you turn back again to the weak and beggarly elemental spirits, whose slaves you want to be once more?" (Gal. 4:8-9).

VI

The concern to avoid androcentrism in our talk about God is an urgent one. In fact, of course, the tradition is unanimous in rejecting the sexual or androcentric connotations of the personal names "Father" and "Son." This is precisely the point of affirming that these names apply literally to the first and second persons of the Trinity. As we reviewed them earlier, the rules for construing literal predications about God require the exclusion of any limitations associated with the meaning of the predicates "father" and "son" when used to refer to creatures. Chief among these are connotations of superiority and subordination in generation, and the male characteristics of bodily beings who are men. In addition, the sexual differentiation presupposed to human generation is excluded, since there is no active/passive partnership in the generation of the Son.[45] When

45. In the *Summa Contra Gentiles* (4.11.19), Aquinas states, "One should note carefully that the fleshly generation of animals is perfected by an active power and by a passive power; and it is from the active power that one is named 'father,' and from the passive power that one is named 'mother.' Hence, in what is required for the generation of offspring, some things belong to the father, some things belong to the mother: to give the nature and the species to the offspring belongs to the father, and to conceive and bring forth belong to the mother as patient and recipient. Since, however, the procession of the

"Father" and "Son" are predicated of God, the *modus significandi* of these predications corrects for all creaturely limitations, including androcentrism. Male characteristics can be attributed to God only by way of metaphor, since such characteristics suppose bodiliness in their very meaning. It is crucial to the reformist feminist cause that the distinction between metaphorical and literal predications about God be recognized and maintained. This distinction provides the principal basis upon which to exclude androcentrism from conceptions of God.

In the absence of such a distinction, revision of traditional trinitarian language will appear to be the only means available by which to achieve this important objective. But in that case and in the name of negative theology, we would run the risk of subverting or obstructing the loving initiative of God the Father, Son, and Holy Spirit through our anxiety to find adequate words in which to address them — rather like a lover whose anxiety to find the right words to speak to her beloved leads her to postpone and delay indefinitely the intimacy beyond words for which her beloved longs. The speakability of the otherwise unspeakable mystery of the triune God is rooted in the gift of God's very self to us in grace.

Customary trinitarian language expresses the reality of the mystery of the triune God and our participation in the communion of life of the three persons. The triune God "who stands in need of no one gave communion with himself to those who need him," wrote St. Irenaeus.[46] Feminist objectives can be served neither by altering the language that names this mystery nor by preferring language that fails to do justice to its reality. No considerations of any kind can be advanced that would warrant the revision of the language in which the Father, Son, and Holy Spirit invite us to speak with them. "O abyss! O eternal Godhead! O deep sea! What more could you have given me than the gift of your very self?"

Word has been said to be in this: that God understands Himself; and the divine act of understanding is not through a passive power, but, so to say, an active one; because the divine intellect is not in potency but is only actual; in the generations of the Word of God the notion of mother does not enter, but only that of father. Hence, the things which belong distinctly to the father or to the mother in fleshly generation, in the generation of the Word are all attributed to the Father by sacred Scripture; for the Father is said not only 'to give life to the Son' (cf. John 5:26), but also 'to conceive' and 'to bring forth'" (vol. 4, trans. and with an introduction by Charles J. O'Neil [Notre Dame: University of Notre Dame Press, 1975], p. 90).

46. From the treatise *Against Heresies* (4.14.2-3) assigned for Readings on Wednesday during the second week of Lent in *Liturgy of the Hours*, 2:177.

The God Who Likes His Name:
Holy Trinity, Feminism, and
the Language of Faith

ALVIN F. KIMEL, JR.

HOW TO NAME God? This question has been acutely put to the American churches in the past decade by feminist theologians, and with profound effect. Substantive changes in the language of faith are now taking place: the triune name of Father, Son, and Holy Spirit is routinely ignored; baptisms are occurring in the names of inclusive substitutes; liturgies are composed that omit references to God as Father or Jesus as the Son, some of which directly address God as Mother and other feminine titles; the masculine pronoun for the deity is said to be inappropriate usage. Important reasons and theologies are advanced to justify these changes. The thesis of this essay is that these changes must result in an alienation from the gospel. The particularities of the biblical revelation that are now so offensive to contemporary sensibility are at the very heart of profession of faith in the Holy Trinity. The triune God has named himself, and he likes his name.

The Grammar of the Triune Name

For we are bound to be baptized in the terms we have received and to profess belief in the terms in which we are baptized, and as we have professed belief in, so to give glory to Father, Son, and Holy Ghost.[1]

1. Basil, *Epistle* 125.3, in *A Select Library of Nicene and Post-Nicene Fathers of the*

This essay, revised and expanded for this volume, originally appeared in *Interpretation* 45 (April 1991): 147-58, and is reprinted here with permission.

In the course of defending the divinity of the Holy Spirit, Basil the Great enunciated the above grammatical rule for Christian faith and worship. His argument is that our common baptism into the name of the Holy Trinity functions to shape the public life of the people of God. As we have been baptized, so must we formulate and confess our creedal belief; as we profess our faith, so must we pray, composing our worship and doxology accordingly. Baptism, creed, liturgy — all together form an interlocking whole, a language of faith; yet within this network of communication the sacrament of baptism plays a formative role. It structures both our profession of faith and our offering of praise. The God who is acclaimed in the ecumenical symbol of the church and the God who is invoked in the communal liturgy is to be the selfsame God into whom we are first baptized.

Holy baptism thus governs and shapes the language of faith, and it does so with divine authority: "Go therefore and make disciples of all nations," Christ Jesus enjoins his followers, "baptizing them in the name of the Father and of the Son and of the Holy Spirit" (Matt. 28:19). Explicitly written as a command of the exalted Lord enthroned in the fullness of eschatological power and presented in the canonical and apostolic tradition, the baptismal mandate exercises a normative authority in the life of the Body of Christ.[2] There is no other, more authoritative tradition over against which to appeal. By the decree of Christ, the church is sent into the world and instructed to initiate believers into the triune name of God. Either we obey this command or we simply cease to be the church. Holy baptism, therefore, is the primal embodiment of the gospel and is properly construed as foundational and constitutive of ecclesial life. From baptism flows our discourse and prayer, ordered by that verbally identified reality into which we are sacramentally incorporated.

Given this morphotic and configurative function of the baptismal naming, Basil insists on the traditional wording, rejecting all alterations and substitutions. "It is enough for us," he states, "to confess those names which we have received from Holy Scripture, and to shun all innovations about them."[3] The canonical mandate, in other words, is received as

---

Christian Church (NPNF), 2nd series, 14 vols. (New York: Christian Literature Co., 1890-1900), vol. 8; see also *Ep.* 159.2. Basil's brother, Gregory of Nyssa, offers similar instruction: see *Ep.* 2, in NPNF, vol. 5.

2. On the contingent finality of sacramental mandate, see Robert W. Jenson, *Visible Words: The Interpretation and Practice of Christian Sacraments* (Philadelphia: Fortress Press, 1978), pp. 6-9; on the baptismal mandate, see pp. 126-35.

3. Basil, *Ep.* 175; see also *Ep.* 188.1; *Ep.* 125.3.

dogma, binding on the community as a whole. The significance of the dogma goes far beyond the establishment of a common rite of initiation. It is grammatical instruction stipulating the speech and practice of the church: God is to be named as Father, Son, and Holy Spirit.[4]

Trinitarian speech pervades the corporate life of Christians. We begin the liturgy with the invocation of the triune God. We join our voices in threefold creedal acclamation in the confession of the catholic faith. The eucharistic prayer is classically given distinct trinitarian form: the Father is praised and thanked for the blessings of creation and salvation, the crucified and resurrected Jesus is remembered and extolled, and the outpouring of the Spirit is besought upon both the community and the oblations of bread and wine. Whenever the church acts in the ministry of Christ, whether to bless, absolve, anoint for healing, or ordain to office, the triune God is explicitly proclaimed, entreated, glorified, named. Even our shortest prayers and collects are concluded in trinitarian doxology: "through Jesus Christ our Lord, who lives and reigns with you [the Father] and the Holy Spirit, one God, now and for ever."

At the center of ecclesial society is the proclamation of the gospel and the recounting of the biblical narrative. We tell the story of the God of Israel, creator of the universe, who gathers a people to himself in holy covenant, binding them to him by name and sacrifice and prophetic word. For hundreds of years, the Lord shapes, breaks, and molds his people, forming them into faithful witnesses and joyful worshipers. Through Abraham, Sarah, Jacob, Moses, Miriam, Aaron, Deborah, David, Isaiah, the Lord executes his salvific will in the history of his Israel. Finally, in the fullness of time, he sends his Son, the promised Messiah, to offer atonement for the sins of the world. . . . We tell the story of Jesus of Nazareth, the Son of this God, born to and into God's people. Prophet, teacher, healer, eschatological bearer of the future kingdom — Jesus confronts Israel with the exhilarating message of the incomparable love of the One he calls Father, a love revolutionary in its unconditionality and grace, a love that demands new garments and new wineskins, conversion and discipleship, death and rebirth. This Jesus, however, is intolerable; his message and presence are too threatening. He is betrayed, denounced, humiliated, and executed as a common criminal. But

---

4. Gregory of Nyssa describes each of the titles within the triune name as "a rule of truth and a law of piety"; see *Against Eunomius*, in NPNF, vol. 5. See also Deborah Malacky Belonick, "Revelation and Metaphors: The Significance of the Trinitarian Names, Father, Son and Holy Spirit," *Union Seminary Quarterly Review* 40/3 (1985): 31-41.

the Father vindicates his Son on Easter morning by raising him from the dead and exalting him to his right hand, establishing him as the destiny and conclusion of the universe. . . . We tell the story of the Holy Spirit, the divine breath that moved over the waters of chaos at the beginning of creation, who spoke through Moses and the prophets, who anointed Jesus with unconquerable power to heal the sick, exorcize evil, and raise the dead. It is this Spirit the risen Christ promises to pour out on the community of faith, and by this Spirit the church is driven into the world to proclaim the gospel and bring sinners into the new creation of the kingdom. Into him each believer is immersed and born anew, baptized into the love of the Father and the Son.

"The Church," writes George Lindbeck, "is fundamentally identified and characterized by its story."[5] At any point in history, the church of Jesus may be picked out as that assembly proclaiming the narrative of the Father, Son, and Holy Spirit and promising it as good news to its hearers. We speak not of deity-in-general but of the God who is self-revealed in the biblical drama: the three divine actors who together, in essential, ontological unity, accomplish the salvation of humankind. The trinitarian narrative functions as the paradigm through which both deity and creation are interpreted and provides the foundational content and vocabulary for our preaching, liturgy, and theology. By this story the imaginative life of the church is renovated; through it the people of God envision their mission and ministry; in it all believers find forgiveness for their past and hope for their future. It is the story of the triune God that is summarized and encapsulated in the triune name. The threefold appellation may thus be said to identify the church, for it encompasses that story which the church tells and must tell in order to be the church. When we are baptized into this name, we are baptized into a way of life, being, and speaking constituted by the evangelical narrative of the trinitarian God. But if the triune name and the manifold trinitarian namings of the language of faith identify the Christian church, this is so because the appellation first and primarily identifies the God of the church. Father, Son, and Holy Spirit is our deity's *proper name.*[6]

5. Lindbeck, "The Story-shaped Church: Critical Exegesis and Theological Interpretation," in *Scriptural Authority and Narrative Interpretation,* ed. Garrett Green (Philadelphia: Fortress Press, 1987), p. 165.

6. See Robert W. Jenson's important discussion in *The Triune Identity: God According to the Gospel* (Philadelphia: Fortress Press, 1982), pp. 1-20. Cf. Catherine Mowry LaCugna, "The Baptismal Formula, Feminist Objections, and Trinitarian Theology," *Journal of Ecumenical Studies* 26 (Spring 1989): 235-50. For an interesting linguistic analysis,

Proper names are distinguished from common nouns in that they signify singular and unique objects rather than classes of objects. A proper name allows us to designate a specific something, separating it from the anonymity of existence for communication, study, use, love. Even deities need proper names. We need to be able to identify which one we are addressing, worshiping, obeying, fleeing.

In the resurrection of Jesus, God declares his name of the new covenant: Father, Son, and Holy Spirit (Matt. 28:19). This name articulates the apostolic experience of God in Christ. It identifies the specific deity we are talking about or praying to as being precisely the God of the New Testament. Each term within the name links us to God's historic self-disclosure; each is grounded in the salvation narrative; each interprets the other two. "Father" refers specifically to the holy transcendence whom the Nazarene knows as *Abba,* to whom he bids us pray, "Our Father, who art in heaven." "Son" designates Jesus in unique filial relationship to the Father: "This is my Son, whom I love; with him I am well pleased" (Matt. 3:17). "Spirit" is the communal love and life and future of the aforementioned Father and Son. Together these mutually coordinated names form one name, a name proper and personal to the Christian God.[7] Thus the holy creator introduces himself to the world.

With the name of Father, Son, and Holy Spirit, our God is clearly identified and our experience of deity linguistically defined. Each believer, by the mandate of the risen Christ, is baptized into this name, initiated

---

see Christian J. Barrigar, "Protecting God: The Lexical Formation of Trinitarian Language," *Modern Theology* 7 (July 1991): 299-310.

My argument presumes both the possibility and the actuality of God's self-naming in our historical experience. That God in fact has named himself in the history of Israel and the person of Jesus Christ seems clear from the biblical narrative and the importance of the holy name of God acknowledged throughout the Scriptures (see, e.g., Exod. 3:13-15; 33:19; John 17:6, 11-12). Feminist discussions of naming God almost universally premise that all historical names originate exclusively in humanity and are thus *our projections upon the deity.* Thus limited by both creatureliness and cultural experience, traditional names enjoy only relative authority. Each generation is obligated to search for new namings more adequate to their religious experience and understanding. This is true of even irenic presentations: for example, see James E. Griffiss, *Naming the Mystery: How Our Words Shape Prayer and Belief* (Cambridge: Cowley, 1990). For more radical analyses, see Rosemary Radford Ruether, *Sexism and God-Talk: Toward a Feminist Theology* (Boston: Beacon Press, 1983); Sallie McFague, *Models of God: Theology for an Ecological, Nuclear Age* (Philadelphia: Fortress Press, 1987); and Brian Wren, *What Language Shall I Borrow? God-Talk in Worship: A Male Response to Feminist Theology* (New York: Crossroad, 1989).

7. Jenson, *The Triune Identity,* pp. 12-13, 17-18.

into a concrete, verbally determined relationship with the triune God of the Scriptures. From this point on, we meet and experience the deity from within the trinitarian narrative proclaimed in the community of faith. We are the people of the Trinity, shaped and formed by the threefold appellation of our God. "Baptism into the name of 'the Father, and the Son, and the Holy Spirit,'" writes Catherine LaCugna, "means incorporation into the power and essence of God, into the history and story of God, into the life and heart and identity of God."[8] The dominical command, therefore, both sanctions the triune name by divine revelation and establishes it as a necessary function in our knowledge of the living God.[9] God gives himself to us in his name and by his name defines our experience of him as triune. We know the deity as the Holy Trinity because we speak, pray, hear, believe, and worship his personal name.

The proper-name function of the trinitarian formula has recently been criticized by Ted Peters. He argues that proper names refer arbitrarily and ostensively and are consequently transliterated from language to language, whereas the triune formula is universally translated. According to Peters, this indicates that "Father," "Son," and "Holy Spirit" are metaphorical titles.[10] Peters' argument can be met by acknowledging that *within the triune name,* "Father," "Son," and "Spirit" are relational, denominating titles of address, each of which signifies one of the three persons of the Trinity, and each of which are analogically correlated to human realities. They are therefore rightly and necessarily translated into equivalent terminology as the gospel moves into new cultures. However, when brought together — as they are, for example, in holy baptism or the Gloria Patri — they function as *one* personal name identifying the *one* Christian God and separating that God from all other deities. This means that the trinitarian formula enjoys a special status as a proper name. As Robert Jenson notes, "A proper name is proper just insofar as it is used independently of aptness to the one named, but it

---

8. LaCugna, "The Baptismal Formula," p. 248.

9. See Thomas F. Torrance, *The Trinitarian Faith: The Evangelical Theology of the Ancient Catholic Church* (Edinburgh: T. & T. Clark, 1988), p. 70.

10. Peters, "The Battle Over Trinitarian Language," *Dialog* 30 (Winter 1991): 47-49. Peters does emphatically affirm the trinitarian names as nonexchangeable symbols inextricably tied "to the event of revelation and salvation itself." Thus, he concludes, "to bypass the biblical terms in favor of some substitutes is to identify with a God other than that of Jesus Christ" (ibid., p. 49). Susan Brooks Thistlethwaite also rejects the proper-name function of the trinitarian formula, also posing the false dilemma of metaphor or name, but her substantive argument is minimal and flawed by misreadings of her sources (patristic and contemporary). See "On the Trinity," *Interpretation* 45 (April 1991): 165-67.

need not therefore lack such aptness."[11] Of decisive importance here is the fact that the baptismal institution stipulates initiation into the *name* (singular) of the Father, Son, and Holy Spirit.[12]

As we have been baptized, so must we confess and pray our faith. We are incorporated into a distinctive language and grammar. The great Anglican divine Richard Hooker saw this quite clearly in the sixteenth century. In defending the Anglican form of the Gloria Patri against Puritan objections, he wrote,

> Baptizing we use the name of the Father, of the Son, and of the Holy Ghost; confessing the Christian faith we declare our belief in the Father, and in the Son, and in the Holy Ghost; ascribing glory unto God we give it to the Father, and to the Son, and to the Holy Ghost. It is "the token of a true and sound understanding" for matter[s] of doctrine about the Trinity, when in ministering baptism, and making confession, and giving glory, there is a conjunction of all three, and no one of the three severed from the other two.[13]

By our baptism we are charged and authorized to name God by his revealed name: Father, Son, and Holy Spirit. This triune name forms the identity of the Christian church and structures the grammar of catholic belief and practice. Christians cannot be *Christian* if they refrain from speaking the trinitarian language. To replace or alter the triune formula is to repudiate the creed, church, God of our baptism.

We may examine two recent proposals. First, "Creator, Redeemer, Sanctifier." This formula does not and cannot function as a proper name: it does not identify; it does not specify which God we are talking about. All putative deities presumably create, redeem, and sanctify, as well as do numerous other things.[14] Furthermore, within classical trinitarian

---

11. Jenson, *The Triune Identity,* p. 18. Is it really the case, as Peters claims, that proper names are never translated from language to language? Native American names, for example, immediately come to mind. Contrary to Peters, Christian Barrigar recognizes that common nouns can become proper nouns. He calls this rhetorical process, "whereby a proper name is given on the basis of a leading quality," antonomasia. See also Jenson's brief response to Peters in *Dialog* 30 (Summer 1991): 247.

12. At the turn of the century the Anglican theologian Francis J. Hall wrote, "The most perfect name of God is that of the Blessed Trinity — *The Father, the Son and the Holy Ghost* — a name which is at once singular in number, and threefold in articulation" (*Dogmatic Theology,* vol. 3: *The Being and Attributes of God* [New York: Longmans, Green & Co.,1909], p. 229).

13. Hooker, *Of the Laws of Ecclesiastical Polity* 5.42.8.

14. Jenson, *The Triune Identity,* p. 17.

theory these *ad extra* activities are understood as contingent cooperative works of the Godhead. The Father creates, redeems, and sanctifies through the Son by the Spirit. Each person of the Trinity is fully involved in the functional activities of deity. Or, to put it slightly differently, God was not always creator, redeemer, sanctifier; he has become such by his free decision.[15] Within the divine life of the Godhead, however, the deity is eternally Father, Son, and Holy Spirit. This is his name before time and forever.

Second, there is "Mother, Lover, Friend." This truly feminist alternative raises serious difficulties of another sort. Perhaps what is most objectionable is that it so clearly seeks to evade the biblical narrative; it is so clearly our own invention. Speak "Father, Son, and Holy Spirit" and immediately we know we are speaking of the God of the New Testament. But to what deity does "Mother, Lover, Friend" refer? What story are we telling when we name divinity thus? And if we are telling a different story, are we not creating a new religion? This and all similar formulas sunder the church from the evangelical narrative by which we identify our God as well as ourselves. They "disrupt the faith's self-identity at the level of its primal and least-reflected historicity."[16] Furthermore, this formula is open to the same criticism as that given "Creator, Redeemer, Sanctifier." Are the terms to be interpreted only in relationship to us, in which case we are presented not with a proper name but with *ad extra* descriptions, or are they to be interpreted *within* the name? It is difficult indeed to reconcile the latter with the biblical story, not to mention Christian sensibility!

The God Who Is Known

Therefore it is more pious and more accurate to signify God from the Son and call Him Father, than to name Him from His works only and call Him Unoriginate. For the latter title does nothing more than signify all the works, individually and collectively, which have come to be at the will of God through the Word; but the title Father has its significance and its bearing only from the Son.[17]

15. Torrance, *The Trinitarian Faith,* pp. 87-89.
16. Jenson, *The Triune Identity,* p. 17.
17. Athanasius, *Against the Arians* 1.34, in NPNF, vol. 4. My interpretation of Athanasius is deeply influenced by some of Thomas Torrance's work: "Athanasius: A Study in the Foundations of Classical Theology," in *Theology in Reconciliation* (Grand Rapids: William B. Eerdmans, 1975), pp. 213-66; "The Doctrine of the Holy Trinity According

In his debate with Arianism, Athanasius was compelled to address the question of how we name God. In their philosophical understanding of deity, his opponents were fond of calling God "the unoriginate," which they evidently believed spoke clearly and accurately of the divine being. The term emphasizes that divinity is self-sufficient in its transcendent reality, plainly distinguished from the contingent creation. Unlike the misleading anthropomorphic and metaphorical terminology of the Bible, the term "unoriginate" is true and precise. Athanasius responded by noting that such naming is a form of negative theology which speaks of God not as he is in his inner reality, not as he is in his divine nature, but only in his relationship to that which is made by him out of nothing. It thinks of divinity exclusively in terms of creaturely being; it apprehends God solely by his works. We believe the universe to be created, contingent, finite, dependent for its existence upon the deity; thus we call God the unoriginate and creator, thereby contrasting him with that which he is not. We construe him in his absolute difference and distance from us. For Athanasius, while what we say in this regard may be true — but as Gregory Nazianzen commented, if we do not know what something is, how can we specify what it is not?[18] — it does not yet grasp God in his internal being. It is analogous to inferring the character and personality of Shakespeare by reading only his plays. Such an approach to divinity is inherently anthropocentric, for it conceives the deity from a center in ourselves and the created order, not from a center in God. Ultimately, we end up knowing simply ourselves turned inside out. We are thus no better off, says Athanasius disparagingly, than the Greeks.[19]

To name God the Father and the Son is to speak of the deity as he is in the immanent reality and relations of his divine essence. It is thus to know him objectively, truly, accurately. When we name God Father, we are naming him neither by abstraction from creation *(via negativa)* nor by infinite extension of creation *(via eminentiae)* nor by self-projection (my-

---

to St. Athanasius," *Anglican Theological Review* 62 (Fall 1989): 395-405; and *The Trinitarian Faith,* especially pp. 47-145.

18. Gregory Nazianzen, as cited by Torrance in *The Trinitarian Faith,* p. 50.

19. Athanasius, *Against the Arians* 1.33. It is important to note that much feminist theology shares this "Greek" ignorance of God. Sallie McFague is representative in her explicit denial of the possibility of knowing deity in its internal being (*Models of God,* pp. 223-24, nn. 2, 3, 5). Theological reflection is grounded not in God's self-communication in Christ but in personal (feminist) experience of self and world. Rejection of the Nicene doctrine of the Holy Trinity is thus inevitable. McFague reduces the trinitarian model to an expression of the transcendence-immanence dialectic (ibid., pp. 183-84).

thology); rather, we are identifying him by the eternal Son, who belongs to the divine being and is proper to the Godhead, who has projected himself into creation in the person of Jesus Christ. The playwright has stepped into his play. In Jesus our theological reflection and knowing are ontologically grounded *in God.* The Father/Son relation, therefore, must have primacy over the creator/creature relation in our apprehension of divinity.

In the Nicene Creed the catholic church confesses the following: "We believe in one Lord, Jesus Christ, the only Son of God, eternally begotten of the Father, God from God, Light from Light, true God from true God, begotten not made, *of one Being* with the Father" (emphasis added). The key phrase, which originates from the creed adopted by the Council of Nicaea in A.D. 325, is the affirmation of the incarnate Christ's oneness of being *(homoousios)* with the Father. While this confession was vague enough to permit a plurality of interpretations at the Council, it clearly excluded Arius and his followers and they knew it. It is to Athanasius that we owe the triumph of the *homoousion* in its evangelical radicality: Athanasius forcefully declared that our Lord's oneness of being with the Father was to be understood in terms of *identity.* Jesus of Nazareth — the creed speaks of the incarnate Son and not the *logos asarkos* ("Word without flesh") — fully possesses the divine *ousia* ("essence"). In the divide between creator and creature, Jesus is to be located clearly and categorically on the creator side. The Nazarene is God; the Galilean rabbi is a member of the Holy Trinity. Thus Jesus Christ in the fullness of his incarnate humanity, the man born of Mary and crucified under Pontius Pilate, the friend of tax collectors and sinners, is constitutive of the deity. In the words of Athanasius, "And so, since they are one, and the Godhead itself one, the same things are said of the Son, which are said of the Father, except His being said to be Father."[20]

God has incarnated himself in time and space. He has come as Man, as the specific human being Jesus who lived and died in the first century in an obscure Middle Eastern country. The theological consequences of this confession are revolutionary. In Jesus we may now know God directly and personally. The deity has presented himself to us as an

---

20. Athanasius, *Against the Arians* 3.4. On the constitutive significance of the Incarnation for the Godhead, see Torrance, *The Trinitarian Faith,* pp. 135-90; Karl Barth, *The Humanity of God* (Atlanta: John Knox Press, 1960), pp. 37-65; and Karl Barth, *Church Dogmatics,* 4 vols., ed. G. W. Bromiley and T. F. Torrance (Edinburgh: T. & T. Clark, 1935-1969), II/2:94-194.

object.[21] This objectivity is of course mediated — we meet God only in his assumed creaturely form — but it is an objectivity nonetheless in which the triune bestows *himself* to our human knowing. As with any other object, we may now pick out our God: "There he is. That one, the son of Mary. He is the One I worship." In the concrete particularity of the crucified Jew, we apprehend the deity, in and by the Spirit, according to his divine nature. We may use the word "revelation" to describe the gift of divine objectivity, but only as long as we understand it to mean more than creaturely modeling or the conveying of information, to mean the communication of God's very self.

Once the Incarnation has taken place, once the eternal Word has made himself object in Jesus, we may no longer look anywhere else to find divinity. God has chosen the time, the place, and the media by which we may meet him. The humanity of Christ is the trysting grounds of our love affair with the Father, Son, and Holy Spirit. The faithful man Jesus therefore *defines* and *interprets* the reality of God. Identical in being with the Father, our Lord embodies — finally, decisively, conclusively — the character, life, and essence of deity. Karl Barth expresses this powerfully:

> The Word of God does not just come to us through the man Jesus of Nazareth, as though we could later have heard it and known it in itself and apart from him. The Word of God is this man as man, and always and inescapably it is spoken to us as the reality of this man and not otherwise. This is God's mercy, that precisely in the reality, no, as the reality of this man, God is Immanuel, God with us, God among us.[22]

This is not christological triumphalism (christo-fascism, as some put it), as though the church is parsimoniously restricting the knowledge of deity to a select few. It is the humble recognition that in Christ we are, by grace, confronted with the fullness of divinity and given access to the immanent triune being. Jesus is the second person of the Trinity, risen into the divine society of the Godhead. Consequently, we may not evade the Nazarene or go behind his back in our quest to find deity, for the holy God has terminated our quest by becoming the object Christ and enacting his trinitarian life among us.

It is crucial to understand that Jesus reveals God the Father precisely

---

21. See Barth, *Church Dogmatics,* II/1:1-62.

22. Barth, quoted by Bruce Marshall in *Christology in Conflict: The Identity of a Saviour in Rahner and Barth* (New York: Basil Blackwell, 1987), p. 129.

in his identity as the begotten Son.[23] Jesus is not the Father but the Son, and it is as the Son that he discloses the Father. The divine Fatherhood and Sonship are correlative: the Father is the Father *of* Jesus, and Jesus is the Son *of* the Father. Neither can be conceived or known apart from the other. The two are united in being and agency: Jesus is the place where the Father is encountered. From Christ we learn who the Father is; in him we learn from the Father who the Son is. We meet both simultaneously and coincidentally in mutually defining relationship. Thus our Lord can insist that he is the sole mediator of our knowledge of the Father: "I am the way and the truth and the life. No one comes to the Father except through me. . . . Anyone who has seen me has seen the Father" (John 14:6, 9). This is the theological explanation why "Father" is used infrequently in the Old Testament to refer to God, and used even less frequently as a term of address. Until Jesus arrives on the scene, the God of Israel is known only in his undifferentiated oneness, addressed principally by the ineffable name of Yahweh. Only the Son can introduce us to his Father.

We may now return to the text of Athanasius with which we began this section. When the church names God as the Father and the Son, it is speaking of the creator in his inner reality, referring to relations subsisting in the divine *ousia*. Unlike the Arians, Athanasius insists that we truly know the deity in Jesus Christ — as Father, Son, and Holy Spirit. When challenged why we may and must use this language, he replies that it is sanctioned and authorized by the divine Word himself who knew "whose Son He was."[24]

A God with History

From the ancient church on, the root trinitarian assertion is that the history God has with us, as Jesus the Israelite with his "Father" in their Spirit, is not merely a manifestation or revelation of God but *is* God.[25]

---

23. See Torrance, *The Trinitarian Faith*, pp. 59-60.

24. Athanasius, *Against the Arians* 1.34. Precisely because the Father/Son language is grounded in God's economic self-communication, its semantical relation to God is *real* and not conventional. See Thomas F. Torrance, *Reality and Evangelical Theology* (Philadelphia: Westminster Press, 1982), especially chap. 3.

25. Robert W. Jenson, *America's Theologian: A Recommendation of Jonathan Edwards* (New York: Oxford University Press, 1988), p. 91. Throughout this section I am indebted to Jenson's creative and provocative work.

That God should have a history is nonsense in view of our inherited understandings of deity. God, after all, is that reality which dwells outside time as the creator of time. He is eternal, the pure actualization of being, immune to the changes and movements of temporality. We may speak of God as the Lord of history, but we well understand this to mean his providential guidance of history from the external vantage point of heaven or supernature. We certainly do not mean he is an actor within history, making history, having history, living through history. On the contrary, God in his timelessness is impassible, ultimately unaffected by the events and happenings of the world.

Yet there at the heart of the Christian gospel is the story of God become Man, a God who is born, who is raised in Nazareth, who breathes and eats and cries and laughs and loves, a God who suffers and dies. This is a God who in Christ both affects and is affected by the world, a God who has, in the words of Jonathan Edwards, "really become passionate to his own."[26] The gospel is thus the claim that the deity has a history — the history of Jesus in Israel. The Word has become flesh; the Crucified is *homoousios* with the Father; the eternal Son lives in and through time. It is the peculiarity of this God that he is identified not by abstract attributes but by narrative — by historical descriptions and biblical stories. We remember what he has done in the past and we anticipate his promises of what he will do in the future: "Christ has died. Christ is risen. Christ will come again." Our God is eternal in that he is faithful in time to his promises. The divine transcendence is properly described as eschatological futurity or temporal unsurpassability.[27]

That the eternity of the biblical God is irreconcilable with the eternity of Greek philosophy is increasingly apparent today, but for almost two thousand years Christians have been convinced that the being of their God must be defined by its transcendence of temporality. Thus the theological problem: How do we keep together the divine timelessness and the narrative descriptions of God's history? Well, it's not easy. Athanasius is a case in point. On the one hand, he is emphatic in his insistence that in Jesus, God has come as Man, a full-blooded human being, with biography and all. On the other hand, all the Hellenistic predicates also obtain: God is incorruptible, immaterial, unchangeable, and so forth. In his fidelity to

26. Edwards, quoted by Jenson in *America's Theologian*, p. 118.
27. See Robert W. Jenson, *God After God* (Indianapolis: Bobbs-Merrill, 1969), pp. 123-35; and Jenson, *The Triune Identity*, pp. 138-84.

Scripture, Athanasius did not attempt to resolve the paradox; but later theologians, particularly in the West, did try, and usually at the expense of the biblical understanding.

When a Greek comprehension of deity is joined to the biblical narrative of God's history with us in Christ, dualism appears at two closely connected points. One, the pre-existent Word, the *logos asarkos,* is posited as the inner-trinitarian ground of creation.[28] God creates and saves the world not through Jesus of Nazareth but through his metaphysical discarnate double. Two, the processions of the immanent Trinity are divorced from the historical missions of the economic Trinity.[29] The begetting of the Son and the spiration of the Spirit become ineffable events unconnected to salvation history. With the occurrence of these two moves, the way is prepared for the proliferation, beginning in the Middle Ages, of treatises devoted to *De Deo Uno,* quite independent of *De Deo Trino.* Thus the divine being of the Godhead is *uninterpreted* by the historical event of Jesus. We determine through our philosophy, ideology, culture, and religious experience what deity is, and then we assert that this deity is somehow and in some way "revealed" through Jesus. Within modern Protestant reflection this ultimately results in the theological irrelevance of the Nazarene and renders the doctrine of the Holy Trinity disposable.

The contemporary renaissance in trinitarian theology — perhaps best summarized under the dictum "The economic Trinity is the immanent Trinity" — has made possible a fresh appropriation of the trinitarian grammar. Robert W. Jenson is the foremost American representative of this new theological paradigm. Jenson asks us to move from a theology of revelation to a theology of constitution: it is not that the stories of Jesus, the Father, and the Holy Spirit vaguely reveal the divine being; they are *constitutive* of it. The historic relationship in the Spirit between Christ Jesus and his Father, lived out in the conditions of first-century Palestine and eternally established in the resurrection and ascension of our Lord, is the triune life of the Godhead. The Christian God has a history, and just as the identity of every human being is defined by the life he or she lives, so the identity

28. Robert W. Jenson, "The Christian Doctrine of God," in *Keeping the Faith,* ed. Geoffrey Wainwright (Philadelphia: Fortress Press, 1988), p. 47.

29. Robert W. Jenson, "A 'Protestant Constructive Response'" to Christian Unbelief," in *American Apostasy: The Triumph of "Other" Gospels,* ed. Richard John Neuhaus (Grand Rapids: William B. Eerdmans, 1989), pp. 65-66.

of our God is defined by his history with us. God *is* the Father who grieves for the death of his Jesus at Calvary. God *is* the Son who prefers the company of harlots and tax collectors to that of religious professionals. God *is* the Spirit poured out on the church on the day of Pentecost who will bring us into the kingdom of the Father and the Son. The Holy Trinity does not lie behind or under these historical events; the Trinity is constituted in and by them. There is no other God but the God who knows himself as this history. "Truly, the Trinity is simply the Father and the man Jesus and their Spirit as the Spirit of the believing community," writes Jenson. "This 'economic' Trinity is *eschatologically* God 'himself,' an 'immanent Trinity.'"[30]

The confession of God as Father, Son, and Holy Spirit directly challenges our antecedent construals of divinity. Specifically, it compels us to reconceptualize the doctrines of divine timelessness and impassibility, which have led theology into a disastrous divorce between the immanent reality of God and his historic self-objectification in Jesus Christ. The biblical history of Jesus is the history of God — this is the radical trinitarian claim. The economic relations between the Galilean rabbi crucified under Pontius Pilate and the transcendent reality whom Jesus names his Father and the eschatological power who creates the future from the ashes of death belong to the internal life of the Godhead. Unlike most theological methods that lead us away from history and the temporalities of the created order into the infinite, unknowable, homogeneous abyss of motionless deity, the doctrine of the Trinity fully grounds our knowledge of the living God in history, in that concrete history which God knows as his own, in that dominical history constitutive of the divine *ousia*. Thus the trinitarian confession will always be offensive to culture and church, for it binds theological reflection to the givens of Scripture and requires us to think divinity through the particularities of the Nazarene. But if we are so bound, so is God. And here is the heart of the offense: the God of the gospel freely establishes his triune identity not in pretemporal hiddenness but in and by specific — and quite visible, audible, and knowable — finite realities and events. We may not, therefore, transcend God's history with us in Christ, for not only does God not endeavor to transcend it but he incorporates it into his eschatological eternity. The trinitarian narrative is foundational within the Godhead. When the deity seeks to know who he

---

30. Jenson, *The Triune Identity,* p. 141. Cf. Jürgen Moltmann, *The Trinity and the Kingdom,* trans. Margaret Kohl (San Francisco: Harper & Row, 1981), pp. 151-78.

is, he looks at Jesus the Israelite; when he seeks to understand who he has been and will be, he tells himself the biblical story of the Father, Son, and Holy Spirit.

The new nonsexist liturgies of the Episcopal Church *(Prayer Book Studies 30)* illustrate the direction of moderate feminism today. They aver a trinitarian theology while simultaneously abstracting from the divine historicity: "We are challenged with being faithful to the creedal tradition of the Church, while, at the same time, naming the God who is 'One in Three and Three in One' in non-gender specific terms."[31] One specific way this is worked out in the texts is the virtual elimination of the vocative "Father." With the exception of the Lord's Prayer, God is addressed only as "God." When the Trinity is understood eschatologically, however, all such efforts to evade the particularities of the biblical revelation are shown to be both futile and apostate. Apart from the constituting temporal events of the evangelical narrative, the doctrine of the Holy Trinity is meaningless. Expunge the trinitarian namings of the language of faith and the triune God does not come to speech.

As Geoffrey Wainwright has observed, Jesus' use of "Father" as an address to God must be distinguished, though not separated, from the figurative use of "father" (or "mother") as a way of describing the deity's care for humankind.[32] The linguistic reason for this is that kinship terms, when used in direct invocation and discourse, have unique reference and

---

31. *Commentary on "Prayer Book Studies 30," containing Supplemental Texts* (New York: Church Hymnal Corporation, 1989), p. C-20. Abstraction from the biblical story, usually combined with a nonchristological apophaticism, underlies the argumentation of virtually all moderate feminist theologians who wish to remain nominally trinitarian while at the same time advocating inclusive language for God. The result is linguistic iconoclasm. See, for example, Gail Ramshaw Schmidt, "De Divinis Nominibus: The Gender of God," in *The Word and words*, ed. William D. Watley (Princeton: COCU, 1983), pp. 15-25; and Elizabeth A. Johnson, "The Incomprehensibility of God and the Image of God Male and Female," *Theological Studies* 45 (1984): 441-65.

If the Father/Son relation is prior to the creator/creature relation in our knowledge of divinity, and if the temporal relations of Jesus, the Father, and the Spirit are constitutive of the Godhead, then the apophatic prehension of deity, achieved by appeal to God's radical transcendence and the negation of created reality, must be called into question. The incomprehensibility of God is posited *in* Jesus Christ, not outside of him. Only at the foot of the cross do we behold the true mystery of Godhead. See Barth, *Church Dogmatics*, II/1: 186-204, 346-48.

32. Wainwright, "The Doctrine of the Trinity: Where the Church Stands or Falls," *Interpretation* 45 (April 1991): 119-20. Also see Robert W. Jenson's contribution in the present volume, "The Father, He . . . ," pp. 103-4.

thus "behave like proper nouns."[33] That is to say, they specifically identify their referents and thereby function as personal names. When, for example, my daughter calls out "Daddy," I simultaneously recognize both her voice and the title, and immediately conclude she is speaking to me and respond accordingly. However, if another little girl calls out "Daddy," I do not respond, for I know the title does not, in this case, apply to me. Within the circle of my family, the vocative "Daddy" personally identifies me to my children and establishes me in a specific kind of relationship with them, and them with me. To the rest of the world I am known as "Al" or "Alvin," but to my children I am known as "Daddy." Indeed, if my children were to begin addressing me by some other name — even if they were to name me by my given name — this act would be a virtual denial of our familial relationship.

Within Christian usage "Father" is not just one of many metaphors imported by fallen sinners onto the screen of eternity. It is a filial, denominating title of address *revealed* in the person of the eternal Son. "On the lips of Jesus," Wolfhart Pannenberg states, "'Father' became a proper name for God. It thus ceased to be simply one designation among others. It embraces every feature in the understanding of God which comes to light in the message of Jesus. It names the divine Other in terms of whom Jesus saw himself and to whom he referred his disciples and hearers."[34] Jesus names the holy God of Israel *Abba*, "Father," thereby expressing, and indeed effectuating, the intimate inner communion between them, a unique relationship of knowing and love. "No one knows the Son except the Father, and no one knows the Father except the Son" (Matt. 11:27). By this historical address God is acknowledged as the hope, joy, ultimate source, and final authority in our Lord's life; by this address he is *constituted* as the Father. The dominical naming occurs *within* the being of the Godhead. It is an event of the divine biography,

---

33. Randolph Quirk, Sidney Greenbaum, Geoffrey Leech, and Jan Svartik, *A Comprehensive Grammar of the English Language* (New York: Longman, 1985), p. 292. The authors note that in English such terms are usually capitalized. It is the failure to recognize the referential, denominating function of familial terms that has rendered unsatisfactory, up to this point, much of the scholarly discussion of metaphor and the Christian naming of God as Father.

34. Pannenberg, *Systematic Theology*, vol. 1, trans. Geoffrey W. Bromiley (Grand Rapids: William B. Eerdmans, 1991), p. 262. Also see Claude Geffre, "'Father' as the Proper Name of God," in *God as Father?* ed. J.-B. Metz and Edward Schillebeeckx (New York: Seabury Press, 1981), pp. 43-50; and Ralph Quere, "'Naming' God 'Father,'" *Currents in Theology and Mission* 12 (February 1985): 5-12.

an eternal act of self-differentiation occurring in time. When uttered by the incarnate Word, "Father" (defined exclusively by Christ himself in the totality of his filial existence) is a creative, performative word of eschatological power — analogous, on a different level, to God's speaking forth the universe in Genesis 1 — which eternally calls into being the One who loves his Son beyond all imaginings, beyond all conditions and limits. The Father *receives from Jesus,* through the power of the Spirit, his hypostatic identity *as Father.*

Here we admittedly move beyond those traditional reflections that protect the impassibility of the Father by constituting his identity solely in his pretemporal begetting of the preincarnate Son: the deity of the Son is conceived purely passively; it is the Father, the fount of all divinity, who is the active, generating agent.[35] The Son thus contributes nothing to the personal reality of the Father, and therefore his temporal naming of God must be construed as only metaphorical human projection, perhaps illustrative of (or by feminist lights, perhaps not!) but ontologically irrelevant to the unoriginated *hypostasis* (person). But when we break down the wall between the immanent and economic Trinities — thereby allowing actual traffic between creator and creature — we can begin to think more dynamically and dialectically about the *reciprocal* relations between the divine persons.[36] Jesus is the Son, for he is eternally generated of the Father, sent into the world to accomplish the salvific will of his God, but the Father is the Father in that he is eternally named and glorified as such by Jesus. The Father is personally defined by the filial address, trusting obedience, sacrificial death, and joyful worship of his begotten Son. He submits himself to the embodied judgment of the Nazarene. "What there is to being God the Father is being addressed as 'Father' by the Son, Jesus," Robert Jenson writes. "*In that* Jesus cries, 'Father, into your hands . . .' and *in that* he who says this will be the final event, *there* is the Father."[37]

---

35. Jenson suggests that the traditional asymmetry of the trinitarian relations and the location of the divine monarchy in the Father may also be due to male sexism and dominance. See *The Triune Identity,* pp. 143-44.

36. According to Wolfhart Pannenberg, "The reciprocity in the relationship of the divine persons makes room for the constitutive significance of the central salvation-historical events for the Godhood of God and thus for the significance of time and change for the divine eternity" ("Problems of a Trinitarian Doctrine of God," *Dialog* 26 [Fall 1987]: 252).

37. Jenson, *The Triune Identity,* p. 175. This does not mean, as Jenson points out, that the Father is created by Jesus; rather, Jesus, as the Son, is an essential, irreplaceable term in the reciprocal interpersonal relationship. There is no Father apart from the historical

From the man Jesus, God hears the words of filial invocation and receives that love, self-giving, and affirmation evoked by his own love for his only begotten child; from his Son he apprehends who he is in his divine Fatherhood. The Father knows himself only in and from his Son.

The reciprocity and mutuality of this relationship in the Spirit structures the inner communion of the Trinity and demonstrates the infinite love of the Father for Christ Jesus. In that God withholds nothing in autonomous self-possession but in love and risk communicates the fullness of his being and life to Jesus, and in that he remains faithful to Jesus through the agonizing rupture of Calvary, and in resurrection subjects the cosmos to his Son's absolute Lordship and authority (Matt. 28:18; Phil. 2:9-11), and in that he awaits from Jesus the deliverance of the kingdom into his hands (1 Cor. 15:20-28), God becomes utterly dependent on his Son for his identity, completely open to Christ's defining confession of him: "Father, the time has come. Glorify your Son, that your Son may glorify you" (John 17:1). Thus the temporal, historical event of Christ's relating to God as Father, so abundantly and clearly presented in the Gospels, is simultaneously an eschatological event whereby the deity constitutes and differentiates the divine being. The consubstantial relationship between the Father and the Son is confirmed and established on Easter morning: by the resurrection there forever stands before the first person of the Godhead the One who calls him *Abba*.

If the Father is constituted by Jesus Christ's invocation of him, then we can see the impossibility of substituting "Mother" (or some other variant) as a term of filial address. Perhaps Jesus could have addressed God as his mother (though cogent reasons might be offered in explanation or

---

person of Christ, yet there is no time when the Father was not. Needless to say, this can be true only if eternity is conceived eschatologically: God is and always has been Father, Son, and Holy Spirit because he always *will* be (ibid., pp. 140-41). Jenson's elimination of a *logos asarkos* raises the speculative question "Would God have been triune apart from his community with us in the man Jesus (if, e.g., he had never created the universe)?" Jenson answers yes but says that we are unable to state *how* — nor need we be concerned about this, for God is Holy Spirit and therefore eternally free in his eschatological self-determination (ibid., pp. 141, 146-47).

It should be noted, however, that in his diagram of the inner-trinitarian relations (ibid., pp. 142-43), Jenson does not specify the Son's filial address as constitutive of the Father. He does assert that the Spirit with the Son frees the Father from pretemporal persistence, but he is somewhat vague and general on this point. May we offer the suggestion that God unoriginate is freed from frozen timelessness by the Holy Spirit through the Son's temporal naming of him as Father.

support of his choice not to do so), in which case the first person of the Godhead would likewise be constituted as Mother. But the decisive fact is that "Father" is Jesus' chosen term, and the identity of the economic and essential Trinities precludes us from tampering with this language. In trinitarian doctrine, historical contingency may enjoy theological finality.[38]

The divine Son commands Christians to address his Father as their Father: "Pray then like this: Our Father, who art in heaven, Hallowed be thy Name" (Matt. 6:9). This filial invocation is a privilege of adoption in Christ Jesus. By baptism we are incorporated into the humanity of our Lord and his eternal relationship with the Father in the power of the Spirit (Gal. 3:26–4:6). In Christ we are inserted into the trinitarian conversation of the Godhead. The prayer, praise, and intercession of God the Son are realized in the lives of his adopted brothers and sisters. "For you did not receive a spirit that makes you a slave again to fear," the Apostle heralds, "but you received the Spirit of sonship. And by him we cry, '*Abba,* Father'" (Rom. 8:15). By the gift of the Spirit the church is drawn into the vicarious worship of its risen Lord; by grace we now share in the eschatological address of the Son. With and through Christ we boldly name God "Father" and enter into intimate fellowship with him. Thus the structure and languaging of our prayer and discourse both manifests the triune society of the Godhead and enacts our participation in it. As Jenson observes,

> Christians bespeak God in a triune coordinate system; they speak *to* the Father, *with* the Son, *in* the Spirit, and only so bespeak *God.* Indeed, they live in a sort of temporal space defined by these coordinates, and just and only so live "in God." . . . The decisive gospel-insight is that if we only pray *to* God, if our relation to God is reducible to the "to" and is not decisively determined also by "with" and "in," then it is not the true God whom we identify in our address, but rather some distant and timelessly uninvolved divinity whom we have envisaged. We pray indeed *to* the Father, and so usually address the Father simply

38. See Jenson, *The Triune Identity,* pp. 13-16, 107. Wolfhart Pannenberg has also recently argued that Jesus' naming of God as Father is final and nonsubstitutable. Unlike our ordinary symbolic and metaphorical language for the deity — which is extrinsic to the divine being and thus exchangeable — the Son's historical naming of God is internal to the Godhead. Consequently, to substitute another name or title for "Father" is to turn to another God. "Where the word 'Father' is replaced by something else," Pannenberg concludes, "there can be no warrant anymore that we are talking about and addressing the same God as Jesus did" (*An Introduction to Systematic Theology* [Grand Rapids: William B. Eerdmans, 1991], pp. 31-32).

as "God." But we address *this* Father in that and only in that we pray *with* Jesus *in* their Spirit. The particular God of Scripture does not just stand over against us; he envelops us. And only by the full structure of the envelopment do we have this God.[39]

Where is God? He is in heaven, we say. Where is heaven? It is wherever Christians invoke the Father with their brother Jesus in his Spirit. By our trinitarian naming the triune God is actualized in time.

The God of the gospel identifies himself in and by the particularities of the biblical narrative. Our prayer to God and our speech about him, therefore, will be true only to the extent that they are controlled by the temporal events of the evangelical history. We may find this frustrating, offensive, and scandalous; but the sovereign God nevertheless remains free to be for us whom he has eternally elected to be in the history of Jesus of Nazareth: Father, Son, and Holy Spirit.

Conclusion

The Holy Trinity is the God who has named himself Father, Son, and Holy Spirit. By this name and by the narrative comprehended within it, the identity of the living God is revealed and constituted. Through it we are given access into the triune life of the Godhead. Current feminist proposals for altering the language of faith therefore have the most profound significance.[40] If I am correct in my preceding analysis, these changes touch the substance of the gospel. To abandon or reject the trinitarian naming is to create a new religion, a new God. Yet this crisis carries within itself a wonderful opportunity: it may and indeed must provoke our theological reflection to a radical appropriation and reformulation of the trinitarian dogma. When this occurs, we will see that the triune God is not a deity of sexism and patriarchy but the God of the gospel who saves men and women from their sin and liberates them for love, discipleship, and joyous fellowship in the Father, Son, and Holy Spirit.

39. Jenson, *The Triune Identity,* pp. 47, 51.
40. One of the most pressing needs today, especially in light of the popular metaphorical theology of Sallie McFague, is the formulation of a *trinitarian* understanding of theological language. The work of Karl Barth is suggestive here. See George Hunsinger, "Beyond Literalism and Expressivism: Karl Barth's Hermeneutical Realism," *Modern Theology* 3 (1987): 209-23.

Trinitarian Worship

GEOFFREY WAINWRIGHT

IN HIS CONVERSATION with the Samaritan woman, Jesus declared, "The hour is coming and now is, when the true worshipers will worship the Father in Spirit and in Truth, for such the Father seeks to worship him" (John 4:23). The hour is coming and now is. Some today would say that that hour has been and gone. Scarcely anyone has a good word for the Father. The Truth as it is in Jesus seems to many to be far too particularistic a basis on which to deal with modern science or other religions. When the Spirit is invoked, it is often to bless opinions and activities that have little to do with the virtues the Paraclete encouraged and enabled in the New Testament. As an elderly Roman Catholic said after Vatican II, "These days the Holy Spirit is telling people to do a lot of things the Holy Ghost would never have allowed." It appears to me that liberal, and perhaps even moderate, Protestantism in North America in particular is in greater danger than ever of losing hold of the doctrine of the Trinity, which has been a touchstone of historic Christianity. To see what is at stake, it will be useful to return to the origins and deep structures of trinitarian doctrine. We shall discover that its roots are sunk in worship, and that it finds its most significant continuing expression in the liturgy.

A good place to begin will be the treatise of St. Basil the Great entitled *On the Holy Spirit*.[1] Written around the year 373, Basil's work expounds and

1. See Migne, *Patrologia Graeca* 32:67-218. Scholarly edition by Benoît Pruche in *Saint Basile de Césarée, Sur le Saint Esprit*, rev. ed., Sources chrétiennes 17 (Paris: Cerf,

---

This chapter is a lightly revised version, now equipped with notes, of a lecture that first appeared in written form in *The New Mercersburg Review,* Autumn 1986, pp. 3-11.

defends trinitarian worship and doctrine in the face of Arian and Arianizing interpretations and attacks. It is the first fully systematic treatise to set forth the two complementary patterns of trinitarian devotion and understanding that have marked the Christian liturgy ever since. The argument centers on two pairs of Greek prepositions used in the formulation of praise to God: "Glory to the Father through *[dia]* the Son in *[en]* the Holy Spirit" and "Glory to the Father with *[meta]* the Son together with *[syn]* the Holy Spirit."

The first formulation appears to be the more ancient, and it was the more widely used in Basil's day. The Arians appealed to it, however, in an attempt to condemn the Nicenes out of their own mouths. This phrasing, it was alleged, implies a subordination of the Spirit and the Son to the Father, which is precisely what the Arians taught, to the point indeed of making the Son and the Spirit creatures of the Father. Basil of Caesarea undertook to defend the Orthodox meaning and use of the doxology with "through" and "in." He argued that all God's activity in creation, redemption, and sanctification takes place "through the Son" and "in the Spirit." It was, therefore, appropriate that our grateful response should occur "in the Spirit" and reach the Father "through the Son." Thus our thanksgiving corresponds to God's dealings with the world, the divine "economy."

This "mediatorial" pattern of God's relation with us and our relations with God does not, however, imply that the Son and the Spirit are creatures or are in any way less than God. To the contrary. Following a procedure already advanced by St. Athanasius in his *Letters to Serapion,*[2] Basil appeals to the faith confessed at baptism. Baptism takes place "in the name of the Father and of the Son and of the Holy Spirit." Not only are the three there ranked together, but our salvation is a work of God, and its agents cannot be less than God. Only God can give participation in God. When, therefore, we think of God in very being, a "coordinated" form of doxology is appropriate. It corresponds to the three mutually indwelling persons. While Basil is not always persuasive in the patristic precedents he cites for his use of the "with" form of the doxology, he has made a fair systematic case for its matching the immanent life of the God whom we know in the economy. Within a decade, the Ecumenical Council

---

1968). Modern English translation by David Anderson in *St. Basil the Great: On the Holy Spirit* (Crestwood, N.Y.: St. Vladimir's Seminary Press, 1980).

2. See Migne, *Patrologia Graeca* 26:529-676. Modern English translation by C. R. B. Shapland, *The Letters of St. Athanasius Concerning the Holy Spirit* (London: Epworth Press, 1951).

of Constantinople would not only reaffirm the Nicene faith in Jesus Christ as "Lord," "the only Son of the Father, eternally begotten of the Father, begotten, not made, consubstantial with the Father"; it would also confess the Holy Spirit as "Lord" and "Life-Giver," "who with the Father and the Son together is worshiped and glorified."

Having had St. Basil lay bare for us the deep structures of trinitarian faith and worship, we can now examine its New Testament origins. Its ground plan can be found there, as well as most of the building blocks with which the church would construct its developed and refined formulations in liturgy and doctrine. Here we can draw help from the important seventh chapter in the work of the Italian Benedictine Cipriano Vagaggini, *Il senso teologico della liturgia.*[3]

In the New Testament, Vagaggini finds a "way of communion between God and humankind" that can be described in the following circulatory fashion:

> Every good gift comes to us from the Father, through the medium of Jesus Christ his incarnate Son, in the presence of the Holy Spirit; and likewise, it is in the presence of the Holy Spirit, through the medium of Jesus Christ the incarnate Son, that everything must return to the Father and be reunited to its end, the most blessed Trinity. This is the Christological-Trinitarian activity of the sacred history of salvation, the plan of God in the world. The whole structure of the liturgy presupposes this activity, without which the liturgy would be incomprehensible.[4]

Christian worship, like the salvation it celebrates and advances, is summed up in the movement "from the Father, through Christ, in the Holy Spirit, to the Father *[a Patre, per Christum, in Spiritu Sancto, ad Patrem]*." While the full cycle can rarely be found in single New Testament passages, there is an abundance of fragmentary arcs that allow us to divine the whole.

The Epistle to the Ephesians is particularly rich in this regard. There is, for example, the opening benediction (1:3-14):

> Blessed be the God and Father of our Lord Jesus Christ, who has blessed us in Christ with every Spiritual blessing. . . . In [Christ] you

---

3. See the English translation by L. G. Doyle and W. A. Jurgens, *Theological Dimensions of the Liturgy* (Collegeville, Md.: Liturgical Press, 1976), in particular pp. 191-246.

4. *Theological Dimensions of the Liturgy,* pp. 191-92.

too have heard the word of truth, the gospel of your salvation, and have believed, and you have been sealed with the promised Holy Spirit, who is the guarantee of our inheritance until we acquire possession of it, to the praise of [God's] glory.

Or the cultically flavored passage, 2:18-22:

Through [Christ] we both [Jews and Gentiles] have access in one Spirit to the Father. So then you are no longer strangers and sojourners, but you are fellow citizens with the saints and members of the household of God, built upon the foundation of the apostles and prophets, Christ Jesus himself being the cornerstone, in whom the whole structure is joined together and grows into a holy temple in the Lord; in whom you also are built into it for a dwelling place of God in the Spirit.

Or again, the doxology of 3:20-21:

Now to [God] who by the power at work within us [i.e., the Spirit; cf. verse 16] is able to do far more abundantly than all that we ask or think, . . . be glory in the church and in Christ Jesus to all generations, for ever and ever.

Or there is the very concise passage in Galatians, 4:4-6:

When the time had fully come, God sent forth his Son, born of a woman, born under the law, to redeem those who were under the law, so that we might receive adoption. . . . And because you are God's adopted children, God has sent the Spirit of his Son into our hearts, crying, "Abba! Father!"

It is also apparent that the Christians of New Testament times had begun to draw conclusions from the work of Jesus Christ and apply them to his person. By the fifties, the apostle Paul was able to draw on an even earlier hymn for the prospect that at the name of Jesus every knee would bow, and every tongue confess that "Jesus Christ is Lord, to the glory of God the Father." Philippians 2:5-11 there makes an astonishing echo of Isaiah 45, one of the most "monotheistic" passages in the Old Testament, and uses of Christ the name "Kyrios," by which the Greek version of the Old Testament designates Yahweh. The one whom Thomas acclaims as "My Lord and my God" (John 20:28) is the risen Jesus, "the Word made flesh" (1:14); he "was in the beginning with God" and "was God," and "through him were made all things" (1:1-2). By 2 Timothy 4:18 and 2 Peter 3:18 Christ is receiving doxology as Lord and Savior. And in the book of Revelation every creature addresses "to the one who sits upon the throne and to the Lamb . . . blessing and honor and glory and might for ever and ever" (5:13). In his Letter to Adelphius, Athanasius fully embraces, and indeed actively exploits, the implication that the worship of Christ would be idolatry, were Christ not truly God.[5]

With the dubious exceptions of 1 Corinthians 6:19-20 and Philippians 3:3,[6] there is no case in the New Testament where the Holy Spirit is an object of worship as distinct from an enabling medium. Yet we have seen the systematic logic of a move from agency to being. And there are notable examples in liturgical history for praise and prayer addressed specifically to the Holy Spirit. Hymns in particular range from the Byzantine Pentecostarion "Basileu ouranie" and the Golden Sequence "Veni, Sancte Spiritus," through a large batch of Wesleyan texts so addressed, to the most recent Pentecostalist choruses. There is a scriptural basis for this in the Fourth Gospel, when Christ speaks of "another Comforter," who comes from the Father at his request and accomplishes divine functions. Usually it is "with the Father and the Son together" that the Holy Spirit "is worshiped and glorified."

To sum up so far: we have seen how, in its origins and structure, trinitarian worship and doctrine is closely bound up with the nature of salvation: its source, its giving and reception, its celebration and enjoyment, its end. All of this implies, according to Christian faith, the one God who works tripersonally and is in very being tripersonal: Father, Son, and Holy Spirit.[7] This deep structure has been transmitted in the official liturgies of the church. It has always needed interpretation and has often been under threat. What, now, are the difficulties in our particular context?

At the outset I hinted at difficulties with the sufficiency and finality, and therefore the reality, of the Incarnation. Some Christians may be tempted to weaken here for the sake, at least in part, of external apologetic in the face of other and shifting worldviews.[8] But the most acutely felt

---

5. Athanasius, *ad Adelphium* 3-4 (Migne, *Patrologia Graeca* 26:1073-77).

6. For Augustine's exegesis of these two texts, see my book entitled *Doxology: The Praise of God in Worship, Doctrine and Life* (New York: Oxford University Press, 1980), pp. 91-93.

7. See William J. Hill, *The Three-Personed God: The Trinity as a Mystery of Salvation* (Washington, D.C.: Catholic University of America Press, 1982).

8. See my essay entitled "The Doctrine of the Trinity: Where the Church Stands or Falls," *Interpretation* 45 (April 1991): 117-32.

internal difficulty in our time and place seems to concern the designation of the second and first persons of the Trinity as Son and Father, the latter being the sharpest problem of all. In efforts to avoid it, some are being led, perhaps involuntarily, away from the Trinity altogether. I shall suggest that here, too, it is the reality of the Incarnation that is at stake when the designations "Father" and "Son" are questioned. But let us for a moment isolate the problem of "Father."

Objections to calling God "Father" are of three kinds. The first has a background in Freudian psychology. "God the Father" or "the Father God" would then be the projection, onto a cosmic or even transcendent screen, of early experiences or unresolved neuroses. On Freud's own terms, we should be in the presence of an illusion. The second kind of objection is related to the social and cultural situation. With the breakup of the patriarchal family, or perhaps even the family as such, it is difficult to find at the human end a reference point for the analogical attribution of Fatherhood to God. The third kind of criticism is the most biting of those expressed from within the church. It alleges that "Father" as a divine name is a reflection and buttress of sexist male dominance among humankind and even in the church. What can be replied on each of these three counts?

If taken strictly, the projectionist interpretation will, after the manner already of Feuerbach, reduce all theology to anthropology; the position cannot be refuted on terms acceptable to such of its proponents, but such proponents have in fact stepped outside historic Christianity. When the position is advanced in a more benign form, it is compatible with the view that the God who loves humankind accommodates to our psychological processes. Yet there is always the danger that we shall idolatrously exchange the Creator for the creature (cf. Rom. 1:18-25). Our "images" of God must be permanently open to correction by God's own self-revelation. But that will bring us back precisely to the Incarnation, which I shall treat again presently.

With regard to our social and cultural situation today, there is (I think) an interesting piece of counterevidence in the fact that several popular television series find it possible and desirable to present families, and even fathers, in a positive — indeed, affectionate — light; and that a leading comedian, Bill Cosby, can write a sympathetic bestseller under the title *Fatherhood*.[9] Theologically, it is in any case important to know which end of an analogy is determinative. According to Ephesians 3:14-15, it is

9. Cosby, *Fatherhood* (New York: Doubleday, 1986).

the divine Father from whom every earthly fatherhood is named. The God revealed by Jesus is the corrective norm for every human father. The Incarnation again![10]

In the matter of sexism, I have no wish to support the oppression of any group of Christians, or indeed any human being at all, by any other. On the contrary. The injunction for those who would be followers of Christ is to mutual deference and service (e.g., Mark 10:42-45). But sympathy for some aspects of a cause, as with the position of women in society and in the church, is no reason for acquiescence in other tendencies of a movement that are dangerous, or even erroneous, but are not necessarily intrinsic to the cause. Proposals for linguistic change that threaten trinitarian worship and doctrine are to be resisted. Let me also state carefully the arguments for retaining the trinitarian name of Father, Son, and Holy Spirit.

Feminist theologians who seek change in the divine name often stress the figurative or (as they say) metaphorical character of human speech in reference to God.[11] Now metaphor is not a simple category any more than the literal is.[12] It might be better to see "metaphorical" and "literal" as rough designations for ranges on a linguistic continuum. To this matter I shall return. But even supposing that all human God-talk were somehow metaphorical, it would not necessarily follow that all metaphors were equally appropriate or authorized or that they all functioned in the same way. We might have reason for holding that some metaphors were not exchangeable but rather indispensable and performed special functions.[13]

---

10. For a "secular" recognition (i.e., one that prescinds from substantial theological questions of normativity) of this kind of movement in connection with religious language, note the following passage from Kenneth Burke: "Whether or not there is a realm of the 'supernatural,' there are *words* for it. And in this state of linguistic affairs there is a paradox. For whereas the words for the 'supernatural' realm are necessarily borrowed from the realm of our everyday experiences, out of which our familiarity with language arises, once a terminology has been developed for special theological purposes the order can become reversed. We can borrow back the terms from the borrower, again secularizing to varying degrees the originally secular terms that had been given 'supernatural' connotations" (*The Rhetoric of Religion* [Berkeley: University of California Press, 1970], p. 7).

11. See, for example, Sallie McFague, *Metaphorical Theology* (Philadelphia: Fortress Press, 1982).

12. For theologically interesting discussions of metaphor, see Janet Martin Soskice, *Metaphor and Religious Language* (Oxford: Clarendon Press, 1985); and Roland M. Frye, "Language for God and Feminist Language: Problems and Principles" (Princeton: Center for Theological Inquiry, 1988).

13. In his collection of essays entitled *Divine Nature and Human Language* (Ithaca:

Among the wide range of figurative language used with divine reference in the Scriptures are the following similes:

> Thus says the Lord:
> "Behold, I will extend prosperity to
>   [Jerusalem] like a river,
> and the wealth of the nations like an
>   overflowing stream;
> and you shall suck, you shall be carried
>   upon her hip,
> and dandled upon her knees.
> *As one whom his mother comforts,*
> *so I will comfort you;*
> you shall be comforted in Jerusalem."
>
> (Isa. 66:12-13, my italics)

> Jesus said:
> "O Jerusalem, Jerusalem. . . .
> *How often would I have gathered your children*
> *together as a hen gathers her brood under*
> *her wings,* and you would not!"
>
> (Matt. 23:37, my italics)

It is in accord with those texts that Julian of Norwich, when speaking of the maternal characteristics of God manifested in Christ, should have in mind the attitudes and acts of the Godhead as such *toward us* — "*our* Mother." Julian does not use "Mother" to designate the relations of the trinitarian persons *among themselves*. They remain Father, Son, and Holy Spirit.

Psalm 103:13 employs the following simile:

> As a father pities his children,
> so the Lord pities those who fear him.

Some of the language of Jesus in the Sermon on the Mount may remain in the same range of metaphor, as when he refers to the divine care for

---

Cornell University Press, 1989), William P. Alston argues against "irreducible metaphors" in theology, denying that what is said in metaphors could not, in principle, be said, at least in part, in other terms. But he does not argue *to* the interchangeability of metaphors in talk of God. To the contrary, he argues *from* the perception that some talk of God, at least, is literal.

the birds of the air and the lilies of the field and argues *a fortiori* for the tender loving care of "your heavenly Father" toward his listeners. The fact that the hymn "Veni, Sancte Spiritus" can call the Holy Spirit also "father of the poor" suggests that paternal care is an attitude of the whole Godhead as such toward us.

In these last cases we have seen comparisons drawn from positive human experience — whether of motherhood or fatherhood — to illustrate God's attitudes toward the world and people. But we have not yet reached the question of the trinitarian name. Here we need to look at the Epistles and, above all, the Gospels for the Father-Son relationship. It quickly becomes obvious that, if we are dealing with a metaphor, it is a highly privileged one. If a distinction between the metaphorical and the literal is to be maintained, I would hold that we have now moved toward the literal end of the scale.[14] Better still, in this case of Father and Son we have to do with *primary* language. Let us examine the key evidence.

Joachim Jeremias has highlighted the significance of Jesus' address of God as "Abba."[15] While the uniqueness of this use may be hard to prove, it is a striking characteristic of Jesus that he should address his prayers by this intimate term which expresses both affection and respect when used by a child to address its father. The Aramaic word is transliterated at Mark 14:36, and we may suppose it to lie behind the Greek "Pater" when this occurs in accounts of Jesus praying in every strand of the gospel tradition. Jesus appears to have chosen this as the most appropriate way of expressing his relationship to the one who sent him and with whom he stays in constant touch (cf. John 11:41-42). The implications of that for Jesus' own identity are brought out in, for instance, Matthew 11:25-27:

> At that time Jesus declared, "I thank thee, Father, Lord of heaven and earth, that thou hast hidden these things from the wise and understanding and revealed them to babes; yea, Father, for such was thy gracious will. All things have been delivered to me by my Father; and no one knows the Son except the Father, and no one knows the Father except the Son and any one to whom the Son chooses to reveal him."

14. This is an *ad hominem* way of stating a point that would really require a full exposition of my understanding of the principle of analogy and its ontological assumptions and consequences in religious and theological use.

15. See especially Joachim Jeremias, *The Prayers of Jesus* (London: SCM Press, 1967).

The Word incarnate can *define* language. In this context, "Father" and "Son" *mean* who the first two persons of the Trinity *are* and what the relation between them *is*. It is the divine ontology that sets the meaning of the terms, not an already established meaning of the terms that dictates the divine being.[16] The content of the Father-Son relationship, when expressed and lived out in the terms of the Incarnation, is to be discerned from the significant words and deeds of Jesus and the events of his life, death, and resurrection.

We cannot know "from the inside" the relationships among the trinitarian persons. The best hints provided in Scripture are those of a mutual indwelling that does not exclude the first person being what the Cappadocians would call "the fount of deity." In any case the relationships are such that, when they are turned "ad extra," the Son can reveal the Father:

> Philip said to [Jesus], "Lord, show us the Father, and we shall be satisfied." Jesus said to him, "Have I been with you so long, and yet you do not know me, Philip? Whoever has seen me has seen the Father; how can you say, 'Show us the Father'? Do you not believe that I am in the Father and the Father in me?" (John 14:8-10)

> No one has ever seen God; the only Son, who is in the bosom of the Father, he has made him known. (John 1:18)

The self-revelation of God in Christ becomes determinative, Christians believe, for all our understanding of God and of God's relation to the world and to us, and consequently of our proper response to God and of proper intra-human relationships.

In sum, it seems to me that the trinitarian name of God is *given* to us with Jesus' address to "Abba, Father," his self-understanding and career as "the Son," and his promise of the Holy Spirit. Christian reflection upon the divine self-revelation and the experience of salvation it brought led to the conclusion of an eternal divine Tri-unity. Classical Christian worship has therefore constantly followed the structure expressed in the two complementary formulations — mediatorial and coordinated — ex-

16. Georges Florovsky spoke of the *transfiguration* of human speech in this connection: "Man is created in the image and likeness of God — this 'analogical' link makes communication possible. And since God deigned to speak to man, the human word itself acquires new depth and strength and becomes transfigured" ("Revelation and Interpretation," in *The Collected Works of Georges Florovsky*, vol. 1: *Bible, Church, Tradition: An Eastern Orthodox View* [Belmont, Mass.: Nordland, 1972], in particular p. 27).

pounded and defended by Basil. And it has normatively employed the given name of the one God — Father, Son, and Holy Spirit — whenever the Trinity has been solemnly invoked. Thus the historic identity of the Christian faith is at stake if that structure is obscured or the best name we have is abandoned. It is vital that the structure and the name be maintained at such nodal points as the following:

- the baptismal questions ("Do you believe in . . . ?") and declaration ("I baptize you in . . .");[17]
- the ecumenical creeds (Apostolic and Nicene);
- the eucharistic prayer;
- ordination to the ministry;
- the solemn benediction ("The blessing of God almighty, Father, Son, and Holy Spirit . . .").

The same pattern is found in familiar texts that have commended themselves down through the centuries: the Greater Gloria ("Glory be to God on high . . ."), the Lesser Gloria ("Gloria Patri . . ."), the Te Deum, and so on. The best hymn writers observe it, as does Charles Wesley in this hymn:

> Father of everlasting grace,
> Thy goodness and thy truth we praise,
> Thy goodness and thy truth we prove;
> Thou hast, in honor of thy Son,
> The gift unspeakable sent down,
> The Spirit of life, and power, and love.
>
> Send us the Spirit of thy Son
> To make the depths of Godhead known,
> To make us share the life divine. . . .

So fundamental is the pattern that it is natural for it to pervade all Christian worship. It is important that it continue to mark new compositions and extemporaneous prayer. Otherwise the older examples would risk being treated as fossils.

---

17. The maintenance of the trinitarian name at baptism is advocated, in a partial though by no means complete overlap of argumentation with the present essay, by Catherine Mowry LaCugna in "The Baptismal Formula, Feminist Objections, and Trinitarian Theology," *Journal of Ecumenical Studies* 26 (1989): 235-50.

The trinitarian name and doctrine is precisely *not* an abstract formula.[18] It belongs to a living context. It must be kept firmly attached to the historical revelation through the telling and retelling of the story recounted in Scripture. It can thus carry with it all the associations of the God who has said and done such wonderful things and has received the praises of the people in such a rich abundance of language. The name and the doctrine need exposition in preaching and teaching. Further reflection may be needed to clarify their use, as took place, for instance, already at the Council of Nicea: "*eternally* begotten of the Father," "begotten, *not made*," "being *of one substance* with the Father."

This may be the place, however, to point out some tracks that would be false even if they were pursued with a view to explicating trinitarian doctrine, let alone replacing the triune name altogether (as some are suggesting). For example, "Creator, Redeemer, Sustainer" is either the listing of three activities toward the world on the part of an otherwise undifferentiated Godhead (a kind of Sabellianism) or else runs the risk of dividing the Godhead in a Marcionite way. It is true that the tradition knows the careful and limited use of a principle of "appropriation," as in the Catechism of the Book of Common Prayer:

First I learn to believe in God the Father, who hath made me, and all the world.

Secondly, in God the Son, who hath redeemed me, and all mankind.

Thirdly, in God the Holy Ghost, who sanctifieth me, and all the elect people of God.

But that is possible only in the context of a strong doctrine of the distinction, relations, and mutual coinherence of the three persons in the one God.[19]

18. Cf. LaCugna, "The Baptismal Formula," p. 242: "'God the Father' in the sense of 'Father of Jesus Christ' is a specific and personal way to name God, not an indefinite name for the divine essence."

19. Cf. LaCugna, "The Baptismal Formula," p. 244: "Distinguishing persons by their function with respect to us does not sufficiently highlight the personal and relational character of God *as God*. The strong and bold claim of trinitarian theology is that not only is God related to us, but it is the very *essence* or *substance* of God to be relational." Or, as John Wesley put it in a letter of 3 August 1771 to Jane Catherine March: "The quaint device of styling them three offices rather than persons gives up the whole doctrine" (*The Letters of John Wesley,* ed. John Telford, vol. 5 [London: Epworth Press, 1931], p. 270).

And such a doctrine is based precisely on the given name of Father, Son, and Holy Spirit. Or again, some are now speaking of "the Creator, the Christ, and the Spirit." That makes it sound as if Christ and the Holy Spirit were creatures; and Arianism, as Athanasius and Basil argued, forfeits our salvation, since only God can save.

So much is at stake in the matter of trinitarian worship that I have felt it necessary to give a fairly firm account of the traditional doctrine, and even at times to make a polemical point or two. But I would like to end on a more directly devotional note. I invite you to contemplate one of the most famous icons in Eastern Orthodoxy. Andrei Rublev depicts the persons of the Trinity in the guise of the three visitors to Abraham and Sara by the oaks of Mamre (Gen. 18). The rhythm of the picture "folds" the three figures into one another in such a way as to suggest the mutual indwelling of the three divine persons in the one Godhead. Various details indicate that the figure we see on the left is the Father, the central figure is the Son, and the figure on the right is the Holy Spirit. Through a characteristic use of inverse perspective, the icon "reaches out" toward the beholder, who can thus be "included" in the scene. Salvation is to be drawn, in a way appropriate to creatures, into the very life of God, to be given by the graciousness of God a share in the communion of the divine persons.[20] The sacramental sign of the beginning of that process is baptism in the name of the Father, the Son, and the Holy Spirit. In the Eucharist, the Holy Spirit touches us and the bread and wine so that we may receive the body and blood of Christ and so be included in the Son's self-gift to the Father. To the one God we cry, "Holy, holy, holy. . . ."

20. For an exposition of the Orthodox view of worship as participation in God, see, for example, George S. Bebis, "Worship in the Orthodox Church," *Greek Orthodox Theological Review* 22 (1977): 429-43: Christian worship is "a continuous and an increasing experience, which is nothing less than a real communion with our God, the Father Almighty, the Creator of all things visible and invisible; a participation in the life of Jesus Christ, whose life is extended and thrives in the Church; and the unending reception of the Holy Spirit, who strengthens our life and prepares us to become members of the divine and heavenly household of God" (p. 429).

The Question of Woman's Experience of God

ELIZABETH A. MORELLI

THE QUESTION to be pursued is this: Is there a woman's experience of God? This question is in need of clarification, but there is a danger in too readily clarifying one's question — the danger that the question may wholly evaporate. The anticipated avenue of investigation may close up. Yet, inverse insights are also valuable. To learn that there is nothing to be understood along certain lines may save others wasted effort, and the very process of uncovering a dead end may be revelatory of unanticipated avenues of inquiry.

When I ask whether there is a woman's experience of God, I am, first of all, concerned with experience in its most generic sense. The term "experience" can be used in a narrow sense to refer to the sensory and imaginative, to the empirical as distinct from the intelligent and rational. But I am using "experience" to mean conscious access of any sort. In this sense, one could talk of intelligent and rational experience as well as sensory experience. Second, with the term "experience" I am not referring exclusively to the cognitive. The question of the experience of God encompasses the question of knowing God, but I wish to include the affective and the volitional dimensions of conscious access to God as well. So, the question has become this: Is there in any sense — cognitive, affective, or volitional — a woman's conscious access to God?

While I wish to use the term "experience" in this broadest sense, I also wish to delimit radically the scope of this inquiry. My question regards the *noetic* rather than the *noematic* correlates of consciousness, the conscious operations or acts rather than the conscious contents or objects. Contemporary feminist critiques of traditional accounts of woman's religious knowledge examine the *noematic.* Sallie McFague, for example, explores feminine and masculine models, images, or symbols of the divine. Her investigation takes place at the level of the religious and theological imagination, on which she uncovers the metaphors and models underlying theological conceptual systems.[1] Her focus is on the conscious content, the images themselves, rather than on the conscious operations that give rise to such images. Similarly, feminist analyses of the language employed in religious texts and liturgies are concerned with the *noematic,* specifically with names given to God.[2] The religious words formulated, the images and models elaborated — all are contents of the conscious operations that are the focus of this inquiry. My question regards the acts that give rise to such formulations, metaphors, concepts.

The question is, then, whether there is a conscious act or operation or set of operations performed by woman that gives her conscious access to God. Is there a unique woman's experience of God? The term "woman's experience" is admittedly awkward, yet "feminine experience" is misleading. A woman or a man may engage in acts or pursuits considered to be feminine or masculine. Accordingly, the phrases "a very feminine woman" or "a rather masculine woman" have commonly understood meanings. The designations "feminine" and "masculine" are derivative terms. They get their meanings from the historically and culturally conditioned body of common wisdom and common nonsense concerning the differences between women and men. We can avoid any unintentional connotations that the term "feminine" may carry by asking whether there is a gender-specific experience of God.[3] Does woman *qua* woman have a unique conscious access to God?

The question is not whether an experience of God is possible but whether there is a woman's experience of God. Of course, if the former question were to be answered negatively, the latter would be moot. Nevertheless, the pursuit of the question of woman's experience of God should shed light on the general possibility. Finally, by employing the term "God," I do not intend to rule out more amorphous senses of the divine.

---

1. McFague, *Models of God: Theology for an Ecological, Nuclear Age* (Philadelphia: Fortress Press, 1987), pp. x-xi.

2. Daphne Hampson, *Theology and Feminism* (Oxford: Basil Blackwell, 1990), pp. 156-61.

3. I do not think it is necessary to introduce into this inquiry the controversy concerning the distinction between sex differences and gender differences. For an introduction to this area of analysis, see *Theoretical Perspectives on Sexual Differences,* ed. Deborah L. Rhode (New Haven, Conn.: Yale University Press, 1990).

I am using the term "God" to designate the ultimately transcendent as well as the most intimately immanent. Such a heuristic notion of God does not exclude the Christian personal God, but neither does it specify this in advance. My question, then, is whether there is a woman's experience of the divine ultimate, not, specifically, whether there is a woman's experience of Christ or the triune God of Christianity.

Having clarified the meaning of our question, let us now turn to the historical reasons for its emergence. I can discern at least two reasons why this question has arisen. The first and perhaps most prominent reason is a tradition of Western thought stretching back as far as the sixth century B.C. The second is a contemporary reason, a reductionist trend in postmodern epistemological reflection.

The long-standing tradition — or, more accurately, bias — is the attribution of rationality exclusively to men. The notion of a set of opposites, such as Hot and Cold, Wet and Dry, and so on played an important role in the cosmologies of the pre-Socratics from the time of Anaximander. In his *Metaphysics,* Aristotle refers to a standard table of ten pairs of opposites, which he attributes to the Pythagoreans. In this table the opposite Female was listed in the column characterized generally by lack and disorder. Female was on the negative side along with the opposites Unlimited, Evenness (as the opposite of the more perfect unity of Oddness), Many, Left, Motion, Darkness, Badness, Curved, and Oblong.[4] While Female as an opposite was itself a form or a universal, it was one of the forms characterized by a lack of form, definition, order, and perfection. In addition, Aristotle's working definition of man (humanity as distinct from plants and merely sentient animals) was as rational animal, an animal possessing intellect. There were, then, two basic tenets that could be combined: (1) Female is the opposite of Male, or woman is not man; and (2) Man is rational. Unfortunately, these two propositions can be combined as the premises of an invalid argument: Man is rational; woman is not man; therefore, woman is not rational. This argument is invalid whether the ambiguous term "man" in the first premise is taken to mean humanity or men. If in using "man" we mean humanity, then the second premise is false, and the argument is invalid. If in using "man" we mean men, then the argument is an example of a standard fallacy. "All A's are B's" does not entail that "All not-A's are not-B's." I am not attribut-

4. Kathleen Freeman, *Companion to the Pre-Socratic Philosophers* (Oxford: Basil Blackwell, 1966), p. 248.

ing this actual argument to anyone, but only illustrating the kind of faulty reasoning that has served to bulwark centuries of misogyny. Because man is defined as rational, and woman clearly is not man, then woman must be in some sense non-rational.[5]

The attribution of an essential, defining characteristic of humanity to only one of its sexes has serious metaphysical implications. If woman is non-rational and rationality is essential to being human, then woman must be, in Dorothy Sayers' words, "not quite human."[6] We can read the most brilliant and ambitious accounts of the human spirit, and find at the back of the weighty tome a small section entitled "On Women" or "The Woman Question." It is disheartening, if not enraging, for the serious student of philosophy, reaching up to the mind of a great thinker, to come upon a remark such as the following by Hegel: "Women are capable of education, but they are not made for activities which demand a universal faculty such as more advanced science, philosophy, and certain forms of artistic production."[7] After having wrestled more or less successfully with the intricacies of dialectical method, one discovers that she does not after all have the faculty to comprehend herself as rationally self-conscious. The same opinion of woman was expressed by Schopenhauer: "For women, only what is intuitive, present and immediately real, truly exists; what is knowable only by means of concepts, what is remote, absent, past, or future cannot really be grasped by them."[8] Woman is understood to be bereft of the wherewithal, lacking the universalizing faculty, to engage in abstract reasoning. (If one should happen to encounter an "analytic" woman, her possession of this masculine trait is considered to be an aberration.)

Returning to the passage just cited from Hegel's *Philosophy of Right,*

5. Actually, Aristotle fares better in this regard than Enlightenment thinkers. He, at least, characterized woman as essentially rational, as possessing intellect; however, he understood woman to possess a rationality inferior to that of man. This inferiority was a function of woman's limited sphere of the exercise of her reason. Woman was not allowed to participate in the public, political arena, but she was capable of exercising reason in the domestic sphere. See Hannah Arendt's *The Human Condition* (Chicago: University of Chicago Press, 1974).

6. Sayers, "Human-Not-Quite-Human," in *Moral Dilemmas,* ed. Richard L. Purtill (Belmont, Calif.: Wadsworth Publishing Co., 1985), pp. 236-40.

7. Hegel, *Philosophy of Right,* trans. T. M. Knox (New York: Oxford University Press, 1973), pp. 263-64. This passage and the following from Schopenhauer's work were quoted by Carol McMillan in *Women, Reason, and Nature* (Princeton, N.J.: Princeton University Press, 1982), pp. 8-11.

8. Schopenhauer, *On the Basis of Morality* (Indianapolis: Bobbs-Merrill, 1965), p. 151.

we read further that "the difference between men and women is like that between animals and plants. Men correspond to animals, while women correspond to plants because their development is more placid and the principle that underlies it is the rather vague unity of feeling."[9] Kierkegaard, who differed from Hegel so radically on major points, reiterates fundamentally the same metaphysical view of woman: "This being of woman (for the word existence is too rich in meaning, since woman does not persist in and through herself) is rightly described as charm, an expression which suggests plant life. . . . She is wholly subject to nature and hence only aesthetically free."[10] As non-rational — or, more precisely, pre-rational — woman has a different being than man, and this metaphysical difference grounds an ethical difference. Woman is not free, not autonomous, and thus she is rightly subject to authority. Insofar as woman is incapable of grasping and applying the categorical imperative, she cannot conduct her life according to the law of reason, except indirectly by obeying one who does.

A litany of maddening opinions on the nature of woman, expressed over the centuries by representatives of various disciplines, could easily be recited. I have quoted these few remarks in order to illustrate that the attribution of rationality to men exclusively has grave ramifications for epistemological, metaphysical, and ethical accounts of woman. It is well-known that similar presuppositions concerning the nature of woman persisted well into this century. The traditional belief in woman's passive, non-rational nature underpins the theories and methodologies of the pioneers of otherwise new fields of thought (Sigmund Freud, Max Scheler, Edmund Beecher Wilson, and Lawrence Kohlberg, to name a few). A number of feminists critical of the patriarchal tradition of male domination, from the time of Mary Wollstonecraft in the late eighteenth century to the present, have nevertheless adopted this presupposition of feminine non-rationality.[11]

9. Hegel, *Philosophy of Right*, pp. 263-64.

10. Kierkegaard, *Either/Or*, vol. 1, trans. David F. Swenson and Lillian Marvin Swenson (Princeton, N.J.: Princeton University Press, 1944), p. 426. Kierkegaard speaks pseudonymously in this passage, as the master aesthete Johannes the Seducer. This accounts for the haughty tone of the remarks, but not, I think, for the essential message, because as far as I know Kierkegaard does not disavow this opinion elsewhere.

11. In her *Vindication of the Rights of Woman* (1792), Wollstonecraft celebrated the "manly virtues" and urged women to "every day grow more and more masculine." See Jean Bethke Elshtain, *Meditations on Modern Political Thought: Masculine/Feminine Themes from Luther to Arendt* (New York: Praeger Special Studies, 1986), p. 27.

For a contemporary example, Carol Gilligan in her critique of Kohlberg's meth-

Historically, the non-rationality ascribed to woman has taken three forms: pre-rationality, extra-rationality, and supra-rationality. Enlightenment thinkers and many post-Kantians characterize woman as pre-rational, as adept at intuitive, pre-conceptual knowing. As such, she is likened to animals (or, as we have seen, to plants) and to children. The main difference between the woman and the child, however, is that the child (boy) has the potential to become fully rational, autonomous, and free, whereas the woman is thought to live her life as a perennial child (girl). The primary cognitive ability characteristic of woman, according to this view, is the intuitive. As Hegel remarks later in that same passage cited previously, "Women are educated — who knows how? — as it were by breathing in ideas, by living rather than acquiring knowledge."[12]

Non-rationality can also mean that which is complementary to rationality, the volitional and the affective. The volitional, insofar as it is grounded in rationality, was not associated with woman. Kant thought woman to be heteronomous, lacking the moral authority of the rational moral agent.[13] Her willfulness was considered to be a function of childish arbitrariness or animal stubbornness rather than the exercise of a free will grounded in the law of reason. The proper domain of woman was considered to be the heart, the emotional or affective.

The affective as non-rational is not necessarily sub-rational. Phenomenologists of the heart have shown that the range of feelings ascends spiritually at least as high or as deep as reason. Max Scheler and Stephan Strasser, for example, have uncovered complex hierarchies of affectivity, which extend from the simplest sensations to the most profound passions.[14]

odology does not critique his Kantian-Rawlsian presupposition of male rationality. Rather, she pursues the question of whether or not women do in fact develop morally as far as men, but along different lines — along the lines of greater interpersonal sensitivity as distinct from legalistic negotiating. See Gilligan, *In a Different Voice* (Cambridge, Mass.: Harvard University Press, 1982).

12. Hegel, *Philosophy of Right*, pp. 263-64.

13. In describing the process of attaining enlightenment, the difficult appropriation of one's own autonomy, Kant remarks, "That the step to competence is held to be very dangerous by the far greater portion of mankind (and by the entire fair sex) — quite apart from its being arduous — is seen to by those guardians who have so kindly assumed superintendence over them" (*Foundations of the Metaphysics of Morals*, trans. Lewis White Beck [Indianapolis: Bobbs-Merrill, 1959], p. 85).

14. Scheler, *Formalism in Ethics and Non-Formal Ethics of Value*, trans. Manfred S. Frings and Roger L. Funk (Evanston: Northwestern University Press, 1973); and Strasser, *Phenomenology of Feeling: An Essay on the Phenomena of the Heart*, trans. Robert E. Wood (Pittsburgh: Duquesne University Press, 1977). For a summary account of their affective

If woman is associated exclusively with the heart, this does not, then, impose a limitation on her potential spirituality. Unfortunately, even Scheler, who embraces affectivity as a more significant field for *a priori* investigation than rationality, does not redeem woman as man's spiritual equal. On the contrary, while woman's domain may be the heart, she is relegated to its basement. Scheler characterizes woman as essentially prone to negative emotions such as envy, jealousy, spite, and, particularly, *ressentiment.* In addition, due to her ontological inferiority, woman is associated with feelings of the lower ranks, sensory and vital feelings and desires.[15]

Scheler explains how *ressentiment,* which is a complex condition of self-poisoning of the heart, originates in individuals or groups on the basis of social conditions or hereditary factors. He considers women to be a pre-eminent example of such a group. While not every woman will fall victim to *ressentiment,* woman's essential nature makes her especially prone to this condition. In his analysis of this susceptibility, Scheler characterizes the domain of woman's most vital interest to be the erotic. He writes, "She is always forced to compete for man's favor, and this competition centers precisely on her personal and unchangeable qualities." Woman is vulnerable to *ressentiment* because "feelings of revenge born from rejection in the erotic sphere are always particularly subject to repression."[16] We can gather from these remarks that woman's primary interest is the erotic on the sensitive and vital levels. The higher levels of affectivity, the feelings and interests corresponding to the cultural values of beauty, justice, and wisdom, require the intelligence and self-reflection of spirit. Due to her nature, and not only to social conditioning, woman is not motivated by the higher spiritual affects. So, we find that even in her own special domain of the emotions, woman is understood to enjoy an inferior status. The key differentiating factor in the affective potential of women and men is the ability to be articulate and self-reflective — in short, the capacity to be spiritual (rational).

Third, the non-rational can mean not that which is inferior to reason nor that which is complementary to reason but that which transcends reason. The non-rational in this sense is the transcendent realm of the mysterious and the holy. In experiencing the mystical, one moves

---

typologies, see Elizabeth A. Morelli, *Anxiety: A Study of the Affectivity of Moral Consciousness* (Lanham, Md.: University Press of America, 1985), chap. 2.

15. Scheler, *Ressentiment,* trans. Lewis Coser (New York: Schocken Books, 1961), pp. 60-62.

16. Ibid., p. 61.

beyond the mediation and articulation of intelligence and reason to the silence of mystery. One moves beyond the experience of any sensory or imaginatively based affect to an experience of the sublime, the *mysterium tremendum*. One moves beyond acts of will to self-surrender to God's will. Has woman, historically, been specifically associated with the non-rational in this sense?

The mystical is understood to correspond to the highest potential of the human as person. Insofar as women have not been considered persons, mystical experience, the experience of the holy, has not been attributed to them. In those cultures and times in which women have been considered to be family property or things, they have not been considered to be persons. In the Koran, for example, women are not thought to possess souls and are thus considered to be incapable of holiness or of immortality.[17] The Christian tradition does recognize a religious personal nature in woman, and with this, a capacity to experience the mystical. Women such as Saint Teresa have been ranked among the greatest mystics. But this gift of mystical union with God seems to transcend all specific differences of age, education, social status, education, and gender. The non-rational in this sense has not been specially attributed to woman, although it has, in some cultures, been specially denied her.

Besides the mystical as ultimately self-transcending, there is also a romantic sense of the spiritual, which has been specifically associated with woman. This spirituality is non-rational, meaning not that it transcends reason but that it lacks rationality. It is a "spirituality" defined by a lack of spirituality. It is a romantic notion of the spiritual grounded in the imagination. Woman as not transcending materiality is thought to be somehow aligned with the dark forces of nature. As "earth mother" she possesses a mysterious power, described by Hilda Hein in her critique of woman's spirituality:

> But it is not an individuating, intellectualizing, or morally elevating property. It is rather an elemental and undifferentiated force that "passes through" and occupies a woman. . . . Woman's spirituality is in no way incompatible with her passivity or with her lack of moral authority.[18]

17. Scheler, *Formalism in Ethics and Non-Formal Ethics of Value*, pp. 481-82.
18. Hein, "Liberating Philosophy: An End to the Dichotomy of Spirit and Matter," in *Women, Knowledge, and Reality*, ed. Ann Garry and Marilyn Pearsall (Boston: Unwin Hyman, 1989), p. 299.

Possessing mysterious power and yet not capable of rational, personal autonomy, woman was logically linked to another source of supernatural power — the devil. Historical practices of enrobing and closeting women and the excesses of witch burning have been attributed to the powerful psychological need to control the dark forces women represent.[19]

In summary, the non-rational can be understood in at least three ways: as pre-rational, as extra-rational, or as supra-rational. The supra-rational as ultimately transcending reason, as the highest, most profound human experience, is not, at least in the Christian tradition, considered to be gender-specific. However, woman has been specifically associated with the mystical in the romantic sense. The extra-rational as affective is also associated specifically with woman, but only in the limited sense of the erotic. The extra-rational as volitional has not been associated with woman, because she is thought to lack or to fail to exercise the rationality that grounds free self-determination or autonomy. Finally, the pre-rational, the realm of the inarticulate and the intuitive, has been most consistently attributed to woman. We shall take up the issue of woman's intuition subsequently, but first let us look at another notable reason for the emergence of the question of whether woman has a unique conscious access to God.

The question of how women experience or know God is not essentially different from the question of how any distinct human group experiences or knows God (or anything). Contemporary epistemologists and cognitive sociologists seek to determine how differences in knowing are a function of an individual's age, ethnicity, gender, sexual orientation, nationality, economic class, education, and so on. "Radical feminists," according to Alison Jaggar, are so called insofar as they accept the Marxist argument that "there is no epistemological standpoint 'outside' social reality and that all knowledge is shaped by its social origins." She adds further, "Claims that knowledge is objective in the sense of being uninfluenced by class interests are themselves ideological myths."[20] Other feminists have found class distinctions alone to be too impoverished to adequately account for the cognitive differences in groups, particularly in groups of women. Catharine Stimpson, for example, calls for a greater recognition of national characteristics: "To understand an Israeli woman,

---

19. Ibid., p. 300. See also Simone de Beauvoir's account of how woman becomes the wielder of black magic in the imagination of threatened man in *The Second Sex*, trans. H. M. Parshley (New York: Bantam Books, 1953), chap. 9.

20. Jaggar, *Feminist Politics and Human Nature* (Sussex: Harvester Press, 1983), p. 378.

one would have to understand the power of the religious courts; to understand an Australian woman, the presence of an overwhelming, empty landscape."[21] Women as a group are thought to know differently than other groups, and subgroups of women are thought to know differently than each other. Thus, a young, black, lesbian professional from Paris is going to experience or know differently than a white, middle-aged, heterosexual, working-class female from Milwaukee; and they are both going to think differently than their male counterparts.

The discovery and affirmation of pluralism in historical viewpoints, cultural mores, socioeconomic classes, religious beliefs, scientific frameworks, philosophic methodologies, and so on has led to a despair of the universal. The postmodern suspicion and denigration of the *a priori* or transcendental was originally expressed in Nietzsche's eloquent and reflective critique of the will to Truth.[22] Henceforth, to seek a universal ground for objectivity, a way of knowing that is transcultural, has been considered to be ideologically recalcitrant or, at best, naive. There is not a single, universal way that human beings experience, think, or reason. Alasdair MacIntyre has shown that the very meaning of reason itself, of what it means to be rational as we have been discussing it so far, is historically conditioned.[23] It follows that if one is to attempt to do epistemology at all, one must study the ways of reasoning or thinking or believing of various, distinct groups. The question of whether woman has a unique conscious access to God, then, arises in the contemporary context, regardless of any traditional differentiation of rationality in terms of gender.

I refer in the preceding paragraph to a "despair of the universal" because of certain nihilistic undercurrents in the postmodern wave. Rather than a celebration of the fact of pluralism, one detects a sense of loss, a loss of the surety that attended the classical notion of necessary truth. But the recognition of pluralism in all its forms does not preclude the possibility of a universal core of human knowing, feeling, and willing. Max

---

21. Stimpson, "Women as Knowers," in *Feminist Visions: Toward a Transformation of the Liberal Arts Curriculum,* ed. Diane L. Fowlkes and Charlotte S. McClure (Tuscaloosa, Ala.: University of Alabama Press, 1984), p. 21.

22. Nietzsche, *The Genealogy of Morals,* trans. Horace B. Samuel (New York: Modern Library, 1927), III.24, p. 782. For an analysis of Nietzsche's critique in juxtaposition to the notion of an *a priori* desire to know, see Elizabeth A. Morelli, "A Reflection on Lonergan's Notion of the Pure Desire to Know," *Ultimate Reality and Meaning* 13 (1990): 50-60.

23. MacIntyre, *Whose Justice? Which Rationality?* (Notre Dame: University of Notre Dame Press, 1988).

Scheler, with his *a priori* order of the heart, and Bernard Lonergan, with his transcendental structure of conscious intentionality, have shown that thorough study of historical and cultural differences only provides further evidence for the affirmation of a universal ground of objectivity. The limitations of this inquiry do not allow me to elaborate and defend this claim here. My intention has been simply to indicate another reason why the question of woman's religious experience has emerged.

The non-rational as outlined previously has three senses, and each is associated with woman, but of the three, the pre-rational or intuitive is most uniformly associated with woman. While feelings and desires may be considered to be woman's domain, still it is the sensitive and pre-rational affects with which she is especially associated. Similarly, woman has been considered uniquely gifted with spiritual powers, but only insofar as those powers are understood to be natural or material — again, intuitive. Let us examine, then, whether or not intuition is a unique noetic constituent of woman's consciousness, and if it is, whether it provides special access to God. In other words, to rephrase one of Heidegger's questions, What is this thing called "woman's intuition"?

First, I would like to eliminate what is not meant by "woman's intuition." I am not referring to the sensitive intuition of Kant's "Aesthetic," which is no more than sensory experience, nor do I mean the eidetic intuition of Husserl's phenomenology. The latter is not fundamentally different from the intelligent abstraction of the intelligible form, found in the Aristotelian tradition. The intuition attributed to woman is not mere sense experience nor is it an act of intelligence, an insight, although both of these noetic correlates are pre-rational. The former is pre-rational as merely empirical; the latter, as pre-conceptual, though intelligent. When a woman says, "I just know. Don't ask me how," she is not claiming greater perceptual acuity — sharper vision or a stronger sense of smell. She is also not claiming greater capacity for abstracting the universal. The content of such "intuition" is not the provisional supposition of theoretical operations. It is, rather, pronounced as a judgment, as knowledge that has been attained. This intuitive knowledge is thought to be reached immediately and wholly, not through the mediation of intelligent grasp, conceptual formulation, and rational verification. Such a claim to "just know" something directly without or apart from the mediation of abstraction and formulation would be considered preposterous, as indeed Kant considered all speculative claims of intellectual intuition. Yet, the myth that there is such a thing as woman's intuition has persisted, even when its possibility in general has been radically critiqued.

What accounts for the persistence of the myth of woman's intuition? We are predisposed to accept this myth, as we have seen, because of the historical association of woman with the pre-rational. There is also the inescapable fact that the claims made on the basis of woman's intuition oftentimes turn out to be confirmed. What is pronounced independently has in fact taken place or does actually transpire. The not uncommon confirmation of woman's intuition is met by the bemused shrug of the rational man. Further, women themselves have been known to take pride in this unique, incomprehensible power. If one is deprived of other socially acceptable exercises of power, it is understandable that what is thought to be a unique source of feminine power would be cherished. As Carol McMillan has pointed out, a number of feminists have begun to argue that women ought to embrace this identification of women with the intuitive. The feminist argument in defense of woman's intuition is not compensatory, but it is philosophically therapeutic.[24] The appropriation of woman's intuition is lauded as part of a general move away from the excessive abstractness of rationalism.

Just as I think the attribution of the non-rational specifically to woman is fallacious, so I think the notion of woman's intuition is also ungrounded. The nature of the mistake in this instance is not biased reasoning but incorrect objectification. Something is going on in woman's consciousness, and she can arrive at the truth, but it is inaccurate to refer to the process as "intuition."

Conscious acts, the *noetic* elements of consciousness, are essentially intentional — that is, directed toward objects *(noema)*. A conscious act invariably makes us aware of its content. The act itself *qua* conscious is also self-present. However, the fact that both content and act are conscious does not mean that one is reflecting on either. For example, at the movies, while engrossed in a film, you may be tasting buttered popcorn, feeling irritated with the kicking of the back of your seat, recalling a similar scene in a previous film, questioning the coherence of the plot, and so on. These and any number of similar conscious operations are not taking place unconsciously. If another were to ask you how the popcorn is, you would be able to answer coherently, yet you were not "thinking" about it previ-

24. McMillan, *Women, Reason, and Nature* (Princeton, N.J.: Princeton University Press, 1982), p. 34.

ously. Your attention was on the film. Conscious acts and contents that are not attended to or reflected upon constitute what Sartre calls pre-reflective consciousness.[25] Lonergan refers to this as what is conscious but not objectified.[26] Both Sartre and Lonergan dismantle the classical, psychoanalytic notion of the unconscious by means of these distinctions. Conscious acts, including affective acts and states and volitional acts, as well as cognitive acts, can occur without being reflected upon. The acts, while themselves conscious and intentional, need not be intended.

What is called "woman's intuition" is, I think, a matter of pre-reflective or unobjectified conscious acts of perception, intelligence, affectivity, and reason. In pronouncing what she "just knows," a woman is simply objectifying the end product of a series of conscious and intentional but pre-reflective operations. When a mother "just knows," for example, that her daughter is going to be involved in a car accident, she may be drawing upon a more attuned sensitivity to her daughter's mood, the manners of her date, the sound of the car's engine, and recollections of previous adventures. Into this data, which might not be available to a less concerned individual, she may get a practical insight regarding what is likely to happen, and this insight may be confirmed by further worried attention to detail, and finally pronounced as a fact. Through sensory, affective, imaginative, intelligent, and rational activity, she has arrived at a probable judgment. Her conscious acts were not reflected upon, not objectified, all her attention being directed toward the object of her concern. So, when the police ask her later how she knew the accident was going to happen, she answers simply, "Woman's intuition." With this illustration I do not mean to imply that women only claim to be intuitive, because they are not often phenomenologists. Yet, as long as one's conscious and intentional operations remain unobjectified, one will tend to fall back upon the most readily available account of cognition. So, someone who may be just as perceptive, intelligent, and rational as any man but who has already identified being a woman with not being rational will, not surprisingly, cite woman's intuition.

It could be argued that especially in an instance like the one described in the preceding example, when a woman claims to know what has not yet happened or what happens at a distance, there is an extra-

25. Sartre, *The Transcendence of the Ego,* trans. Forrest Williams and Robert Kirkpatrick (New York: Farrar, Straus & Giroux, 1957).
26. Lonergan, *Method in Theology* (New York: Herder & Herder, 1972), p. 34n.5.

sensory dimension to be considered. I do not mean to rule out the possibility of extrasensory data, but as simply data it is not knowledge any more than ordinary sensation is. If a woman is to employ such data in order to arrive at knowledge, intelligent and rational acts are still required. The pronouncement, at least, must be formulated, and this requires insight and conception.

The only difference between a cognitive claim such as "It's a simple matter of deduction, my dear Watson" and the claim "I just know it — woman's intuition" is a habit of objectifying and appropriating conscious operations traditionally accepted as gender-appropriate. The process of knowing in any case involves the same set of conscious and intentional operations, more or less attended to or objectified. As Lonergan has shown, there is a universal, transcultural, and, I would add, gender-transcendent structure of conscious intentionality. This is not to say, of course, that the *noematic* correlates are the same. Different sensations, interests, images, expectations, and desires do give rise to different affects and questions, and in turn these occasion different insights and formulations. So, to return to the example of the worried mother, what she noticed, which gave rise to her prediction, would vary according to her interests, preoccupations, training, and so on, and might very well differ from what her husband might notice. Yet, the process of arriving at her conclusion involves the same set of conscious and intentional operations that anyone employs to know anything.

"Woman's intuition" is an imprecise and abstract term for a set of conscious and intentional operations that is neither distinctly intuitive nor specifically female. The *a priori* set of acts constitutive of the process of knowing consists of both abstractive, logical, rational acts and so-called intuitive or pre-conceptual acts such as sensing, imagining, and questioning. Even the act of abstracting, which I believe Schopenhauer had in mind when he referred to the universalizing faculty, is, strictly speaking, pre-conceptual. Just as there is no such thing as "woman's intuition," so there is no "universalizing faculty" attributable only to men.

If, as I have argued, the process of conscious intentionality is not gender-specific, it follows that there is no conscious access to God unique to woman. The answer to the original question of this inquiry is simply an inverse insight, the discovery that there is nothing there to be understood. Nevertheless, I would like to conclude with a positive suggestion. Is there a conscious access to God for us regardless of gender? Lonergan answers this question with his notion of the pure desire to know, the immanent source of transcendence to ultimate mystery.[27] Scheler answers this question with his account of the highest level of values, the holy, and the highest affective act of the person, love.[28] Finally, Kierkegaard answers this question with his account of faith, the self-transcending act of willing to be oneself transparently before God.[29] The primary conscious access to God for Lonergan, the early Lonergan, is cognitive;[30] for Scheler it is affective; and for Kierkegaard it is volitional. Which account is truer; which mode has primacy? If we ask what is common to these three accounts, we find that in each one our access to God is understood to be the most fundamental core of the human spirit. If we can be content for the time being with this most heuristic notion of human access to God, we can return to our original question. Insofar as we understand our access to God to be the very ground or core of the human spirit, then we cannot attribute to woman *qua* woman a specific conscious access to God. To do so would be to assert that woman is not quite human, or that there are two distinct human natures.

27. Morelli, "A Reflection on Lonergan's Notion of the Pure Desire to Know."

28. Scheler, *Formalism in Ethics and Non-Formal Ethics of Value,* chap. 6.

29. Kierkegaard, *The Sickness unto Death,* trans. Howard V. Hong and Edna H. Hong (Princeton, N.J.: Princeton University Press, 1980), p. 14 and Part Two.

30. This cognitive emphasis is apparent in his *Insight: A Study of Human Understanding* (New York: Philosophical Library, 1957). In later works, the pure desire to know is described as one manifestation of a single principle of transcendence, which unfolds as intelligent inquiry, rational reflection, moral consciousness, and religious love.

Creation as Christ: A Problematic Theme in Some Feminist Theology

DAVID A. SCOTT

Introduction

FEMINIST THEOLOGIANS announce as their starting point women's oppression and exploitation in a patriarchal and sexist culture. Generally speaking, their theological writings have two sides. One is critical: the analysis and assessment of the structures of destructive dualisms that oppress and exploit women, men, nature, and whole cultures. The other is constructive: positive proposals that would replace dualistic views with a holistic vision of the relation between God and creation, spirit and matter, men and women, humanity and the environment, the First and the Third Worlds. Obviously, the critical and constructive efforts are two sides of the same coin.

This essay focuses on one facet of feminist critique and proposal: the relation of God and creation, which involves the doctrines of God as Trinity, God Incarnate in Jesus Christ, and God as Creator. I intend to show that, in their justified rejection of destructive theological dualisms, some feminist theologians ascribe to the creation, or to some aspect of it, attributes which classical Christian theology reserves for Jesus Christ, the Incarnate Word of God. In other words, I intend to identify a pervasive theme of feminist theology: the "christification" of creation. To my knowledge, this feature of some feminist theology has not been noted.

I argue that this theme needs to be questioned and criticized. This theme or doctrine attacks basic Christian beliefs. Well-intentioned as it may be, it often proceeds from a misunderstanding or misrepresentation of Christian teaching, and, despite the intention of feminist authors, it may actually undermine legitimate feminist goals.

David A. Scott

Destructive Dualisms

Grace Jantzen, an editor of the Anglican theological journal *Theology*, offers the following description of feminist theological critique of traditional Christian theology:

> What is central to feminist theology . . . and what makes it crucial for everybody and for all forms of theological scholarship, is that feminists argue that Christian theology has for centuries been in the grip of a series of interlocking and destructive dualisms.[1]

Jantzen then states that one dualism underlies the others:

> The basic theological dualism is the split between God and the material universe. The doctrine of creation *ex nihilo* is usually centred on an understanding of God as pure spirit, utterly other than the material universe which is created by divine fiat. This world, thus created and set apart from God, is essentially matter (minds are introduced by a separate act of divine creation . . .), and the attributes of matter are the polar opposites of the attributes of God. God is all knowing; matter is mindless, irrational. God is goodness itself; matter in itself is without value, mere stuff.[2]

From this, "the basic theological dualism," other destructive dualisms flow. One is anthropological: the dualism of mind and body. Mind or soul is alleged to be the essence of the person; the body is a prison house from which the human soul or human spirit can hope to be released only by death; then the spirit can enjoy an incorporeal immortality. The real self — mind or spirit — is akin to God; the body is a part of the physical universe from which it came and to which it will return. The body detracts and diverts the soul from its spiritual home — God — and from the journey back to God. The role of the mind is to control the body and its passions, as God transcends the physical creation and rules it according to providential guidance.[3]

This anthropological dualism relates to a second intra-worldly de-structive dualism: that between men and women. Although women are

---

1. Jantzen, "Who Needs Feminism?" *Theology* 93 (September/October 1990): 339-45.
2. Ibid., p. 340.
3. Ibid.

credited with having a rational soul, they are more closely associated than men with the material world. Therefore, the irrationality, instability, and passivity of matter mark women. Men, by contrast, are deemed more rational, more capable of control of their passions and emotions, more able, more powerful, more stable — indeed, better in every way! In relation to women, therefore, men should be in control and, indeed, beware of women whose nature-rooted sexuality can distract and divert male rational self-control and world-control. From this dualism, flowing from that of God and world, arises the image of women as danger to male, rational virtue.

Jantzen identifies two further intra-worldly destructive dualisms flowing from the basic dualism of God and world. One is the dualism of technology and nature; the other is the dualism of the First (sic!) World and the rest of the world, especially the so-called Third World. The dualism of mind over matter, grounded in the metaphysical/theological dualism of God and world, privileges mind in the form of technological control over nature, objectified as a value-free arena for human exploitation and manipulation. The same metaphysical dualism, says Jantzen, legitimizes in the minds of white, Western males their economic, military, and cultural imperialism of other cultures, especially "undeveloped" agricultural (i.e., "rooted in nature = feminine") cultures.

I cite Jantzen's exposition of "what is central to feminist theology" at some length for two reasons. First, feminist theologians differ among themselves, and as a consequence any author who intends to engage it fairly must identify what he or she understands by the phrase "feminist theology." Second, I take Jantzen's statement, brief as it is, to be representative and typical of feminist critical analysis of the classical Christian theological tradition. A central point of that critique, again, is that traditional Christian theology (specifically in its doctrine of *creatio ex nihilo*) provides the "ideological underpinnings"[4] of the destructive dualisms just described.

If Jantzen's statement of what is central to feminist theology is accurate and representative, it renders plausible a theme that pervades Christian feminist writings. This is the attributing to the creation or to aspects of the creation attributes which classical Christian theology reserves for Jesus Christ. That is, in apparent response to dualistic thinking, imputed to traditional Christian theology, some feminist theologians describe

4. Ibid., p. 345.

the relation of God and the world not in terms of transcendence and absoluteness but in terms of immanence and interdependence. In so doing, they ascribe to the world attributes traditionally reserved for the Incarnate Word. To demonstrate this assertion is one of the main purposes of this essay. We turn now to this task.

Feminist Theology of the World as God's Incarnation

1. Sallie McFague's Model of the World as God's Body

In her recent book entitled *Models of God*, Sallie McFague proposes that Christian theology consider the model of the world as God's body as an alternative to the traditional Christian understanding of God's relation to the world. One of McFague's criteria for proposing any model of our relation to God is that it help articulate "an understanding of the Christian gospel as a destabilizing, inclusive, nonhierarchical vision of fulfillment for all creation."[5]

According to McFague's own understanding of theological models and metaphors, they do not so much refer to God as they are aimed at sparking our imagination and our efforts to work for fulfillment for all creation. That is why McFague can present the model of the world as God's body and also say that she does not mean that the world literally *is* God's body. Models are not true or false claims about God; indeed, McFague claims that theology attempts not to describe God but to give voice to a kind of wager about reality — a wager, in McFague's case, influenced by Christianity, her other criterion for the validity of a model.[6] The purpose of the model or metaphor is that it is part of the effort to "image the most significant ways to speak of God's presence in one's own time."[7]

How, exactly, might this metaphor or model help promote an inclusive, nonhierarchical vision of fulfillment for all creation? Primarily through leading us to image the world as "self-expressive of God, . . . as a 'sacrament' — the outward and visible presence or body of God, . . . not an alien other

5. McFague, *Models of God: Theology for an Ecological, Nuclear Age* (Philadelphia: Fortress Press, 1987), p. 60.
6. See the important endnote concerning the referent of theological models, according to McFague: *Models of God*, p. 192n.37.
7. Ibid., p. 61.

over against God but expressive of God's very being." Accordingly, the metaphor will lead us to think of "the entire universe [as] expressive of God's very being — *the* 'incarnation,' if you will."[8] In other words,

> What this experiment with the world as God's body comes to, finally, is an awareness, both chilling and breathtaking, that we as worldly, bodily beings are in God's presence. . . . We meet the world as a Thou, as the body of God where God is present to us always in all times and in all places. In the metaphor of the world as the body of God, the resurrection becomes a worldly, present, inclusive reality, for this body is offered to all: "This is my body."[9]

McFague states that this model is monist or, more precisely, panentheist: "It is a view of the God-world relationship in which all things have their origins in God and nothing exists outside God, though this does not mean that God is reduced to these things."[10]

McFague proposes this model of the world as God's body as a replacement for what she calls the "monarchical model," which she charges with numerous flaws: it encourages attitudes of militarism, dualism, and escapism; it condones control through violence and oppression; it has nothing to say about the nonhuman world.

I believe I have described McFague's notion of the world as God's body sufficiently to substantiate the striking analogy between her proposal and the traditional Christian doctrine of the Incarnation of the Word of God. While McFague nowhere says so, she could have arrived at her doctrine of the world as God's body by drawing directly from the classical understanding of God as the Incarnation of the divine Word. And while she denies that her model asserts that the world literally is God's body, this does not prevent her from transferring categories from classical christology to her way of speaking of the creation.

In classical Christian theology, Jesus Christ, the incarnate Son, is asserted to be (1) the *embodiment* and *enfleshment* of the eternal Word of God, (2) the *revelation* and *human expression* of God, and (3) the *sacramental presence* of God in and to the world. Each of these roles McFague logically assigns to the world. Hence it is only consistent with her practical substitution of the world for the traditional Christian view of Christ that

8. Ibid., pp. 61, 62.
9. Ibid., p. 77.
10. Ibid., p. 72.

the language which Jesus used of the bread and wine at the Last Supper and which Christians use to refer to the consecrated elements — that is, "this is my body" — be applied to the earth as such.

It would be difficult to find a more explicit demonstration of the "christifying" of the creation. Sallie McFague's model of the world as God's body invites us to think of the earth as traditional Christianity has thought of Jesus Christ — as the revelation of God, as the sacrament of God, as the resurrected body of God — indeed, as the incarnation of God.

2. Carter Heyward on God as the Power of Right-Making Relationships

Sallie McFague wrote *Models of God* specifically in the face of the threat of ecological and nuclear destruction of the environment. She includes the whole cosmos in the scope of her theological vision. Accordingly, she speaks of the world as God's body, and she criticizes some feminists for excessive focus on interpersonal and social-justice issues.

An Anglican theologian who does concentrate on human relationships is Isabel Carter Heyward, Professor of Theology at Episcopal Divinity School in Cambridge, Massachusetts. Heyward does not ignore the destructive relationship between humanity and the world promoted by sexist and patriarchal dualisms, nor does she ignore social-justice issues. But her focus is on interpersonal relationships. Heyward's theology provides further evidence of the theme we are tracing: ascription to creatures of attributes that classical Christianity reserves for Jesus Christ. The road to this ascription in her theology begins with her move of identifying God with the power of interpersonal relationships marked by mutuality.

In her first book, *The Redemption of God: A Theology of Mutual Relation,* Heyward states that experience of "self-in-relationship" is "the ultimately nomic experience."[11] By "nomic" Heyward means the power to give meaning and normative structure to life. Thus, God's reality is to be equated not simply with self-in-relationship but rather with the healing, whole-making, life-enhancing power that is encountered in relationships marked by mutuality.

In a more recent book, *Touching Our Strength,* Heyward continues her claim that "God" refers to power in mutual relationships:

11. Heyward, *The Redemption of God: A Theology of Mutual Relation* (Lanham, Md.: University Press of America, 1982), p. 2. "The power in relation is God," Heyward claims.

When I speak of God in this book, I am referring to a sacred source of power, erotic and liberating. Like the christian and jewish deity, this power is committed to right relation/justice; and, like the Goddess, this power is committed also to women, girls, the earth, and many delights. She includes some dominant christian images of God, but is far more delightful, mysterious and vast.[12]

More specifically,

God is our power in mutual relation. It is with and by this sacred power that we are able to nurture relationships as resources of growth as cocreative women and men. By God, we can act, responsibly (morally/ethically) and joyfully, on behalf of the liberation of all people and creatures, including ourselves, from bondage to wrong relation. God, our sacred power, is both "personal" and "transpersonal." God is the active source of our creative, liberating power — she with whom we are open (in prayer). We embody the sacred when we generate right relation, acting with one another as resources of the divine Spirit. Insofar as we do so, we "god" (verb).[13]

What is striking about this citation from a glossary that Heyward provides at the end of her book is not only how she identifies God with power in mutual relations but also how she teaches that humans embody God when they generate right relations. More than that, when they generate right relations, humans actually "god." By this I understand her to mean that humans do not just participate in divine power in and through their own creaturely power but, more radically, actually generate deity in and through their own working in, for, and at mutual relationships. This, I take it, is why

---

12. Heyward, *Touching Our Strength: The Erotic as Power and the Love of God* (San Francisco: Harper & Row, 1989), p. 163n.1.

13. Ibid., pp. 188-89. Heyward's position is, in fact, self-contradictory, or perhaps she would say paradoxical. On the one hand, perhaps constrained by the idea of God, which denotes something beyond human life, she writes, "God is our relational power — our power in mutual relation. It is from this God that you and I draw our power to be in life in the first place, and to sustain our lives in relation." But then she states, in effect, that God needs us in order to be real: "In sustaining and becoming ourselves in relation, we are giving birth to more of this same sacred power who needs us, her friends, to bring her life and help nourish her life on the earth. She is being born among us, and yet she is seldom fully present, fully herself. To that extent, she is not yet but becoming. Where there is brokenness, fear, despair, or violence, the power may not be — yet. But with our help, she is becoming" (ibid., pp. 23-24).

Heyward can speak of humans in right relation as being "resources of the divine spirit"; this is what she means by that phrase.

Heyward's view of humanity's relation to God is both similar to and different from that of McFague. What is similar is Heyward's notion of humans as "godding," which implies that God and the world are not separate. Indeed, their relationship should be understood panentheistically: God is in the world, and the world is in God. The difference between McFague's and Heyward's views lies in the scope of the divine presence and manifestation. According to McFague, the whole cosmos embodies God. As Heyward sees it, God is the empowering presence of right-making relationships and relationships of mutuality. God is most closely identified with what Heyward calls "the erotic," which she describes not as the world in general but more as a feature of human vitality.

The implication of Heyward's position that God is "godded" — that is, actualized in and through the efforts of persons in right-making relationships — is that, in contrast to the assertion of classical Christian theology, deity cannot be uniquely identified with the person of Jesus Christ. While acknowledging that in the tradition "God's 'personal' presence has been most popularly imaged as that of a 'Father' and his 'Son,' Jesus/Christ," Heyward insists that God cannot be "contained in any single human life, including that of Jesus."[14] Nor may we confess redemption as the exclusive achievement of Christ. As the title of Heyward's first book suggests, God does not accomplish salvation through Christ's death once and for all on the cross and through his resurrection by the power of the Spirit; rather, we contribute to God's redemption and erotic renewal of humanity in and through right-making relationships. For Heyward, the redeeming role of Jesus Christ actually applies to us. She writes, "She [God] is born and embodied in our midst."[15]

In the writings of Carter Heyward, we find a clear proposal to transfer the christological and salvific predicates traditionally confessed of Jesus to a part of creation — viz., human relationships of justice and mutuality. Heyward thus exemplifies the movement of feminist writers to apply to the world or parts of it divine attributes or functions that classical Christian theology reserves for the second person of the Holy Trinity.[16]

14. Ibid., p. 189.
15. Ibid., p. 102.
16. It should be clearly stated that such a substitution is by no means universal in feminist theology. See, for example, the work of another Anglican feminist theologian, Patricia Wilson-Kastner, *Faith, Feminism and the Christ* (Philadelphia: Fortress Press, 1983).

3. God Births the Earth — Liturgical Texts Proposed by the Episcopal Church

In the fourth century the Council of Nicea confessed Jesus Christ as "the Son of God, begotten of the Father as only begotten." Three hundred and fifty years later, the Eleventh Council of Toledo declared that the Son was begotten "from the womb of the Father." In contrast, a striking feature of the work of some Christian feminist theologians is their taking the image of being born or begotten of God and applying it to the world. This, then, is yet another ascription to creation of an attribute that classical Christianity gave exclusively to the Word made flesh: that he was begotten, not made.

As developed by theologians in the third and fourth centuries and enshrined in the Nicene/Constantinopolitan Creed, classical Christianity confesses God to be Father, Son, and Spirit. God is One, yet not a simple mathematical unity but the rich unity of perichoretic threefoldness. In the classical formula, God is one essence in three persons. Important for our purposes is the orthodox affirmation that the relations or complexity which constitutes God's oneness involves specific kinds of relationship. The specific relationship which concerns us in this essay is that of generation: the Son or Word, the second person of the Trinity, is generated or begotten of the Father.

As the early trinitarian theologians insisted, the relationship established through the generation by the Father of the Son is not to be understood in material ways. Sexual procreation does not occur in God. But the language of "begetting" or "generating" was considered important as contrasted with "producing," which was simply a creation out of nothing by the will of God. That is, as the Nicene/Constantinopolitan Creed states explicitly, the Son is begotten, *not* made. With this, the early church theologians were making a decisive and astounding claim about God's being. The claim is that, from eternity to eternity, God is the act of total self-conferral; God confers his very own nature on the Son and does so in the eternal generation or begetting of the Son. Thus, God's essence is marked by a fecundity and creativity that is a loving self-communication of God's nature. Holding nothing of himself back, God *is* the act of creative *self*-giving, and parents' communication of their human nature to their child is but a pale and secondary reflection of this act.

Classical Christian theology contrasts emphatically God's eternal life of generative self-communication with God's creation of the cosmos. Classical Christianity teaches that God *made* the world; God did not generate or beget the world. That is, the created world is not of God's own nature. Rather, the creation has its own unique constitution and nature, marked by real existence, dependent on God's creative and sustaining will yet real in its own right. Thus, by insisting in the Nicene/Constantinopolitan Creed that the Son is begotten, not made, the early theologians intentionally and consciously made a fundamental distinction between the eternal Word's relation to God and the creation's relation to God. This was the distinction between the *generation* of the Son and the *creation* of the world. The begotten Son, the second person of the Trinity, issues forth from the being of the Father. He shares the divine substance and nature. He is of the Godhead. The creation, on the other hand, is made out of *nothing* by the will and pleasure of the Creator. It is not of the divine nature; it does not participate in the eternity and being of God, but enjoys its own kind of reality — dependent, contingent, and real in its specific creaturely way.[17]

With this classical Christian distinction between the eternal begetting of the Son and the creation of the world in mind, it is striking to find in the recently issued *Supplemental Liturgical Texts* of the Episcopal Church statements that describe God giving birth to the world. For this essay, of specific interest is the "Second Supplemental Eucharistic Prayer." The Commentary accompanying the texts states that this second eucharistic prayer "has the central metaphor of God bringing to birth and nourishing the creation."[18] Of particular concern is the following passage from the prayer:

> O God, from before time you made ready the creation. Through your Wisdom, your Spirit moved over the deep and brought to birth the heavens: sun, moon, and stars; earth, winds, and waters; growing things, both plants and animals; and finally humankind. You made us in your image, male and female, to love and care for the earth and its creatures as you love and care for us, your children.[19]

Pertinent also is a prayer to be said by the celebrant of the eucharistic liturgy in concluding intercessions by the whole congregation. The prayer reads: "O God, who brought all things to birth in creation and gave us

17. This issue is well developed by Thomas F. Torrance in chapter 2 of *The Trinitarian Faith: The Evangelical Theology of the Ancient Catholic Church* (Edinburgh: T. & T. Clark, 1988).

18. *Commentary on Prayer Book Studies 30, Containing Supplemental Liturgical Texts* (New York: Church Hymnal Corporation, 1988), p. 58.

19. Ibid., p. 70.

grace to become your daughters and sons: draw us together that we may live in the Spirit as the family of Christ, to ages of ages. *Amen.*"[20]

Note two things about the first prayer. First, the prayer's words "from before time you made ready the creation" might mean that the creation existed "before time" and God was "readying it" by "moving over the deep." But if the creation existed before time, it can be thought to have existed from eternity — that is, to be co-eternal with God. And this would precisely be the case if God eternally begets, births, or generates the world. If the world is co-eternal with God and generated of the being of God, then the world *is* divine in some sense.

The second thing to note is the explicit use of birthing as a metaphor for God's original relation to the creation. This metaphor is not supported by any passage in Scripture — where the controlling image of God's act of creation is producing through command — but, most importantly, it implies that the creation is of God's nature, since a child is of the same (human) nature as its mother. It was precisely for this reason that classical Christian theology insisted on the eternal generation of the Son from the Father and differentiated this act from God's creation of the world. That which is generated of God is God.

These statements about God bringing the creation to birth appear in supplemental liturgical texts developed in response to a perceived need for inclusive language and imagery. Their intention, clearly, is to utilize birthing images, and in this sense feminine images, to describe God's action of creating. Thus a defender of these passages could claim that they do not intend to make a theological statement about how God created the world.

Such a defense is very weak. Whether intended or not, the actual words of the prayers in question borrow the language of generation (birthing, begetting) in the language of creating. In other words, this language confuses what classical Christian theology intentionally, and with a sense of enormous significance, carefully distinguished. The language of the Second Eucharistic Prayer and the concluding prayer invite Christian worshipers to think of the creation, and therefore of themselves, *in the very same* categories that classical Christian theology reserves for the Son of God, the second person of the Trinity. These prayers thus invite worshipers to count themselves as children of God after the fashion of Christ's eternal, uncreated Sonship — that is, to view themselves as proceeding

20. Ibid., p. 81.

from the essence of deity and therefore as being by nature (not by adoption, which is the New Testament teaching) children of God. This is a clear contradiction of classical theology.

How can we explain the source of this description of creation as generated or birthed, since it is not biblical? One possibility is the incorporation into feminist theology of ideas from ancient goddess religions, one of which is that the world was produced from the primordial mother goddess through an act of sexual intercourse with her consort. In fact, one of the most influential feminist theologians, Rosemary Radford Ruether, has done this. For example, in her book entitled *Sexism and God-Talk: Toward a Feminist Theology* she proposes "pagan sources" as one resource for feminist theology. Specifically she has in mind "pagan veneration of nature," "myths and cults of Goddesses," and "ancient Near Eastern religions," which are "seen as providing autonomous and different resources that illuminate both what Biblical religion rejected and what it appropriated from them in transformed fashion."[21] In this book Ruether describes the religious image of the goddess as "an impersonalized image of the mysterious powers of fecundity."[22] Ruether goes on to describe this resource for theology thus:

> We can speak of the root human image of the divine as the Primal Matrix, the great womb within which all things, Gods and humans, sky and earth, human and nonhuman beings, are generated. Here the divine is not abstracted into some other world beyond this earth but is the encompassing source of new life that surrounds the present world and assures its continuance. This is expressed in the ancient myth of the World Egg out of which all things arise.[23]

Whereas the Episcopal Church's proposed liturgy of divine birthing of the world simply adopts the image and language of the generation of the world from God, Ruether herself combines the primordial matrix theme of Babylonian goddess religion with other themes, notably the biblical prophetic tradition. Thus she proposes that we think of deity as the Shalom of our being and designates the word "God/ess" to denote this power. She defines it this way:

21. Ruether, *Sexism and God-Talk: Toward a Feminist Theology* (Boston: Beacon Press, 1983), pp. 39-41.
22. Ibid.
23. Ibid., p. 48.

[God/ess is] the foundation (at one and the same time) of our being and our new being [and] embraces both the roots of the material substratum of our existence (matter) and also the endlessly new creative potential (spirit). . . . God/ess liberates us from this false and alienated world, not by an endless continuation of the same trajectory of alienation but as a constant breakthrough that points us to new possibilities that are, at the same time, the regrounding of ourselves in the primordial matrix, the original harmony.[24]

This citation shows that Ruether is dissatisfied with the image of God simply as the Ground of Being, as an impersonal source from which the creation emanates in some automatic way. Rather, she suggests a paradoxical image of the divine: God/ess is the power that both roots us as primordial matrix and directs us to the future, to "new possibilities" (which certainly include social and not just individual aspects). God/ess also comprehends both matter and spirit.

Ruether's teaching about divine creativity contrasts sharply with traditional Christian teaching. Orthodox Christianity teaches that, as Father-Son, God's eternal nature is infinitely and eternally fecund and generative. Christian theology also teaches that God's creative act of producing the world from nothing is grounded in the generativity which God *is*. At the same time, orthodox theology carefully distinguishes between God's generativity as Father-Son and the act of creation *ex nihilo,* between begetting and creating. By contrast, by accepting the premises of Babylonian goddess religion, Ruether reduces God's generativity to God's relation to the cosmos. Inevitably, this theological move implies that we think of nature as in some sense divinely sacred. This doctrine suggests the *kami* (spirits of nature) of Japanese Shintoism, the fertility rites of Canaanite Baalism, and the modern sacralization of *Blut* and *Boden* in Nazi ideology. It should lead us to ask how Ruether protects her theology from the destructive implications of such sacralization of nature.

Problems with Confusing Christ and Creation

The working premise in this essay is that feminist theology is a critical reaction against what Grace Jantzen, cited at the beginning of this essay,

24. Ibid., p. 71.

calls "a series of interlocking and destructive dualisms." What I have shown thus far is that some feminist theologians attribute to the world functions (such as incarnation, redemption, and "begottenness") which classical theology reserves for Jesus Christ, the Incarnate Word of God. In the remainder of this essay, I wish to raise two problems with or questions about this "christification" of the creation.

1. Distortion of the Classical Doctrine of Creation

One question to be posed to some feminist theology is whether it distorts classical Christian teaching in the process of presenting feminist "holistic" alternatives. Specifically, when some feminist theologians imply that the classical Christian doctrine of creation from nothing underlies and ideologically supports sexist dualisms, are they accurate? Is it true that the traditional doctrine of creation from nothing is itself a destructive dualism and the source of all the others? Or is it an underlying destructive dualism only when it is misrepresented?

To make my point, I will summarize what I consider to be an accurate presentation of the Christian doctrine of creation from nothing and then compare it with some feminist claims about the classical doctrine.

Donald Bloesch provides a useful summary statement of the classical, orthodox Christian doctrine of creation from nothing:

1. God exists prior to and independent of the creaturely world of time and change.
2. God created the world "out of nothing" (in Latin, *ex nihilo*) by an act of will. This second statement means that God did not create the world from pre-existing "matter" or out of God's own divine substance; creation is made, not born.
3. The world exists apart from God, in the sense that it has its own real, though dependent, contingent existence, coherence, and order.
4. God is wholly immanent as the sustainer of all creaturely existence, as its protector, provider, and rejuvenator. This last point means that the whole creation and each of its parts and systems depend upon God's sustaining them in being every moment.[25]

25. Bloesch, *Battle for the Trinity* (Ann Arbor: Servant Publications, 1985), p. 29.

If this is an accurate presentation of the traditional, orthodox Christian doctrine of God as creator of the world *ex nihilo,* then the following statement is not a fair representation of the doctrine: "The doctrine of creation *ex nihilo* is usually centred on an understanding of God as pure spirit, utterly other than the material universe which is created by divine fiat."[26]

In the first place, this statement does not describe the classical doctrine because according to the latter, God creates both matter and spirit. God does not just create matter; God creates every aspect of creation, its spiritual and its material aspects, however they may be properly understood in their natures and relationships. This is implied in the second of the four statements just cited.

Second, the classical doctrine patently does not teach that God is "utterly other" than the creation. This contradicts statement four. Sallie McFague, for example, does not clearly distinguish what she rejects from the classical doctrine of creation from nothing when she states that the traditional doctrine of creation is "dualistic and hierarchical" and when she contrasts her model of the world as God's body with the "monarchical model," according to which the world is "an alien other over against God" and God is "distant from the world."[27]

In fact, as statement four declares, God is immanent as Creator to or in the creation as its power of existence and sustenance. This means that according to the classical doctrine, God is *not* an alien other over against the creation, and the classical doctrine does *not* teach that God is distant from the world. Granted, the doctrine of God usually associated with eighteenth-century Deism *does* describe God as utterly other than and transcendent to the creation. According to the Deist notion, God is pure cause and the world is effect; God does not continue to sustain the creation in being once it is made, but rather confers its own principle of continuing being to it. The theological targets of Jantzen and McFague appear to be Deism, not classical Christian theology. But they present their targets as classical, orthodox Christianity.

Third, the traditional doctrine does not imply the subordination of created matter to created spirit or created mind. This claim is made or implied when, for example, Jantzen says that the inferiority of matter to creaturely mind "reflects and is reflected by" the "dualism" between God

26. Jantzen, "Who Needs Feminism?" p. 340.
27. McFague, *Models of God,* pp. 61, 68.

and the world.[28] This claim is also implied when Rosemary Radford Ruether describes what feminist theology must reject (without clearly distinguishing it from classical doctrine), saying that "feminism must question the model of hierarchy that starts with nonmaterial spirit (God) as the source of the chain of being and continues down to nonspiritual 'matter' as the bottom of the chain of being and the most inferior, valueless, and dominated point in the chain of command."[29]

In fact, the subordination of matter to spirit or mind is *not* the logical implication of the classical doctrine of creation from nothing. Precisely because the creation is not an emanation from God, born of God's substance, creaturely matter and creaturely spirit are equally different and equally sustained by God. Spirit and matter may be different, but they are equally good and valued, according to the classical doctrine, because both derive from God and are sustained by God in the same way and for the same purpose. Since God as Creator is categorically — that is, ontologically — other than the creation, *all* aspects of the creation are equally present to and equally different from God. Matter is neither more nor less "god-like" than spirit or mind, and vice versa. Precisely this point is underscored in the orthodox understanding of the person of Christ as two natures, divine and human, in one flesh. His flesh, in the form of the eucharistic elements, for example, is as important to the members of Christ's body — the baptized — as Christ's teaching. The resurrected Lord is the crucified one — his embodied death is included in the resurrection victory, not just his mind.

I believe I have presented enough material to make the point of my first question: Does the critique of feminist theology really touch the classical, orthodox doctrine of creation *ex nihilo*? Is the feminist critique aimed at the real Christian thing or to something similar but basically different? As feminists describe their theological target, do they misrepresent classical, orthodox Christian doctrine? This is not just a petty pedantic quibble, since the so-called holistic alternatives are molded to be counterstatements to the dualistic doctrines that these feminist theologians criticize. In short, the question of clarity and accuracy in representing what Christianity actually teaches touches the substance of feminist theology's constructive theological proposals.

28. Jantzen, "Who Needs Feminism?" p. 340.
29. Ruether, *Sexism and God-Talk*, p. 85.

2. *The Burdens of Being Christ*

In different ways, as we saw, Sallie McFague and Carter Heyward state or imply that the creation is the incarnation of God. McFague's metaphor — the world is God's body — suggests that the whole creation incarnates God. Heyward's notion that humans "god" in their efforts at right-making relationship suggests that God is incarnate in human efforts toward just and mutual relationships. Further, I noted that liturgical statements that the world is birthed by God invite the worshiper to think of himself or herself as of the divine nature, as proceeding, like Jesus Christ, from the essence of deity.

Such teaching undermines fundamental Christian faith-claims. One such claim is that Jesus Christ is the unique incarnation of God. Don't the feminist alternatives mentioned rather suggest that if Jesus Christ has any significance, it is that he is merely a particularly vibrant example or representative of what, potentially at least, the whole creation or persons in right relation are? In other words, the feminist teaching that any human can "god" God or that the earth incarnates God destroys the uniqueness of Jesus Christ. It replaces the classical doctrine of Christ's uniqueness with another claim: that of Christ's paradigmatic or exemplary status. As example or paradigm, Jesus Christ incarnates not God but a principle: the principle of creation's deity or the principle of humanity's potential for "godding."

Thus Christ is reduced to a manifestation or expression of a God/creation unity that is real apart from and independent of the person of Jesus. This cuts the nerve of evangelism and mission. If Jesus Christ is not the unique, God-intended means in and through whom persons come to a right relation to God, then to evangelize in the name of Christ is religious imperialism, imposing an example merely meaningful to us in our cultural context upon others in their cultural context.

Further, demoting Christ from being the unique Incarnation of God to being only an example of a universally true God/human unity undermines the centrality of Jesus Christ for the human knowledge of God. For a theologian to affirm this universal unity means that he or she could in principle derive his or her knowledge of God from some source other than God's revelation in Christ. This ultimately makes the theologian himself or herself the arbiter of revelation; indeed, the theologian's own experience becomes revelatory or elevated to the status of revealed source. In this regard, Carter Heyward's statement is instructive: "I am re-imaging humanity, God, and Jesus in order to speak my truth."[30] Ironically, the establishment of personal (or women's) experience as the critical standard for all truth about God and creation necessarily generates a destructive dualism between those with the "right" consciousness and anyone else with a different consciousness or experience. Conflict is inevitable, for what is at stake is not the interpretation of a commonly acknowledged objective standard of revelation but the validity of the standard as such.

Finally, if Christ is not the unique Incarnation of the Word but merely exemplifies an already real or potential union between us and God or the creation and God, the note of triumphant victory in Christian preaching is substantially undermined. For according to this feminist teaching, Jesus at most can motivate us as an example of what we either are or have the potential to be, depending on our own efforts. Ultimately, we are responsible for producing "a life of freedom and fulfillment for all," according to McFague, or even "the redemption of God," to cite Heyward.

This duty puts McFague in the odd position of defining the theological task not as traditional theology does — that is, naming God in the light of God's naming of himself in revelation, and thus witnessing to the redemption God has achieved. Rather, theology for McFague necessarily becomes a redeeming work, the theologian herself, through her creativity, cooperating with God to achieve the this-worldly perfect society that can come only through human efforts. Theologians, our redeemers — a remarkable thought!

This is not a caricature of McFague's conception of the theological task. Throughout *Models of God* she stresses that this task is one of human construction for the promotion of an ideal society in this world. For McFague, theology is primarily a work of the theologian's creative imagination, a matter of constructing images and metaphors that are required by the demands of the present, as interpreted by the theologian. "Theology is mostly fiction," she writes: "it is the elaboration of key metaphors and models."[31] These creative constructions themselves are intended to move human beings toward being good.

McFague does seek to show that her vision of a utopian future is in continuity with the Christian tradition. To make that plausible, how-

30. Heyward, *The Redemption of God,* p. 14.

31. McFague, *Models of God,* pp. xi-xii. In her words, "Metaphorical theology is a postmodern, highly skeptical, heuristic enterprise, which claims that in order to be faithful to the God of its tradition — the God on the side of life and its fulfillment — we must try out new pictures that will bring the reality of God's love into the imaginations of women and men of today" (ibid., p. xii).

ever, she reduces the gospel as proclaimed in the Bible to the idea that "the universe [sic!] is neither indifferent nor malevolent but that there is a power (and a personal power at that) which is on the side of life and its fulfillment."[32] And she reduces and distorts the substance of the New Testament to *parables,* as destabilizing forms of discourse; to *table fellowship,* as embodying the principle of inclusivity; and to *the cross,* as the principle of equality.[33] Another distortion is her claim that Jesus Christ does not "do something on our behalf" on the cross. The most that Jesus' cross means to McFague is that "at the heart of the universe is unqualified love working to befriend the needy, the outcast, the oppressed."[34] Christ's cross does not mean that God has done or is doing anything apart from our own efforts to produce an egalitarian, just world. The emphasis throughout McFague's book is not on what God has done or is doing but on what we must do — our creative efforts.

This requires McFague to ransack the religious traditions of her own culture for resources for the fabrication of new, allegedly more effective images. In this process, she does not draw back from pasting traditional labels on her efforts — "God," "creation," "Christ," "Christian," "gospel." Is her purpose to maximize the rhetorical clout of her constructs to further her this-worldly utopian vision of a "radically egalitarian, nondualistic way of being in the world"? Doesn't that come close to elitist manipulation of the "masses" through the use of religious symbols, the kind of charge Karl Marx made against Christianity? Only McFague would have the theologian do it intentionally and consciously. The task of the theologian, as she represents it, is rife with the dangers of manipulation, elitism, and outright deception, since the theologian uses words related to God as redeemer but really means a human project being engineered by educated, socially well-placed elites.

Also, when a theologian constructs his or her own religion to promote some this-worldly ideal society and encounters the ferocity of evil, he or she is vulnerable to sadness and despair. I am not surprised to hear these notes sounded in a later statement from Carter Heyward in *Touching Our Strength:*

> I am writing between sadness and hope. My faith in you, in myself, in our sacred source seems irrepressible, though why I cannot tell in

32. Ibid., p. x.
33. Ibid., pp. 49-55.
34. Ibid., p. 55.

this moment, for around and within me is much despair. I'm afraid it will not be long before we know we are not exaggerating when we speak of fascism here at home. We are destroying ourselves, our flesh and blood. It is not "those people" who are shooting up with dirty needles; not "those others" taking their own lives in shame and terror; not "them" battered to within an inch of their lives. Unless we know at the core of our integrity that we are they, neither this book nor any resource on love will make much sense to us now.[35]

Such sadness pervades Heyward's book. It witnesses commendably to a heart sensitive to the pain of the world. But Heyward's despair logically flows from identifying our efforts at mutual relationships as the place where "god" happens. Such a theology in principle bars itself from the joy of the Christian gospel's proclamation that in Christ's death and resurrection sin and death have been in principle overcome.

Conclusion

Feminist theology constructively proposes holistic models to replace destructively dualistic models of God and world, mind and body, male and female, reason and nature, First World and Third World. Some feminist theologians claim that the doctrine of creation from nothing is responsible for these destructive dualisms and propose new ways of speaking theologically about the world. One trend in some feminist theology is to attribute to the world qualities that traditional, orthodox theology reserves exclusively for Jesus Christ, the Incarnate Word. I have surveyed feminist theologians speaking of the world as God's incarnation, of human creatures enacting redemption and even redeeming God, of the world as being begotten by God, not made by God.

Thus I have identified a tendency in some feminist theology to "christify" creation, and I have posed two critical questions. First, does the critique of the doctrine of creation from nothing have the classical, orthodox doctrine in view or a perversion of that doctrine? I suggest that what feminist theologians attack is a parody of the doctrine, and therefore ask whether feminist constructive proposals may be keyed to a mistaken version of Christian teaching. Second, doesn't the tendency to think of

35. Heyward, *Touching Our Strength*, p. 88.

creatures as classical theology thinks of Christ undermine mission, attack the doctrine of creation, exalt the theologian as the locus of revelation, and generate disingenuous, if not deceitful, theological programs?

If the preceding analysis and critique bear critical testing, one important implication follows. Classical orthodox doctrines — for example, those of God as Trinity, creation *ex nihilo,* and Jesus Christ as the unique revelation and redeemer — may be better theological resources for our time than some of the feminist proposals we have examined in this essay.

Worldview, Language, and Radical Feminism: An Evangelical Appraisal

STEPHEN M. SMITH

WE LIVE IN A TIME of massive cultural conflict. Some sociologists tell us that it reflects a split in the middle class between those in the business community and those in the "knowledge class" (Peter Berger),[1] or between "traditionalists" and "expressive individualists" (Robert Bellah).[2] However it is described, we sense it and wonder how to be faithful Christians in this conflict.

This conflict is in reality a clash of worldviews; it is not new in the history of ideas. What is new is that it is being fought on so many fronts: sexual morality, the authority of Scripture, the possibility of revelation, the nature of God-language, and liturgy. What makes it so difficult to analyze at the rational level is that worldviews are forms of enchantment, to use C. S. Lewis's image, which cast their spell over us and shape our consciousness and identity at their deepest levels, and rarely come completely to rational, propositional expression.[3]

Central to this conflict is the act of naming. Naming is the ability

---

1. Berger, *A Rumor of Angels,* expanded edition (New York: Anchor Books, 1990), pp. 143-66.

2. Bellah et al., *Habits of the Heart: Individualism and Commitment in American Life* (Berkeley: University of California Press, 1985); see especially pp. 33-35, pp. 47-48, and chap. 6.

3. Lewis, *The Weight of Glory* (Grand Rapids: William B. Eerdmans, 1949), pp. 1-15. In *The Silver Chair,* one of the volumes in the Chronicles of Narnia, Lewis describes this process in a mythic narrative form as the Queen of the Underworld seeks to cast her spell and convince her would-be victims that there is no transcendent reality (see chap. 12).

to shape the meaning of an event, phenomenon, or practice by determining the vocabulary we use to speak of it. Is homosexuality to be named as an "alternative" along the "spectrum" of sexual expressions, or is it a moral failure and a sin? Is abortion to be named a necessary private act of women who would claim their "reproductive freedom"? Are those who see abortion as the killing of human life to be described as pro-life or anti-choice or anti-abortion? Is the Fatherhood of God to be called a patriarchal, sexist projection or the gift of divine self-naming? Naming shapes our perception of reality. Much is at stake.

In the cultural conflict of our time, the right or authority to name is crucial. Different worldviews generate different names for the same phenomenon. These different names determine whether the phenomenon is believed to be good or bad, desirable or undesirable. Names express worldviews and worldviews determine names.

An interesting case is the collapse of the East European socialist states in late 1989. As they were seen to be — to put it nicely — dead ends, the proposition of the good of state economic control simply lost legitimacy. Until that time it seemed that Western socialists were given the moral authority to name market economics by the pejorative term "capitalism." But when socialism not only failed but was rejected by the people who had lived under it, those in the West could name their experiment, and they called it by the laudatory term "free market economics." History seems to be giving them the right to name it at this moment. In this case, naming is a spoil of historical success.

Abortion is another example. In *Abortion and the Politics of Motherhood*, sociologist Kristin Luker demonstrates that those in the pro-life movement see the world as created by a transcendent Creator who gives it moral norms and who gives great value to the human person. Accordingly, abortion has to be named as killing human life and opposing abortion as pro-life. These names seem to flow inevitably from a larger vision of the world. Luker also describes those in the pro-choice movement as individuals with a worldview that affirms the quality of life, the centrality of reason, and the human capacity to manage and control life. We can clearly see why the term "pro-choice" is so apt.[4]

In his book entitled *Aborting America*, Dr. Bernard Nathanson

---

4. Luker, *Abortion and the Politics of Motherhood* (Berkeley: University of California Press, 1984), pp. 158-91. The crucial chapter on this issue is titled "Worldviews of the Activists," in which the depth of the worldview differences is made plain for all to see.

explains that he was a leading abortionist who, in his studies of the development of the fetus, became convinced that real human beings were being exterminated in abortions.[5] When he became compelled by the sense that valued human lives were at stake, he had to switch sides. But he still remained an atheist. Later he came to see that he needed to account for his sense of the value of human life. He could do this only by affirming its transcendent grounding, but in acknowledging this he knew he had sinned gravely by taking human life. He sought forgiveness and found it in Christ and his church. Nathanson had the courage to break the spell of the secular worldview and its names, even though it meant facing his guilt, a guilt hidden behind the "value-neutral" naming of the secular worldview. Providentially, he discovered that the God who values life and opposes its taking forgives and renews in Jesus Christ.

In this essay I will propose that there is a profound, albeit mysterious, connection between language and worldview. For simplicity's sake, I will define a worldview as a metaphysical vision that defines reality, identity, morality, and destiny. In other words, it deals with issues of the ultimate. It asks who or what God is, who we are, what we are to do, and where we are going. This will be the working definition.

I propose that in the church there is a battle of worldviews being waged between classical theists and religious monists. I contend that embracing or being enchanted by the monist worldview will eventually result in the use of language patently different from that presently used in the church's worship and preaching. Accepting religious monism will eventually require a renaming of God to bring the names used in prayer, worship, and theology into line with the God of monism. The books I will examine — Bishop J. A. T. Robinson's *Honest to God*, Bishop John Spong's *Living in Sin?* and Professor Sallie McFague's *Models of God* — are ones I have chosen not because they are eccentric or extreme, but because they are widely influential, because they understand this clash of worldviews from the monist perspective, and because they demonstrate the inevitable outworking of monism in the naming of God. They illustrate and clarify the battle of worldviews and the consequences of a coherent advocacy of a monist position.

Both classical theism and religious monism can be described in terms of the fourfold outline of worldviews just provided. Classical theism affirms a transcendent Creator who is revealed in Jesus, the incarnate Son of God.

5. Nathanson, *Aborting America* (New York: Pinnacle Books, 1979).

This worldview is based on the beliefs that Jesus died for sinners and rose again (reality), that humanity is fallen (identity), that there is a transcultural moral structure (morality), and that there is a hope of heaven and a danger of hell (destiny). Religious monism holds the unity of the creator with the creation in that nothing exists outside of God (reality). This worldview is based on the beliefs that Jesus is at most the most perfectly actualized human, that humanity is not fallen but is ignorant and unfulfilled (identity), that morality is relativistic and experiential (morality), and that there is a hope of self-actualization (destiny). As we shall see, the radical feminist renaming of God proceeds quite logically from the monistic worldview.[6]

I. Worldview Clashes in the Church:
Honest to God and the Monist Project

Although the historical roots of the monist movement we are going to discuss reach back much further, let us begin with its entry into consciousness of average churchpeople: the publication in 1963 of Bishop J. A. T. Robinson's theological landmark entitled *Honest to God*, perhaps the most widely read work of theology in our century.[7] It was tremendously popular: three years after publication it had sold nearly one million copies. Two decades later, it is still in print.

At one level the book is quite attractive. The bishop, a New Testament scholar, was deeply concerned to reach the modern skeptic. In the tumultuous sixties, when everything was being questioned (except, of course, the wisdom of questioning everything), here was a courageous man who was honest enough to ask publicly the "big question": Is the orthodox worldview a necessary component of Christianity? Robinson pulled no punches. He claimed that this orthodox "way of thinking is the greatest obstacle to an intelligent faith," and that something "should [be] put in its place" (p. 43).

6. Terminological clarity is difficult because meanings at this time are in a state of flux and because they can be used both to identify and value or to condemn. Monism is a term taken from the discussion in McFague's *Models of God: Theology for an Ecological, Nuclear Age* (Philadelphia: Fortress Press, 1987). It covers *both* pantheism (all is one) and panentheism (God and cosmos are distinguishable but *not* separable). Dualism also covers many views such as the gnostic vision that matter is evil. I will use *monism* as McFague does — to describe the notion that God and cosmos are distinct. This is a Christian first principle that is found in Genesis 1 and is the first statement of all ecumenical creeds.

7. Robinson, *Honest to God* (Philadelphia: Westminster Press, 1963). Subsequent references to this volume will be made parenthetically in the text.

What was (and is) striking about the bishop's book was his use of the term "projection" for the orthodox worldview. He claimed that belief in a transcendent God the Father was "a projection, an idol" (p. 41) that was no longer persuasive or even believable and needed to be replaced. To support this analysis, he used Feuerbach and Freud (as he should have). The question he raised was this: Can we construct an alternative worldview that will promote and protect "the faith" for our time? Bishop Robinson's project was to construct a religious worldview recognizably Christian yet able to win over those naturalists and skeptics unable (allegedly) to believe in a transcendent God.

What he proposed he borrowed from Rudolf Bultmann and Paul Tillich. From Bultmann, Robinson got his hermeneutical strategy: to see behind the Bible's "prescientific mythology" (e.g., the resurrection of Jesus in space and time) to existential truths of self-understanding. From Tillich, Robinson got his alternative monist worldview in which God is called the "ground of being." God is no longer to be conceived of dualistically as a transcendent Trinity of persons wholly other from the creation; rather, he is to be conceived of as the " 'ecstatic' character of *this* world" (p. 56). Thus God can be "encountered in his fullness only *between* man and man. . . . God, the unconditional, is to be found only in, with *and under* the conditional relations of this life" (p. 60; emphases in original).

The bishop rejected the orthodox worldview as a now unbelievable projection and proposed another more compatible with the modern mind. The logic of his case would force him to concede that his alternative is equally, and more self-consciously, a projection. But here is the difference: the new projection is a version of monism. In monism all is one, not one thing but one in the union of being: "Being is nothing apart from beings," to quote a recurrent phrase in John Macquarrie's monist theology.[8] This is the worldview battle, if it can be reduced to a bumper sticker: dualism versus monism. Or, to draw the battle lines more fully: classical theism

---

8. Macquarrie, *Thinking About God* (New York: Harper & Row, 1975). In chapter 10 of this volume, "God and the World: Two Realities or One?" (pp. 110-20), we have a very clear monist case, although Macquarrie uses the term *organic*, not *monist*. He does compare his worldview with theistic dualism. He contends that God and the cosmos are "distinguishable but not separable within an organic whole" (p. 111). He calls this view panentheism and rejects pantheism. He provides a systematic working out of this worldview in his *Principles of Christian Theology*, 2nd ed. (New York: Charles Scribner's Sons, 1977), pp. 84-148.

with its distinction between Creator and creation versus religious monism with its unity of Being-in-beings. It should be noted that the term "dualism" is *not* being used in a gnostic sense of affirming an evil creation, but rather refers to any worldview which affirms the difference and distinction between Creator and creation.

It is interesting to note that some naturalist and skeptical philosophers saw this paradigm shift clearly. Alasdair MacIntyre claimed that Bishop Robinson was an atheist with a thin (and desperate) coating of religious verbiage.[9] Logical positivist A. J. Ayer observed that Robinson was "coming round to a position a number of us have held for some time."[10] Secular monists recognized Robinson as going their way.

Interestingly, Archbishop Michael Ramsey noted that Robinson appeared "to reject the concept of a personal God as expressed in the Bible and the Creed." Robinson responded by saying, "I reject emphatically any suggestion that what I have written is contrary to the Catholic Faith."[11] Robinson's response was remarkable. Didn't he understand what he was arguing for? Perhaps he didn't understand that the worldview he rejected was a crucial part of the Catholic faith. Perhaps he was so enchanted by his monism and moved by the virtue of his missionary intentions that he didn't understand what he was doing. Whatever the reason, the bishop's response to the archbishop appears to be a study in denial.

Whether or not Robinson completely understood what he was doing, *Honest to God* gave the church a persuasive, popular case for religious monism legitimated by a scholarly bishop. Let us go back to the question of naming. If Robinson is correct, then classical Christian theism is a false projection and God must be renamed (though Robinson himself remained comfortable with the biblical language). Despite his response to Archbishop Ramsey, Robinson sensed these implications of his project and claimed that he was involved in a "reluctant revolution whose full extent

9. MacIntyre, "God and the Theologians," in *The Honest to God Debate*, ed. David L. Edwards (Philadelphia: Westminster Press, 1963), pp. 215-28. This volume, published within months of *Honest to God*, contains many significant analyses and responses. Robinson considered MacIntyre's challenge sufficient to respond directly to it (pp. 228-31).

10. Ayer, in Keith W. Clements, *Lovers of Discord* (London: SPCK, 1988), p. 197. The entire chapter, pp. 178-215, is very helpful. For another analysis of this book, see Robin Gill, *Theology and Social Structure* (London: Mowbrays, 1977), pp. 83-103.

11. This exchange is cited in Eric James, *A Life of Bishop John A. T. Robinson* (Grand Rapids: William B. Eerdmans, 1987), pp. 121, 122-23.

I have hardly begun to comprehend" (p. 27). Now we *are* beginning to comprehend it and to see such renaming proposed by serious theologians and supported by many in the leadership of the major churches. It is a conceptual revolution, a revolution in worldview that redefines God, identity, morality, and destiny.

The grand story of the Bible is of God, who names himself. This gracious act of revelation is central. We might say that the Old Testament is concerned with who the real God is. Is God the Lord, or is God found among the idols of the pagan nations who are monistically identified with powers of nature and fertility? Is he the transcendent Creator, Redeemer, and Judge, or is he a power in and of nature? The God of the Bible names himself. The Son himself gives the final form of that name as "Father, Son, and Holy Spirit" at the end of the Gospel of St. Matthew. If this grand story is true, monism is a false projection leading to a false understanding of reality, identity, morality, and destiny. It is false at every crucial point.

However, if Robinson's project is correct, we must understand the message of Scripture in a much different way. Let us be clear that the Bible describes a God who is clearly distinct from his creation, who has willed it into being. The cosmos is not eternal, and it does not flow from the divine. Humans are not in any sense divine beings but God's beloved creatures, now tragically flawed. God intervenes in the story to save his creatures. Bushes flame and speak, mountains smoke, laws are given, waters are stopped, and prophets speak after having visions — then, of course, God the Son comes to live among us, suffers for our sins, and breaks the bonds of death. But if Robinson is correct, all this is projection and indeed false projection. We cannot believe in a story in which God has named himself. We must name God. Theology has become self-conscious projection. Yes, Jesus is still important as a "man for others" and a "window into Being," but he cannot be God the Son except in the sense that we all (potentially) are! Certainly there is a morality — indeed, a "new morality" — that we can all intuit, but monism "delivers" us from transcendent, transcultural norms. Heaven and hell are merely metaphors for knowledge or ignorance of our union with Being.

New Age religion is also a form of religious monism. It has concluded that we are divine, though it is not clear what that means. Whatever it means, I would contend that all forms of monism wreak havoc with a meaningful understanding of self. Perhaps that is why they are so susceptible to myths of androgyny.

Further, if religious monism is true, then it is the task of the theological leadership to do the naming. No longer will the theologian simply clarify the faith given in Bible and creeds and apply it to the challenges of the age. Here is the truly significant task: the naming of God, constructing visions of reality that can aid us in our social projects or our quest for "wholeness." No longer need we be hindered by transcendent claims of morality and meaning; the possibilities of world and self-construction are endless. To stay in the church, all we need do is to show some connection with the "historical Jesus," if only as the first example of the truly self-actualized person each of us may one day become.

Episcopal Bishop John Spong has this understanding of the task of religious leadership. He describes the role of the "new Bishop" to be "defining God, producing liturgies, reinterpreting creeds . . . and determining the boundaries of moral and immoral behavior."[12] The only price monism asks is that one set aside one's archaic concept of a truly transcendent God who names and reveals himself.

II. Bishop Spong and Monist Application

Bishop John Shelby Spong is a very controversial man. He has appeared on countless television talk shows and has argued with remarkable eloquence for a more "inclusive" sexual ethic. He has challenged the church to be more actively engaged in the challenges of our times and culture. *Time* magazine described his recent book on sexual ethics, *Living in Sin? A Bishop Rethinks Human Sexuality,* as the most radical work on such a topic by a Christian bishop.

But why look at Bishop Spong? As an Episcopalian I am quite concerned about the leadership of my communion, but for our purposes Bishops Robinson and Spong when taken together form a historical parable of the consequences of a religious monism working itself out in the life of the church. Bishop Spong is a committed monist; he is quite aware that he has the task of "defining God" and constructing a religious worldview for our time. I use Bishop Spong because he gives such a clear illustration of the coherent — indeed, courageous — implementation of the monist vision in the church, an implementation for which Bishop Robinson prepared the way but which he did not apply as thoroughly as Bishop Spong. Bishop Spong is also a symbol of the magnitude of conflict in the church and of its crisis of identity.

12. Spong, *Living in Sin?* (San Francisco: Harper & Row, 1988), p. 223.

John Spong began his public journey in 1973 with *Honest Prayer,* the matter of prayer clearly being a crucial issue for a monist. In this book we can see the ideas we saw in *Honest to God.* At this point Bishop Spong's thoughts were not yet well formed. He clearly pitted himself against "dualist" thought and continually referred to God as "the Source of Life."[13] For him, then, God is greater than but not separate from the world. Heaven is redefined as God's earthly presence. God "does not live in some other worldly place called heaven"; he is "the Ground of Being . . . the Depth of Life" (pp. 46, 51). Further, "God is not a superperson . . . but he is the Power of Love. He is the Meaning of Life" (p. 79). What is prayer? "The life of prayer is for me the responsibility to open myself in love to the transcendent in everyone I meet" (p. 29). Clear enough? This is a consistent monist redefinition of prayer. Prayer is a "quality" relationship with another, not a relationship with the transcendent. The tragedy for the monist is that without categories he is as vulnerable to the demonic as to the Spirit of God. The bishop's final comments on the Lord's Prayer are a remarkable exercise in monist redefinition. To hallow God's name is to become "our deepest and truest selves" (p. 122). To affirm God's glory is to be "fully alive" (p. 123). The Lord's Prayer becomes a soliloquy for self-actualization.

Recently Bishop Spong took a brief sabbatical at Harvard, where he spent much time engaging "the challenge of science."[14] "I believe that the word 'God' points to that which is ultimately real," he wrote afterward. "I believe that humanity itself represents the emerging of consciousness within this many billion year old universe." Carl Sagan and any naturalist could have said this. What A. J. Ayer wrote of Bishop Robinson could be equally applied to Bishop Spong. "I believe that this emerging consciousness will someday be seen as nothing less than that which we now call spirit and divinity," he continued. The bishop need not wait for "someday." New Age monism already sees this and has boldly announced our divinity. Again we can see the confusion of identity as it plagues the monist worldview.[15]

---

13. Spong, *Honest Prayer* (New York: Seabury Press, 1973), pp. 8, 123. Subsequent references to this volume will be made parenthetically in the text.

14. Spong, "The Task That Lies Ahead," *The Voice,* April 1990. All quotes in this and the following paragraph are from this essay.

15. This confusion can be seen in Bishop Spong's most recent book, *Rescuing the Bible from Fundamentalism* (San Francisco: Harper & Row, 1991). After discussing the I AM sayings of Jesus in the Gospel of John, the bishop concludes that "the Christian is the one called so deeply . . . into being that he or she can say with Christlike integrity, I AM" (p. 209).

Earlier I noted that a monist within the church had to tie this perspective to Jesus to justify his claim to be Christian. Not surprisingly, the bishop's next line is "I believe that Jesus, whom I call Lord, is that unique life where humanity and divinity flow together." Since he also believes that "divinity" flows through all of us, Jesus can be no more than our Guru, the exemplar of God-consciousness or divinity for Western Christians. By "Lord" the bishop can mean no more than this. Here again is a vague but discernible monist vision that renames both humanity as the divine incarnation of evolutionary consciousness and God as the "ultimately real."

We can now focus on Spong's *Living in Sin?* to see what monism looks like in radical feminist dress as it is applied to sexual ethics. Because of Spong's proposals in sexual ethics, this book is considered quite radical — which indeed it is. He makes the case that since we are on the other side of the sexual revolution and sex is now separated from marriage, and since we cannot reverse the "tide of history," we must have the "courage" to bring some stability to this new situation. To do this, the church is being called to bless people who choose to live together in various ways — heterosexuals in trial liaisons, homosexuals in committed unions (much like heterosexual marriages), and the elderly in pragmatic pairings (those, for example, who choose to live together rather than marry and lose part of their Social Security payments).

This case has a measure of plausibility. But the preceding proposals are only the beginning. The bishop sees the real battle not simply as a revision of sexual morality to meet changed circumstances, but as a battle of worldviews, in particular a battle over authority. "The debate in the church . . . ," he says, "is over the authority of Scripture and the role of both Scripture and the church" (p. 116).

Bishop Spong then attempts to show why the Scriptures are a thin reed to rely upon for guidance in these areas. First, the Scriptures are awash in contradictions. "In the Bible there are conflicting accounts of creation, conflicting versions of the Ten Commandments, conflicting understandings of who Jesus is and was, conflicting details concerning what happened on the first Easter," he claims (pp. 111, 112). On the literal level the Bible is inadequate. But this is a relatively small matter to the bishop, who believes that the second and real problem is that the Bible represents a patriarchal projection, a projection created by males to serve their interests and help them dominate women and indeed all of creation. As Spong explains it, "Human beings always form their understanding of

God out of their own values, needs, and self-understanding. We do make God in our own image. We deify whatever we perceive to be the source of security and awe" (p. 122).

Here again is Bishop Robinson's assertion that classical Christian theism is a projection. But now Bishop Spong has wedded it to the cause of radical feminism. With this cause in mind, he sees the Bible as permeated on "every page" with a "pervasive anti-female bias" (p. 120). The Bible represents the male reaction to the power of the more ancient mother-goddess. Unlike the nurturing mother-goddess identified with the creation, Yahweh is a "solitary male God" (p. 120) distinct from and ruling over the creation, and thus a projection of the male quest for legitimacy and dominance. The God of the Bible is anti-woman.

But the bishop has good news. We are leaving the dark night of sexism and patriarchy, and a new age is emerging with its new consciousness. First was the monistic, peaceful age of the goddess. Then came the violent age of the male quest for power, culminating in biblical religion with its transcendent masculine Creator. But now comes a return to monism, mutuality, and the affirmation that all is good. Indeed, this is the very function of the bishop's Christ, who is to "make that goodness [of creation] real and apparent. That is what salvation is all about" (p. 160). Now in the new age we must follow the bishop who is "willing to live fully, freely, and openly, scaling the barriers that inhibit life" (p. 160).

If all this does not dissuade us from leaning on Scripture for sexual ethics, the bishop reminds us that the person who spoke most about sexual issues was the Apostle Paul. He was never married, "seemed incapable of relating to women," and was torn by "inner conflict" (p. 151). Surely we need not consider his "ill-informed, culturally biased prejudices" (p. 152) in the area of sexual ethics — or anywhere else, for that matter — since he seems incapable of telling us how good we are and helping us to "scale barriers."

Yet behind this self-contradictory, sexist projection written by ill-informed, biased males, behind this twisted word is nevertheless(!) a Word. And it is this: all is good. All is united to the "ground of all being." Jesus connects us with our "original goodness," giving us "courage" to be all we are created to be (p. 161). So much for the living God in his self-revelation! To free himself to make new proposals for sexual ethics, the bishop has had to reduce the Bible to a historical relic that has almost no value and indeed is dangerous because it presents the ideology of patriarchal repression. The "word" behind the words in the Bible is no more than a vague, monist sentiment that all is good since it is united to the ground of being.

I contend that in the writings of Bishop Spong we have an illustration of the monist theological project in full flower — or better, in complete decay. All that is left is ever more complete condemnations of the Bible and its God and ever more "progressive" proposals for blessing other forms of sexual behavior, based on no other authority than the accepted practices of contemporary society and offering no hope of healing and redemption.[16] In Bishop Robinson we saw the proposal of a new, monist worldview without a clear understanding of what changes that would entail. In Bishop Spong we see the application of the monistic worldview to sexual morality, which clearly paves the way for the renaming of God.

III. Sallie McFague and Monist Naming

In *Honest to God* we see the classic theistic worldview abolished and a monist proposal being crafted. In it, calling God "Father" is still acceptable if one knows what all that sort of language "really means" as we move beyond such primitive anthropomorphic projections. In *Living in Sin?* the theistic projection with its language is no longer seen as benign — it now represents the male religious will to power. The language of God the Father in heaven *must* go to deliver us from an oppressive male God and help us to our own self-actualization. But at this point Bishop Spong has yet to make the next move in calling the church to rename God, although he tells us that part of a bishop's job description is "defining God."

Bishop Spong applied his worldview to sexual ethics and the role of the church, yet he made no explicit linguistic proposals. But clearly, if God has not named himself, why can't we do the naming? In fact, if God has not named himself, we *must* do the naming. If we operate with a monist model, other names for God suggest themselves as more appropriate than "Father." "Mother" may top the list. Naming is merely the linguistic component of the theological task of constructing alternative worldviews and models.

16. As exhibit A of this contention, I would direct the reader to Carter Heyward's *Touching Our Strength* (San Francisco: Harper & Row, 1989). In applying monist principles to sexuality, Heyward, an Episcopal priest, claims that "our erotic power is sacred." Further, "God is not above sex or gender, but rather is immersed in our . . . erotic particularities" (p. 103). Even "sadomasochistic eroticism" may be "a relational conduit through which we move toward mutuality . . . with God" (p. 108).

This is what the feminist theologian Sallie McFague argues in her book entitled *Models of God.*[17] She argues for a worldview that she describes as "monist and perhaps most precisely designated as panentheistic. . . . The world does not exist outside or apart from God" (p. 72). She claims as her tradition such notables as Schleiermacher, Hegel, Tillich, and the contemporary process theologians, a tradition she characterizes as "monistic," defined as affirming "the basic oneness of all reality, including the unity of God and the world" (p. 93). The cosmos is God's "body." This God cannot intervene in history because all is "historical-cultural evolutionary process" (p. 73). Further, since the old model of God and its supporting worldview is "monarchical" and hierarchical, it is the cause of "many kinds of oppression," and to encourage that way of thinking is "pernicious" (p. 67). Classical theism is now seen as "idolatrous" and "opposed to life" (p. ix).

Thus McFague not only would engage in an attempt to overthrow classical theism (as did Bishops Robinson and Spong) but advances beyond them to advocate a new language. What is needed is both to "unseat . . . the royal model" and to replace it with a model that will be sufficiently attractive to "move people to live by it and work for it" (p. 80). To move people, personal metaphors are needed; Robinson and Spong's impersonal language of "the ground of being," while probably more formally accurate, will not do. We need personal models, and McFague proposes that we call God "mother, lover and friend . . . models that have been strangely neglected in the Judeo-Christian tradition" (p. 84). Of course, they have been "neglected" because they are not given in the biblical revelation, but McFague seems so enchanted by her own creation that she has missed the obvious. Her linguistic proposal is designed to express her monist worldview in contrast to "the radically transcendent models for God in the Western tradition" (p. 85).

McFague's justification for such a proposal is the crisis of our times. Nuclear proliferation and the problems of our environment compel her to construct this model of God to express a monistic, organic, evolutionary worldview that she believes will be healing and redemptive. The "dualistic, monarchical" worldview of classical Christianity she considers to be the source of our problems. How monism can help us with the ecological crisis is beyond me. Isn't the fire that destroys the forest an expression of

---

17. McFague, *Models of God.* Subsequent references to this volume will be made parenthetically in the text.

God as much as the beauty of the unburned forest? How can I transcend it in order to act in a way that will do it "good" when there is no objective good? The good simply is; whatever is, is right. Why would a religious monist oppose pollution? Like any body, God's body produces both the pleasant and the unpleasant. Finally, how can one fight evil when, as McFague admits, in her world evil is "part of God's being" (p. 75)? It is not at all clear how McFague's projection could ever move us to achieve such formidable goals. Can that which is so self-consciously created really move others?

Of course, this new model demands that other theological ideas and doctrines be reconceptualized. Jesus is now "a paradigm of God's way with the world" (p. 55). He was "radically egalitarian," and his parables were a "destabilization of *all* dualisms" (p. 51, emphasis in original). McFague's Jesus was a religious monist who was "opposed to hierarchies and dualisms" (p. 46). The cosmos is "God's body," which is "bodied forth from God, it is expressive of God's very being" (p. 110). In other words, "The universe [is] the visible creation coming from God's reality and expressive of God," Here we are given a picture of "God giving birth to her body" (p. 111). In principle the universe is eternally begotten of God, not created; it is God of God, of one being with the Mother.

In *Models of God*, McFague proposes an alternative worldview, and she has had the courage (or hubris) to rename God in a way consistent with her worldview. McFague is surely correct in contending that language and worldview must cohere. Here we see a consistent monist facing the question of language.

IV. Reflections on Monism Come of Age

This essay began with a general observation about the struggle between worldviews in our culture. The church shares this struggle, except that its battle is between dualism (in its trinitarian theist form) and religious monism. This clash of worldviews is profound. These contrasting worldviews radically differ on all crucial doctrines of the Christian faith. Monism is quite simply a total rejection of classical orthodoxy. In monism God is most properly named "Mother," in whose body and being we share and who does not — indeed, cannot — speak a word to us from outside ourselves. If he enters into the matter at all, Jesus is merely the first or the best example of someone in tune with the cosmos and the Mother — or else an idol created by a patriarchal, oppressive worldview. The individual derives identity from being an incarnation of the God-cosmos connection at the level of consciousness. Morality is relative in that it is essentially self-derived as that which enhances the fulfillment of the self. Our destiny is that we will be "remembered" by "the ground of being" or perhaps live on in some undefined form in process of fuller self-actualization.

In its exclusivistic references to the real transcendence of a personal triune God, the Bible is clearly a problem for monism. It has to be seen either as pre-scientific and mythological or as a male sexist projection. Biblical faith is thus either naive or evil. But somehow one can legitimately stay within the church by finding a Jesus behind the text who embodies the virtues required by this monistic vision.

As I've already indicated, in two areas in the life of the church the clash of worldviews is especially evident in our time. Sexual ethics is the most public. From a monist perspective, sex is not only good but part of the quest for self-fulfillment, provided the relations are "mutual" and not exploitative. As Roman Catholic monist Matthew Fox declares, "Love beds are altars" because sex is "an encounter with the living God."[18] (Are we on the edge of having that quote reversed and moving into the realm of cult prostitution? In the logic of religious monism it is not at all absurd. It happened before!) The church must affirm and bless many new forms of sexual activity, if indeed no transcendent God imposes transcultural moral norms.

The other area in which the clash of worldviews is evident is that of worship and liturgy. In the Book of Common Prayer of the Episcopal Church, the dualistic worldview of classical Christian theism is expressed consistently and coherently — at least as far as the plain meaning of the words is concerned. The liturgy of the church celebrates a living God who "created everything that is, [by whose] will they were created and have their being."[19] In one eucharistic prayer the congregation is required to proclaim that "by your will they were created and have their being."[20] The Nicene Creed, which must be said at every Sunday service, celebrates the Father almighty, the eternal Son who is eternally begotten of the Father,

---

18. Fox, *The Coming of the Cosmic Christ* (San Francisco: Harper & Row, 1988), pp. 177-78. Perhaps a more systematic statement of Fox's monism can be found in *Original Blessing* (Santa Fe: Bear & Company, 1983).

19. *The Book of Common Prayer* (New York: Church Hymnal Corporation, 1979), p. 93.

20. Ibid., p. 370.

and the Holy Spirit, the Lord, the giver of life. For the monists in the Episcopal Church there must be revision of this liturgical expression of the orthodox worldview.

In 1987 the Standing Liturgical Commission of the Episcopal Church published a compilation of *Liturgical Texts for Evaluation.*[21] In an alternative Eucharist for "The Nurturing God" we are clearly on the way to a monist liturgy. Trinitarian language has been dropped wherever possible, except in the Nicene Creed and the Lord's Prayer, whose traditional forms did not (yet) allow radical revision. Male pronouns for God and hierarchical terms like "Lord" are rigorously excluded. One option for replacing the traditional opening acclamation to the Eucharist, "Blessed be God: Father, Son and Holy Spirit," is "Blessed be the One, Holy, and Living God" (p. 113). Creation is a "bringing" of all things "to birth." God's Spirit "issued forth and brooded over the deep, bringing to birth heaven and earth" (p. 122). In this liturgy the celebrant is to pray that God would "draw us with cords of compassion to your heart, at the heart of the world" (p. 125). Again, the issue is not merely language; language reflects worldview.

In response to surprisingly strong and widespread criticism, the next version of the rites, published in 1989, eliminated a bit of the explicitly monistic language, though it continued the avoidance of male pronouns for God and hierarchical terms like "Lord." The Spirit is still described as having "brought to birth" the creation. Further, the fundamental intention of the previous version is maintained. "The central metaphor" is again "God bringing to birth and nourishing the whole creation."[22] The primary linguistic commitment remains.

Perhaps it cannot be claimed that there is an explicit monism in these texts, but clearly there is the linguistic expression of a monist vision. With the sharp reduction in the use of traditional trinitarian language and its replacement with terms and ideas like the "birth" of the cosmos from the Spirit, who issued forth from God, who is the "heart of the world," it is clear that language most congenial to that worldview is being employed. These texts certainly seem to be part of an attempt to create a monistic liturgy and ultimately to enshrine the monist worldview as the

21. *Liturgical Texts for Evaluation* (New York: Church Hymnal Corporation, 1987). Subsequent references to this volume will be made parenthetically in the text.

22. *Commentary on Prayer Book Studies 30* (New York: Church Hymnal Corporation, 1989), p. 58.

worship of the church, where in the liturgical churches it will have the deepest effect upon the people. Language expresses worldview. Change the worldview, and the language must follow. Change the language, and a new worldview can enter into the life of the church.

For the church this battle has two profound results. The first is that no church affected by monism can be a real community. Community is built upon a shared language and a shared mission, which are generated by a shared worldview. If different worldviews are allowed equal status in the name of inclusiveness or pluralism, such shared meanings and mission cannot arise. For those of us who constantly experience this erosion of communal foundation, it is the cause of great pain. Without community, a particular church can be only a collection of different interest or advocacy groups with much deep misunderstanding and conflict. It *cannot* be a communion. Since every worldview is "imperialistic" in that it claims to be true (even when it claims we can know no truth), the church will be a place of contention and will be unable to function as the Body of Christ.

The second result is that with the monistic alternative widely established in the denominational leadership and in the ministry through seminary indoctrination, and established in the worship of at least some parishes, we will see more battles of the two worldviews. Sexual ethics and liturgy are now the issues, but we can guess which others might be next. There may well be movements to write an alternative creed. Since the Nicene Creed defends and reflects the theistic trinitarian worldview, its replacement must eventually be advocated. We will also expect to see new hermeneutical proposals providing the monistic interpretation of Scripture to get at the "Word behind the words." There will also be proposals for uniting at the local level with other religions. Monists may want to hold joint services with Buddhists or Hindus, since their faiths are so similar. There will be much activity in the near future attempting to show that the monist worldview is the true basis for all enlightened ecological action. Finally, since monism is really a form of nature religion, some will attempt to tie religion into the patterns of nature, as is already being done in radical feminism.

The ultimate tragedy of the monistic challenge to classical orthodoxy is that the entire enterprise is self-defeating. How can intelligent men and women really take Christianity seriously when its fundamental reality is a vague, undefined, impersonal "force" or "ground" that is being "named" by a skeptical elite in such a way as to advance their social and moral projects? Intelligent skeptics will look at all monist revisionism much the way A. J. Ayer did decades ago and rightly observe, "You are finally coming around. Just a bit more and you'll be an atheist like me."

The church faces a crisis of identity possibly unmatched since the second century. An alternative worldview, not just a theological variation, contends with classical orthodoxy for the mind and heart of the church. Either God has named himself and given us a true worldview that answers life's ultimate questions and sets us on a path to real virtue and eternal life, or we really don't know what to make of the ground of being and must name he/she/it as best we can in ways appropriate for our time. To understand the struggle in liturgical revision and language for God is to understand this clash of worldviews.

Recently *The Atlantic* ran a lengthy analysis of the "troubled world" of our seminaries written by a noted scholar who clearly articulated the clash of worldviews in our churches. Near the conclusion of the analysis, Harvard biblical scholar Paul D. Hanson offered an explanation — probably quite shocking to some — of how he viewed the situation. First, he noted that "the pendulum is now where not a revision but a negation of tradition is espoused in the classroom." Second, he contended that "when we lose sight of the transcendent God, we begin to create our own gods."[23] I would only note the obvious: when we create gods, we must also name them.

The issue is finally this: who is at the center of our world? If we are, then the divine will tend to be conceived in impersonal terms, and we will demand the "right" to name he/she/it as we "scale barriers" (to use Bishop Spong's phrase) in our quest to "be all that we can be." Or there indeed *is* a triune, transcendent Creator-Redeemer who has named himself and given us a great story to enter, a morality to live out, and a real hope to press toward. We are back on Mount Carmel.

23. Hanson, cited in Paul Wilkes, "The Hands That Would Shape Our Souls," *The Atlantic* 266 (December 1990): 86.

The Movement and the Story:
Whatever Happened to "Her"?

BLANCHE A. JENSON

"WHEREVER THE GOSPEL is preached in the whole world, what she has done will be told in memory of her" (Mark 14:9).

This amazing passage has a place of singular importance on the title page of Elisabeth Schüssler Fiorenza's book entitled *In Memory of Her.* So situated, it makes the intended impact: this splendid title engages the imagination. The book's content provokes my question. My concern in this essay is limited: Can feminist theology live with the biblical narrative?

The nineteenth-century feminist movement gave us The Woman's Bible. The present feminist movement is giving us an explosion of theologies, and the resulting discussion agitates both synagogues and churches. People of goodwill are not sure what the proper response is.

Sisters once united in the project of feminist theology have now separated as various paths of scholarship, reflection, and commitment have proved appealing. A decade ago Judith Plaskow and Carol Christ collaborated to produce the influential book entitled *Womanspirit Rising.* In their recent book, *Weaving the Visions,* they confess the changes these years have brought and admit they have not always been happy ones: "Carol has more deeply embraced Goddess and nature spirituality, while Judith has clearly committed herself to the transformation of Judaism."[1]

For many Jewish and Christian women, the actual doing of theology from a feminist perspective has led out of religious traditions once followed. Mary Daly was an early exponent of this move. Some agree with

---

1. *Weaving the Visions: New Patterns in Feminist Spirituality,* ed. Plaskow and Christ (San Francisco: Harper & Row, 1989), p. v.

Daphne Hampson that "feminism represents the death-knell of Christianity as a viable religious option."[2]

Others like Plaskow have chosen — often for very different reasons — to remain within their traditions to reform or re-vision them. Schüssler Fiorenza is one such within the Christian tradition. The influence of her work and that of other revisionists is the occasion for this collection of essays.

To understand feminist theology, we must recognize its dependence on feminist theory. Feminist theory begins with experience, the experience of oppression. Because the Western world has been constructed as a patriarchy, women have been regarded as nonpersons. Liberation from this oppression is the goal of the feminist movement.

Consciousness-raising groups, so common in the seventies, worked to identify the oppressor. In the naming of the oppressor, the oppressed expected liberation and anticipated empowerment. Within these discussions — both national and international — it became evident that not all women could fit neatly into the white middle-class structure of the United States. Differences among sisters in the various cultures of the world were noted, and these differences are now regarded as essential to discussion within the movement.

But those within the church found a common ground. The oppressor was the Bible, with its androcentric authorship and the male-dominated community that claimed it as its scripture. Mary Daly, Rosemary Radford Ruether, Letty Russell, Sallie McFague, Elisabeth Schüssler Fiorenza — these early feminist theologians became household names as people within the churches sought to understand or participate in feminist theology.

While there is no *one* feminist theology, and while not all women are feminists, *nor* are all feminists women, there is an almost agreed-upon starting point and goal. Christ and Plaskow put it this way: "Recognizing that women's perspective had not been included in the Jewish or Christian naming of God, human beings, or the world, feminist theology began with women claiming and naming our own experiences and exploring the ways in which incorporating women's experience might transform traditional religion or lead to the creation of new tradition."[3] Rebecca Chopp describes its evolution: "Feminist theology began not merely to correct

2. Hampson, *Theology and Feminism* (Oxford: Basil Blackwell, 1990), p. 1.
3. *Weaving the Visions*, p. 3.

but to change, not merely to be suspicious but to proclaim: to proclaim God and freedom, hope and humanity, in new ways and new forms." The language shifted: rather than demanding "let us in," feminists began saying, "share our vision." According to Chopp, "The radical activity of feminist theology is . . . nothing short of a transformation of Christianity itself."[4]

In seeking an answer to the question posed by this essay, I have chosen to examine books written by three feminist theologians who wish to remain within the Christian tradition. Elisabeth Schüssler Fiorenza's book is responsible for the question. The books by Rebecca Chopp and Pamela Dickey Young were almost random choices I made from among the plethora of new material that has been written since *In Memory of Her* was first published. I cannot claim to have done full justice to these works. My concern is limited but I believe essential if we are to make decisions about the appropriateness of feminist theology within the church.

Schüssler Fiorenza set out to reconstruct biblical history by searching for women mentioned within the New Testament. Her claim is that the group of women around Jesus was a "discipleship of equals" and that it is only in the later church that male dominance removed women from this space. She believes that "as long as the stories and history of women in the beginnings of early Christianity are not theologically conceptualized as an integral part of the proclamation of the gospel, biblical text and traditions formulated and codified by men will remain oppressive to women."[5] However, because she believes the Bible to be both the source of women's power and the source of their oppression,[6] she attempts to "provide new lenses that enable one to read the biblical sources in a new feminist light, in order to engage in the struggle for women's liberation inspired by the Christian feminist vision of the discipleship of equals."[7]

Schüssler Fiorenza advocates reconstruction on this basis: "The personally and politically reflected experience of oppression and liberation must become the criterion of appropriateness for biblical interpretation and evaluation of biblical authority claims." She continues, "A feminist

---

4. Chopp, *The Power to Speak: Feminism, Language, God* (New York: Crossroad, 1989), pp. 17-18.

5. Schüssler Fiorenza, *In Memory of Her: A Feminist Theological Reconstruction of Christian Origins* (New York: Crossroad, 1984), p. xv.

6. Ibid., p. 35.

7. Schüssler Fiorenza, "In Search of Women's Heritage," in *Weaving the Visions,* p. 38.

theological hermeneutics having as its canon the liberation of women from oppressive patriarchal text, structures, institutions, and values maintains that — if the Bible is not to continue as a tool for the patriarchal oppression of women — only those traditions and texts that critically break through patriarchal culture and plausibility structures have the theological authority of revelation."[8]

The main body of Schüssler Fiorenza's book, an imaginative reconstruction, leads finally to the recommendation of an "ekklesia" of women. Here, she says, "baptism is the sacrament that calls us into the discipleship of equals." And she asserts, "To embrace the gospel means to enter into a movement, to become a member of God's people who are on the road that stretches from Christ's death to Her return in glory."[9] Schüssler Fiorenza closes her discussion with a series of vivid assertions and questions:

> Finally, a feminist Christian spirituality is rooted in the "ekklesia" of women as the "body of Christ." Bodily existence is not detrimental or peripheral to our spiritual becoming as the "ekklesia" of women but constitutive and central to it. Not the soul or the mind or the innermost Self but the body is the image and model for our being church. How can we point to the eucharistic bread and say, this is my body; as long as women's bodies are battered, raped, sterilized, mutilated, prostituted, and used to male ends? How can we proclaim "mutuality with men" in the body of Christ as long as men curtail and deny reproductive freedom and moral agency to us? As in the past so still today men fight their wars on the battlefields of our bodies, making us the targets of their physical or spiritual violence. Therefore, the "ekklesia" of women must reclaim women's bodies as the "image and body of Christ." It must denounce all violence against women as sacrilege and maintain women's moral power and accountability to decide our own spiritual welfare, one that encompasses body and soul, heart and womb.[10]

She concludes the book with this sentence: "In breaking the bread and sharing the cup we proclaim not only the passion and resurrection of Christ but also celebrate that of women in biblical religion."[11]

Because this early work of feminist reconstruction has become

8. Schüssler Fiorenza, *In Memory of Her,* pp. 32-33.
9. Ibid., pp. 344-45.
10. Ibid., pp. 350-51.
11. Ibid., p. 351.

foundational for more recent work, it is important that we observe carefully Schüssler Fiorenza's historical and theological moves. We will return to these later.

In her recent book entitled *Feminist Theology/Christian Theology: In Search of Method,* Pamela Dickey Young describes the work of the feminist theologian as first critique and then reconstruction: "Every theological doctrine and concept had to be examined anew in light of the growing awareness that women had been oppressed in the church at least as systematically as in other parts of society." In reconstruction, she explains, "feminist theologians seek to revise various doctrines in ways that take account of women's presence, of women's experience. They . . . revise these doctrines so that they will not contribute to the continued oppression of women."[12]

She hopes to provide an affirmative answer to the question "Can one be a feminist and a Christian at the same time?" Two criteria must be satisfied: the matter must be credible to the feminist, and it must be appropriate to the Christian tradition. She is aware that many feminists believe this to be impossible and that attempting the task is a risky enterprise. Jesus, the male savior, is a stumbling block. Young's theological move is one we should note carefully.

"Any God who is the universal omnipresent God Christians claim is not subject to the biological definitions and limitations of human beings," Young asserts.[13] She goes on to make this argument:

> Although for Christians it is in Jesus that they see God's presence, God's love and care exemplified, that the decisive revelation has taken place in a man, is in a very real sense accidental. There could be any number of historical events that could re-present God's grace to persons in a definitive way. . . . It is human social structures and not God's choice that makes the appearance of a male savior figure more likely. God did not choose Jesus in the sense that God chose him above all others. Rather, God chose Jesus as God could choose many other events that are fitting re-presentations of God's grace. After God's choice must come human recognition for an event to be seen as God's action or revelation.[14]

12. Young, *Feminist Theology/Christian Theology: In Search of Method* (Minneapolis: Fortress Press, 1990), pp. 13-14.
13. Ibid., p. 98.
14. Ibid., p. 99.

Young does not believe that God could never be re-presented in a female form, but notes that "because of our long history of the oppression and degradation of women patriarchal cultures and societies are more apt to recognize the representation of God in a male. And so . . . the 'choice' is more human than divine."[15]

Rebecca Chopp's work of reconstruction has the provocative title *The Power to Speak*. She does not focus primarily on the problem of a male savior; she concentrates on speech, on the Word/word. According to Chopp, it goes without saying that "feminist theologies are about emancipatory transformation." For her, theological reconstruction is one "of openness and not closure," although "distinct terms, values, and norms emerge to guide feminist discourse." Feminist discourse when proclaiming the Word of God will be "guided by the terms of specificity, difference, solidarity, embodiment, anticipation and transformation."[16]

Chopp asserts, "Only if the Word can reveal itself in woman's marginality . . . as something other than master identity, primal referent, and governor of the governed, will feminist theology find a new Word and new words."[17] And how is Scripture to be used?

> The formal answer is that feminist theology uses the Scriptures as collections of proclamations, as models of Christian discourses of emancipatory transformation. The Bible speaks authoritatively within the Word . . . in regard to its credible claims of freedom: its stories, its visions, its images, its hopes, its failures, its history, and its future. All feminist discourse must approach the Bible with suspicion for its contents are not "pure" discourses: the Scriptures themselves demonstrate the tragic distortion of speaking of freedom through the very configuration of woman as less than and "other" than man.[18]

According to Chopp, "feminists must constantly read the Bible with a hermeneutics of marginality: receiving it as a monument of patriarchal oppression, but also knowing the Bible through its credible claims of freedom."[19] The feminist will read to identify both sorts of words — those

15. Ibid., p. 99.
16. Chopp, *The Power to Speak*, pp. 18, 22, 23.
17. Ibid., p. 25.
18. Ibid., pp. 41-42.
19. Ibid., p. 43.

that elevate and those that devalue women — treating the Scriptures as "sacred" in a different sense. According to Chopp, "The Scriptures are 'sacred' because, in relation to community and to feminist discourses of emancipatory transformation, they are stories of people seeking to speak of freedom."[20] The "Scriptures are thus 'sacred' not because they are connected with Christianity and thus have to be holy, but because through the Scriptures, in the power of Word and words, Christians speak to sanctify the world, offering visions, attitudes, images, narratives, and poetry to restore the world to transforming grace."[21]

Before further comment on these three attempts to reconstruct Christian theology to fit feminist credibility, I want to look briefly at Daphne Hampson's very different recent book entitled *Theology and Feminism.*

Well over a decade ago, Daphne Hampson argued for the ordination of women in the Anglican churches of Britain. Since that time she has left the Christian church, believing feminism and Christianity to be incompatible. In her recent book she explains that incompatibility and then develops what she believes to be a post-Christian proposal for the religious woman. I find her arguments for leaving the church extremely interesting when juxtaposed against the ideas of the three theologians whose works we have just reviewed.

Hampson contends that "Christianity proclaims the revelation of God in history, the belief in the uniqueness of Christ, and the inspiration of the literature which tells us of these things."[22] Accordingly, it cannot free itself from its offensive patriarchal past. Christian worship must include mention of Christ, the reading of the Bible, and reference to the people of Israel and the connection with the early church. Further, she says, "Christians believe in particularity. . . . They believe that God was in some sense differently related to particular events, or in a way in which this is not true of all other events or periods in history. Above all they believe that must be said of Christ which is to be said of no other human being. . . . They must say of Jesus of Nazareth that there was a revelation of God through him in a way in which this is not true of you or me."[23] Hampson explains that she has come to reject Christianity because of its particularity and because its history is bound to

20. Ibid., p. 44.
21. Ibid., p. 45.
22. Hampson, *Theology and Feminism*, p. 5.
23. Ibid., p. 8.

that of Jesus: "Presumably as a feminist one will only accept into one's formulation of one's religious position ideas which do not conflict with one's ethical position."[24]

Her desire is to be a religious person who works at a conceptualizing of God "in which the present is normative and the past is only drawn upon in so far as that seems appropriate."[25] Her criticism of feminist theology that wishes in some way to remain within the Christian tradition is harsh:

> In the case of feminist theology, what seems to have replaced talk of God is largely talk of women's experience. It is not even women's experience of God; it is simply women's experience. Thus Elisabeth Schüssler Fiorenza tells us of the community of women in the early church, celebrating their courage in adversity and their egalitarian politics. Rosemary Ruether looks to alternative traditions within the Christian heritage, suggesting that here we may find communities, the knowledge of which will empower us. Mary Daly advocates the self-realization of women and the overcoming of oppression in a new age. . . . Sallie McFague does consider what metaphors we should use for God. But . . . it is unclear to me whether she is in fact speaking of God, or rather of an attitude to life.[26]

Hampson wants theology — talk of God.

However, as Hampson points out, the critical question that feminism poses for Christianity is whether it is ethical: "Is it not the case that a religion in which the Godhead is represented as male, or central to which is a male human being, necessarily acts as an ideology which is biased against half of humanity? Is it not the case that such a religion is by its very nature harmful to the cause of human equality?"[27] Hampson believes it is necessary "to find a way to conceptualize God which is independent of the Christian myth, a myth which is neither tenable nor ethical."[28] Hampson elaborates on the need for this new conceptualization: "For any woman apprized of what the history of women has been, the question of theodicy raised by the previous conception of God has made that conception of God unthinkable. That God, moreover,

24. Ibid., p. 9.
25. Ibid., p. 11.
26. Ibid., p. 170.
27. Ibid., p. 53.
28. Ibid., p. 171.

was most clearly not made in her image, and became superfluous as she came to herself and acquired a feminist consciousness."[29]

I have introduced Hampson into the discussion because her persistent polemic against the Christian faith aids in our analysis of the ideas of the three theologians whose works were previously cited. Her identification of particularity and history as necessary for the Christian church I believe to be correct. Is Hampson, in her decision to leave the church, simply more radical than the other three theologians, or are the other three engaged in a hopeless enterprise? When either particularity or history is relativized, can we say the resulting theology is appropriate for the Christian church?

Feminist theology in its reconstructive stage is serious and intellectually sophisticated, and it is a definite response to the serpent's question "Has God really said . . . ?" The church ought not to ignore the challenge it poses or suppose that minimal changes in language will in any way satisfy. The question of this essay — Can feminist theology live with the biblical narrative? — may now be stated more precisely: Can the biblical story in its particularity and history survive feminist reconstruction?

The passage with which I began this essay is from Mark's Gospel. He tells the story of a woman who came into Simon's house with an expensive jar of ointment with which to anoint Jesus. Some of those present became angry as they watched her ministrations; they said the ointment should have been sold and the money given to the poor. But Jesus defended her: "She has performed a good service for me. For you always have the poor with you, and you can show kindness to them whenever you wish; but you will not always have me. She has done what she could; she has anointed my body beforehand for its burial" (Mark 14:6-8). What follows this passage is the verse Schüssler Fiorenza so effectively isolates. But notice — the narrative is not about women but about one particular woman. It is not about liberation; it announces death. It says something very uncomfortable about the poor. And the content of the "good news" is not identified.

For Schüssler Fiorenza the "unnamed woman who names Jesus with a prophetic sign-action . . . is the paradigm for the true disciple."[30] But through this apprehension of the woman, her particularity in the story is lost. The reconstruction blurs the distinction between Jesus of Nazareth

29. Ibid., p. 173.
30. Schüssler Fiorenza, *In Memory of Her,* p. xiv.

and this woman. Her act and the argument that resulted are lost; she becomes a symbol. Further, Christ becomes a "Her," and both baptism and the Eucharist assume new content and character: the Eucharist becomes focused on women's bodies, and baptism becomes an act of initiating into the "discipleship of equals." The gospel to be proclaimed is the "discipleship of equals," but we are not certain about whose disciples we are to be. Mark's story is lost: the woman's particular act is forgotten, and there is no longer reason to remember "her."

Pamela Dickey Young grants that the sacraments may at times be useful, but she does not find them essential to the Christian faith. In fact, in her reconstruction the biblical story with its many interior stories becomes accidental — more a human than a divine choice. The particularity of the Jew from Nazareth and his mother, Mary, become simply part of the offense of patriarchy — a human rather than a divine choice. Her God is one who establishes boundaries within which we can exercise our freedom. The acting God of the Scriptures appears despotic, arbitrary, and therefore unbelievable.

For Rebecca Chopp, the real task is proclamation. To this end, the Bible must be read through a series of privileged concepts. If, for instance, transformation and emancipation cannot be read from the text, that text will have little or no use.

I said earlier that feminist theology builds on feminist theory. Feminist theory begins with the experience of oppression by males. It is through this experience that all texts must be read and examined. Furthermore, only those texts that speak words of liberation to the woman can be regarded as having value. Whether it is the problem of the male Jesus or the proposal of emancipatory discourse, the imposition on the text is exterior — it is defined by our cultural situation. The problem now is the text, with its particular history and its place and value within the Christian community. The established theory must be imposed upon the text to determine whether or not this part of the tradition's story speaks liberation for women. In effect, this method replaces the story with theory. Feminist theology, because it has already defined the problem and outlined the solution, does not live easily with either the particularity or the complications of the biblical story.

Daphne Hampson recognizes that this is so and sees no problem in making a complete break with the past. This is not the case with the other three theologians discussed here. Each one, for slightly differing reasons, wants to maintain the continuity with the past that the Bible offers. Each of the three knows that for many women, both in the past and in the present, the Bible has been a source of strength even while it has been a source of oppression. The solution is to distinguish the bad from the good. Ostensibly, the "new lenses" that Schüssler Fiorenza seeks to provide and the privileged concepts that Chopp suggests will correctly distinguish what is liberating and therefore good from what is oppressive and therefore bad.

But there is still a problem: both the new lenses and the privileged concepts are culturally determined. The assumption is that we know how to define emancipation, that we know what transformation would look or feel like, that we know what mutuality is, that we know what ethical behavior is appropriate to God, that we can conceive God. The assumption is that we know how to distinguish good from evil.

The church has assumed the opposite. The church has confessed its dependence upon the biblical story for definitions of words, for the meaning of reality. The church through its liturgy has reminded its members of the acting God and those people to whom particular commands or promises were given. Baptism has drawn individuals not into a discipleship of equals but into a particular community of faith in the name of a particular God. And the Eucharist has been the remembrance of the particular Jew, Jesus of Nazareth.

The church has introduced its children to their ancestors through the biblical stories read in the gatherings of the faithful. The church has cultivated the moral imagination of its members through the stories of the saints. And as with family histories, real stories complicate neat theories.

We will, of course, theorize; we will produce theology in words or pictures — the libraries and the art galleries of the world bear witness to our creativity. But lest our theologies tyrannize — we cannot forget the Nazi move to change the offensive Jewish Jesus into a blue-eyed Germanic type — they must fit with the history and particularity of the story. The Bible, however, is not always easy to live with or within. It appears too exclusive for our commitment to inclusivity. Its God is jealous. Its stories are not examples of democratic behavior.

But they are interesting. They engage our imagination. They perplex us. A young child I know, after hearing the story of Peter and John healing the lame man outside the temple, surprised the adults present with her amazed comment: "They could do it too!"

A good story is one that can surprise and engage the hearer in time because the hearer is a human whose connections — whose ways of relatedness — are not just of the present moment but move both backward and forward in time. It is the claim of the church that the biblical story, with its interior stories, speaks truth despite historical and cultural differences between text and believer. That does not mean that we will not bring questions or objections to the text. It does mean that the text must not be lost or distorted by ideology.

The question with which this essay began was whether feminist theology could live with the biblical story. As I see it, the answer is no. I agree with Hampson — the particularity and history of the biblical narrative cannot be relativized. The story cannot stand the control the theory demands. To remember "her" is simply too messy.

But we do not live by theory alone. Feminists know this well. A great part of the feminist movement has been the effort to provide space and time for "her story," the individual stories of women. For many women this has been at least a momentary experience of liberation. For many it has also been an experience of disillusionment, for if the story is just the woman's story, she is not related; she is left alone. And a woman's experience of oppression is finally only the experience of herself.

So what is there to say in the end? As long as feminist theology is controlled by feminist theory, the biblical narrative will be controlled, leaving us with "safe" stories. But will they speak reality? Might it be that the feared oppressor is really the biblical God?

Pamela Dickey Young is concerned with the presence and experience of women, Elisabeth Schüssler Fiorenza's stated concern is "her," and Rebecca Chopp wants the silent woman to come to proclamation — all worthy goals for which I also hope.

I am writing this during the first week of Advent, and I would like to offer this reconstruction. The story is of the pregnant, waiting Mary. The birth will occur: there is that moment when she will release the child she has carried. All will be different. We may empathize with Mary; many of us have also been bearers of children. But only to her have these words been spoken: "This child is destined for the falling and the rising of many in Israel, and to be a sign that will be opposed so that the inner thoughts of many will be revealed — and a sword will pierce your own soul too" (Luke 2:34-35). Only she has truly conceived God.

From Mary, the bearer of the Word, we learn the meaning of our words. From Mary's son we learn the story. And when it is preached, what she has done will be told in memory of HER.

The Incarnation of God
in Feminist Christology:
A Theological Critique

RAY S. ANDERSON

THE CHRISTOLOGICAL QUESTION formulated by Anselm of Canterbury — *Cur Deus Homo?* — has re-emerged in contemporary feminist christology with a quite different concern. For Anselm, the question of why God became man pointed directly to the answer as found in the death of Jesus Christ, who, in offering up the sinless life of a perfect human, rendered full satisfaction to the honor of God, which had suffered loss through the sin of Adam inherited by the whole human race. For Anselm, the purpose of the incarnation of God was to make atonement for sin through the perfect humanity of Christ. It was the death of this innocent "God-Man" that explained the purpose of the incarnation. Anselm developed his doctrine of the incarnation as the logical answer to the problem of sin and the need to make satisfaction to divine justice.

For feminist theologians who continue to be interested in the concept of incarnation, the question no longer arises out of the atonement for which incarnation is the answer. Instead, the incarnation is itself the problem. "Why God should become *Man* (read *male*)" is the problem. It is not only that the word *man* fails as a generic term for humanity in light of the cultural (and biblical) association of male dominance with the term. The implicit sexism that lies concealed within language itself is just one part of the problem. An equally serious problem, in my estimation, is with the historical person Jesus of Nazareth, a male, as the incarnation of God in human flesh. One can call God "Mother" by switching metaphors, but one cannot make Jesus into a female.[1]

1. It should be noted, however, that periodically throughout the Christian tradi-

Some of the more radical feminist theologians repudiate totally the concept of an incarnation in the form of a male figure. While not disputing that Jesus of Nazareth was male, Naomi Goldenberg, for example, argues that the concept of Jesus as a male embodiment of deity contributes to the suppression of women and leads to a sense of inferiority.[2] Mary Daly charges that the maleness of Jesus has been used by clergy as an excuse to suppress women. As a result, she rejects the concept of incarnation as obscuring the power of the "New Being" in each human being.[3] Susanne Heine begins a sermon by saying, "Jesus Christ: a man again. God's Son: a man with divine authority. Again a hierarchy of men in which women do not appear, or only at the very bottom of a long ladder, where they are hardly mentioned." She then quotes the Swiss pastor Kurt Marti, who hopes for a female Messiah: "'Ah, if only a God, if only a God were made flesh in the flesh of a rather fat girl!' Jesa Christa, says Ernst Eggiman, Joan of Arc, Angela Davis? 'Father, send us a daughter?'"[4]

The scope of this essay must be both narrowed and focused. The

---

tion, the concept of Jesus as mother emerges. One example can be found in the writings of Julian of Norwich, the fourteenth-century anchorite who viewed Jesus as a "mother who seeks to find and heal all of her children." Her meditations on the motherhood of Jesus include these thoughts: "Our substance is the higher part, which we have in our Father, God almighty; and the second person of the Trinity is our Mother in nature in our substantial creation, in whom we are founded and rooted, and he is the Mother of mercy in taking our sensuality. And so our Mother is working on us in various ways, in whom our parts are kept undivided; for in our Mother Christ we profit and increase, and in mercy he reforms and restores, and by the power of his passion, his death and his resurrection he unites us to his substance" (cited by Patricia Wilson-Kastner in *Faith, Feminism, and the Christ* [Philadelphia: Fortress Press, 1983], p. 102). It might be noted that, although Julian gives the title "mother" to Jesus, she uses the masculine pronoun when referring to his historical personhood. See also Eleanor McLaughlin, "'Christ My Mother': Feminine Naming and Metaphor in Medieval Spirituality," *St. Luke's Journal of Theology* 18 (1975): 356-86; and Caroline Walker Bynum, *Jesus as Mother: Studies in the Spirituality of the High Middle Ages* (Berkeley and Los Angeles: University of California Press, 1982).

2. Goldenberg, *Changing of the Gods* (Boston: Beacon Press, 1979), p. 22.

3. See especially *Beyond God the Father: Towards a Philosophy of Women's Liberation* (Boston: Beacon Press, 1973), pp. 69ff. In Daly's later book, *Gyn/Ecology* (Boston: Beacon Press, 1978), she makes no mention at all of Christ.

4. Heine, *Matriarchs, Goddesses, and Images of God: A Critique of Feminist Theology* (Minneapolis: Augsburg, 1989), p. 137. Heine's own position is not so radical. When God moves in the human world, she says, he moves in the reality of the difference between the sexes: "Incarnation. The alien becomes near. God comes near to the feminine in the masculine thou. Therefore, once again, Jesus Christ, not Jesa Christa. Jesus Christ, the man, and for men too an alien: the man who comes near, the man who serves" (ibid., p. 145).

literature on feminist theology is growing so rapidly and is already so voluminous that a survey would be a study in itself.[5] The linguistic problem concerning masculine nouns and pronouns referring to God, as previously noted, is one that warrants serious discussion but that must lie outside the scope of this essay. What is of concern here is the issue of the incarnation of God in the person of Jesus of Nazareth and how this doctrine is handled in feminist christologies. We can set aside those feminist theologians who do not deal with the incarnation at all and look more closely at three representative theologians whose christology does attempt to deal with the doctrine of incarnation.

I have chosen three who represent something of a spectrum among feminist theologians. Elizabeth A. Johnson, Associate Professor of Theology at the Catholic University of America, accepts the doctrine of the incarnation as a historical event within the Christian tradition but sees it primarily from a post-resurrection perspective as representing the ontological humanization of all persons without regard to the particular male person Jesus of Nazareth. For her, incarnation affirms the humanity of all persons, male and female. Patricia Wilson-Kastner, Professor of Homiletics at General Theological Seminary in New York, understands incarnation as the manifestation of God's divine love as a cosmic reality, for which the historical Jesus represents *a* human life, not *the* human life. For her, incarnation affirms the reality of divine self-giving as a basis for reconciliation and hope for all of humanity. Sallie McFague, Professor of Theology at Vanderbilt Divinity School in Nashville, Tennessee, views the incarnation as the core paradigm of divine presence for which new metaphors must be created in order to make sense to women today. For her, incarnation is a "model" by which we understand continuing "incarnations" of divine presence and love through human relationships.

I will attempt, first of all, to expound briefly each of these three feminist christologies with respect to their view of the incarnation, and then to offer a theological critique. My goal is that we might understand more clearly *how* some feminist theologians think of Jesus of Nazareth as the very incarnation of God in the flesh, and then *what* the theological content of the incarnation means for us as an essential dogma for Christian faith.

---

5. One of the better surveys of feminist theology to date can be found in Anne Carr, *Transforming Grace: Christian Tradition and Women's Experience* (San Francisco: Harper & Row, 1988). See especially her bibliography (pp. 245-66), in which she lists more than 300 titles.

Three Feminist Christologies —
Johnson, Wilson-Kastner, McFague

In her most recent book, *Consider Jesus — Waves of Renewal in Christology,*
Elizabeth Johnson reviews recent trends in Roman Catholic scholarship
in the area of christology from the perspective of the church's life of
preaching, teaching, prayer, and pastoral action.[6] In Chapter Seven, "Feminist Christology," Johnson suggests that the fundamental christological
question "Who do you say that I am?" receives quite a different response
when answered from the experience of believing women. Similar in many
ways to liberation theology, where the context and praxis of experiencing
salvation in history provide the hermeneutical criteria, feminist theology,
Johnson suggests, arises out of a particular oppressed group — in this case,
women. From this perspective, the traditional view of the incarnation,
which focuses on Jesus of Nazareth as a male person in whom God is
present and through whom God is addressed as "Father," fails in two ways.
It fails first by excluding women in making the male normative for humanity as created in the divine image, with women only indirectly related to
God through the male. This way of understanding the incarnation, Johnson suggests, supports the androcentric tendency that pervades most societies, along with patriarchal structures that define women by relation to
the men to whom they belong. The second failure of the traditional view
of the incarnation of God in the male person Jesus is that it does not
express adequately the nature of God, who is "beyond gender" and in
whom both masculine and feminine *qualities* can be found without attributing either feminine or masculine *aspects* to God.[7]

In support of her argument, Johnson cites Tertullian, who wrote
that women are "the devil's gateway" who "destroyed the image of God,
Adam," and Augustine, who wrote, "Woman does not possess the image
of God in herself, but only when taken together with the male. . . . But
as far as the man is concerned, he is by himself alone the image of God
just as fully and completely as when he and the woman are joined together." Thomas Aquinas, following Augustine's biology, held that "woman

6. Johnson, *Consider Jesus* (New York: Crossroad, 1990). See also her essay entitled
"The Incomprehensibility of God and the Image of God Male and Female," *Theological
Studies* 45 (1984): 441-65.

7. In "The Incomprehensibility of God and the Image of God Male and Female,"
Johnson makes the distinction between *qualities* and *aspects* (pp. 456ff.).

is a misbegotten man."[8] With an androcentric theology of incarnation, such caricatures become normative anthropology and orthodox theology as "written by men!"

With respect to the incarnation, Johnson states that Jesus was a human male in whom God was present uniquely and fully: "God who is beyond gender became a human being." This fact, says Johnson, is "beyond question." But what must be questioned, she adds, is the theological conclusion drawn that the maleness of Jesus reveals the maleness of God, or that the only proper way to represent God is in male images. She points out discerningly that even male theologians who are too sophisticated to project maleness onto God say things like, "God is not male; he is Spirit." To which she responds, "Why does it always have to be 'he'? It is because we are operating within an androcentric framework, supported by the maleness of Jesus, which presumes that God always has to be considered male" (p. 106).

"Could God have become a human being as a woman?" asks Johnson. The question strikes some people as silly or even worse, she replies. But the answer must be yes. Why not? "If women are genuinely human and if God is the deep mystery of holy love, then what is to prevent such an incarnation?" But she concludes, "Owing to the way christology has been handled in an unthinking androcentric perspective, Jesus' maleness has been so interpreted that he has become the male revealer of a male God whose full representatives can only be male. As a package, this christology relegates women to the margins of significance" (p. 107).

Johnson makes no attempt to probe further into the inner relation that Jesus has with God as expressed in the biblical language of the Son of the Father. She sets aside the ontological aspect of incarnation (Jesus' being as intrinsically divine being) for the sake of the functional aspect (the role that Jesus played in revealing God). Jesus preached justice and peace for both women and men. Jesus prayed to God as *Abba* (father), which connotes intimacy and mutuality rather than paternity. Jesus called women also to be his disciples, and women stood by him up to the end, whereas men forsook and betrayed him. In his resurrection, Jesus poured his Spirit out upon both women and men, with women as well as men baptized, contrary to the Old Testament ritual of circumcision for men only. Jesus continues as the liberator from oppression and the one who restores true humanity to all (pp. 108-12).

---

8. Cited by Johnson in *Consider Jesus*, p. 101. In this section, subsequent references to this volume will be made parenthetically in the text.

In Johnson's christology the doctrine of incarnation as viewed through the resurrection no longer focuses upon the unique person Jesus of Nazareth but focuses instead upon humanity as a cosmic, universal, and spiritual reality: "If God has become one of us, then that means something for the whole human race. Human nature itself is gifted with God's identification with us in our own nature. . . . 'Human nature is the grammar of God's self-utterance.' Our human nature is so made that God can speak in and through us" (pp. 32-33). If the incarnation is in any way related to the overcoming of sin in this christology, it is by way of affirming the fundamental dignity and value of all humanity in such a way that "whatever disfigures or damages a human being is an insult to God's own self" (p. 32). As an event within the evolutionary history of God's creative self-giving, the incarnation is the "Omega Point" with both ecological and cosmic implications, and with justice and peace and universal salvation promised for all the peoples of the earth and the cosmos itself (pp. 142-43).

When we turn to the work of Patricia Wilson-Kastner, particularly her book entitled *Faith, Feminism, and the Christ,* we find an attempt to "reconstruct Christology and its fundamental concerns in the light of feminist values."[9] In light of the problems for women who are confronted with an incarnation of God in a male, Wilson-Kastner asks, "Must all Christologies and Jesus Christ himself, therefore, be dismissed as hopelessly corrupted with an intrinsic sexism that is necessary to their very being?" Some theologians, she writes, are convinced that Jesus' male personhood is of the essence of his meaning as the Christ. Others, herself included, hold that "Jesus became flesh so as to show forth the love of God among us, a love which is not merely an expression of good will, but the power of an energy which is the heart, core, and cohesive force of the universe" (p. 93). The maleness of Jesus, she argues, is just one part of the accidental and incidental aspects of the concrete situation in which this incarnation of love occurs; it is not decisive, nor is it normative.

According to Wilson-Kastner, this calls for a reconstruction of the living tradition of the church throughout the ages, including the writings of various theologians, liturgies, confessions, and even the Scriptures themselves (pp. 90-91). The "search for the historical Jesus" (to quote Albert Schweitzer) is not one of ultimate importance, says Wilson-Kastner. What

---

9. Wilson-Kastner, *Faith, Feminism, and the Christ* (Philadelphia: Fortress Press, 1983), p. 8. In this section, subsequent references to this volume will be made parenthetically in the text.

is important for the sake of the fundamental insights of feminism, as well as the purifying of Christian theology, is a view of incarnation through the lens of an inclusive humanity whereby Christ serves as a link between the human and the divine, the cosmos and its conscious inhabitants. Such a christology will be feminist not by making Christ into a female or merely attributing feminine characteristics to him, but in coming to understand Christ as embodying values and ideals that are sought for and valued by feminists (p. 92).

The doctrine of the incarnation is thus subsumed under a doctrine of creation. God's creative activity is a continuing process, unfolding throughout the ages of history, revealing itself through increasing diversity and complexity, but also focusing upon a dynamic of love that seeks the unity of all things. This "logos of God," through which all things come into being, became incarnate in the person of Jesus of Nazareth as an "extension of that which God has been doing from the beginning." Through the incarnation, the "whole cosmos is drawn into a complete and free acceptance by God" (p. 96). In the crucifixion of Jesus Christ as the incarnation of God's creative love, the good of creation is redeemed from the evil that threatens its unity and perfection: "In this redemptive activity, the crucified Christ does not affirm that everything is caught up together in one undifferentiated whole in which diversity is ignored, and multiplicity erased. *In the cross* all that diversity, which is often the cause of division and alienation among humans, is embraced and unified in Christ. The crucifixion creates a dynamic whole through one human being's experience of the world's divisions and brokenness" (pp. 99-100).

In her christology, Wilson-Kastner views the incarnation more through the cross as a dynamic transformation of humanity than through the person of Jesus as both divine and human in nature. Instead of the uniqueness of a "birth of God," it is the uniqueness of the "death of God" as the embodiment of divine love that constitutes the particular form of Christ as savior. Thus the biological maleness of Jesus is of no significance, because on the cross all such divisions resulting from sexuality, race, and religious discrimination are overcome. Humanity as represented by such biological, social, and political divisions is transformed into the new humanity to which resurrection points. In this way, the crucified God (Jürgen Moltmann) and the resurrected human provide the theological content of the doctrine of incarnation (p. 109). Based on this, Wilson-Kastner offers a reconstruction of the doctrine of the incarnation through death and resurrection that seeks to satisfy both biblical testimony to Christ as well as the instincts of feminists:

> One of the most fundamental insights of feminism is that the various divisions of hierarchy — alienation of humanity from the animate and inanimate world about it, dualism of body and spirit — all need to be healed and overcome in us. In the resurrected Jesus, God has assured us that such healing has entered the world through the Spirit and is at work among us, and that this is the promise which God is fulfilling among us. The cosmic vision of feminism is not an illusory dream of naive individuals, but in its most thoroughgoing and radical form is the vision of the gospel, the promise made by God to the world through Jesus Christ. The struggles of feminism find their fullest context and their strongest promise of fulfillment in the risen Christ. (p. 114)

It becomes quite clear that Wilson-Kastner has no desire to develop a doctrine of the incarnation on the biological and historical grounds of Jesus of Nazareth as one conceived and born "as God become human." Nor does she attempt to explicate the significance of the biblical language that expresses the relation of the historical Jesus to God as "Son of the Father." A christology in which incarnation is viewed from the perspective of the transformation of such male-oriented and biologically specific concepts into "undifferentiated" humanity cannot afford to take as theological dogma the concept of ontological "sonship" as the basic form of divinity possessed by Jesus Christ. On the other hand, Wilson-Kastner concludes, "To discard completely the Father-Son terminology of trinitarian language would present serious difficulties, because one could easily lose sight of the interpersonal aspects of that relationship" (p. 133). Accordingly, she wishes to preserve something of the "inner life" of the trinitarian God, in which we are "invited to participate." Just what this "inner life" of the triune God means in terms of epistemology and soteriology Wilson-Kastner does not make clear to us in her christology.

Our third representative in the study of feminist christology is Sallie McFague, whose book entitled *Models of God: Theology for an Ecological, Nuclear Age* draws out christological implications of her earlier work on metaphorical theology.[10] While other feminist theologians have a tendency

---

10. McFague, *Models of God* (Philadelphia: Fortress Press, 1987). See also *Metaphorical Theology: Models of God in Religious Language* (1982; reprint, Philadelphia: Fortress Press, 1985). In this section, all subsequent references to *Models of God* will be made parenthetically in the text.

to subsume the incarnation under the doctrine of creation in an attempt to avoid the scandal of particularity represented by the biological maleness of Jesus, McFague is more intentional in this regard. Her understanding of Jesus is mediated by cosmological structures of thought that focus primarily on the incarnation as a paradigm of God's relation to the world. The doctrine of redemption thus finds its meaning in the ecological restoration of all that exists in the cosmos through the personalizing effect of God's presence as sacramentally mediated through human love.

At the outset, McFague makes clear her radical Kantian dualism between the phenomenal world and the noumenal realm, which is essentially unknowable. "All language of God 'misses the mark,'" she writes (p. 23), and "no language about God is adequate" (p. 35). The meaning of all language "applies properly only to our existence, not God's" (p. 39). Consequently, she affirms, "theology is mostly fiction," but "some fictions are better than others" (pp. xi, xii)! In light of this agnosticism concerning realities beyond the world of our own sensory experience, the use of metaphors serves heuristic purposes in theology. Metaphors do not claim to define truth as an absolute reality but serve to stimulate the imagination and enable the theologian to think in an "as-if fashion" (i.e., heuristically). "Heuristic theology," McFague continues, "though not bound to the images and concepts in Scripture, is constrained to show that its proposed models are an appropriate, persuasive expression of Christian faith for our time" (p. 36). In McFague's way of thinking, paradigms are metaphors that have "staying power," and thus serve as focal points for the explication of the meaning of Christian faith in terms of a "this-world" horizon for interpreting God's relation to the cosmos.

For McFague, christology is one paradigm among many others in the pluralistic world of metaphors and models. In attempting to interpret the confession of Christian faith in Jesus Christ as God, one turns to the "paradigmatic figure Jesus of Nazareth":

> To see the story of Jesus as paradigmatic means to see it as illuminative and illustrative of basic characteristics of the Christian understanding of the God-world relationship. . . . The question as we approach the issue of the paradigmatic figure Jesus of Nazareth is not whether everything we need in order to do theology in our time can be generated from that figure but whether there are clues or hints here for an interpretation of salvation in our time. . . . If one understands the life and death of Jesus of Nazareth as a parable of God's relation

to the world, and if to be a Christian means to be willing to look "God-wards" through his story, then one is constrained to say in what ways that story is significant now. (p. 46)

I have quoted McFague at length in order to show clearly the cosmological perspective that determines her christological approach. From the christological paradigm that consists solely of the narrative of Jesus' life and death, she draws forth three clues about the kind of metaphors needed to represent God's relation to the world. Through the lens of liberation as a praxis hermeneutic, she discovers that the story of Jesus leads to the *destabilization* of existing concepts and social structures that are oppressive, an *inclusive* rather than exclusive approach to persons, and a *nonhierarchical* vision of fulfillment for all of creation (pp. 48-49). Jesus' use of parables, his table fellowship with outcasts, and his humiliation and death on the cross contribute to McFague's threefold christological paradigm. On this basis she then develops a "model" of trinitarian understanding of God through the three metaphors of God as Mother, God as Lover, and God as Friend.

What formal christology exists in her book is found in the section "God as Lover." McFague deals in two ways with the biblical concept of the incarnation of God in human flesh. First, she asserts that "creation as a whole (God's body) is a sacrament or sign of the presence of God" (p. 136). Incarnation, then, is not a unique or "one time only" occurrence of God becoming human; instead, incarnation serves as a metaphor of God as "lover of the world" who loves "not with fingertips but totally and passionately, taking pleasure in its variety and richness, finding it attractive and valuable, delighting in its fulfillment" (p. 130).

Second, McFague asserts that incarnation can be understood metaphorically: "Human beings, particularly those human beings especially open and responsive to God, are sacraments or signs of God the lover. God becomes incarnated, 'in the flesh,' both in the body of the world as a whole and in the bodies and spirits of certain creatures who have special capacity to respond to God as lover and hence to manifest that love." It follows, then, that "Jesus is not ontologically different from other paradigmatic figures either in our tradition or in other religious traditions who manifest in word and deed the love of God for the world." He is "our historical choice" as the premier paradigm of God's love, but he is not uniquely the incarnation of God in human form (p. 136).

McFague's view of sin and evil is enfolded into this christological vision of God as lover of the world in its many-faceted and complex forms.

Essentially a mystery that defies explanation, evil is pervasive in the form of all resistance to divine love, which is manifested by hostility between people at every level; by social, institutional, economic, and political oppression; and especially by the violation of the cosmos — the very cosmos in which people live — through lack of ecological reverence for creation as the "household" of God (pp. 137ff.). To say that Jesus Christ is the savior of the world is thus to say that God's presence in this broken and hostile world is present wherever there is human love and ecological concern which aims at healing, reconciliation, and restoration. Salvation is "not something received so much as it is something performed," McFague explains: "it is not something that happens to us so much as something we participate in. . . . We participate then in our salvation" (p. 145).

McFague argues that the doctrine declaring Jesus Christ to be the "one savior" of the world made sense only in a time which understood that the one thing needful was atonement for personal sins, ransom from the devil, or reconciliation with an angry God. "But if the one thing needful is reunification of the shattered, divided world, there must be many saviors," McFague argues. "Jesus of Nazareth, as paradigmatic of God as lover, reveals God's passionate, valuing love for the world. . . . But as revelatory and powerful as that life was and continues to be, it cannot stand alone as accomplishing salvation if salvation is seen as the piecing together of the fragmented body of the world in one's own time and place. That work must be done and done again, by many minds, hearts, hands, and feet" (p. 150).

This brief exposition of christological themes in three feminist theologians is not intended to suggest that there is *a* feminist christology any more than there is *a* feminist theology. There are feminist *theologies* and consequently a variety of feminist *christologies*. The three that I have chosen, despite radical differences in their methodology as well as in their content, do attempt to explicate a doctrine of the incarnation of God as a christological tenet or, at least, a paradigm. Each deals with soteriological aspects of the incarnation, and each attempts to relate the importance of Jesus Christ to a contemporary worldview.

Assessment and Critique

My own assessment and theological critique will be modest, and cautious as well, in light of the profound issues relating to the incarnation of God in human personhood, not the least of which is the significance of his biological maleness. I understand and appreciate the difficulty in asserting that the incarnation took place in the historical particularity of the man Jesus of Nazareth, who is called Son and who called God "Father." In my critique I will attempt to defend this assertion as necessary to our true knowledge of God and our assurance of salvation. At the same time, I will attempt to show how we can overcome the implications of a gender-specific language in retaining the biblical expressions of God as Father and Son. We can and must learn from each other as theologians, and male theologians especially can learn much from female theologians who wisely and insightfully remind us that maleness, despite historical precedence in doing theology, does not constitute a theological privilege or a hermeneutical advantage.

Let me begin by pointing to what I consider to be some common assumptions and themes in the three views of the incarnation considered in the preceding pages. These are by no means assumptions attributed only to feminist theologians. I simply happen to find them in the three views examined in this essay. They can also be found in the theologies of many others, both men and women.

First, there is an epistemological dualism of a Kantian nature that pervades these christologies. Kant argued that being in itself was unknowable to us as a metaphysical object of thought. A Kantian type of dualism is one in which the essential nature of an object or being is hidden from us. We can know something only as it gives itself to us within the limits of our world of sensory experience. While this dualism is explicit in the theology of Sallie McFague, it can also be found in that of Patricia Wilson-Kastner as well as Elizabeth Johnson. In this dualistic perception of reality, what is taken to be the essence of God is ineffable and unknowable, not because God is other than humans but because the human subject as finite creature sets the boundaries for knowing at the point of self-perception and self-experience.

Johnson, for example, says, "Human nature is a deep questing of holy Love seeking to give Godself away."[11] For her this posits a problem of the relation of language to the being of God, as is evident when she discusses the biblical concept of God as Father. Taking this term to be a "male metaphor" that does not specify an aspect of God's being, she says, "makes us realize deeply the mystery of God who goes beyond all our images and concepts." I would agree with Johnson that God is ultimately incomprehensible to our finite minds, but he is not inaccessible to our

11. Johnson, *Consider Jesus*, pp. 30-31.

minds because, contrary to Kant, his being is in his act. Accordingly, there is a semantic and not merely a symbolic relation between word and being.

Patricia Wilson-Kastner criticizes the Cartesian and Kantian approach to epistemology that separates the self as a knowing subject from the outer world. From the perspective of a feminist, the knowing subject is a psychophysical reality which perceives the greater reality of which it is a part and is integrated into the greater reality it perceives. Thus, she argues, following Michael Polanyi, the knower is part of the whole she or he knows. This leads to an epistemology which is inclusive of all that human nature and experience represent as phenomena which are essentially integrated rather than segmented. In this way, sexual differentiation at the biological level gives way to an integrated human experience that provides epistemological clues to the incarnation of God in human form.[12]

So far, so good. The dualism between male and female is overcome in favor of an integrated humanity in which both masculine and feminine are included. This approach succeeds in overcoming the strict Cartesian dualism between subject and object, but it is questionable whether it overcomes the basic Kantian dualism between the experience of objects other than oneself of a transcendent nature and the essence or nature of those objects of experience. For example, when dealing with the term *God,* Wilson-Kastner states that it should be understood as a general representation of the "functional aspect of the divine as the one worthy of worship rather than [used] as a personal designation." The term *God,* she argues, can still be "useful" even though it does not denote an essential being knowable to us in terms of God's own nature. Accordingly, the images and metaphors by which we speak of God are to be judged by their epistemological adequacy in functioning as part of the whole of our experience in the world.[13]

This kind of dualism, which treats concepts and words as only "images" of reality that we construct with our minds, has a long philosophical tradition and has been embraced by many modern theologians as a solution to the failure of metaphysics (following Kant) to specify the nature of being in and of itself.[14] I suspect that feminist theologians who

12. Wilson-Kastner, *Faith, Feminism, and the Christ,* p. 40.
13. Ibid., pp. 33-34.
14. See Thomas F. Torrance, "Emerging from the Cultural Split," in *The Ground and Grammar of Theology* (Charlottesville: University Press of Virginia, 1980), pp. 15-43. According to Torrance, "It is the anachronistic persistence of the conception of the world as a closed, deterministic realm of causal connections that keeps alive the damaging dualisms that give rise to such pseudo-interpretations and pseudo-theologies, which are still so

seek to overcome the implicit sexism in gender-specific language concerning God find this epistemological dualism a solution as well. When the semantical relation between objective reality and words and concepts is broken, words no longer have essential meaning, only metaphorical meaning. The relation of words and concepts thus becomes "mythical" in the sense that nonspecifiable and unknowable "being" can be spoken of only in terms of what is specifiable and known. For this reason, Sallie McFague boldly calls for the "remythologizing" of Jesus Christ in metaphors and concepts more congenial to our contemporary experiences and minds, and calls both Bultmann and Tillich to her side in support of such a revision of christology.[15]

This leads me to conclude that the fundamental problem for many feminist theologians is the relation of language to being, which explains why they propose that the words which Jesus uses to speak of God as "Father" be considered not "names" but rather a "way of speaking" of a relation which Jesus has with one who is beyond human comprehension and description. But what becomes ironic in this dualistic approach is that when words such as *father* are broken free from an ontological and semantic reference in the very being of God as the one "named," the words become gender laden and treated merely as anthropological terms that theologians are free to reject in order to "name" God for themselves. Some suggest that the word *mother* can function just as well as if not better than *father* for those whose image of God needs to be maternal rather than paternal in order to evoke positive feelings. The question about the use and meaning of words that have their content determined by the reality *denoted* rather than by what is *connoted* is the place to begin this discussion. This issue, however, cannot be carried forward any further in this essay, as I indicated at the very outset, because the agenda here is different.

A second assumption that appears to pervade these feminist chris-

---

rife . . . Thus, with the exposure and collapse of the false epistemological dualism with which so much modern biblical interpretation is bound up, the ground is clear for us to engage in a fresh theological interpretation of the biblical material, through which it will be presented to us in a very different light. Theological structures may be developed only if they are directly grounded in, and epistemically controlled by, the objective intelligibilities of the biblical revelation, such as the intrinsic significance of Jesus, the Word made flesh" (pp. 27, 32). See also Thomas F. Torrance, "The Making of the 'Modern' Mind from Descartes and Newton to Kant," in *Transformation and Convergence in the Frame of Knowledge: Explorations in the Interrelations of Scientific and Theological Enterprise* (Grand Rapids: William B. Eerdmans, 1984), pp. 1-59.

15. McFague, *Models of God,* pp. 32, 79.

tologies is an implicit adaptation of process theology as a metaphysical concept which relates God to the world in mutual interaction so as to overcome the more traditional transcendence/immanence construct. The process theologians no longer think of God's being as distinct from the being of the world and thus perceive God as the "cosmic coefficient" in the evolutionary continuum and creative process of all events in this world. This way of conceptualizing God's being as coterminous with the evolutionary process of all "creative" events in the cosmos merges the concept of incarnation with that of creation. Or, to put it another way, it is a shift from a christology focused upon soteriology to a christology grounded in cosmology. If one still uses the word *incarnation* with respect to Jesus Christ, it means that this person is an exemplification, perhaps in an extraordinary way, of the incarnational dynamic of God's "being in the world." The effect of this way of thinking is to describe God more in terms of being a functional coefficient in the inherent creative process of the world. The ontological existence of God, if one still wishes to use such language, is thus bound up with the dynamic ontology of the "creative process" of the world, which is a unity of interactive potentialities, forces (both negative and positive), and possibilities.

Following the thought of Teilhard de Chardin, the higher possibilities of psychic, personal, and spiritual being emerge from the lower structures through an evolutionary process by means of spontaneous "eruptions" of higher forms of life. In this way, Jesus can be understood by process theologians as such an "eruption" of love, compassion, and spirituality that a new and higher way of life is now possible, as the cosmos is infused with the power of a "Christ life." Process theology can now view the resurrection of Christ as a metaphor, or sacrament, of the resurrection of the cosmos from its nihilism and destruction in its struggle with the evil forces within it. Sin is to allow the forces of division, hostility, and alienation to delay or defeat this growth toward holiness and wholeness.

The appearance of Jesus Christ is thus understood as part of this creative process, an exemplification of the divine factor in the process itself. The doctrine of incarnation is subsumed under the doctrine of creation, christology explained in terms of cosmology, and soteriology interpreted as the creative process at work in overcoming its own intrinsic deformities (evil) in order to achieve its intrinsic goal (good).[16] There are many saviors

16. Sallie McFague, for example, draws directly upon the process theology of John Cobb, as well as process theologians Schubert Ogden, David Griffen, and Charles Hart-

who embody the "Christ Spirit" and who work toward the humanization of all people and the ecological peace and unity toward which the creative process groans and travails.

Feminist theologians can be attracted to this theology as a means of disarming and relativizing the attribution of divine status to the male Messiah, Jesus of Nazareth, as the very incarnation of God. The historical particularity of Jesus of Nazareth disappears along with the "maleness" of Christ. This offers an immediate solution to the problem of attributing to God aspects of maleness and, more important, gives females equal participation in the incarnational relation of God to the world through the creative humanity of both male and female.

Patricia Wilson-Kastner, for example, understands the incarnation of the divine Word as an event that occurs on a continuum of continued divine creativity: "The Word did not create by a one-time fiat, but constantly creates through an ever-active giving birth to creation, constantly sustains the ever-shifting currents of life in the cosmos. Within this context of God's continuing creativity, the incarnation of the Word is an extension of that which God has been doing from the beginning."[17] She does not view the crucifixion of Jesus Christ as making atonement for personal sin and the expiation of the judgment of God against the sinner. Rather, she sees atonement for sin as giving way to reconciliation of the cosmic unity and the destruction of the divisive forces that cause alienation among humans: "The crucifixion creates a dynamic whole through one human being's experience of the world's division and brokenness. And in one moment of time everything is unified as it had once been in the primordial harmony of creation."[18] When the shift from christology to cosmology as determinative of incarnation occurs, the atonement as forgiveness of sin and reconciliation with God is no longer grounded within the divine being

shorne. See *Models of God*, pp. 193, 201. For Cobb's own relationship to feminist theology, see "Feminism and Process Thought: A Two-Way Relationship," in *Feminism and Process Thought*, ed. Sheila Greeve Davaney (New York: Edwin Mellen Press, 1981).

17. Wilson-Kastner, *Faith, Feminism, and the Christ*, p. 96. In fairness, it should be noted that Wilson-Kastner does not wish to be as strongly identified with process theology as with the thought of Teilhard de Chardin, for whom transcendence is part of the evolutionary development and process of matter into personal, psychical, and spiritual being (ibid., p. 53). For Teilhard de Chardin, all aspects of life — inorganic, organic, personal, and spiritual — are united in a common origin and participate in a common destiny. Thus interrelationship and "spontaneous" development are fused into a principle of life and being.

18. Ibid., pp. 99-100.

through the incarnation of God's self who lived, died, and was raised again; rather, the cross points to a cosmic event whose effect is yet to be realized through the creative power of love unleashed into the world.

Elizabeth Johnson does not express the concepts of process theology in her christology, but prefers the "cosmic embodiment" theology of Karl Rahner and his concept of "anonymous Christians." She nonetheless suggests a shift from Jesus Christ as Savior from sin to Jesus Christ as "Savior of the whole world, of the natural world and all of its creatures." She urges the restoration of the "theme of creation" in christology, which was neglected in favor of a focus on deliverance from personal sin: "In Jesus Christ's incarnation God and the world, the infinite and the finite, divine and creature, are brought into intimate contact. Jesus Christ is the summit of creation, the Omega Point, and evolutionary history is but the straining of all creatures toward him as their goal."[19] This eschatological and cosmic vision is indeed found in the New Testament theology of redemption through Christ. What is absent from Johnson's feminist christology, however, is a reconciliation of humanity to God as the inner life and covenant that God prepared before the foundation of the world in the eternal life and love of God as creator, reconciler, and redeemer.

It is easy to see why feminist theologians are attracted to a cosmological rather than a christological hermeneutic, and thus find process theology a viable method. The particularity and uniqueness of incarnation in the form of the male person Jesus of Nazareth as representing an aspect and action of divine being can be set aside in favor of a concept of incarnation as expressive of divine love, compassion, and solidarity with all of humanity — indeed, with the very cosmos itself. This "functional" christology has no need to explicate the inner life of God as revealed through the male person Jesus of Nazareth. This person can be considered to be a "paradigm" of the divine intention to heal the broken and fragmented world, an expression of the continuing interaction between God and the world.

For the same reason, it is easy to see why feminist theologians are sympathetic to the praxis hermeneutic of liberation theology. Elizabeth Johnson devotes an entire chapter to liberation christology, showing how theological reflection done from the context of oppression takes seriously salvation "in history" rather than merely "salvation history." Liberation theology, writes Johnson, "is more functional than ontological, focusing

19. Johnson, *Consider Jesus*, pp. 139, 142.

more on the saving, liberating power of Jesus Christ than on his inner makeup."[20] This liberating power is key, because it is not hard to demonstrate historically an exclusive, hierarchical, and patriarchal oppression of women through male domination. Nor can one deny that the biblical culture and context is also pervaded by this same patriarchal and male-dominated emphasis in both social structure and thought form. A quick review of almost two thousand years of Christian theology would reveal a male bias in the translation of Scripture, the formulation of creedal statements, the determination of the office of administration and ministry in the church, and theological pronouncements upon the nature and role of women in society.

While entire races (the people of Israel included) have been subjected to slavery and oppression periodically throughout history, the subjection of women and their exclusion from economic, social, political, and intellectual centers of power has been virtually universal and continuous throughout recorded history. To read and interpret the Bible from other than a male-dominated perspective requires a radical "rereading" and rethinking by those who are part of the oppressed rather than the oppressors. Liberation theology offers the tools of a social/historical (Marxist) analysis and theological hermeneutic ready-made for women to use to proclaim their own liberation from oppression and, far more importantly, to undertake theological reflection upon God's nature and purpose in a context where both women and men bear the divine image equally.

In looking at the way in which feminist theologians deal with the incarnation of God, I hope that I have been fair in attempting to tease out some of the basic assumptions on which these theologies are based. My approach has been to look for theological assumptions, not feminist assumptions, because my critique is aimed at assumptions and implications with regard to the doctrine of the incarnation of God in the person Jesus of Nazareth. When theologians identify themselves as feminist theologians, what needs to be examined, as with any other theologians, is their theological assumptions. In the case of the incarnation, the matter of the biological

---

20. Ibid., p. 93. Anne Carr suggests that the concept of the "liberating God" can be more helpful than the concept of the "incarnational God." In her way of thinking, the incarnation can be understood as a "sacrament" that binds all of creation into a unity in which "God and creation or the world are not in competition but are irrevocably united, joined, made one in God's self-gift to humankind and so to the world. . . . The relationship of the divine and human and of God and creation in the incarnation is rather a relationship of irrevocable union, reverence, and compassionate love" (*Transforming Grace*, p. 149).

maleness of Jesus as well as his self-designation as the Son of the Father is a matter of theological concern for all theologians, not just for feminists.

As one sympathetic and deeply committed to the propositions that women are created as fully as men in God's image and that God's self is differentiated and known by us in ways other than by gender attribution, I offer these comments by way of a theological critique.

The question "Who is Jesus Christ?" demands an answer prior to any concept of incarnation. For the Apostle Paul, Jesus was God's Son, "descended from David according to the flesh and designated Son of God in power according to the Spirit of holiness by his resurrection from the dead, Jesus Christ our Lord" (Rom. 1:3-4). Jesus spoke of himself in the same language of divine sonship when he said, "All things have been delivered to me by my Father; and no one knows the Son except the Father, and no one knows the Father except the Son and any one to whom the Son chooses to reveal him" (Matt. 11:27). Many New Testament scholars hold this to be an "authentic Jesus saying," expressive of his own unique filial relation with God in language borrowed from the human family.[21]

For John, Jesus is the divine Logos who became flesh (John 1:14), and so the concept of incarnation finally was expressed as a theological formulation of the early Christian testimony to the divine origin and nature of Jesus of Nazareth. In the centuries that followed, theological reflection upon the question of Jesus' divine origin and nature led to the statement that Jesus of Nazareth was *homoousios to patri,* of the same essence as the Father (Nicea, A.D. 325). The full trinitarian doctrine of God as a unity of three "persons" — Father, Son, and Holy Spirit — became the central core of orthodox theology.

It is a matter of some interest to our discussion that some of the early attempts to define the nature of Jesus took a cosmological form, particularly with Arius, who eventually denied the essential deity of Jesus as "uncreated" divine being for the sake of preserving God's essential being from the creaturely form of the divine Word as incarnate in Jesus Christ. It was Athanasius, among others, who approached the christological question from the soteriological perspective rather than the cosmological, and who argued that if the one who was incarnate and who died on the cross

---

21. See, for example, Edward Schillebeeckx, *Jesus: An Experiment in Christology* (London: Collins, 1979), p. 266. See also Robert Hamerton-Kelly, cited in W. A. Visser 't Hooft, *The Fatherhood of God in an Age of Emancipation* (Geneva: World Council of Churches, 1982), pp. 120-21.

was not essentially one *(homoousios)* in being with God the Father, then the atonement, forgiveness of sin, and full reconciliation with God had not been achieved. Thus incarnation as the conception, birth, life, death, and resurrection of God as eternal Son, the same in essence as the Father, was held to be the ontological linchpin of our salvation.[22]

Through incarnation God takes hold of our creaturely and finite being in its estrangement and brokenness and restores it ontologically, rather than merely functionally, to a real relation to God. Expressed another way, this means that the relation of Jesus as the obedient Son to God as loving and sending Father has its origin within the very being of God's existence. This is what is meant by the "pre-existence" of Jesus of Nazareth in the form of the divine Son of God before the historical event of incarnation. There is no pre-existence as such of Jesus the male Jew, born of Mary. Jesus was conceived as God in Mary's womb by the Spirit of God. But, as the later creeds of the church were to say concerning his deity, Jesus of Nazareth is of the same essence *(homoousios)* as God. The ego/center of the historical person Jesus of Nazareth is the pre-existent divine Logos, which, through the life of Sonship lived by Jesus, can now be understood as the eternally "begotten" Son of God.

Failure to understand the incarnation as revealing to us the inner being of God has serious consequences for our knowledge of God. Only if the divine Logos has become incarnate in the form of the man Jesus Christ can we have access to the inner logic of God's self-revelation. Failure to understand the incarnation in this way has serious implications as well for our understanding of the atonement as God's gracious determination to restore and reconcile humans to their created nature and destiny as

---

22. "The *homoousion* is associated with two fundamental truths about Christ. The first is the eternal generation of the Son, stressed by Origen and St. Athanasius. . . . As Christ is the eternal God's offspring, he also exists from all eternity. . . . Christ is the Father's very own self-revealing and creative activity, without whom he neither creates anything nor is known. . . . The second truth is that Christ consists of two natures, the human and the divine. If we deny in Christ the divine nature, the *homoousion* cannot be applied to the relation of God and Christ. . . . From the above statements we declare that neither Christianity without the incarnation nor the Creed without the *homoousion* is acceptable to us. The first constitutes the essence of our Faith. Christianity without the incarnation of God is meaningless and useless. Christ without being *homoousios* to the Father is neither the Revelation of God nor our Redeemer" (Archbishop Methodios of Thyateira and Great Britain, "The Homoousion," in *The Incarnation: Ecumenical Studies in the Nicene-Constantinopolitan Creed,* ed. Thomas F. Torrance (Edinburgh: Handsel Press, 1981), pp. 10-11.

bearers of the divine image. Only if the incarnation provides an ontological and not merely a functional relation to God through the life of this man will we have assurance of God's gracious provision for humans to share in God's own divine and eternal life. If Jesus Christ is viewed only as a "parable" of the incarnation of God in each person's life, we have lost the historical connection between God and humanity as a unique and unrepeatable event. When each person's humanity is viewed as the historical point of incarnation, then God becomes relative to history, not revealed in history. In Jesus Christ we are presented not merely with God but with God's own humanity as the ontological source of our knowledge of and relationship to God. When feminist theologians abandon the ontological and epistemological nature of the incarnation for the sake of a "functional" christology with cosmological formulations of Christ's "being for us," the "slippery slope" where meaning slides into mere metaphor appears. Sallie McFague is more direct and honest than most when she says that "theology is mostly fiction" and that "some fictions are better than others."

The specific problem of the biological maleness of Jesus as the incarnation of God needs now to be addressed more fully. As previously mentioned, this isn't a problem only for feminist theologians; it is a concern for all theologians. When the inner relation of divine being is revealed to us through Jesus of Nazareth as the very incarnation of God's self, differentiated in the form of God's being as one who begets and one who is begotten, the dualism inherent in human thinking about God is overcome. Behind the terminology of "Son" and "Father" is not mere "being beyond gender," as Elizabeth Johnson has put it. Instead, beyond the gender differentiation implied in these terms is the essential differentiation within God's own being. The nature of this differentiation within God's own being is the subject of John's prologue, in which he clearly identifies the divine Logos of God as distinct from God and yet "with God" from the beginning. The historical person Jesus of Nazareth the male Jew, "descended from David according to the flesh," is the very "Son of God," the eternally "begotten" of God. In becoming human, the eternal Logos as already "begotten" becomes the male person Jesus. The assertion that Jesus of Nazareth is the divine Logos incarnate entails the unavoidable conclusion that God, in becoming human, became man, not woman. The historical particularity — and scandal — of the incarnation of God begins with the man Jesus. But rather than *divinizing* the male at the expense of the female, the incarnation *humanizes* both male and female by bringing their biological and gender differentiation under judgment for the sake of revealing the true nature of God and the true status of humanity as created in the divine image, male and female.

The flesh assumed by the divine Logos in John's theology of incarnation (1:14) is indeed male flesh. But it is also, primarily and essentially, *human* flesh, and in an important sense, the flesh of Israel — the flesh of both Abraham and Sarah, through whom the people of the covenant were chosen, formed, and judged as representative of all humanity. God's incarnation into human flesh was not incarnation into humanity in general but incarnation into the specific humanity of the people under promise and also under judgment as vicarious representatives of all humanity. The humanity of Israel, as a vicarious sign and witness of God's gracious election of all persons to receive grace and live in fellowship with God, constitutes the hermeneutical clue about the humanity of God in Jesus Christ. It is through these people of God, chosen as representative of all humanity, that the doctrine of creation in the image and likeness of God emerges as a theology of human personhood — differentiated as male and female, co-equal and mutually bound in their humanity one to the other. The failure of these people of God is the failure of humanity to express the divine image in the love of God and the love of one another.

The flesh assumed by God in Jesus of Nazareth is thus humanity already determined to be differentiated as male and female, male or female, and under both promise and judgment. The biological maleness of Jesus of Nazareth is as much a sign of God's judgment against the division and hostility between male and female as it is a sign of God's promise that the image will be restored as both male and female in true equality and mutuality. This promise was anticipated by the Old Testament prophet Joel and announced as fulfilled by Peter on the day of Pentecost: "I will pour out my Spirit upon all flesh, and your sons and your daughters shall prophesy" (Acts 2:17; Joel 2:28-32).

The inner relation with God that Jesus experienced and revealed discloses to us a differentiation within the being of God which is the source of all creativity, freedom, grace, and love. The attribution of the title "creator" to God describes God's relation to the world, but even more, it points to God's creative life as expressed by the concept of Jesus as the "begotten" Son of God. "For to what angel did God ever say, 'Thou art my Son, today I have begotten thee'?" (Heb. 1:5). Within God's own being there is the differentiation of "begetting" and "begotten," which is the source of all creativity. This is why the Nicene Creed insists that Jesus is "begotten, not made."

The doctrine of incarnation discloses to us the source of creativity as found in God's being, not in God's "making" or in the function of God with respect to the world. Through incarnation we understand that the "making of the world" took place within the creative relation and differentiation of God as one who begets and one who is begotten. What is "beyond gender" in Jesus' relation to God is not undifferentiated love, compassion, and grace as attributes, but the differentiated being of God as the source of love which is creative, compassion which is rooted in love, and grace which seeks and sustains the bond of love despite all that threatens and resists.[23]

Theological constructs of God's being that follow the biblical language of Father, Son, and Holy Spirit can be understood only through a doctrine of incarnation in which God is first of all the Father of Jesus. Beyond the gender connotations in the words *Father* and *Son* lies the essential core of God's being as both the "origin" or source of all being and the response of all being to God. It is not only that Jesus is a paradigm of how humanity can embody the divine, but that the "Father knows the Son, and the Son knows the Father" (Matt. 11:27). It is not only that God is the dynamic principle of origin and consummation but that "the Father loves the Son" (John 17:23, 26). I suppose that one could say that the Creator loves the Redeemer as a functional attribute of God. But this would not ground love in the very being and nature of God in the same way as saying that the one who begets loves the begotten. It is this essential core of divine love that the terms *Father* and *Son* are meant to convey beyond male and female gender terms. One might also say that God loves as Mother loves Daughter, but then there would be no ontological and semantical link with these terms to the incarnation of God that took place in Jesus the historical person who called God his Father. Once again, I am arguing for the necessity of the historical particularity and uniqueness of incarnation as it took place in Jesus of Nazareth.

Some attempt to substitute terms such as *Creator* for *Father* and *Redeemer* for *Son* as a way of creating liturgical language that is without gender reference to God. Similarly, some call God "Mother" and Jesus

---

23. "If then Christ in the bipolar unity of his incarnation and his suffering is the living centre of man's historical occurrence, then he must also be the centre of the cosmic event. . . . The whole creation then, included in man, participates in the curve of incarnation, cross and exaltation in which Christ included in himself that humanity which he saved from death" (J. H. Walgrave, O.P., "Incarnation and Atonement," in *The Incarnation*, p. 173).

"Lover," as does Sallie McFague, for the sake of overcoming the male terminology that hinders many women in their devotional approach to God. But without a theology of incarnation that grounds all liturgical and devotional expression of our relation to God in Jesus Christ as God incarnate, the Son of the Father, our devotion will fall back into our own subjectivity, and we will be cast back relentlessly upon ourselves to sustain our life of faith.

It is not only that the man Jesus died upon the cross to effect salvation through his own obedience unto death, but the same Jesus after his resurrection from the dead continues to be the source of salvation for all who are baptized into his life of obedience, prayer, and worship as the Son to the Father. If maleness died upon the cross in the form of the weak and powerless man, this is the powerlessness of both male and female to effect their own good apart from the life of God. In the resurrection of this same person both maleness and femaleness have been restored to their true humanity. Women had long been powerless in the cultural patriarchal society of Israel as the object of God's covenant promise. The virgin Mary, as representative of powerless humanity in the form of woman, becomes the "mother of God." Her son, Jesus Christ, as representative of power and self-determination in the form of man, becomes the "crucified God."

This same Jesus, who brought sinful humanity under judgment on the cross as the man that he was, was raised from the dead as certification of his divine sonship (Rom. 1:3-5), and through the power of the Holy Spirit, we, both male and female, are given a share in that life as sisters and brothers, daughters and sons, of God. This is why the Apostle Paul is fond of the concept of adoption through Jesus Christ, because since "God sent forth his Son, born of woman," we, through the "Spirit of the Son," receive adoption as children (sons) of God, echoing his prayer, "Abba! Father!" (Gal. 4:4-6). In this theology of incarnation it is neither creation nor the cosmos that constitutes the status of persons as children of God, but it is Christ's own divine "Sonship" that enters into solidarity with the human race, having already a "solidarity" with God's own being as one eternally "begotten" of God. The ground of all true knowledge of God is thus given to us in that incarnational reality whereby Jesus, fully human, also is known by God as fully divine, expressed in the filial language of Father/Son. This is the import of Matthew 11:27, which tells us, "No one knows the Son except the Father, and no one knows the Father except the Son." If one abandons this incarnational and ontological structure of divine revelation and reconciliation, the cosmos and all that is within it collapse into their own utter senselessness and lostness — a disintegration concealed from our minds with lovely metaphors, like the flowers covering the casket of a departed loved one.

If I am criticizing certain feminist christologies from the perspective of the doctrine of the incarnation, it is not because the concerns of the feminist theologians are wrong but because the theological models they have chosen will, in the end, not be adequate to satisfy their intentions.

Susanne Heine, herself an advocate of liberating humanity from the self-deception of a patriarchal tyranny for the sake of full personhood for women, scolds the feminist theologians who take up theological and philosophical concepts uncritically only for the sake of creating a "feminist science" that supports their cause. "The divinized idea of the feminine did damage to women," she writes:

> What would Jesa Christa be? Not a redemption for women and a temptation for men to subject God. Incarnation means neither removing the human nor bringing near what is always near to us.
>
> Incarnation. The alien becomes near. God comes near to the feminine in the masculine thou.
>
> Therefore, once again, Jesus Christ and not Jesa Christa.
>
> Jesus Christ, the man, and for men too an alien: the man who comes near, the man who serves.[24]

"Jesus Christ . . . for men too an alien." Yes, the incarnation is not only a scandal of particularity with regard to the claim that the eternal God became temporal and the infinite finite, but a scandal to every person, male and female, who stands exposed as having violated the humanity of others, as having oppressed others for the sake of one's own advantage. "Why did God become man?" asked Anselm. We answer, so that both man and woman might find in God a savior and find in themselves healing for division and brokenness.

24. Heine, *Matriarchs, Goddesses, and Images of God,* p. 145. At the beginning of this volume, Heine explains, "I write with a degree of scorn, and indeed sometimes with anger. The illogicality of some lines of argument can take one's breath away, and I get angrier and angrier because I see and also experience the degree to which women harm their legitimate intentions in this way. They make it easy for the opponents of their humane purposes to dissociate themselves, whether through mockery or by sympathetically recommending a psychiatrist. . . . What is evident in other disciplines, a capacity for cross-checking and methodological reflection, should also be noted and taken seriously by a feminist theology" (ibid., pp. 5-6).

Christianity or Feminism?

LESLIE ZEIGLER

ANY ATTEMPT TO EVALUATE or even to discuss feminism in relation to Christianity has certain similarities to threading one's way through a mine field blanketed by a heavy fog. The literature is vast, the issues (at least on the surface) are complex and badly intertwined, the danger is real, and the stakes are high — the gospel itself.

My thesis is a simple one: most feminist theologians are presenting us *not* with the Christian faith but with a quite different religion, and their efforts are being aided and abetted, as well as camouflaged, by the Christian churches themselves, particularly by the mainline Protestant churches. I will deal with this problem first by referring to the present state of these Christian churches — their uncertainty regarding their true function and their theological disarray — and then by turning to the feminists' agenda, particularly their approach to Scripture and to theology.

As an introductory clarification, I cannot state too emphatically that I am not questioning in any respect the legitimate claims of feminists regarding equal rights for women politically or economically. Nor am I overlooking the fact that women have been and are discriminated against in the churches. I agree wholeheartedly with Elizabeth Achtemeier that the basic question is not *if* women should enjoy status and discipleship within the church but "*how* that God-given freedom is to be gained." As she says, "For the Christian, the freedom of both females and males is mediated precisely through the biblical witness to Jesus Christ; and apart from that mediation, we have no freedom from the world, with its enslavement to sin and death and to other human beings."[1] The hope of all of us, as Christians, is based upon the gospel.

Further, I want to clearly state that I am assuming at least the following perimeters must be acknowledged if one is to legitimately claim to be within the Christian tradition. First, the authority of the Scriptures must be recognized. Without the Bible there can be no church. Second, the crucial significance of Jesus Christ must be recognized. The Christian faith stands or falls with God's self-revelation in Jesus of Nazareth. And third, this self-revelation is the basis for the requirement of speaking of the Trinity. If we wish to speak of the Christian God and not some other god, we must be clear regarding the meaning of the trinitarian formula or symbol for God.

To be a Christian does not mean that some religious sentiment — some "spirit of love" or "concern for life" — takes possession of one's heart. The Christian affirms, along with those early members of the community who gave us the Scriptures, that Jesus is "Lord and Christ" (Acts 2:36). This is not only a theological affirmation but also a historical statement. It affirms that God has done something for human beings at a particular time, in a particular place, and in a particular manner. It also involves an affirmation that one understands oneself as a member of that particular historical community which has its origin in that particular act of God: the life, death, and resurrection of Jesus of Nazareth. The events of Jesus' life — incorporating, of course, those events which produced the community of which he was a part — are mediated to us through the Scriptures. And whenever the church ceases to hear the essential message of the Scriptures, it ceases to understand what it means to be the Christian church and falls captive to whatever may be the dominant ideology of the moment — whatever other "gospel" may be currently popular.

The trinitarian formula identifies the God who made himself known in the biblical story — the story of redemption and the promise of salvation as given us in the history of Israel and the Incarnation. "Father, Son, and Holy Spirit" specifically names the particular God with whom Christian life is concerned — the Father is the Father of our Lord Jesus Christ, and the Holy Spirit is the Spirit of the Father and the Spirit of the Son, *not* the spirit of our own enthusiasms or even of the wisdom of the present or any other age. The Trinity — Father, Son, and Holy Spirit —

---

1. Achtemeier, "The Impossible Possibility: Evaluating the Feminist Approach to Bible and Theology," *Interpretation* 42 (1988): 46, 48; emphasis in original.

identifies the God of the Christian gospel and distinguishes that God from all other gods and that gospel from all other "gospels."

The feminists, however, are vigorously engaged in calling the Christian gospel into question. The general charge is that crucial renovations are necessary or else the structure must be abandoned — condemned as not fit for human (at least for women's) habitation. But the renovations being called for are such that the new structure no longer houses the Christian faith but constitutes a quite different religion. All of the necessary perimeters of the Christian tradition I have mentioned are either ignored or specifically rejected.[2] And the feminists have enjoyed considerable help from the church in their undermining program.

Undermining the gospel is by no means a new activity for the church. The church came into existence in a tradition that was well acquainted with such activity. About 750 B.C. Isaiah began his message to his fellow Israelites with this statement: "The ox knows its owner, and the ass its master's crib; but Israel does not know, my people do not understand" (Isa. 1:3). Today this lack of understanding is widespread, and Peter Berger helps us comprehend a very important aspect of this present situation.

In 1961 Berger published *The Noise of Solemn Assemblies,*[3] in which he charged that American Protestant Christianity had become a cultural religion. It was no longer a Christianity that recognized itself as standing over against and beyond any particular culture, no longer a Christianity that recognized a transcendence which always involves both judgment and grace. Instead, there was a cultural church — a well-established and generally self-satisfied institution serving to legitimate "the American way of life."

Some twenty-five years later, Berger sees important changes having occurred in American society but *no* change in the relationship between the church and society.[4] "The 'assemblies' are the same . . . (and more

2. In *Theology and Feminism* (Oxford: Basil Blackwell, 1990), Daphne Hampson argues very convincingly that feminist theology is incompatible with Christianity, and those feminists who attempt to remain in some relationship to the Christian faith do so because of the influence of their particular biographical context. They cannot do so on the basis of their theology.

3. Berger, *The Noise of Solemn Assemblies: Christian Commitment and the American Religious Establishment* (Garden City, N.Y.: Doubleday, 1961).

4. Berger, "Different Gospels: The Social Sources of Apostasy," in *American Apostasy: The Triumph of "Other" Gospels,* ed. Richard John Neuhaus (Grand Rapids: William B. Eerdmans, 1989), pp. 1-14. A condensed version of much of this material is found in Peter Berger, "Reflections of an Ecclesiastical Expatriate," *The Christian Century,* 24 Oct. 1990, pp. 964-69.

'solemn' than ever)," he says; "the 'noise,' to be sure, has changed."[5] Heresy on the part of the church is at least as alive and well as ever. The most significant change in society is a bifurcation of the middle class that has taken place since World War II:

> Whereas previously there was one (although internally stratified) middle class, there now are two middle classes (also internally stratified). There is the old middle class, the traditional bourgeois, centered in the business community and the old professions. But there is also a new middle class, based on the production and distribution of symbolic knowledge, whose members are the increasingly large number of people occupied with education, the media of mass communication, therapy in all its forms, the advocacy and administration of well-being, social justice and personal lifestyles.[6]

The new middle class understands itself, of course, as "liberal" or "liberating" in contrast to the strictness and virtues of the traditional or more "conservative" old middle class.

Although, as Berger has pointed out, the mainline Protestant churches still have as members individuals from the old middle class and also the working class, their younger clergy, and particularly their denominational officials and intellectuals, have strongly (in many instances, almost completely) identified with the political agenda of the new middle class, and this means, of course, identification with the feminist agenda. Feminism has become "the prevailing orthodoxy, which is why 'inclusive language' (which serves to stigmatize and exclude those who dissent from the orthodoxy) is pushed with such vehemence."[7]

In this respect, my experience coincides precisely with Berger's analysis. Among the churches' denominational officials and among their intellectuals (exemplified by faculty members teaching religious studies in seminaries and colleges or universities), it is almost impossible to obtain even an acknowledgment of the justification of questioning the feminist agenda. Attempts to encourage a discussion of the theological issues involved in the use of inclusive language for God are met with either a stonewalling resistance or a curt rejection — "The past is settled. We need to be concerned with the present and the future."

5. Berger, "Reflections of an Ecclesiastical Expatriate," p. 968.
6. Ibid., p. 966. See also "Different Gospels," pp. 4-5.
7. Berger, "Reflections of an Ecclesiastical Expatriate," p. 968. See also "Different Gospels," p. 5.

Obviously, a church such as Berger has described, one that understands its function as legitimating the interests and values of its culture, is going to provide very fertile soil for the cultivation of one of the basic interests of that culture. Thus the feminist agenda is not only provided a safe haven in which to take root but also given a home in which it is carefully nurtured and a headquarters from which it is often robustly promoted.

Two theologians, Robert W. Jenson and Helmut Thielicke, have given us revealing insight into the particular theological defects of this church that no longer recognizes its master's crib.

Robert Jenson agrees with Berger that for much of mainline Protestantism, political ideology has replaced the gospel. In looking for a possible cause for this situation, he states that he cannot believe that it is dedication to politics itself that is responsible, "since Protestantism can also and just as happily replace belief with quite different substitutes — perhaps most notably cultivation of one 'therapy' or another." So he raises these questions: "Why . . . did Protestant theology and piety react to modernity in the self-destructive fashion that has been in fact characteristic of it? Is there a *theological flaw* in Protestantism . . . ? And can the flaw be fixed?"[8]

Jenson believes that the flaw is in the doctrine of God, and if it is to be fixed, what is required is a renewed understanding of the Trinity, which in turn requires a renewed understanding of christology. The church must again learn to "*offend* the self-evidences about God" and to say, "God is everything we have not supposed he is, in that the narrative about Jesus is the narrative about him."[9] Jenson explains what this will entail:

> Jesus the man will be identified as God, and God the Son will be understood to be *as* God the subject of the narrative by which the human life of Jesus is identified. . . . Then very directly the history enacted between him and the Transcendence he addressed as Father and the Spirit of their converse *is* God.[10]

Thus the christological renewal "consists in uncovering the *truth* of God and trinitarian dialectics in *displaying* it."[11]

In his prolegomena to the Christian faith, Helmut Thielicke is

8. Jenson, "A 'Protestant Constructive Response' to Christian Unbelief," in *American Apostasy,* p. 57; emphasis in original.
9. Ibid., p. 71; emphasis in original.
10. Ibid., p. 72; emphasis in original.
11. Ibid., p. 74; emphasis in original.

concerned with the relationship of theology to modern thought forms. He makes his analysis, of course, in view of those issues most debated at the time of his writing — Rudolf Bultmann's demythologization program and the "death of God" issue — but his conclusions apply with equal force to our present theological atmosphere, and they strongly support Jenson's views. Thielicke points out that the relationship of theology to modern thought forms involves two fundamentally different approaches, which he designates as Cartesian and non-Cartesian. The Cartesian approach is characterized by an emphasis upon the autonomous "I" — "a general and pre-Christian self-understanding of man as a separate theme which must be dealt with before the theological agenda is tackled." If God's address, the kerygma, is to be appropriated by its recipient, the self, then an examination of that self brings to light "the possibility, presuppositions and conditions under which the message is intelligible and relevant and can be appropriated."[12]

Despite the best intentions of those following this procedure, the end result is that the method takes control and provides a sort of "sieve" through which God's address reaches us. The kerygma has been cut to our measure — to that which we, on the basis of the elements of the structure of ourselves, can understand and appropriate. Regardless of what we may understand these basic elements to be — regardless of whether we prefer an existential analysis such as that of Bultmann or an ontological analysis of finite and self-questioning existence such as that of Paul Tillich, or whether we take our cue from some form of process philosophy or from phenomenology (or from the "sensibility of our time," as present-day feminists would put it) — the end result is the same. We control that which addresses us. We hear only that which, in the final analysis, we have determined we are capable of hearing.

In contrast, the non-Cartesian approach sees the self as constituted by its relationship to God, and hence God's address is both creative and challenging. *It* calls *its* recipients, including their basic presuppositions, into question, not vice versa. In Thielicke's terms, the problem with Cartesian theology is an inadequate understanding of the Holy Spirit (which, of course, means an inadequate understanding of God), and a corresponding inadequate understanding of the human self. As he expresses it, the Holy Spirit *creates* its hearers — our identity is determined by the

---

12. Thielicke, *The Evangelical Faith,* vol. 1: *The Relation of Theology to Modern Thought Forms* (Grand Rapids: William B. Eerdmans, 1974), p. 50.

God who addresses us and who incorporates us into that history of which Isaiah was also a member, and in which we become who we are and who we should be as we recognize our master's crib.

As we shall see subsequently, the feminists provide us with ideal examples of those views that illustrate the heretical (or, in many instances, apostate) results of the flaw in the understanding of God which Jenson calls to our attention. They also provide us with examples of the extreme of the Cartesian position that Thielicke describes — a position that prevents Scripture from speaking to us any word but our own. But before turning to the feminists, we will consider briefly some leading expressions of this theological flaw and the Cartesian approach in today's "unbelieving" church, in preparation for noting how these expressions are supporting the feminist agenda.

One of the most widely acclaimed "spirits of our age" is "pluralism." Not only is pluralism honored; it has in many respects attained the status of a celebrated motto, the banner to be flown by all decent, caring Christians. We obviously live in a world made up of people with quite different perspectives, people with a basic commitment to various religions or even to no religion at all, as well as people representing a variety of perspectives within any one faith community. In such a world, it is held, living together peaceably requires that the "sincere" commitment of each of these groups be honored, and not only honored but celebrated, since honoring all sincere and "creative" ways of living and believing can only serve to enrich each group within the total assemblage.

In this perspective there is no room, of course, for any claim to truth in any absolute sense. With respect to the question of the relationship of Christianity to other world religions, it has led to considerable interest in an understanding that rejects the "notion" of the uniqueness of Jesus Christ or of Christianity being true in any universal or normative sense. We have a number of voices recommending a "theocentric" christology or raising anew the claim that there are "many ways to the same center" — that all traditions are talking about the same God. Accordingly, if we are to have authentic interreligious dialogue, Jesus Christ must take his place *not* in terms of there being "no other name" (Acts 4:12), but as one name among others by which we may be saved.[13]

13. As examples of this discussion, see Paul F. Knitter, *No Other Name? A Critical Survey of Christian Attitudes toward World Religions* (Maryknoll, N.Y.: Orbis Books, 1985); and *The Myth of Christian Uniqueness: Toward a Pluralistic Theology of Religions,* ed. John Hick and Paul F. Knitter (Maryknoll, N.Y.: Orbis Books, 1987).

In connection with the name of Jesus Christ being one name among others, one cannot help but be reminded of the offer made by the Roman emperor to our spiritual ancestors. The emperor very graciously told those early Christians that he would be happy to give Christ a place in the pantheon of gods. They, of course, politely said, "No thanks," and the emperor fed some of them to the lions. But now, it seems, some of our own "leaders in the faith" — some of our own professional theologians — are proposing that for which their forebears died.

The work of Gordon Kaufman has combined two basic elements of modern thought, and his views have been particularly congenial to the feminists. He begins his discussion by centering on the threat of the possibility of nuclear disaster. The fact that we now possess the chemical ability to destroy ourselves through a nuclear holocaust is understood as presenting us with a radically new, unprecedented religious situation. According to Kaufman, we "must recognize and acknowledge that humankind has moved into a historical situation unanticipated by biblical writers and subsequent theological commentators alike, a situation of much greater human knowledge, power and responsibility than our religious tradition had ever imagined possible."[14] In this new situation of humanity's "coming of age," says Kaufman, we must also recognize that traditional images of God, particularly personalistic conceptions and images of divine providential care, "have become not only outmoded; they have become misleading and dangerous."[15] Further, we recognize that these symbols and images do *not* refer to a Reality with Whom we must deal and Who deals with us — one with Whom we must come to terms. Rather, these images are humanly created concepts, concepts that have been developed in a history and that can be transformed in further history. Hence it is our present responsibility as theologians to engage in the most radical kind of deconstruction and reconstruction of these symbols, particularly of the most central ones (God and Jesus Christ), with the aim of providing a theology suitable for a nuclear age, an imaginative construction that will help save us from destroying ourselves.

Here we have obviously gone off the scale of Thielicke's analysis. The

---

14. Kaufman, "Nuclear Eschatology and the Study of Religion," *Journal of the American Academy of Religion* 51 (1983): 13.

15. Ibid., p. 9. Kaufman has further described and developed his program of deconstruction and reconstruction in the following: *An Essay on Theological Method* (Missoula, Mont.: Scholars Press, 1975); *The Theological Imagination: Constructing the Concept of God* (Philadelphia: Westminster Press, 1981); and *Theology for a Nuclear Age* (Philadelphia: Westminster Press, 1985).

Cartesian approach has reached an extreme which he was not considering — that of the elimination of any address *to* us which then *could* be cut to our own measurement. We are left with only our own imaginative ingenuity.

We now turn to the approach of the feminists themselves to Scripture and to theology. First, there is the problem of the Bible. As our preceding discussion at least hints, and as even the most superficial glance at the relevant literature clearly shows, the feminists enter an arena where uncertainty regarding biblical authority and interpretation is the order of the day, adding their voice to the disturbance already present.[16]

Essentially by definition, feminists are committed to "the promotion of the full humanity of women,"[17] which involves, specifically, promotion of the liberation of women from all forms of patriarchal oppression in the church and in society.[18] In this task the Bible becomes one of their major hurdles, as it would be very difficult to find a feminist who does not regard the Bible as totally androcentric and pervaded by patriarchy. It was written by men, it has been interpreted throughout the centuries solely by men, it has been used by the church to subordinate women to men, and its influence is regarded as being a major cause of the existence of the oppressive patriarchal structures and attitudes in modern Western society. Hence the dilemma faced by the feminist who wishes to maintain a relationship with the Christian tradition is whether to give up on the Bible or try to find a way for it to have some place in her life. Can it in some way, despite its patriarchalism, be found to serve the cause of liberation from that patriarchalism?

Various and sundry attempts have been made to find ways of doing this.[19] Both Letty Russell and Rosemary Ruether have looked for some

16. For an excellent introductory summary of the issues involved, see *Biblical Interpretation in Crisis: The Ratzinger Conference on Bible and Church,* ed. Richard John Neuhaus (Grand Rapids: William B. Eerdmans, 1989).

17. Rosemary R. Ruether, *Sexism and God-Talk* (Boston: Beacon Press, 1983), p. 18.

18. This common theme is found in the work of all the feminist writers. See, for example, Elisabeth Schüssler Fiorenza, *Bread Not Stone: The Challenge of Feminist Biblical Interpretation* (Boston: Beacon Press, 1984), pp. ix-xvii.

19. For presentations of the feminist approach to Scripture, see, in addition to Schüssler Fiorenza's *Bread Not Stone,* the following: *Feminist Interpretation of the Bible,* ed. Letty M. Russell (Philadelphia: Westminster Press, 1985); Letty M. Russell, *Household of Freedom: Authority in Feminist Theology* (Philadelphia: Westminster Press, 1987); *The Bible and Feminist Hermeneutics,* ed. Mary Ann Tolbert (Chico, Calif.: Scholars Press, 1983); *Feminist Perspectives on Biblical Scholarship,* ed. Adela Yarbo Collins (Chico, Calif.: Scholars Press, 1985); Katherine Doob Sakenfeld, "Feminist Perspectives on Bible and Theology: An Introduction to Selected Issues and Literature," *Interpretation* 42 (1988): 5-18; and

aspect or theme of the Scriptures themselves that can be correlated with "women's experience." Ruether finds the prophetic-liberating tradition of the Bible helpful; Russell prefers to make use of "God's intention to mend all creation," which she sees as enabling everyone, especially women, to work as his partners in this task. Others, such as Elisabeth Schüssler Fiorenza, reject this correlation approach in favor of the use of an untarnished "women's experience," which she understands, in common with feminists in general, as not just women's experience but, specifically, "women's experience in their struggle for liberation from oppression."

Regardless of the specific approach taken, however, it is clear that the key or norm for understanding the Bible is "women's experience" — the experience of the feminists themselves. Their own experience determines what is acceptable in Scripture and what is not — what may be understood as in some way expressive of "divine revelation" or "the true nature of things" and what may not. As Ruether expresses it, "Whatever diminishes or denies the full humanity of women must be presumed *not* to reflect the divine or authentic relation to the divine, or to reflect the authentic nature of things, or to be the message or work of an authentic redeemer."[20] Schüssler Fiorenza proposes a feminist model of biblical interpretation which serves to identify sexist and patriarchal texts, and a "feminist hermeneutics of proclamation" which "must insist" that all texts thus identified "should *not* be retained in the lectionary and be proclaimed in Christian worship or catechesis."[21]

The feminists have handed us, without even a trace of a blush, not only a new "canon" but also specific directions regarding how it should be read. And this new canon is *not* a new authoritative guide for Christian faith and action but *a tool* for use in promoting the feminist agenda. Here we have, in terms of Thielicke's analysis, an "unadulterated" Cartesianism. Neither Scripture nor the Holy Spirit is allowed to address us — to speak *any* word that is not our own. The feminists, along with Kaufman, have very effectively cut themselves off from that gospel which is the hope of all of us, them included.

We now turn to the significance of Jesus of Nazareth — "Lord and Christ." The feminists, however, do not wish to recognize *any* lord, and particularly not the Lordship of Christ (or the Sovereignty of God), because

---

Mary Ann Tolbert, "Protestant Feminists and the Bible: On the Horns of a Dilemma," *Union Seminary Quarterly Review* 43 (1989): 1-17.

20. Ruether, "Feminist Interpretation: A Method of Correlation," in *Feminist Interpretation of the Bible*, p. 115; emphasis mine.

21. Schüssler Fiorenza, *Bread Not Stone*, p. 18.

this represents the patriarchal oppression from which they are seeking liberation. A brief history of the feminists' attitude toward Jesus and their attempts to construct "christologies" as provided by Susan Thistlethwaite is very instructive for the insight it provides into the feminist understanding of an adequate christology.

As Thistlethwaite states, the "Jesus was a feminist" approach of the early 1970s, based on his apparent "remarkably egalitarian, at times even preferential, treatment of women," was brought up short by the dissent of Jewish feminists, who objected that this position was yet another slam at the Jews in that it presented first-century Judaism as "unrelievably patriarchal."[22] Ruether's presentation of Jesus as the bearer of a liberating message that "aims at a new reality in which hierarchy and dominance are overcome as principles of social relations"[23] is regarded to be still another slam — although a more subtle one — at Judaism, and once this is recognized, it cannot be sanctioned without qualification.

"Relational christology," which Thistlethwaite herself has advocated, following the lead of Tom Driver[24] and Carter Heyward,[25] is regarded as an advance. In this perspective, christology is pursued in the context of ethics and an understanding of existence as relationship. It requires the rejection of all terms, titles, and concepts regarding Christ that focus on his once-for-all uniqueness and the recognition that the reality of Christ is a relation of mutual dependence. Traditional christology is understood as threatening human freedom and undermining human responsibility, in contrast to which relational christology insists that "God has chosen to give human beings responsibility" for our history, "and it is our fault if we do not take it. Likewise, it is to our credit if we do. . . . Christology comes about through human relationality. Human beings bring God into the world."[26]

22. Thistlethwaite, *Sex, Race, and God: Christian Feminism in Black and White* (New York: Crossroad, 1989), pp. 92-108.

23. Ruether, *Sexism and God-Talk*, p. 136.

24. Driver, *Christ in a Changing World: Toward an Ethical Christology* (New York: Crossroad, 1981). Driver regards traditional christology, with its understanding of Christ as unique (the center, model, or norm of human life), not only as obsolete but as a major hindrance to proper ethical behavior for our time. Hence this view must be replaced by a christology which, while it is formulated, is subject to *our* ethical judgment — a judgment based on our conscience (see especially pp. 21-31).

25. Heyward, *The Redemption of God: A Theology of Mutual Relation* (Washington, D.C.: University Press of America, 1982).

26. Thistlethwaite, *Sex, Race, and God*, p. 96. See also Thistlethwaite, *Metaphors for the Contemporary Church* (New York: Pilgrim Press, 1983), pp. 93-100.

But even this relational christology proves to be flawed. It recognizes clearly that we bring God into the world in our relations to each other, but it fails to recognize clearly "the uniqueness and the difference of the 'other,' " and hence fails to be truly liberating. Women's experience is the context for Thistlethwaite's relational christology, but as this experience has been that of white Christian feminists, the experience of Jewish feminists and black feminists becomes obscured. No particular feminist experience can serve without to some degree belittling, and hence oppressing, the others.

The "spirit of pluralism" has reared its head again. The question "Who do you say that I am?" must be answered on the basis of the experience of the respondent, and all sincere answers must be honored. Thistlethwaite concludes her discussion with this statement:

> If Jesus rose anywhere for me, he rose in the survivors of abuse. This is what resurrection means to me . . . : Victims of Incest can Emerge Survivors. . . . [But I respect] the claims of others that "your experience is not my experience." *This is my encounter with the struggle to survive and to prevail.*[27]

In this perspective, the name of Jesus Christ has become many names, each brought into the world in the service of the particular experience of the one "struggling to survive and to prevail." Pluralism has prevailed, and the flaw in the doctrine of God to which Jenson referred has become an obvious fracture. Rather than the narrative about Jesus telling us who God is, it is the narrative of each feminist's own individual existence that "brings God into the world." Christology, like the Bible, has become a tool to be used in the cause of the feminist agenda.

The use of inclusive language for deity has received widespread publicity in the church and has even resulted in a partial acceptance in the form of the publication, under the auspices of various denominational headquarters, of inclusive language (or, sometimes, "language-sensitive") lectionaries, hymnals, prayer books, and some biblical translations. These publications serve to illustrate Berger's observation that the churches' denominational officials and intellectuals have strongly identified with the political agenda of the new middle class — "the prevailing orthodoxy."

Although a number of scholars have published clear and convincing arguments demonstrating that the use of female language for God results

---

27. Thistlethwaite, *Sex, Race, and God,* p. 108; emphasis mine.

in a denial of the gospel,[28] it is very difficult to find a feminist writer who even acknowledges the existence of this material other than regarding it as unreasonable or even irrational opposition to the feminist program — stigmatizing the dissenter, as Berger stated. Attempts to deal with the specific arguments presented are almost nonexistent. The feminists see the use of female language for God as *the* necessary plank in their program for liberating women from patriarchal oppression in the church, and if that liberation requires destruction of the gospel, so be it. Many of them quite openly suspect that this may be the case, and the arguments of those who point out that this is what *is* being done do not, therefore, seem worthy of too much attention. Indeed, the destruction of the gospel is not incidental to the inclusive-language program; it is, as many feminists claim, precisely what is needed for the success of their cause.

It needs to be stated first that proposals for the use of inclusive language for God (or for any other usage, for that matter) are nearly always presented on the basis of prior assumptions regarding the nature and function of language itself — assumptions that are introduced as self-evident or sometimes regarded as so self-evident that they do not even need to be presented. Foremost among such assumptions are the notions that language controls attitudes ("shapes thought"), that generics in the English language ("man," "mankind") are actually gender-specific (including charges that people *do* use them as gender-specific, and always have, even if only subconsciously), and that therefore a change to inclusive language (to language that does not "exclude women") will result in a change in attitudes (eliminate sexism, for example). All these assumptions have been questioned by both linguists and sociologists as decidedly problematic, if not seriously mistaken. Linguist Joseph C. Beaver, for example, has argued cogently that the feminist activists misunderstand how language actually works,[29] and sociologists

28. Among the most telling are the works of Elizabeth Achtemeier and Roland M. Frye, upon whom my discussion is heavily dependent. See Elizabeth Achtemeier, "Female Language for God: Should the Church Adopt It?" in *The Hermeneutical Quest* (Allison Park, Pa.: Pickwick Publications, 1986), pp. 97-114; and also "The Impossible Possibility"; and see Roland M. Frye, "Language for God and Feminist Language: Problems and Principles," *Scottish Journal of Theology* 41 (1988): 441-69. A shorter version of this article is found in *Interpretation* 43 (1989): 45-57.

29. Beaver, "Inclusive Language Re-examined," *Dialog* 27 (Fall 1988): 301-3. See also George H. Tavard, "Sexist Language in Theology," *Theological Studies* 36 (1975): 700-724, especially pp. 703-12; Bruce Vawter, "On 'Inclusive Language,'" *Dialog* 25 (Winter 1986): 64-67; and Vernard Eller, *The Language of Canaan and the Grammar of Feminism* (Grand Rapids: William B. Eerdmans, 1980).

Briggitte and Peter Berger have argued that the feminist proposals are politically motivated, expressive of class identity and conflict, and will not serve the purpose of emancipation in the long run.[30] These crucial linguistic problems are almost completely ignored by the feminist theologians.

The feminists' God-naming program is based on their essentially universally held view that the Christian God is a male God. Under the influence of Mary Daly's battle cry "since God is male, the male is God," this view has led to the argument that the Bible's use of masculine language for the deity serves to legitimate the domination of women by men, both in the church and in society. The first order of business in the task of liberation of women thus requires the "feminization" of God — the introduction of the use of female language and female images for God.

When it is pointed out that the use of masculine language for God does *not* mean that the biblical God is male, that that has *never* been the teaching of the central Christian or Jewish faith, the feminist response, when one is made, is simply to the effect that that is the way the language is frequently heard, and hence it is offensive to women. No consideration is given to the fact that, while it *may* be heard in that fashion, such hearing constitutes a gross misunderstanding of the Christian faith, and the solution is education in the meaning of the faith rather than contributing further to a misconception which actually constitutes a rejection of that faith. Rather, the claim is made that the text must be condemned on the basis of its use, even if that be a recognized misuse.

For example, as Elizabeth Achtemeier points out, Ephesians 5:21-33, a text universally condemned by the feminists, clearly calls for husband and wife "to be *subject to one another* in Christ, acting toward each other as if toward the Lord . . . and rendering to each other that sacrificial love with which Christ loves his own."[31] Rather than being demeaning, this text provides a very significant obligation for Christians to strive to meet. Sharon Ringe does admit that "careful exegetical study of Ephesians 5:21-33 reveals patterns of mutuality in the marriage relationship and revolutionary claims that *men can be self-giving.*"[32] (Does this "revelation" really

---

30. Berger and Berger, "Excursus — Goshtalk, Femspeak, and the Battle of Language," in Berger and Berger, *The War Over the Family* (Garden City, N.Y.: Doubleday, 1983), pp. 301-3.

31. Achtemeier, "The Impossible Possibility," p. 53; emphasis in original.

32. Ringe, "Reading from Context to Context: Contributions of a Feminist Hermeneutic to Theologies of Liberation," in *Lift Every Voice: Constructing Christian*

require careful exegetical study?) But, she argues, whatever its intent, this text has been used "to grant a benediction to violence," and hence a responsible interpretation must take this into account. And Susan Thistlethwaite, although recognizing that study of the passage does not support physical violence against women, looks for other forms of abuse and subjection, such as verbal intimidation or deliberate humiliation, which could be regarded as compatible with the text "since only wives are admonished to 'respect' their spouses."[33]

As Roland Frye has pointed out, rejection of Scripture may be seen in Rosemary Ruether's declaration that "feminist theology cannot be done from the existing base of the Christian Bible." This is so because, as Ruether goes on to say, the Old and New Testaments have been shaped, formed, transmitted, and canonized to "sacralize patriarchy." A new canon is needed, and she looks for the necessary texts by some "reading between the lines" of the patriarchal texts, but primarily she looks outside these canonized texts in those of gnostic or other communities declared heretical by either the Christians or the Jews, or looks among the nonbiblical texts of the ancient Near East or of classical Greece.[34] More recently, feminist writers have carried this view even further, extending possible sources for feminist theologians to include the religious traditions and folktales of Native American tribes, African tribes, Asian traditions, and Haitian voodoo.[35] "Pluralism" has become essentially unlimited, and the use of the term "Christian" theology has obviously taken on a quite esoteric meaning, one that bears little relation to the traditional understanding of Christianity.

The feminist change of language for God involves the substitution of other terms for the masculine "Father," "King," "Lord," and so on when speaking of God, and particularly for the trinitarian formula "Father, Son, and Holy Spirit," as well as the "balancing" of the masculine by feminine or impersonal images for God. Most commonly, we have the substitution of "Mother," or at best "Father and Mother," for "Father," and some such

---

Theologies from the Underside, ed. Susan Brooks Thistlethwaite and Mary Potter Engel (San Francisco: Harper & Row, 1990), p. 288; emphasis mine.

33. Thistlethwaite, "Every Two Minutes: Battered Women and Feminist Interpretation," in *Feminist Interpretation of the Bible,* pp. 104-5.

34. Ruether, *Womanguides: Readings Toward a Feminist Theology* (Boston: Beacon Press, 1985), pp. ix-xi. See also Frye, "Language for God and Feminist Language," p. 442.

35. See, particularly, *Lift Every Voice,* and *Weaving the Visions: New Patterns in Feminist Spirituality,* ed. Judith Plaskow and Carol P. Christ (San Francisco: Harper & Row, 1989).

formula as "Creator, Redeemer, Sustainer" for the Trinity. With respect to nonmasculine images for God, we have a smorgasbord of offerings, ranging from the impersonal, such as "Rock," "Fire," and "Cloud," to such creations as "Mother-eagle" and "Baker-woman."

Such changes are justified by claiming that the Bible itself uses female images for God and that the use of female language is a "literary device" which compels us to overcome the "idolatrous equation of God with androcentric notions of humanity."[36] However, as Achtemeier points out, these changes are not only literary devices.[37] They constitute *very* substantive changes in the meaning of the text. Further, as Roland Frye demonstrates, in making such changes the feminists are making a fundamental linguistic and literary mistake. They are confusing two figures of speech that have quite different functions — simile and metaphor.[38] Regardless of the specific terminology that may be used to designate the figures of speech involved, the fundamental distinction remains between a figure of speech which merely states a resemblance and one which "boldly . . . declares that one thing *is* the other." The Bible contains similes that compare God to a comforting mother (Isa. 66:13), to a woman in childbirth (Isa. 42:14), to a mother eagle (Deut. 32:11), and to a mother bear robbed of her cubs (Hos. 13:8). But the Bible does not address God as "Mother." These similes serve to illustrate "some phase of God's intent or attitude, as defined in the simile's context, but they are not and do not claim to be transparent to personal identity," as are metaphors, which predicate a name.[39] To say God may in a particular circumstance act *like* a mother bear robbed of her cubs is vividly meaningful; to say God *is* a mother bear robbed of her cubs is ludicrous.

But biblical metaphors function differently. As Frye puts it, "The predicating metaphors God the Father and the Son of God become transparent to the divine reality, words by which the divine persons are called, addressed, recognized, or known." These impressions function as the foun-

---

36. Rita M. Gross, "Female God Language in a Jewish Context," in *Womanspirit Rising: A Feminist Reader in Religion,* ed. Carol P. Christ and Judith Plaskow (San Francisco: Harper & Row, 1979), p. 171.

37. Achtemeier, "Female Language for God," p. 99.

38. Those theologians who deny that religious language can have *any* predicative or naming function make Frye's distinction irrelevant, but they are also not speaking of the Christian God.

39. Frye, "Language for God and Feminist Language," pp. 462-69.

dational symbols and images for the entire structure of belief, "the vertebrate anatomy to which different parts of the living body of faith connect and through which they function."[40] And Achtemeier describes the disastrous results when the backbone of the faith is broken — when God is imaged as Mother. When such terminology is used, the relationship of God to the world as the Creator transcendent to his creation is inevitably replaced by the birthing image. And the consequence of a female deity giving birth to the world is that "all things participate in the life or in the substance and divinity of that deity — . . . *the creator is indissolubly bound up with the creation.*"[41]

The result, of course, is that we have a very different God than the Christian Creator — the Father of our Lord Jesus Christ — and a very different faith. But this criticism scarcely gives pause to the feminists. The transcendent Creator is precisely the God they want to replace. He exemplifies a basic dualism of domination/subordination that they regard as a false view of reality. His replacement, derived from the use of feminine God-language, is described in various ways — the "Primal Matrix," or "womb," within which all things are generated, the life force or energy that things share. Regardless of how the replacement is described, however, the point is that human beings, as well as all creation, now share or participate in divinity. The feminists have adopted the quotation "I found God in myself and I loved her fiercely" almost as a slogan, and there can be no better commentary on it than that by Achtemeier: "That is the ultimate idolatry, in which the Trinity is destroyed, the holy otherness of God from creation is lost, and human beings have usurped the place of their Creator."[42]

The trinitarian formula — Father, Son, and Holy Spirit — specifically identifies the particular God with whom Christians have to do, the God who has made himself present in history as the Father of Jesus Christ. It is immaterial whether one regards this formula as the proper name for God — as do Robert Jenson,[43] Carl Braaten,[44] and Alvin Kimel,[45] among

---

40. Ibid., p. 467.

41. Achtemeier, "Female Language for God," p. 100; emphasis in original.

42. Achtemeier, "The Impossible Possibility," p. 56.

43. Jenson, *The Triune Identity* (Philadelphia: Fortress Press, 1982).

44. Braaten, "The Problem of God-Language Today," in *Our Naming of God: Problems and Prospects of God-Talk Today,* ed. Carl E. Braaten (Minneapolis: Fortress Press, 1989), pp. 11-33; see also Braaten, "Inclusive Language and Speaking of God: The Gospel at Stake," *Word and World* 11 (Winter 1991): 59, 61.

45. Kimel, "The Holy Trinity Meets Ashtoreth: A Critique of the Episcopal 'Inclusive' Liturgies," *Anglican Theological Review* 71 (1989): 25-47.

others — or whether one is satisfied with saying that it "specifically identifies" the Christian God, as Ted Peters[46] is. The point is that the formula is not replaceable. The use of proposed replacements such as "Creator, Redeemer, Sanctifier" give us another god and another faith. Paul Minear, with reference to the revised benediction "the blessing of God Almighty, the Creator, the Redeemer, and the Sanctifier," has stated, "A Jewish friend, a rabbi and a scholar, says that he could join in this revised benediction without difficulty, but not in its trinitarian edition."[47] Obviously, the change in meaning is considerable.

These terms refer to activities ascribed to deities in general; they do not identify the Christian God. As Jenson has pointed out, such changes "disrupt the faith's self-identity at the level of its primal and least-reflected historicity."[48] Accordingly, if we are really concerned for the integrity of the church, it would be "vital testimony to rise and leave the place"[49] where such parodies of God's name are employed. In another context Jenson uses considerably stronger language, saying he would no more "dare participate in a service coming under the authority" of such modifications than he would dare participate in a "voodoo ceremony" he had been invited to observe.[50] A number of other authors could be cited who deal with the disastrous results of changing the trinitarian name for God,[51] but we will turn to an examination of Sallie McFague's incredible proposal for using the terms "mother," "lover," and "friend" for God. McFague's work serves as an excellent example of the degree to which "anything goes" on

46. Peters, "The Battle Over Trinitarian Language," *Dialog* 30 (Winter 1991): 44-49.

47. Minear, "The Bible and the Book of Worship," *Prism* 3 (Spring 1988): 52-53.

48. Jenson, *The Triune Identity*, p. 17.

49. Jenson, "A 'Protestant Constructive Response' to Christian Unbelief," p. 73.

50. Jenson, "The Inclusive Lectionary," *Dialog* 23 (Winter 1984): 6.

51. See, for example, Donald G. Bloesch, *The Battle for the Trinity: The Debate Over Inclusive God-Language* (Ann Arbor: Servant Publications, 1985). Also, an excellent treatment of the fourth-century christological and trinitarian debates, with particular emphasis upon the doxology — "Father, Son, and Holy Spirit" — is provided by Deborah M. Belonick, "Revelation and Metaphors: The Significance of the Trinitarian Names, Father, Son and Holy Spirit," *Union Seminary Quarterly Review* 40 (1985): 31-42. She concludes, "In the theology of the early church, the traditional Trinitarian terms are precise theological terms. Therefore these terms are not exchangeable. Through them humanity encounters the persons of the Trinity, and through them relationships among members of the Godhead are defined. . . . There is no historical evidence that the terms 'Father, Son and Holy Spirit' were products of a patriarchal culture, 'male' theology, or a hierarchical church" (p. 36).

the basis of the justifications she has presented for making her proposal. Those justifications express with great clarity generally held feminist views, views held in the context of, and nourished by, the theologically flawed church of which Berger and Jenson speak.

To begin with, McFague[52] outlines what she refers to as the "new sensibility" of *our time* (emphasis hers), and argues that Christian theology must be commensurate with this new sensibility; otherwise, no matter how helpful it may have been previously, it can now be harmful. This new sensibility involves three major aspects.

First, it involves an "evolutionary, ecological perspective" which takes with utmost seriousness the view that "from the cells of our bodies to the finest creations of our minds" we are a part of the whole: electrons, neutrons, rocks, water, soil, atmosphere, plants, animals, and human beings — all are dynamically interrelated. Appreciation of the extent to which we are embedded in this evolutionary ecosystem — our interrelation with *all* entities — is an *essential* prerequisite for doing theology for our time. And this understanding, of course, is held to make indefensible all talk of absolute divisions between human beings and other beings, whether animate or inanimate, as well as dualism, such as spirit/matter, subject/object, male/female, and mind/body.[53] No consideration is given to the obvious problems with this perspective, particularly the problem of providing for human responsibility and the age-old problem of evil.

The second aspect of the new sensibility involves the nuclear issue — the knowledge that we now have the power to destroy ourselves and other forms of life. Here McFague follows the lead of Gordon Kaufman: she sees this as a knowledge new to human history, a knowledge of our time that requires a fundamental change in understanding the relationship of God to the world. It makes indefensible the view of a bygone age in which God is understood as externally related to, and sovereign over, the world. The dualism "between God's power and ours" must go, to be replaced by an understanding in which God is related to the world in "a unified, interdependent way," and which allows for a profound acceptance of human responsibility for the fate of the earth.[54] Again, on McFague's own terms, on what basis can one speak of this essential human responsibility?

52. The following discussion of McFague's proposal is based on her book entitled *Models of God: Theology for an Ecological, Nuclear Age* (Philadelphia: Fortress Press, 1987).

53. Ibid., pp. 1-9. Rosemary Ruether has argued the same point. See *Sexism and God-Talk*, pp. 85-92.

54. McFague, *Models of God*, pp. 14-21.

The third aspect of this new sensibility is "consciousness of the constructive character of all human activities, especially of . . . our world views, including our religions." The most basic characteristic of *all* language about God is that it is human construction which "misses the mark" — that it corresponds to "what the tradition calls the *via negativa*." Thus, *no* theological language can be said to serve to identify God.[55] Yet McFague wants to hold that metaphorical language need not be without referent — that the models of God she proposes are not arbitrary. The argument she presents to support this is particularly significant:

> Models of God, such as mother, lover, and friend, . . . are not arbitrary, because, along with the father model, they are the deepest and most important expressions of love known to us, rather than because they are necessarily descriptive of the nature of God. But are these loves descriptive of God *as God is?* . . . It seems to me that to be a Christian is to be persuaded that there is a personal, gracious power who is on the side of life and its fulfillment, a power whom the paradigmatic figure of Jesus of Nazareth expresses and illuminates; but when we try to say something more, we turn, necessarily, to the "loves" we know. . . . I do not *know* who God is, but I find some models better than others for constructing an image of God commensurate with my trust in a God as on the side of life.[56]

This statement is very revealing of the flaws of McFague's proposal. First, if to be a Christian is to at least regard Jesus of Nazareth as unique, McFague's definition does not qualify. Jesus is merely a "paradigmatic figure" who "expresses and illuminates" the way she would understand someone who is "on the side of life and its fulfillment." In other places in her discussion, McFague speaks of a number of others, "the many saviors of the world," whose lives are reflections of the belief that "the universe is neither malevolent nor indifferent but is on the side of life and its fulfillment."[57] As Daphne Hampson has commented, this is certainly more akin to humanism than to Christianity.[58]

Further, given the basis of McFague's criterion for the construction of models for God, the "loves" we know, and taking seriously the new

55. Ibid., pp. 21, 23.
56. Ibid., p. 192n. 37; emphasis in original.
57. Ibid., p. 152.
58. Hampson, *Theology and Feminism,* p. 160.

sensibility of our time — our fundamental interrelatedness to all entities — why wouldn't the faithful and devoted love of my favorite canine companion serve as a "canine" model for God? Actually, it would seem that, on her own terms, she could not object to this. She admits that her proposal of the three models of mother, lover, and friend was a "deliberate attempt to unseat" the trinitarian names of Father, Son, and Holy Spirit "as descriptions of God which will allow no supplements or alternatives" — to require the important admission that *"God has many names"* to be made. She also states that she sees nothing sacred about a trinity — "a trinity is not a necessity nor should the divine nature be in any way circumscribed by it."[59] But this "important admission" is a denial of the Christian faith, in which God is the one identified by the trinitarian formula, and a plunge into the *via negativa* tradition of the unidentifiable God of "many names" but *no Name*.

Throughout her discussion, McFague overlooks the fact that the *via negativa* (in and of itself) does *not* express the Christian gospel and tradition. She is quite correct: the *via negativa* makes it clear that all efforts to describe the divine nature *are* ultimately inadequate, *apart from* the basic affirmation of the Christian faith, the affirmation that God is known in the narrative of the life of Jesus of Nazareth, and the identifying formula — Father, Son, and Holy Spirit — resulting from that affirmation.

At this point I should mention that McFague is more circumspect than many of her fellow feminists in proposing "names" for God, in that she maintains a preference for personal metaphors, whereas most other feminists are very ready to propose nonpersonal terms.[60] However, she prefers personal metaphors not because she thinks they more truly "name" God but because she thinks certain specific personal metaphors are needed to reflect a relationship to God appropriate *for our time*. She regards the metaphors "mother," "lover," and "friend" as expressive of a relationship of "mutuality, shared responsibility, and reciprocity" between God and the world, and hence needed to offset the traditional and unsuitable metaphors that are "hierarchical, imperialistic and dualistic, stressing the distance between God and the world and the total reliance of the world on God."[61]

59. McFague, *Models of God*, pp. 181, 182, 184; emphasis in original.

60. One of the most intriguing statements by a writer who proposes multiple metaphors for God, including depersonalized ones, is that of Rebecca Oxford-Carpenter: "If poet Wallace Stevens could write about 'thirteen ways of looking at a blackbird,' how many more ways must exist to envision the infinite and eternal God?" ("Gender and the Trinity," *Theology Today* 41 [1984]: 23).

61. McFague, *Models of God*, p. 19.

McFague also tells us that she will "address head on" the objections to the employment of female metaphors for God. Instead of addressing the objections, however, she proceeds to offer what she refers to as the reason *for* using female language — namely, the very unconvincing argument that doing so serves to demonstrate that the traditional language is *not* nonsexual but is male. First, she states that to speak of God as father has obvious sexual connotations, despite all claims to the contrary, but this has been "masked" because of the "Hebraic tradition's interest in distinguishing itself from Goddess religions and fertility cults, as well as the early and deep ascetic strain in Christianity." But by introducing female metaphors, which are blatantly sexual, "the sexuality of both male and female metaphors becomes evident." We are thus made aware that there is "no gender-neutral language if we take ourselves as the model for talk about God, because we are sexual beings." Hence traditional language *is* male, not nonsexual. Further, "since the *imago dei* is twofold, female as well as male, both kinds of metaphors ought to be used."[62] McFague does not mention, of course, that the traditional language does *not* "take ourselves" as the model for talk about God.

McFague agrees with Achtemeier that the use of the term "Mother" for God entails the image of birthing, instead of the traditional understanding of creation, for the relationship of God to the world. But she regards this as an advantage, not a problem. It undercuts the traditional dualism of God and the world (as well as the dualisms of matter/spirit, mind/body, and humanity/nature), and gives us a picture of the "affinity and kinship" of God and the world that is commensurate with the holistic, evolutionary sensibility of our time.[63] As Achtemeier makes clear, however, it also provides us with the ultimate idolatry — usurping the place of God for ourselves.

The feminists, in pursuit of their goal of liberation from patriarchy, have attempted to co-opt Christianity as a tool for use in achieving their purpose. And a church that has trouble recognizing its master's crib has functioned willingly, although perhaps partially unwittingly, as an ally in that co-option, thereby helping to destroy its own foundation and the very source of liberation for us all, feminists included. We can only hope Jacques Ellul was correct when he said, "Christianity never carries the day decisively against Christ."

62. Ibid., p. 98.
63. Ibid., pp. 109-16.

Index